THE LAST GREAT NECESSITY

Creating the North American Landscape

Gregory Conniff
Bonnie Loyd
David Schuyler
Consulting Editors

George F. Thompson
Project Editor

The Last Great Necessity

Cemeteries in American History

DAVID CHARLES SLOANE

The Johns Hopkins University Press

Baltimore and London

The Johns Hopkins University Press, 701 West 40th Street,
Baltimore, Maryland 21211
The Johns Hopkins Press Ltd., London

The paper used in this book meets the minimum requirements
of American National Standard for Information Sciences—
Permanence of Paper for Printed Library Materials,
ANSI Z39.48–1984

Library of Congress Cataloging-in-Publication Data
Sloane, David Charles.
The last great necessity: cemeteries in American
history / David Charles Sloane.
p. cm.—(Creating the North American landscape)
Includes bibliographical references and index.
ISBN 0-8018-4068-6 (alk. paper)
1. Funeral rites and ceremonies—United States.
2. Cemeteries—United States—Landscape architecture.
3. United States—Social life and customs.
I. Title. II. Series.
GT3203.A2S56   1991
393′.1′0973—dc20   90-41906

To
Beverlie Conant Sloane

Love Always

An ample permanent and attractive resting place for our dead,
seems to be the last great necessity of our city.

—Elias W. Leavenworth, dedication of Oakwood Cemetery,
Syracuse, N.Y., 3 November 1859

CONTENTS

ILLUSTRATIONS

TABLES

ACKNOWLEDGMENTS

An enormous number of people have helped bring this book to publication. I owe a great debt to those associated with the cemetery industry who talked with me, toured cemeteries with me, and allowed me access to their archives. Particularly helpful were James Black, Bob Bruce, Jeanne Capidulupo, Seth Colby, James Glavin, Clyde Gordon, Jim Huggins, Edward Laux, Alfred Locke, Duncan Munro, Samuel Stueve, Fred Whaley, John Wheeler, and the office staffs of the Cemetery of Spring Grove in Cincinnati, Forest Lawn Cemetery in Buffalo, Pinelawn Memorial Park in Pinelawn, N.Y., Vestal Hills Memorial Park in Binghamton, N.Y., and Woodlawn Cemetery in the Bronx. The staff of Oakwood Cemeteries in Syracuse, especially Janice Hornick, provided invaluable help during my research. David Hanna, then of the Gorham Bronze Company, gave personal and professional aid on many occasions.

The Division of Cemeteries, New York State's regulatory body, also provided valuable help. Howard Carr, Richard Brady, and Pierce O'Callahan gave me free rein over their files and spent much time explaining the intricacies of financing and regulation.

The sorts of materials upon which this book is based is not collected systematically by academic libraries. Instead, information must be sifted from collections in historical societies, public and private libraries, and cemeteries. To have done so would have been impossible without the help of many librarians. I thank them all. The most helpful public libraries were in Boston, Buffalo, Cincinnati, Kansas City, New York City, Rochester, San Francisco, and Syracuse. The Cincinnati, New York, Long Island, Rochester, and Onondaga historical societies hold excellent materials. Private archives at the Trinity Church Library and the Garden Library at Dumbarton Oaks Center were invaluable. The State Library of New York and the Library of Congress held important information. The university libraries at Berkeley, Brown, Cincinnati, Cornell, Harvard, Los Angeles, Princeton, and Rochester also held valuable material. The librarians of Syracuse University and Dartmouth College have been unfailing helpful. John Crane has become a close friend.

Numerous scholars influenced the development of this book. My greatest debts are to Sally Gregory Kohlstedt, who has been a faithful reader, critic, and friend for over a decade; and Ted Mitchell, who read the manuscript, discussed parts of it endlessly, and has been a wonderful scholarly companion and good friend. Barbara Rotundo read and greatly improved the manuscript. At Syracuse University, Michael Flusche, Peter Goldman, Ralph Ketchum, Frederick

Marquardt, David Robinson, Otey Scruggs, William Stinchcombe, and William Stueck urged me to rethink issues that improved the book. During my preliminary work on this project, my fellow graduate students gave me enormous personal and professional support. Henry Shapiro, Alan Ward, and Blanche Linden-Ward helped me understand issues regarding Mount Auburn Cemetery and the Cemetery of Spring Grove. Charles Backus read and criticized part of the manuscript at a critical time. Mary Taylor and Pierre Bastianelli, Dartmouth Medical School illustrators, graciously printed many of the photographs.

The editorial staff of the Johns Hopkins University Press has been generous and helpful. Project Editor George Thompson efficiently but gently guided me through the maze of the publishing process. Jane Warth was an extremely effective editor.

David Schuyler provided me with valuable criticism and sources.

Syracuse University provided me with travel funds through the Roscoe Martin Fund in 1981 and 1983. The university also supported my research with a travel grant in 1982 and with a University Fellowship in 1981 and 1982. I thank the history department for its encouragement.

The most important sources of help and support have been friends and family. Jack and Rosemary Sloane shared over thirty years of experience in the cemetery business in Ohio and New York. This book is only a small return for a lifetime of love. Lawrence Sloane read and criticized the manuscript and responded whenever I asked for advice. R. Gregory Sloane provided information and ideas at every stage. Chris and Steven Sloane made sure I remained humble, and Joan, Sandra, Sara, Nora, William and Stephanie Sloane pleasantly distracted me while always remaining interested and supportive.

I was especially fortunate that Ralph and Audrey Conant not only tolerated a son-in-law who sometimes ignored them, but that Ralph spent many hours editing and Audrey encouraged me every step of the way. Chas, Jamie, and Jake Boynton are too young to understand how many times they and their parents made a tired and grumpy researcher forget his problems and start laughing.

I cannot thank all the friends and family who have helped shape and support this book. Rube Gerber, David Feld, Marti Morec, and Max Feld, Steve Eimer and Kevin Cartwright, Lynda Anderson, Jane Brody and Richard Enquist, Margaret Young, Karen Degerberg and Andy Sandler, Carl and Tillie Stollenmeyer, Betty Sloane, Molly and Irving Zahn, Tina and Bob Williamson, provided hospitality and conversation to a traveling researcher. My many friends in Hanover helped make writing a joyous experience. Steve Kairys and Fred Meier read early drafts of the material on cremation. Marv Sorkin read the entire manuscript, bringing to it his skills as a writer and editor. David Drach spent hours discussing the manuscript, and Carolynne Krusi has been a wonderful friend and critic, and truly generous in every way, especially in sharing Paul, Adam, Rebecca, and Ben.

This book is dedicated to my wife, Beverlie Conant Sloane. She never allowed me to forget that these are the best years of a scholar's life. I deem it the great privilege of my life to live and work with her.

The Last Great Necessity

OAKWOOD CEMETERY, 1859

The sky threatened rain in the early hours of 3 November 1859, but later turned bright and beautiful, much to the satisfaction of the organizers of the day's festivities. The occasion was the dedication of Oakwood Cemetery, in Syracuse, New York. After a decade and a half of planning, promotion, bickering, and frustration, the new cemetery was to be celebrated by the community and consecrated.[1]

Over one-third of the city's fifteen thousand people attended the dedication. They watched three bands, the mayor and common council, the clergy, the fire department, representatives of the Odd Fellows and YMCA, and the Fifty-first Regiment of the New York State Militia march three miles from downtown Syracuse to the cemetery. There they listened to music, poetry, a benediction, and addresses.

Elias W. Leavenworth, the primary force behind the new cemetery, gave the introduction. A leading local lawyer, former congressman, and amateur horticulturist, Leavenworth had fought in 1841 against a proposed new cemetery, believing that it would be too close to the city and not large enough to solve the community's burial crisis. In 1852 he had gathered interested individuals for a meeting to discuss following the lead of Boston, Cincinnati, New York City, Rochester, New York, and other cities in opening a new cemetery. After his efforts toward opening a new cemetery failed, Leavenworth began again in 1858 with the help of local banker Hamilton White. Finally, in 1859, Leavenworth's group of civic leaders succeeded in buying one hundred acres from Charles Baker and hiring landscape gardener Howard Daniels of New York City to improve the grounds.

Leavenworth recognized how hard members of his group of supporters had worked to establish the cemetery. He remembered the public apathy the group had encountered. At the dedication ceremony, he therefore briefly discussed why the new cemetery was so important and why it was a necessity for a prosperous and growing city to have a new cemetery. Nature and the community had labored "diligently and successfully for the wants of the living," Leavenworth reminded his audience. "Water and gas, railroads and canals, a

PINE RIDGE AVENUE.

Touring Oakwood Cemetery, Syracuse, N.Y., 1871

During the mid-nineteenth century, strolling through the cemetery was a popular pastime. One reason for its popularity was that the new rural cemeteries enveloped visitors in an environment that was naturalistic and totally different from that of their daily urban life. (Henry P. Smith, *History of Oakwood,* 1871. Courtesy of Oakwood Cemeteries.)

salubrious climate, a fertile soil, prosperous agriculture, commerce and manufacturing, have . . . filled our laps with plenty and made our homes the abodes of happiness and peace. . . . But . . . we [have] forgotten what was due the dead." Leavenworth insisted that "an ample, permanent and attractive resting place for our dead, seems to be the last great necessity of our city."

Leavenworth's listeners heartily agreed. They knew that past graveyards had been abandoned to builders and had suffered the indignities of vandalism. To them, Oakwood Cemetery symbolized their commercial and cultural success, marking Syracuse as both a permanent, happy, and civilized place for the living and a safe, secure place for the dead. The cemetery also manifested contemporary wisdom that in-city graveyards and churchyards were potential health hazards, as well as unattractive and inappropriate places for the living to mourn the dead.

Instead, Oakwood Cemetery evoked images of a quieter country life—so much so that founders of new cemeteries throughout America named them *rural cemeteries: cemeteries* from the Greek word for "sleeping chamber," because they were considered temporary resting places during the wait for Judgment Day; *rural* because their landscapes embodied the founders' respect for nature and provided a counterpoint to the chaotic commercialism of the city, over which the founders felt a strong moral disquiet.

Leaving the city streets of Syracuse, visitors entered the tranquil burial place by strolling down Pine Ridge Avenue and crossing over Linden and Maple avenues. The renewed belief in an individual's chance for salvation reinforced the ideas that the grave was a sleeping chamber and that the cemetery was a solemn, but not gloomy, place. Visitors came to the new rural cemetery expecting a place of nature and art, a museum of history, and a fitting commemoration of both families and individuals, open to all in the democratic community.

OAKWOOD CEMETERY, 1990

Over one hundred and thirty years after it was established, Oakwood Cemetery is encircled by residential neighborhoods and Syracuse University. The cemetery has many of the problems it had been established to solve, including noise, vandalism, and a diminished sense of sanctity. During the 1970s, Oakwood had merged into a holding company, Oakwood Cemeteries, which included three monumented cemeteries, a memorial park, and a crematory. Oakwood Cemeteries is a million-dollar corporation with a full-time staff of over twenty people and a sophisticated marketing program, selling hundreds of thousands of dollars of services each year.[2]

The "last great necessity" that Leavenworth envisioned that day in 1859 has been transformed by the cemetery's managers, lot-holders and trustees in reaction to significant changes in American customs. Evolving community feelings, demographics, modern methods of health care, and attitudes toward nature and death have led Oakwood Cemeteries to expand its work force, sell its lots more aggressively, defend its borders vigilantly, and reach out to new clientele. Oakwood has been involved in several controversies. Commentators wondered about the safety of the area after the body of a raped and battered woman was found in Oakwood. The New York State Cemetery Board questioned the financial arrangements of Oakwood's management contracts with other cemeteries in the area. Neighbors angrily demanded that Oakwood Cemeteries' crematory not be used, believing the effluent was endangering their children's lives. Although Oakwood has generally been a safe place used by walkers, bird watchers, and others, has voluntarily given up a lucrative part of its cremation business to satisfy its neighbors, and has satisfactorily answered every inquiry about its finances, the cemetery appears vulnerable to further incidents.

This book explains how and why the American cemetery has been transformed from an institution celebrated and fêted by the nation to one seemingly outside the daily lives and even sacred moments of many Americans.

THE LAST GREAT NECESSITY

CHAPTER ONE

An American Mosaic of Death

THE MOSAIC

Over San Francisco Bay, a man reaches out of an airplane and carefully empties into the water the cremated remains of a friend dead of AIDS. In Chicago, a large group of Ukrainian-Americans attends the church funeral and the burial of a leading merchant in its community, then gathers together at his home to celebrate the continuation of life and to honor his contribution to the community. On the Upper West Side of New York City, the body of a wealthy dowager is mechanically lifted into a mausoleum crypt in Trinity Cemetery. She outlived her friends and relatives, and thus her interment is witnessed only by workmen.

Amid the forests and glens of New Hampshire's White Mountains, a family gathers to remember Grandmother, now interred in the small family cemetery overlooking the land that the family has owned for a century. In Syracuse, New York, a year after the burial of their father, a Jewish family gathers friends and relatives to witness the unveiling of his gravestone. He was interred in a small cemetery with very rocky soil, situated along a dead-end street on a steep hillside overlooking a former meat-packing plant and a new highway bypass. A few miles away, an African-American mother, devastated by the death of her young son, eludes the grasp of her husband and friends and, as a large funeral party watches, tries to jump into his grave. Her minister and husband lead her back to the waiting car.

THE MOSAIC'S PATTERNS

There is a vast diversity of American burial customs and burial places. As many as one hundred thousand European-style burial places have been identified nationally. The result of the tragedies and hopes of three centuries of settlement, these burial places reflect many aspects of American technology, business practices, demographics, cultural norms, social relationships, and material culture. Yet the American mosaic has a discernible pattern.

Two centuries of interaction between the cemetery and American society has left the cemetery, once central to the urban scene, a necessary, but not necessarily desirable, neighbor in the suburbs. The transformation began in the decades after the American Revolution, when centrally located graveyards were removed to the outskirts of growing towns. Then, large, new rural cemeteries were located farther away from the city as counterpoints to the commercial atmosphere of urban life.

The rural cemetery of mid-nineteenth-century cities was planned with a picturesque atmosphere, inefficient but aesthetically pleasing serpentine roadways, and economically impractical wide pathways and natural land reserves. Unlike earlier graveyards, most of the new cemeteries were owned and managed by private, secular associations established solely for the development of the cemetery. Families gathered together under the umbrella of the association to preserve and protect their family lots.

Disturbed by the crowding and spatial confusion in the first generation of rural cemeteries, new cemetery designers streamlined the landscape and new owners altered the management of the cemetery beginning in the 1850s. The resulting *lawn-park cemeteries* were more rational and efficient in design, more dependent on professionals to develop and maintain the landscape, and less likely to serve as wide a population as the rural cemeteries because the cities were more ethnically, religiously, and culturally diverse. The cemeteries also underwent decorative changes as Americans mechanized and standardized monument production. This movement coincided with the distancing of most Americans from death with the development of public hospitals, professional funeral management, and other aspects of the twentieth-century process of dealing with death.

The twentieth-century cemetery was renamed the *memorial park* by founders who wished to obscure the morbid connotations they believed the public perceived in the word *cemetery*. The memorial park was simpler and more accessible than the lawn-park cemetery. Society no longer desired a mysterious relationship with the grave. Customers wanted the cemetery to be comfortable and familiar, reflecting mainstream American practices such as the acceptance of the hospital as the place to die, the removal of the funeral from the home, and the purchase of the cemetery lot *preneed* as a simple business transaction. Thus, cemetery designers freely used the elements of the increasingly popular suburban landscape in developing the look and atmosphere of the memorial park. Founders placed, on the lawns and terraces of the landscape, patriotic and nonsectarian religious statuary, which reinforced the visitor's familiarity and comfort with the landscape.

Four cemeteries served as models for cemetery design and management: New Haven Burying Ground in New Haven, Connecticut; Mount Auburn Cemetery in Cambridge, Massachusetts; the Cemetery of Spring Grove in Cincinnati, Ohio; and Forest Lawn Memorial-Park in Glendale, California. Each cemetery influenced a generation or more of cemetery designers, managers, and mourners. Each reflected new attitudes toward the symbolic landscape, the institutional structure, and the cultural attitudes associated with people's perceptions of the relationship between death and nature.

Leaders such as James Hillhouse of the New Haven Burying Ground, Perkins Nichols of the Marble cemeteries in New York City, Jacob Bigelow of Mount Auburn, Adolph Strauch of Spring Grove, Hubert Eaton of Forest Lawn, landscape architect and cemetery-manual author Jacob Weidenmann, cemetery designer and manager Ossian Cole Simonds of Graceland Cemetery in Chicago, and Edward "Doc" Williams, creator of the first cemetery empire, identified and implemented needed changes, which improved the cemetery by contemporary standards.

AMERICAN VERSUS EUROPEAN CEMETERIES

The similarities within American cemetery types become clearer when compared to their European counterparts. Although Europeans have many national distinctions, their burial practices, which have consistently influenced American cultural decisions, can be distinguished from American practices. There are five primary aspects of differences: private ownership, family control, commercial activity, natural landscapes, and cremation.[1]

Europeans have a long tradition of allowing the church and government to oversee the interment of the dead. When in-city churchyards were prohibited in the early nineteenth century, Europeans turned to municipal governments to designate new burial places on the periphery of the city. Except for the British, few Europeans emulated the Americans who formed private corporations to bury their dead.

Inside the government and religious cemeteries, the permanent family lot has never become the norm. Père Lachaise, established outside of Paris in 1804, was the first Continental cemetery to allow middle-class families to purchase perpetual burial rights. Prior to this, the grave was rented, typically for between six and twenty years, after which the remains were removed to the charnel house. Père Lachaise opened an era in which the privacy of the dead was more respected by society.

Lot-holders could never be sure that economic pressures or overcrowding would not result in the dead being moved, cemetery land being reused, or undeveloped land being appropriated for other services. In the nineteenth century, American lot-holders assumed the management of cemeteries, whereas French lot-holders remained at the mercy of others, who established maintenance schedules and set regulations about visitors, monuments, and landscaping. They were also at the mercy of others because many cemeteries continued to demand rents. Even today, many Europeans continue to rent their family plots for a ten to one hundred year period. If the family has moved, lost touch, or died out, the plot can be resold and the remains removed.[2]

Europeans could be sure that their governments were not in the business

TABLE 1.1
Characteristics of American Cemeteries

Name	Period	Design	Location	Monumental Style
Frontier graves	17th–20th c.	None	Site of death	Plain (name, date); simple or no markers
Domestic homestead graveyard	17th–20th c.	Geometric	Farm field	Some iconographic markers, if any
Churchyard	17th–20th c.	Geometric or formal garden	Next to church	Artistic iconographic markers, if any
Potter's field	17th–20th c.	Geometric	City borders	Plain markers, if any
Town/city cemetery	17th–20th c.	Formal garden	City borders	Three-dimensional markers; monuments; sculpture
Rural cemetery	1831–1870s	Picturesque, natural garden	Suburb	Three-dimensional markers; monuments; sculpture
Lawn-park cemetery	1855–1920s	Pastoral, parklike	Suburb	Three-dimensional monuments; sculpture; close-to-the-ground markers
Memorial park	1917–present	Pastoral, suburban	Suburb	Two- or three-dimensional, flush-to-the-ground markers; central-section sculptures

Monument Material	Type of Manager	Primary Distinction	Paradigm	Examples
Wooden, stone	None	Isolated; no design	None	B. Nukerk, Syracuse, N.Y.
Wooden, stone	None	Small; family-owned; functional design	None	Farm burial grounds New England and Mid-Atlantic
Wooden, stone, slate	Part-time sexton	Religious ownership; functional design	English churchyards	Trinity, New York City St. Philip's, Charleston, S.C.
Wooden, stone	Sexton	Public ownership; functional design	Gospel according to St. Matthew	New York City burial grounds
Stone, marble	Sexton	Family- or government-owned; formal design	New Haven Burying Ground	Dartmouth, Hanover, N.H.
Marble, granite	Trustee Superintendent	Private ownership; garden aesthetic; mausoleums	Mount Auburn, Cambridge, Mass. Pére Lachaise, Paris	Oakland, Atlanta Greenmount, Baltimore Oakwood, Syracuse, N.Y.
Granite, stone, bronze	Trustee Entrepreneur Superintendent	Entrepreneurial; park-aesthetic; mausoleums	Spring Grove, Cincinnati	Oak Woods, Chicago Lakewood, Minneapolis Swan Point, Providence, R.I.
Bronze, marble, granite	Entrepreneur Sales manager Superintendent	Entrepreneurial; suburban aesthetic; mausoleums	Forest Lawn, Glendale, Calif.	Pinelawn, N.Y. Sharon, Mass.

of burying the dead for profit. Americans increasingly have not had the same reassurance. Since the mid-nineteenth century, numerous for-profit cemeteries have been founded throughout America. Many of the entrepreneurial cemeteries have provided lot-holders with exemplary service and have maintained beautiful grounds. Others have defrauded their customers and left lot-holders with a shell of a cemetery, often full of overgrown grass and unmaintained mausoleums. Private control has inevitably led to commercialism and to the excesses of entrepreneurship.

In for-profit and nonprofit American cemeteries, the landscape has remained much more natural than in European cemeteries. Whether the Campo Santo of the Italians, the *garden cemeteries* of the French, or the churchyards and cemeteries of the English, the European memorial has always received more attention than the surroundings. Although this was also true of early American graveyards, later American cemeteries were elaborately planned to provide large natural spaces around family monuments and markers. Conversely, Europeans have clustered their graves.

Fewer Americans than Europeans have been cremated. Perhaps due to the divisiveness of the religious-scientific debates of the late nineteenth century or the trauma of two world wars, many Europeans have stripped the death ritual of its emotion. Instead of choosing elaborate funerals and ostentatious markers, they have cremated their dead, placed urns in communal storage, and added their names in a book of remembrance. The Catholic church prohibited cremation from the 1870s until the 1960s, but twentieth-century Europeans increasingly embraced the practice. Philippe Ariès has argued that, although Americans first manifested the twentieth century's less emotional relationship to death, Europeans have accepted its dictum of denial much more fully in their customs than Americans have in theirs.[3]

HISTORICAL IMPLICATIONS OF THE MOSAIC

The American cemetery is a window through which we can view the hopes, fears, and designs of the generation that created it and is buried within it. By examining the cemetery from the late-eighteenth to the late-twentieth century, we can find clues to how the mosaic of death changed within America's social and cultural framework. The cemetery has been a community organization, defined by the institutions, families, or individuals that control its management, engineered and designed by professionals and the boards of directors they serve, and reflective of the sentiments of lot-holders.

The most obvious clues to the mosaic are found in the landscape. The grounds of the typical cemetery rarely have been dramatically redesigned. The monuments, representative of a time and a group of cultural concepts, still stand. Although the trees and shrubs have grown and changed, the general appearance of the cemetery often has remained similar. These elements combine to provide an excellent primary source on how Americans of a certain time felt about death, art, nature, and society.

The importance of the American cemetery is not limited to the evolving landscape. The physical development of the cemetery cannot be separated from the development of the changing institutional structure. Issues such as the involvement of the lot-holder in the embellishment and maintenance of individual lots were influenced by the evolution of the cemetery's business practices. Separating the landscape from the management of the business became especially difficult after the Civil War, when more cemeteries became private business corporations. The formation of the cemetery landscape by lot-holders, cemetery designers, and cemetery managers and owners was intricately related to the marketing and management of the institution.

American cemeteries are also manifestations of the importance of the family, professional managers, representative of class distinctions, symbolic of the importance of privacy, and suggestive of the reliance on private enterprise. Tensions existed between private and public, rich and poor, God and science, amateur and professional. Strikingly, the family dominated the landscape of the dead. Yet even the visibility of the family ebbed through the two centuries examined in this book.

DEATH AND THE CEMETERY

Prior to the mid-1800s, removal of graveyards and churchyards from the center of cities was not considered unusual, although relatives sometimes objected. Washington Square in New York City, Lincoln Park in Chicago, Upstate Medical Center in Syracuse, and businesses throughout the nation are situated on the sites of earlier churchyards and graveyards. According to contemporaries, the swift growth of the cities necessitated the reburials.

By the twentieth century, local, state, and federal laws severely limited such violations of the grave. Today, disinterment on cemetery lands for the purpose of using the land for residential or commercial purposes requires complicated legal agreements, which are sometimes impossible to negotiate. The taboo against disturbing the dead is so powerful that the inviolate nature of the cemetery is now accepted as a stereotypical example of an impossible task. During the television coverage of the 1986 World Cup final in Mexico City, one commentator noted that changing the attitude of the ruling body of world soccer would be "like moving a graveyard," a task begun with few expectations of success.

Ironically, as the grave has become legally inviolate, Americans have become increasingly indifferent to the cemetery as a sacred space or as a community and cultural institution. The cemetery's role as a repository of the history and memories of the local community is fading. Other cultural institutions, such as art museums, local historical societies, and botanical gardens, assumed the earlier functions of the cemetery. As this happened, Americans replaced community cemeteries with service cemeteries. The institutionalization of the cemetery reflects a greater distance between the residents of the community and the graves of their ancestors. As Charles Rosenberg has noted about hospitals, death is now in the "care of strangers." Final disposition of the dead is left to specialists trained to view death as their profession.[4]

Throughout our nations's history, though, the cemetery has remained an important place for millions of mourning Americans. Cemetery designers and managers succeeded in attracting lot-holders only when they provided solace to Americans in desperate need for comfort from life's most terrible, but inevitable, fate. America's "last great necessity" was acceptable only when the landscape invited the living and celebrated the dead.

A SINGLE cemetery, even one as prominent as Mount Auburn, Spring Grove, or Forest Lawn, offers a limited view of the changes that occurred during the two centuries of cemetery development. Instead, evidence for these trends is taken from cemeteries throughout the nation. Founders, managers, and lot-holders of these cemeteries experienced the successes and failures associated with the changing customs of burying the dead.

The book focuses on New York State as a means of showing the continuities and changes that have occurred in the American cemetery. For example, in early nineteenth-century New York City, certain ideas and events propelled the community to reject city graveyards and to search for a suitable alternative. Later, both city and countryside embraced the new customs embodied in the rural cemetery. Finally, New York State was a gauge of the relationship between cemeteries and the government. Twice, once in 1847 and again in 1949, the New York State legislature passed landmark legislation regarding the organization and management of cemeteries.

As other examples used throughout this book demonstrate, the changes in New York State were similar throughout the nation. As New York City residents struggled with the issue of removing graveyards from their densely inhabited areas, they looked to civic leaders in Philadelphia, Boston, and Charleston for guidance. The new monuments and family lots that rural New Yorkers found compelling enough to alter their practices were also enticing to residents of New England, the Midwest, and parts of the South. Both in 1847 and 1949, New York's legislation occurred simultaneously with similar legislative discussions in a variety of states. New York provides a representative barometer of the national reaction to a new model.

Protestants organized and managed most of the cemeteries discussed, although they were considered nonsectarian and buried the dead of any religion. Examples are drawn from a wide range of cemeteries, including those managed by Catholic and Jewish communities, but the emphasis is on the attitudes of the Protestant middle class toward death and burial from the 1790s to the

1980s. The Protestant majority developed and patronized the model modern cemeteries. In the twentieth century, religious distinctions among cemeteries diminished. As immigrant ethnic and religious communities fragmented, their cultures became less distinctive. Twentieth-century memorial parks are more likely to serve all faiths.

Nevertheless, Protestants, Catholics, Friends, Mormons, Jews, African-Americans, Ukrainians, Germans, city dwellers, country folk, heterosexuals, and homosexuals have not all had the same burial customs. Funeral, burial, and memorial customs differed among groups and between eras. Yet, within that religious, ethnic, and social mosaic, there is the American cemetery.

The Living among the Dead,
1796–1855

The Revolution provoked both political and cultural upheaval in America. The old colonial ways were unacceptable in this age of independence. Americans had to establish a new history, as well as a renewed sense of identity. These changes did not happen without a struggle. Americans wrestled with abolitionism, temperance, prison reform, asylums, women's rights, the new factory system, alternative religions, changes in family life, and other issues.

In this atmosphere, Americans decided that the colonial graveyard reflected older ideas, passé theologies, and social conflicts. The dead were unprotected and moved from place to place as cities and towns grew. Furthermore, many people believed that the dead threatened the living. They thought that graveyards exuded gases that aided the transmission of disease within cities. They also continued economic distinctions in life as well as death, honoring the successful and obscuring the failed.

Although Americans agreed on the need for reform, there was no obvious alternative to the graveyard. They tried improving the graveyard by giving it a more protected location and by encouraging families to own and embellish it. Americans later decided the graveyard was unacceptable and therefore created a new burial place, the cemetery. Although the cemetery was an urban institution, its design embodied rural values that Americans were worried about losing. Influenced by new European events and ideas, Americans situated rural cemeteries outside cities on large tracts of farmland and developed them into gardens of graves.

Rural cemeteries were promoted as an answer to the confusion and complexity of urban life, and they became symbolic landscapes for the city and country. Country graveyards imitated their monuments, embellishments, and roadway systems. North and South, East and West embraced the concept of the rural cemetery. The new cemeteries reflected common concerns and provided acceptable solutions. The dead were given a new home that was inviting for the living.

CHAPTER TWO

Displacing the Dead

"A CONFUSED MEDLEY OF GRAVES"

The modern cemetery evolved from American dissatisfaction with the grave-yard. In 1805 an article in the *Literary Magazine and American Register* catalogued the ills surrounding contemporary burial places and suggested an improve-ment that was summarized in its title, "A Rustic Cemetery." The article reflected the growing consensus that the graveyard's tranquility was disrupted in the new commercial cities and that it symbolized a time that was past. The article casti-gated the churchyard as a place "where [the] avarice of the living confines within narrow limits the . . . dead; where the confused medley of graves seems like the wild arrangement of some awful convulsion of the earth."[1]

The article's complaints were part of a growing chorus of attacks on Amer-ica's burial customs, in both the city and the country. Colonial practices, whether isolated frontier graves or neatly kept, centrally located churchyards, were becoming difficult to maintain in the commercial atmosphere that was invading the sleepy towns of New England, invigorating growth throughout the North-east, and turning New York City into the nation's largest and most economically powerful city. The consequences of these trends were manifest in Philadelphia long before they were in Cincinnati, but throughout the nation Americans increasingly found public and private burial places of the past unacceptable.

EARLY BURIAL CUSTOMS IN AMERICA

Prior to the development of the new cemeteries in the nineteenth century, Americans interred their dead in four types of places. The earliest burials were by pioneers in unorganized, isolated places. As the population grew, settlers became more formal in honoring their dead. A burial place situated on a family farm might also be used by neighboring families. Next, churchyards were established alongside the new churches, in some cases even before the churches could be built. Some churchyards not only offered members the right to inter their dead in an adjoining burial place but also allowed some to entomb their dead beneath the church itself, in public or private vaults. Finally, most towns maintained a potter's field, designated for the destitute or those not accepted into other burial places. Potter's fields were transient places and were often abandoned after a severe epidemic.

Pioneer Graves. The earliest colonial burial customs were influenced by a combination of the pioneers' European heritage and daily life. The first burial sites, except for those of Native Americans, were apparently isolated graves located wherever death occurred, or nearby already established Native American burial grounds. Little thought was given to marking the grave site because the gravedigger seldom expected to be able to protect and maintain the site. Away from the security of a European settlement, the grave was better left anonymous. Contemporary European customs, which did not highly regard the corpse and relegated most dead to trenches and ossuary houses, reinforced such attitudes toward the grave site.[2]

The nature of pioneer graves is illustrated by the story of Benjamin Nukerk, the first white settler recorded to have died in what later became Onondaga County in central New York State. He had come to the land of the Onondagas with two men and plenty of rum and whiskey to trade. His sudden death in 1787 left Ephraim Webster, the area's earliest pioneer, with the "melancholy task" of burial. Although he was initially disturbed by the Onondagas, Webster dug the grave, using a "slab of cedar, somewhat shaped in the form of a shovel." Almost a century later, the slate burial marker, which was inscribed with Nukerk's name, date of death, and age, still stood a small distance away from a large number of unmarked graves of Onondagas.[3]

Nukerk's grave was fortunately marked with a durable stone. Gravestones were rare throughout the colonial period. Few settlers, even in the cities, had carving skills. Country residents were likely to use a fieldstone or a wooden slab crudely scrawled with the deceased's initials. Within a few years, most of these markers disintegrated or were used by a farmer erecting a stonewall. Many graves were simply left unmarked, the memory of the mourners being the community's only guide to its dead.

Domestic Burial Grounds. The lonely grave was soon replaced by clusters of graves as the pioneers' homesteads grew into small settlements. In 1830, when Harriet Martineau traveled through the American frontier, she described a common sight, the family graveyard: "Wherever there is a solitary dwelling there is a domestic burying-place, generally fenced with neat white palings, and deliberately kept, however full the settler's hands may be, and whatever may be the aspect of the abode of the living." Commentators such as Martineau viewed these small burial grounds as symbols of civilization and domestication, in contrast to the harsh behavior of the frontier settlers.[4]

Set among the trees on the outskirts of one of the fields, the domestic graveyard usually occupied a high point on the land. Whether open for pasturing or enclosed by a stone wall, the graves were shaded by the trees ringing the field. Markers were placed irregularly around the small enclosure, with an occasional child's grave disturbing the line of the row because of the smaller size of the grave. The farmer periodically cut away the overgrown grass, and his wife tended any flowers planted inside the wall.

In burying their dead away from the church and close to home, settlers acted in marked contrast to their European contemporaries. Europeans had no tradition of family burial places, although there were examples of estate burial places unattached to churches. For British Protestants, "occasionally there were instances where the rich could afford to entomb their dead in great mausolea in the grounds of their houses." But these were the exceptions. Even if a French landowner chose to create a domestic burial ground, most of the unattached burial places were somehow sanctified with the relics of saints or actually became the site of a new church associated with the family of the deceased and the peasants who were loyal to that master.[5]

Domestic burial grounds were prevalent in all of the colonies, but were less popular in New England, where the Puritans were more likely to follow English custom and bury their dead around a central community building, the meeting house. Even outside the larger communities, in isolated towns such as Hanover, New Hampshire, families joined together to form neighborhood burial grounds. The majority of the people in the larger coastal settlements, who who were nominal church members, were buried in ever-growing burial grounds, such as that beside King's Chapel in Boston, or in vaults underneath the churches, as with the graves of John and Abigail Adams in Braintree (now Quincy), Massachusetts.

Southerners also had churchyards, particularly in the larger towns and where the Anglican church was strongest. Yet, as the domestic burial grounds at Washington's Mount Vernon and Jefferson's Monticello in Virginia clearly demonstrate, the dead often were buried at home on farms and plantations. The popularity of Washington's tomb as a visiting place reinforced the acceptability of domestic burial grounds. The deterioration of the tomb by the 1820s was also a reminder of the risk a family assumed when burying its dead on privately held ground. National concern about Washington's tomb, heightened by an attempt to steal the remains, resulted in the construction of a new Gothic Revival tomb in the 1830s. Many domestic burial grounds at southern plantations did not receive similar attention and were eventually abandoned.

African-American slaves were particularly susceptible to losing their rights to burial places. As with most northern free African-Americans, southern slaves were interred in either separate sections or completely segregated burial places. Slave burial places were community graveyards rather than family plots. The racist slave-holding society's attempt to strip African-Americans of legitimate familial and community relationships encouraged them to develop and protect the areas in which they could express their sense of family and community. The master's relationship to the slaves apparently strongly influenced the elaborate-

George Washington's Tomb, Mount Vernon, Va., 1839
George Washington was an important symbol of the new nationalism that swept America in the nineteenth century. The Gothic Revival tomb shown here was his second resting place. The first held his remains from 1799, the year of his death, until the 1830s, when national interest led Mount Vernon's caretakers to reinter his remains. Americans' concern for his tomb was one of several issues that led the Mount Vernon Ladies Association to purchase his estate in 1858 and begin preservations. (Engraving by W. H. Bartlett.)

ness of the funeral and cemetery. Few pre–Civil War gravestones of African-American slaves have been discovered, but evidence suggests that, just as they struggled to ensure their right to a funeral, they saw the cemetery as another important aspect of their fragile community.[6]

Susan Cooper, the daughter of James Fenimore Cooper, reported in 1850 that "small family burying-grounds, about the fields, are very common" among northerners. She suggested the prevalence of farm burials "had its origin . . . in the peculiar circumstances of the early population, thinly scattered over a wide country, and separated by distance and bad roads from any place of worship." Although churchyards existed in many of the small communities, distances and hardships reinforced the isolation in life and death on the frontier. The lack of clergy and churches led settlers to make the funeral a community affair, symbolic of the settlement's continuation despite the individual's death. As communities became less isolated and grew into larger villages and towns, the custom was formed of establishing a community burial ground that was not associated with churches. This American experience with a domestic, nonsectarian burial place was a foundation for the secularization of the burial process.[7]

The Churchyard. Many settlers followed European practices and interred their dead in the churchyard. From Trinity in New York City to St. Philip's in Charleston, South Carolina, churchyards served generations of city dwellers. Whether to be buried alongside the church or entombed underneath it, parishioners hoped for a comfortable closeness to heaven and a sentimental attachment to their church community.

Churchyards were the primary burial place in contemporary Europe, and by 1800 had been so for several centuries, but intramural churchyard burial had not always been the practice of Europeans. Fearing the proximity of the dead, Greeks and Romans carefully restricted them from the living, commanding through the Law of the Twelve Tables that "no dead body be buried or cremated inside the city." Instead, the Appian Way and other roads leading out of the cities of the Roman Empire were lined with family vaults "constructed on private estates or communal cemeteries owned and managed by associations that may have provided the early Christians with the legal model for their communities."[8]

Indeed, the early Christians retained the prohibition against burial of the dead in close proximity to the living. "As late as 563 . . . a canon of the Council of Braga [forbade] burial in the basilicas of the holy martyrs: 'One cannot refuse to the basilicas of the holy martyrs the privilege that the towns retain inviolably for themselves, of allowing no one to be buried inside their walls.'"

In time the Church reversed this attitude and "the dead ceased to frighten the living, . . . the two groups [coexisting] in the same places and behind the same walls." This new attitude toward the dead reflected the growing importance that the Church gave to the Resurrection. Due to the biblical account of

Slave Burial at Night, 1881
A night funeral accommodated the desire of slaves to have friends and relatives from neighboring plantations at the ceremony and the desire of masters to have death disrupt the work of the plantation as little as possible. The ceremonies ranged from hasty burials overseen by masters to lengthy, elaborate, African-influenced rituals, which ended with each mourner passing by the grave and throwing a handful of dirt into it. (Drawing by W. L. Sheppard, in Hamilton W. Pierson, D.D., *In the Brush; or Old-Time Social, Political, and Religious Life in the Southwest,* 1881. Courtesy of Dartmouth College Library.)

Jesus's entombment and Resurrection and because cremation was popular with the Romans and other pagans of the ancient world, Christian eschatology came to equate a proper burial with the possibility of salvation. Some early ecclesiastical writers suggested that such a position was ridiculous because an omniscient God was certainly capable of restoring bodies, but their arguments were rejected. A decent earth or vault burial, in a safe and protected place, became a part of popular Christian practice, demanded by all who hoped to join the saints on Judgment Day.

Reflective of this new attitude, which started in the time of Pope Gregory I (late sixth century), new church canons allowed bishops, abbots, priests, and chosen lay church members to be buried in the church itself and all others to be buried alongside the church in the churchyard. The reason for this change in the canons, one American source in the 1820s suggested, was that "relations and friends [of the dead] on the frequent view of their Sepulchre would be moved to pray for the good of the departed souls." Ariès has suggested that everyone wanted to be as close to the holy martyrs as possible because they were the only ones assured of resurrection on Judgment Day.[9]

The new burial place put one closer to the martyrs, and presumably to heaven, but not everyone got equally close. A social hierarchy of burial was quickly established, in which the "lesser folk contented themselves with the uncertain outdoors" in the churchyard. The wealthiest people determined that the "safest spot in any churchyard burying place was the ground next to the east wall of the church." Those with the least status could only afford the north wall, "thought [by the English] most vulnerable to evil spirits, for every earthly trouble from winter gales to Vikings came from that direction." Such a pattern placed the most successful within the warm church, those with the least status in its shadow, and those striving for status outside the building, but at least in the sunshine.[10]

The large number of interments eventually exhausted the space available for burials. Continental Europeans then began to remove decomposed bodies from the grave and place the remains in ossuaries or, as they were increasingly called, charnel houses, that were built within the churchyards. Bones and skeletons were often elaborately displayed during the Middle Ages. Whether displayed in a decorative manner or thrown in a heap, the dead were increasingly likely to be disturbed from the grave.

Long after many Continental Europeans abandoned the churchyard, the English continued the practice, possibly because they were less likely to disturb the dead. James Stevens Curl reports that, as late as the nineteenth century, "corpses were laid in leaden coffins in church crypts, or in brick-lined graves under the church floors; they were buried in wooden coffins in churchyards; or they were interred in small burial grounds that were usually associated with a church or chapel." English churchyards, like most churchyards associated with the churches of the Reformation, were less likely to have a charnel house and an ossuary. Protestants generally disdained the practice of recovering the grave by displacing the corpse. Only in the graveyards of the poor and in the busiest of urban churchyards were graves likely to be trenches with numerous occupants over the generations.[11]

Trinity Church, the seat of the Anglican bishop of New York, reflected this heritage. Trinity's church vaults and churchyard were the primary burial places for the city's English elite and also much of the rest of the Protestant English population. Contemporaries estimated that by 1800, after one hundred years of use, Trinity churchyard held the remains of over one hundred thousand New Yorkers. Vaults were spread throughout the church and tunnelled out from the church into the ground surrounding the building. The burial ground encompassed only a few acres, and no corpses were removed, so the space was reused many times. Burials raised the level of the churchyard by several yards during the century. The churchyard literally rose toward heaven; by the nineteenth century, it sat well above the surrounding streets.[12]

Other churchyards on the Atlantic seaboard underwent a similar build-up over the years. An 1859 report suggested that in St. Philip's churchyard in Charleston, space for approximately two thousand graves had been filled with about ten thousand bodies. In the Circular churchyard in the same city, the first burial had occurred in 1690 in a yard that measured about twenty thousand square feet, which seemed capable of holding about one thousand bodies, but over five thousand had been buried there.[13]

Catholics also chose churchyards as their primary burial places. Everywhere Catholics settled, the church established burial grounds for the faithful. In 1822 Felix McGuire, John McGuire, Patrick McChristen, and James A. Flynn, trustees of the third Catholic church of the western district of New York State, bought a corner lot in Rochester for the purpose of building a church "and for a Cemetery or burial ground, and for no other use or purpose." In New York City, St. Peter's was the first Catholic church consecrated (in 1786), and twenty-three new churches were constructed in the next eighty years. As the Catholic population grew, churchyards became very busy places. The New York City inspector's report for 1839 noted that 2,543 of 8,732 (29 percent) burials in the preceding year were in Catholic graveyards.[14]

Religious graveyards, whether Protestant, Catholic, or Jewish, were remarkably similar in their layout, monuments, and management. Graveyards appeared torn up from new burials and were rarely larger than a few acres. Graves were not carefully plotted, so lines of them often weaved across the grounds. Later, in the nineteenth century, well-meaning caretakers "beautified" many churchyards by straightening the lines of memorials and establishing pathways for visitors. Contemporary accounts suggest that few pathways existed, as space was at a premium. Ornamentation of the graveyards was sparse for the same reason. A few trees and scattered shrubs were the expected plantings.[15]

Neither churchyards nor domestic graveyards were the sacred, closed places that cemeteries became in the nineteenth century. Churchyards and domestic graveyards were rarely fortified or fenced, at least after the settlement was safe from conflict with Native Americans. Instead, such spaces were used for markets, fairs, meetings, walks, and talks. In some cases, the lush grass of the graveyard was purchased by a local farmer, who earned the right to pasture animals among the graves. This sharing of space continued contact between the living and the dead, but the lack of concern for the sacredness of the graveyard

VIEW OF COPPS HILL, BOSTON.

Copp's Hill Burial Ground, Boston, 1851

Copp's Hill was first used as a burial ground in 1659. John Winthrop and Cotton Mather are buried here. By the end of the eighteenth century, it represented the typical in-city graveyard. It was not protected by a fence, the rows of markers were orderly but sometimes askew, and the level of the graveyard had risen since it was first used as a burial site. (Engraving in Thomas Bridgman, *Epitaphs from Copp's Hill Burial Ground,* 1851.)

made displacing the dead and obliterating the graveyard much easier. As the nineteenth century approached, the living began to develop a new relationship to the dead, and the number of fenced or walled graveyards increased.[16]

A Native Art. Americans erected wood and stone markers within the cramped and rather barren grounds of domestic burial grounds and churchyards. Using local stones, such as slate, schist, and soapstone, local artisans crafted gravestones that reflected contemporary theology, economics, and demographics. Artisans carved stele-shaped individual markers, which remained the typical style of stone from 1750 to 1830. These carvings, along with painting, represent some of the finest early American art.[17]

The earliest carvings appeared in the 1670s, ornamenting stones. Previous stones had provided only the deceased's initials, age, and years of birth and death. Stones of the first few decades were filled with skulls and crossbones, coffins, skeletons, and the dominant figure, the death's-head. The ornamental stones contrasted starkly with the lack of imagery in the meeting houses and churches of Protestant New England, the region where the carvings were most elaborate and extensive. Puritans believed that such imagery would be an obstacle in a person's relationship with God. The meeting house was a place of solemn observance, a sacred place in a profane world.

The churchyard burial ground, however, was outside ecclesiastical boundaries, so it could serve as a didactic landscape for the living. The death's-head and the skeleton reminded passers-by that death was inevitable, teaching them that they should live piously in hopes of salvation. Centrally located, the burial grounds offered a constant reminder of these beliefs and a place of quiet meditation for the community.

In the 1740s, the death's-head was joined by the soul-effigy, a winged representation of a soul ascending toward heaven. The soul-effigy was a particularly favorite of carvers and, presumably, customers. The image remained popular as late as the final years of the eighteenth century. Certainly the soul-effigy was a gentler, more sentimental image than the death's-head or the skull and crossbones. The soul-effigy was more optimistic, reflecting a growing belief in a greater chance for salvation.

Although the death's-head or the soul-effigy were the dominant grave-stone carvings during the eighteenth century, neither monopolized this vibrant and vital art. Portraits, hourglasses, crossbones, mourners, and urns were found on many stones. Some carvers became well known beyond their towns. They sold stones in adjoining towns and cities, even in nearby states. A few carvers transported their work from New England, the site of many of the most prolific cravers, as far as South Carolina. The designs, especially the soul-effigies, seemed to speak to a wide geographical and religious spectrum of colonial society.[18]

After the Revolution, the soul-effigy gradually disappeared, and grave-stone carving in general became more standardized and less artistic. Yet one last great episode of carving occurred. Americans turned from the more abstract images of death to classically influenced symbols of mourning, specifically the urn and willow. The urn and willow swept through the nation's graveyards, replacing a wide range of previous motifs. An enormous variety of styles and combinations were carved using the three basic ideas of the urn, willow, and mourner.

Many of the urn and willow carvings appeared on marble stones. As Reverend William Bentley reported to his diary in 1803, white marble "has been within a few months introduced for gravestones" in Salem, Massachusetts. He worried that the new gravestones were more expensive; they were eighteen dollars each, whereas the usual slate ones were twelve dollars each. Bentley noted that gravestones had become increasingly popular in the last thirty years. Prior to that, gravestones were infrequently raised in Salem. Only when "a Stone Cutter" moved to town did the number of stones suddenly increase.[19]

Church Vaults. In the largest cities, burial sites included not only the churchyard but also the church. The Brick Presbyterian Church on Beekman Street in New York City was one of the city's most prestigious. The Presbyterian membership was a rapidly growing, wealthy group. The church offered ground burial in a churchyard surrounding the church and in a larger burial ground on the

Early American Gravestone Styles, c. 1700–1820s

Gravestone styles changed dramatically between the seventeenth and nineteenth centuries. The skull and crossbones, the death's-head (at left), and other graphic iconography gradually was succeeded by softer images, such as the soul-effigy and, later, the urn and willow (at right). In the years before 1830, gravestone carvings were examples of American folk art at its finest.

corner of North (later East Houston) and Chrystie streets. A small number of family vaults, approximately ten by thirteen feet, were also offered for sale by church officials when the new church was opened on Beekman Street in the 1760s. By 1817 there were thirteen family vaults along the front of the church; these vaults extended under the street.[20]

Vault burial was available to many city residents. Churches offered both private vaults that could be purchased by families and public vaults in which any member of the congregation could be entombed. In a rapidly growing city in which accessible land was extremely valuable, subterranean vaults were considered an excellent use of space. Some churches became virtual warrens of vaults, which stretched out beyond the building into the churchyard and under the street. In 1823 it was reported there were over 570 vaults underneath New York City churches. These vaults varied dramatically in size and cost and were the burial place of a significant number of Americans.[21]

A vault was the property of the family, which was responsible for its upkeep. In a series of fascinating letters to his daughter in New Orleans, John Pintard, founder of the New-York Historical Society, commented on his melancholy task of maintaining the family vault under St. Espirit's Church in lower

Manhattan. Pintard's family apparently purchased the vault in 1704. For 116 years, deceased members of the Pintard family had been entombed beneath the city streets. Pintard reported in 1796 that he had found it "necessary . . . to empty the decayed coffins of their contents" to "make room for successors." By 1820 Pintard had designated that the coffins holding "my remains and your dear mothers *[sic]*" would "rest on that [coffin of] my dear & venerable uncles, for the floor is more than two deep of coffins."

In the early nineteenth century, St. Espirit's closed and the congregation moved to St. Clement's. Pintard found removing the family remains to the new vault under St. Clement's "the most painful services." He carefully prepared the new vault, located under the vestry in the rear of the church. He wrote that the vault was "being constructed like a cellar with doors, locks, & keys. Tho' not so large is more so than most modern vaults. I have had it shelved at the lower end so as to contain Coffins without resting on each other." Pintard was forced by space limitations to combine the remains of several of the most decayed ancestors into two coffins.[22]

In the eighteenth century, church interments and entombments were the responsibility of the sexton, who was a general church superintendent. Burial duties were only a small part of his responsibilities. At one church, trustees declared that the sexton's duties included "ringing . . . the bell, opening, sweeping, dusting, and lighting the church; and sweeping and cleaning the streets adjacent, as required by law; opening, sweeping, and lighting the session room, at all such times as are now usual in the day or evening, for the accommodation of the session, trustees, lectures, and prayer-meetings of the church." The sexton's yearly salary of $125 was heavily supplemented by "other emoluments arising from the church," such as burial fees (worth perhaps as much as $225 per year) and collection of pew rents, from which the sexton received 5 percent.[23]

Potter's Fields. Those who could not afford a vault or a grave were buried in the *potter's field,* the term used in the Book of Matthew (23:7) and applied to any burial place for the indigent. Few graveyards were established exclusively as potter's fields prior to the nineteenth century. Earlier communities often set aside a plot in the community burial ground, and churches held open parts of a vault or a plot within the churchyard. Sometimes these plots were designated for "strangers," who presumably would not have the means to pay for their own grave. Most towns were forced to provide such a service early on, as was Chicago, which created a common burial ground in the 1820s.

One of the difficulties in tracing potter's fields is that few existed for very long. New Amsterdam officials organized a potter's field as early as the 1620s. Over the next century and a half, this burial place was consecutively replaced with new ones on Broadway, just outside the gates to the city (1662), and on Pearl Street (1765). During the Revolution, the British used the Old Negroes

Burying Ground, located in a swampy area in what is now City Hall Park, as a public cemetery.

After the Revolution, a new burying place for African-Americans was established at 195 Chrystie Street. That same year, the Common Council appropriated a swampy triangle three miles north of the city as a new almshouse burial ground. In his diary, Gabriel Furman described the fate of this graveyard. In December 1821, he walked through the graveyard and was affected by the graves of the yellow-fever victims of 1794 through 1798. In March 1822, he passed by again "and found the monumental stones all set against the . . . wall, the field having been ploughed and planted with corn." In November 1823 he noted that the House of Refuge for Juvenile Delinquents had occupied the adjoining building and, presumably, the graveyard. This spot later became Madison Square.[24]

In the South as well as the North, public and private graveyards were racially segregated. Often separate graveyards were established for African-Americans and whites. In Charleston, an 1859 report noted that in the Upper Wards there were fourteen graveyards for whites and twelve for "the colored, not including the Potters Field." Historians of Chicago have noted that the city's burial places have been segregated from the very beginning. Both the old and new burial grounds in New Haven had sections set apart for the "Colored." Only for a short time, in some places with the founding of the rural-cemetery movement, would Americans decide that racially segregated cemeteries were unnecessary.[25]

EARLY AMERICAN FUNERALS

The burial place was only part of the larger, evolving custom of tending and burying the dead. As the location and structure of the graveyard changed, so did the funeral ceremony. The privatization of the funeral in the nineteenth-century city reinforced the family orientation and private nature of the grave site. The cemetery evolved as much from the changing attitudes toward death and the manner of handling the dead as it did from the development of urban society. The funeral continued to reflect the tension between the private nature of death and the public display of grief, which would manifest itself throughout American history.

From the earliest times in the colonies, the funeral was a communal event. A burial on the farm was a family happening: "Events date from it and centre on it." When there was a death, family members prepared the body, tended to the household, informed the neighbors, and arranged for the service. Friends and relatives gathered at the home of the deceased. If there was no clergyman, the eldest member of the household read a simple service. Around sunset, the males carried the body to the grave for a short burial ceremony. Afterward there might be a meal and a gathering at the home. The grave, dug by family members or the church sexton, was positioned so that the body faced east; this was in keeping with the hope of Resurrection.[26]

The funeral was as much a social as a religious event, defining the community and its people. In the more rural areas, the funeral was proof of the friendship and unity of the small town, because the entire community participated in the remembrance of the dead. In 1805 Julian Ursyn Niemcewewicz, a Pole who was visiting America, witnessed a funeral cavalcade that suggested the social relationship of death and burial: "We met a procession of about thirty wagons filled with men and women who were going six miles . . . to an interment. . . . But, while partly a religious duty, it is much more an Event, a holiday even, if you prefer, which brings them together for gossip and drinking and thus breaks the uniform monotony of the ordinary day."[27]

In seventeenth-century New England communities, ministers did not participate in funerals. They attended the ceremony as members of the greater community. More important than the minister's sermon, which often was given a few days after the burial ceremony at church services, was the sense of the gathering of the family and the celebration by family and friends of the continuation of their community.

Still, death remained inextricably intertwined with religion and specifically with the church. The home was the site of the burial party, and the church congregation made up the community from which the deceased departed. Most individuals, even in an age of increasing emphasis on the individual soul, retained tight bonds with their religious community. Yet an emotional concern for the individual was becoming more acceptable among Protestants in the seventeenth century. Americans kept emotion sternly in check, for they recognized that death still was the beginning of a new, eternal existence, for which most people were not prepared.[28]

The funeral began to change in the eighteenth century. When people moved to larger towns, most lost the fervor of early Puritan and other religious colonial communities; this resulted in formalized social relationships. Now only the wealthiest of families could afford to invite the entire town to a funeral, and even they would not want all their neighbors to attend. Gradually the funeral became more of a religious event, although it retained its social function. By the mid-eighteenth century, clergy performed services prior to the burial. The services might be in the home, but the clergyman was the center of the ceremony. The postburial feast became increasingly popular as the family attempted to retain control of the process. The family presented small gifts to the clergyman and the pallbearers.[29]

The emergence of other religions and denominations, which had their own churchyards, further formalized the funeral and burial process. The earliest churchyards were intended to serve the entire religious community. The Dutch settlements on the Hudson River soon became infiltrated by the English, and the once purely Protestant settlements now were populated by Protestants, Catholics, and Jews. People became more selective in choosing their neighbors and friends. Yet throughout the colonial and early national periods, a stranger who had died in an American town was buried in the same graveyard with much the same ceremony afforded the oldest resident of the community.[30]

Because churchyards were considered sanctified spaces, members of other religions and outcasts such as suicides were prohibited from burial. John Pintard reminded his daughter in 1829 that, previous to the Revolution, a suicide was buried "where 4 Roads met," to deter such an act. In one instance, a crossroads was marked with an inscription beginning, "*Stop Traveler,*" and setting forth the name and particulars, which Pintard and his friends were made to read as children.

Nineteenth-century society was increasingly unwilling to accept such sanctions against suicides. Pintard remembered, to his regret, that more recently such profane actions were not met with corresponding vigilance. Indeed, in 1810, Sarah Hull committed suicide. "The circumstances of her death," Pintard related, "brought an immense concourse of people to witness a parade, only due to distinguished public worth." Soon after, the old practice of quietly removing a suicide to a family burial ground during the night slowly stopped as more public ceremonies became socially acceptable. Pintard, a man of the old school, was tempted to "lucubrate on a misguided subject," but he recognized that surviving friends would disagree. Yet he ended his epistle to his daughter by reminding her that "such mistaken motives ought not however prevent doing what is right."[31]

Churchyards maintained a sense of community, but that community was not inclusive. No longer would neighbors automatically be told of a death. Instead, written notices gradually replaced the custom of having an individual invite each person to the funeral. These written notices often were sent by messenger to friends and relatives, but they also began to appear in newspapers. A typical notice appeared in the New York *Evening Post* on 5 July 1823: "Early this morning, in the sixty second year of her age, Elizabeth Kermit, relict of Henry Kermit, deceased. The friends and acquaintances of the family are requested to attend her funeral, to-morrow morning, at 9 o'clock precisely, from her late residence, No. 86 Greenwich street."[32]

Eighteenth-century funerals had become more elaborate than seventeenth-century ones, and people questioned whether such funerals were morally justifiable. In 1753 the Massachusetts legislature acted to curb the perceived excesses by restricting expenditures and cautioned against excessive spending. Such legislation apparently had little influence. In 1797 Caleb Davis's funeral cost $844. However, attempts at changes continued into the new century. In 1819 John Pintard wrote his daughter that he had voluntarily stopped giving scarves to pallbearers, setting aside the $50 that would be saved for the Society for the Support of Poor Widows. Although there was a general concern about the expense of funerals, the real criticism came in a more broad-based attack on the appropriateness of early American graveyards within the commercial city.[33]

OVERCROWDING IN EUROPEAN GRAVEYARDS

In 1780 Parisians living in the apartment buildings next to the ancient and venerable Cimetière des Innocents were shocked by a rumbling in their basements. Soon many were overwhelmed by the stench rising from below, and several became seriously ill from mephitic gas. French officials quickly realized that the overcrowded graveyard had broken down the basement walls and sent over two thousand partially decomposed bodies into the basements. They at once applied quick lime to mitigate the incident's impact. The officials quickly reconsidered plans for relocating the city's dead to a less crowded graveyard not situated in the middle of the growing city.[34]

The macabre incident was the most tragic example of the overcrowding of European graveyards in the late eighteenth century. Throughout the Continent and Great Britain, the churchyards and municipal graveyards that had been receiving Europe's dead for centuries were simply exhausted. Cimetière des Innocents was prime example. A Paris burial ground since at least 1186, when Philippe Auguste had surrounded it with high walls "because it had been made a place of the grossest debauchery," Cimetière des Innocents was the burial place of approximately 10 percent of the city's dead annually. It was estimated that over one million bodies had been buried, decomposed, and removed to the Le Grand Charnier des Innocents, the graveyard's charnel house. Bodies were rarely allowed to stay in the ground longer than a few years, particularly in the eighteenth century, when the pressure on the graveyard was at it highest.[35]

Yet the situation at Cimetière des Innocents was not unique. London's graveyards were also very crowded. John Evelyn had hoped that, after the great fire of London of 1665–66, magistrates would remove all the churchyards from the city, but they did not. Thus, instead of a "grated enclosure of competent breadth," which might have served all the parishes, individual churchyards remained throughout the city. Enclosed by residences and businesses, on land that was becoming exceedingly valuable, the churchyards continued burying in eight-foot-deep trenches in order to accommodate the large number of dead.[36]

The disaster in Paris eventually led French officials to open the catacombs, which served as the city's burial place from the 1780s until the nineteenth-century external cemeteries were organized. London and other cities also began reconsidering the practices of the past. New dissenter cemeteries, such as Bunhill Fields, were located outside the built-up parts of London. New churchyards were encouraged, in order to relieve the burdens on older ones.

Still, the *Quarterly Review* noted in 1819 that "there has existed a prejudice against new churchyards!" Churchgoers wanted to be buried in the place that held their ancestors and their friends. Only slowly could people be lured from past practices.

As a student of Spanish burial practices has demonstrated, the transition from the churchyard to the external cemetery was resisted by people who saw the move lowering their status. In Spain, the wealthiest members of the community, along with the clerics, continued to be entombed in the churches, whereas the middle class and the poor were shunted to the periphery. The class-conscious middle class, particularly the merchant elite, was unwilling to be buried with the poor and exiled from the church. Only years of promotion and enforcement gradually improved the status of the peripheral graveyards.[37]

While the location and the style of the new cemeteries were under discussion, consensus had been reached that the in-city churchyard and graveyard were at least nuisances and probably health hazards. Informed by the scientific work of Joseph Priestley and Antoine-Laurent de Lavoisier, critics became insistent that the grave presented a peril to the innocent bystander because its decaying matter created a dangerous atmosphere for disease and more death. The French in particular perceived disinterred bodies as potentially lethal not only for the cemetery's neighbors but also the whole city. Cimetière des Innocents closed, and the search for a new style of burial ground was begun.[38]

THE NEW HAVEN BURYING GROUND

In the small but growing coastal cities, Americans had concerns similar to those of Europeans, although the overcrowding was far greater in the latter's cities, which were older. In the 1780s and 1790s, many residents of American cities, particularly those who followed developments in European science and medicine, began campaigns to close in-city graveyards and move them outside of towns. In New Haven, Connecticut, such a campaign led to experimentation with a new type of burial place, a private association of lot-holders joining together to save the living and preserve the dead.

The New Haven Burying Ground, as the new cemetery was named by founders in 1796, replaced the older burial ground, established prior to the erection of the town's first meeting house in 1639. The older burial ground had served as the community's primary burial place for 157 years, during which there had been an estimated four thousand to five thousand burials. By the 1790s, the dead were buried in a seventy-thousand-square-foot octagon, which was centered on the central green behind the brick meeting house. According to contemporaries, the graveyard crept across the green as the space allocated to the older burial ground was filled. The recurrence of yellow fever in the 1790s, especially in 1794 and 1795, dramatically increased the death rate, causing a crisis on the green. The town usually had about 80 deaths per year. Yellow fever and other illnesses left at least 116 dead within a few months in 1794.[39]

Not surprisingly, the older burial ground was the subject of several scathing attacks. Most of the attacks were less concerned with health considerations than with aesthetic ones. In 1795 Reverend John Pierce wrote of his trip to New Haven: "The beauty of the green is greatly impaired by the Burial ground in the centre, which, it is contemplated, to hide from public view by weeping willows." Timothy Dwight, writing in retrospect, noted that a burial ground should be "a solemn object to man." He considered the older burial ground to have been "rendered too familiar to the eye to have any beneficial effect on the heart." "From its proper, venerable character," he continued, "it is degraded into a mere common object, and speedily loses all its connection with the invisible world in a gross and vulgar union with the ordinary business of life."

Dwight wrote that "this ground was filled with coffins and monuments, and must either be extended farther over the beautiful tract unhappily chosen for it, or must have its place supplied by a substitute." Rising commercialism and the hustle and bustle of the town challenged the long-held ideal of the New England community, with meeting house and graveyard in the center of life.[40]

Along with many other New England towns, New Haven was changing in the early years of the new nation. After the long period of stagnation caused by the troubles surrounding the political grievances of the colonists, which ended in revolution, New Haven was expanding physically and economically. The original nine squares, long the center of town life, were by 1812 all intersected by cross streets in order to increase the number of accessible building lots in the town. These building lots were home to prosperous merchants, many of whom were engaged in the lucrative shipping trade that led to the expansion of New Haven's wharves. As economically exciting as the growing shipping trade was the construction in 1798 of Eli Whitney's arms plant, which signaled the beginnings of "a driving impulse toward civic improvements and economic progress."[41]

The most important civic improvement begun during this period was natural beautification. After long celebrating the conquering of nature, some in New Haven attempted to remarry city and country by beautifying the city streets with elms and other trees. Colonists had held that a piece of land must be rid of its trees in order to be cultivated. Urban residents of New Haven in the 1790s welcomed back nature as a part of the city. They viewed the reintroduction of nature as a moral virtue destined to make city life less harsh, less immoral, and less barren. James Hillhouse's commitment to returning nature to the lives of the city residents helped motivate him to participate in the plan for a new cemetery.[42]

Hillhouse served Connecticut as legislator, congressman, and senator for thirty years. Deeply involved with the development of New Haven, he was a spokesman for many of its enterprises, including the cemetery.[43] While Hill-house was a leader of the community, an individual who, in Leonard Bacon's words, "aimed at the public good" and "lived for his country," personal perspectives on burial customs also compelled him to act.

The epidemics of 1794 and 1795, as well as the general atmosphere of ill health in New Haven, made Hillhouse "not unmindful of the uncertainties of human life." According to contemporary sources, Hillhouse's involvement may have originated in his inability to secure "a sacred and inviolate burial place" for his family. Apparently Hillhouse had considered "making a family burying ground on his own property." He decided against a domestic graveyard after a visit to an estate formerly occupied by one branch of his family, where "he noted with regret, that when the property passed out of the possession of the family, the family burying ground went with the rest into the hands of strangers." The descendants retained only the right to visit. The family had to rely on others to ensure that the property was "honorably protected" and not "neglected, injured, or entirely obliterated."[44]

Thus Hillhouse had three motives for establishing a new burial place and three corresponding objectives for the new cemetery. Fearful of the insecurity of private farm burial, concerned about the epidemics raging almost annually in New Haven, and mindful of the inappropriateness of public burial on the green, Hillhouse sought a grave site permanently secure, situated away from the congested parts of town, and naturally attractive. Unwilling or unable to secure such a burial place through the town, his church, or his family, Hillhouse joined with thirty-one others from the town's wealthy families to incorporate a private association dedicated to establishing and maintaining a burial ground within New Haven. The new cemetery was a remarkable achievement; its institutional structure was unique, and the design of the grounds was considered innovative by contemporaries.

Permanence and security were the primary goals of the new association; a private corporation insured that a family could protect the graves of their ancestors. Incorporation was a relatively new concept in America. The British Crown had never conceded the colonies the right to create private corporations. After the Revolution, Americans exercised this right of government more freely, and, beginning in 1782, incorporation was increasingly used. The City of New Haven itself, incorporated in 1784, held one of the first incorporation charters in the new nation. In the 1790s, the use of the charter was extended from municipalities to private groups and associations. States had incorporated roads, bridges, banks, and insurance companies, but New Haven was the first cemetery incorporated in America.[45]

Incorporation established ownership and control: "Any person or body politic, their heirs, successors, or signs, who shall be the proprietor or owner of a lot which now is, or hereafter shall be located or laid out in said burying ground, shall be a legal member of said corporation, and entitled to one vote for every lot he or they shall own or possess." The proprietors, usually the head of the family, were the owners of the cemetery. The local minister, the town-paid sexton, or any other religious or governmental authority no longer decided if a person could be buried within the burial place, or if the graves should be moved. The cemetery belonged to the families who, through their investment in lots, joined with one another in securing the safety of their dead.

As a result of the decision to establish the new cemetery through a voluntary association of private individuals, the cemetery was legally recognized as a sacred place outside the commercial life of the society. Received from the state of Connecticut, the charter of the new corporation specified that it was exempt from taxes and liabilities imposed on ordinary businesses and individuals. The graveyard had previously been protected from such liabilities through its association with a church or government. The state, through the New Haven charter, was declaring that the cemetery itself was dedicated to a sacred purpose that made it an exception to the rules governing private businesses. This recognition reinforced the cemetery's segregation from commercial life and its role as moral educator within society. It also would prompt considerable controversy when some nineteenth-century cemetery proprietors restructured the cemetery to enable them to profit from sales of lots and cemetery services.

As a result of the separation of the dead from church and state, the family became central to the new institution. Although nine sections were put aside for religious congregations, Yale College, the poor, "Negros," and "Strangers," the remainder of the cemetery was divided into family lots. The landscape revolved around the family. The extensive family lots were centered around a monument proclaiming, often in large letters, the family name. Dwight noted that the "monuments . . . are almost universally of marble, in a few instances from Italy, in the rest found in this and the neighboring states."[46] Families spent large amounts of money celebrating the kinship, rather than the individual achievement, of those buried within the lot.

The horticultural plans for the new burial ground combined elements of eighteenth-century English gardens, American domestic graveyards, and the flowering orchards of the surrounding countryside. A committee consisting of Joseph Drake, Isaac Mills, Elias Shipman, Simeon Baldwin, and James Hillhouse assumed the task of ornamenting the "burying ground with such kinds, and so many trees, as they shall judge advisable." The cemetery was laid out as a grid, with avenues emanating from a central roadway at the entrance.

The new corporation placed Lombardy poplars along the roadways. The poplars grew fast and straight, quickly providing the grounds with shade and ornamentation. The straight trees accented the geometric design of the grounds, emphasizing the regularity and stability of the institution. A few weeping willows were scattered throughout the grounds. The weeping willow had recently emerged in Europe and America as a symbol of a burial place, suggesting a "sense of propriety in disposing of the remains of the deceased."

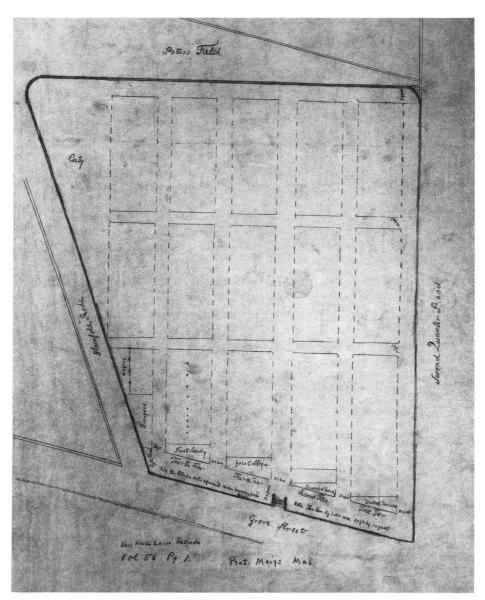

Josiah Meig's Plan of the New Haven Burying Ground, New Haven, Conn., 1797
In 1796 the New Haven Burying Ground was established, and its grounds were laid out
by Josiah Meigs. The new burial place marked a transition from old to new practices.
Note that "Yale College," "Strangers," and "Negros" were among the groups who had
special lots. The private sections were divided into family lots, but the New Haven
Burying Ground remained committed to providing burial sites for the whole community. (Courtesy of New Haven Colony Historical Society.)

As with the terrain of colonial graveyards, the terrain of the new burial ground was not reordered nor the plantings so abundant as to make the graveyard a pleasure ground.[47]

The corporation's individual proprietors were to add plantings to those provided by the corporation. The founders perceived the corporation as a holding company, with the proprietors responsible for the cemetery's appearance. The grounds were sold in large family lots, extending thirty-two feet by eighteen feet. Each family lot was to have plantings surrounding the central monument. Most proprietors quickly erected obelisks adorned with their family name and placed around them a low hedge, a fence, and a new tree or two. The new burial ground was a place where families could securely bury, honor, and remember their dead for generations.

European and American visitors to New Haven were impressed with the new burial ground. Dwight accompanied many Americans and Europeans into the cemetery, "not one of whom had ever seen or heard of anything of a similar nature." In 1821 Englishman William Tudor praised the New Haven Burying Ground and suggested that it could be the model for reform in English cemeteries. He was struck by the landscape ideas that New Haven symbolized and wrote: "The yew, the willow, and other funereal trees, would form suitable ornaments within [our graveyards]. . . . Such a cemetery would be an interesting spot to visit; and when dispirited by unkindness, misfortune, or that listless satiety, that makes life insipid, a walk among the graves of our friends might sooth the mind into composure."[48]

The appearance of the New Haven Burying Ground reflected the forces that were causing other towns and cities to reconsider their custom of in-city burial places. The graveyards that had served towns and villages for a century were now overcrowded and inconveniently located. Entrepreneurs wanted the center of the city for business or at least as a place of pleasure for the living. Above all, there were growing worries about the safety of the living in the presence of the dead.

THE ATTACK ON IN-CITY BURIAL GROUNDS

On 31 March 1823, New York City's Common Council passed "A Law respecting the interment of the Dead." This legislation ordained that, "after the first day of June next," no individual could "dig or open any grave or cause or procure any grave to be opened in any burying ground cemetery or church yard . . . which lies to the Southward of a line commencing at the centre of Canal Street on the North River and running through the centre of Canal Street to Sullivan Street thence through Sullivan st. to Grand Street thence through Grand St. to the East river." Offenders were to be fined a sum of $250 for "every such offence."[49]

New York City's 1823 action, and discussions of similar legislation in cities from Charleston to Boston, was a response to the failure of medicine and government to alleviate the yellow-fever epidemics that had terrorized America since 1793. The origin and transmission of yellow fever was a widely debated topic, and the legislative discussions both reflected and fueled that debate. Although the 1823 legislation was enacted to promote the health of New York City, its response to the crisis suggested that changing American attitudes toward the dead, death, and the grave site were being influenced by more than health considerations.

Certainly there was justification for concern about the public's health. Yellow fever was not simply a problem in New Haven; it was a national issue. Yellow fever had reappeared in New York City in 1793, after a fifty-year absence. The disease continued to reappear over the next decade, then disappeared from 1805 to 1819. The worst of the early epidemics occurred in 1798, when over fifteen hundred lives were lost. By 1818 the city felt secure from yellow fever, but the fever returned in 1819, then again in 1820, killing forty-one people. When the fever swept through the city starting in July 1822, the year's death toll was the worst since the 1790s.[50]

The disease was the subject of a medical debate with public-policy ramifications. Physicians debated whether yellow fever was a noncontagious disease indigenous to America or a contagious disease brought to America from the disease-ridden West Indies by infected people, as well as contaminated food and other imported goods. Supporters of the latter theory argued that the only ways to stop the virulent spread of this disease were an effective quarantine of infected ships and an immediate isolation of people infected with yellow fever.[51]

A shipping quarantine was unpopular because it dramatically affected the business climate of the import-dependent American economy. Business was further disabled when people abandoned cities because of fear of yellow fever. Thus government officials, fearing the effect on commerce, regularly delayed the announcement of the disease. In 1822 the original diagnosis of three people living on Rector Street in New York City occurred three weeks before the public was warned of the danger of yellow fever.

Some physicians rejected the need for any quarantine, arguing that the disease was indigenous, spread through a miasma, a gas or atmosphere hovering over the earth. They suggested that the disease was not contagious, but instead was given off by the sick into the miasma, which was then carried by "animalcules" through the air to infect the next person.

Physicians demanded close inspection of markets, thorough cleaning of streets, installation of new systems of garbage collection, and other measures to cleanse the city of decaying matter. Physicians also proposed distancing the dead from the living. As early as 1806, the city's Board of Health pleaded "that the interments of dead bodies within the city, *ought to be prohibited*." The reason was that "a vast mass of decaying animal matter, produced by the superstition of

Trinity Church and Churchyard, New York City, 1847

Trinity churchyard was the primary burial spot for Protestant New Yorkers for over a century. In the small area surrounding the church, over one hundred thousand bodies were interred. This large number led some critics to charge that the churchyard was a danger to the neighbors' health. (Lithograph by John Forsyth and G. W. Mine, after a drawing by Richard Upjohn. Courtesy of New-York Historical Society, New York City.)

interring dead bodies near the churches, and which has been accumulating for a long lapse of time, is now deposited in many of the most populous parts of the city. It is impossible that such a quantity of these animal remains, even if placed at the greatest depth of interment commonly practiced, can continue to be inoffensive and safe."[52]

Although New York City did not accept the board's judgment, the issue did not disappear. In 1807 a commissioner of health informed the city inspector that the African Zion Methodist Episcopal Church "emitted, frequently, a smell which was very offensive to the neighbors." Because the miasma was impossible to locate except through the fetid odors of decay, such a condition was a serious health concern. The church had no burial ground, relying upon a single burial vault for the entombment of its deceased members. The church had buried approximately 150 members a year for the last five years. As a result, "upon opening the door of this vault," the city inspector reported, "the smell is at this season (August) of the year, peculiarly offensive." The city inspector asked the Common Council to prohibit interment in the vault, fearing "it may be productive of terrible consequences to the neighbourhood." The Common Council agreed and allowed the church a section of the public burial ground for future burials.[53]

The Common Council did not prohibit burials in similar situations involving white churches, but over the next decade it refused petitions by several churches to enlarge or to add below-ground burial vaults. In 1813 Dr. Isaac Ball, in an attack on such burial practices in the *Medical Record,* mentioned that he had been told by the sexton of the Old Dutch Church that, when he descended into the vaults, "candles [lost] their lustre, and that the air was so sour and pungent that it stung his nose like pepper-dust." The return of yellow fever in 1819 provoked residents near New York City's potter's field to criticize sharply the practice of digging a grave large enough for ten to twelve coffins and leaving it open until filled. The Common Council's Committee on Public Land and Places recommended that at least two feet of dirt cover all corpses.[54]

Believers in miasmatic transmission felt that the 1822 epidemic proved the relationship between the graveyard and the origins and transmission of yellow fever. Francis Allen noted that only the "most obstinant theorist" would not accept the position that "the putrid exhalations arising from grave-yards, will not only feed and strengthen yellow fever when once introduced, but will generate disease equally malignant as yellow fever." In a pamphlet castigating local government officials, Allen maintained that allowing burials to continue in the middle of New York City was tantamount to murder of its residents and that the latest yellow fever epidemic could be traced to Rector Street, across from Trinity churchyard. Indeed, the city closed the churchyard during the epidemic. Further, the epidemic was severest around Trinity and spread only sporadically through the rest of the city.[55]

Opposition to Allen's theories was considerable. Daniel Walters wrote in

the *New York Medical and Physical Journal* that although "some ingenious persons
. . . labour hard to prove that the source of the mischief was to be found in the
burying ground attached to Trinity church, . . . it is only necessary to state the
fact, that the poison which actually did cause the disease, was spreading daily in
every direction, . . . for one month before it reached the vicinity of the
churchyard." Walters, along with Joseph Bayley, argued that a shipment of
sugar was the culprit, bringing the disease into the port and touching off the
epidemic. They felt that the traditional action of a shipping quarantine, if
imposed early enough, would have kept the disease from New York City.[56]

David Hosack, who believed that yellow fever could not have originated in
New York, recognized that decaying matter, such as corpses, increased the
impurities in the air, thus allowing miasmas to occur and to spread the disease.
For this reason, Hosack opposed allowing graves to be dug in the graveyards of
the city, though he believed that vaults, which were less frequently opened and
more securely sealed, were permissible.

The struggle among the physicians influenced the public's perception of
the problem and the government's response. When Mayor Stephen Allen made
his original plea that something be done to counteract the continuing epidemics, he straddled the medical fence, declaring that the shipping quarantine
should be strengthened and that environmental concerns should be addressed.
Simply by moving beyond the quarantine, Allen opened a debate about the
efficacy, even necessity, of such measures. Francis Allen and Dr. Felix Pascalis—
a French-born San Domingan refugee—provided facts and arguments for the
aldermen seeking the prohibition of new interments. David Hosack and others
supported a limited repeal of the legislation; this repeal would allow private
vaults to be used. Although the physicians could not agree and left the debate to
the politicians, the public's health remained the motive for the debate over
prohibition of interments.

NEW YORK CITY AND THE DEAD

Trinity Church's desire for three new burial vaults, each of which would have
held two hundred bodies, initiated the 1823 controversy. The new vaults were
to be located "within one foot of the wall which separates the burying ground
from Lumber-street." Given the public opposition to existing burial vaults,
graveyards, and churchyards, the decision to petition for expansion was a
gauntlet that the church threw down at the Common Council. The Common
Council countered by taking up proposed legislation on interments, which had
been tabled the previous December.[57]

The Common Council agreed that current practices had to be changed. It
passed a ban on earth burials within the area; this ban was based on accepted
medical theories. Then the debate moved on to a discussion of banning all
interments. Mayor Allen's original bill of December 1822 had proposed that all

graves and *public* vaults be banned, but that the *private* family vaults continue in use. Mayor Allen believed that the primary danger was the grave, which when opened uncovered soil that was "more or less saturated with the remains of decayed bodies, and the sun operating on this mass of corruption impregnated the air for some distance with disagreeable effluvia." Mayor Allen's position was a middle one, accepting the importance of environmental issues, but avoiding total disruption of established customs.[58]

The Common Council had a long and acrimonious debate focused less on the medical need for such a prohibition, which its members did not unanimously accept, than the social need not to discriminate against poorer members of the community who could not afford to purchase private burial chambers. One member asked: "Why shall we make exceptions in favor of the rich—of old families who have vaults—and prohibit the poor and middling classes of this community from burying their dead where their fathers were buried?" The Common Council agreed, passing the prohibition with only three dissenting votes.[59]

The vote did not end the controversy, but only fueled the debate about its propriety. Over the next two years, the opposition sought out support and tried various means to overturn the prohibition. Opponents viewed the ban as a direct attack on private property and the charter rights of churches. Furthermore, the ban was inexcusable because the vaults were not health hazards or public nuisances, as the Common Council apparently was claiming. Interestingly, opponents argued only for a limited repeal of the law that would have continued the ban on public vaults. Opponents did not view the ban on the poor's burials in public graves and vaults as a similar invasion of privacy.

The Common Council reconsidered the measure twice, both times reaffirming its original decision. When Hosack and several other prominent physicians continued to oppose the ban publicly, a member responded that when some physicians maintain that "our atmosphere is too pure to generate yellow fever" and others just as adamantly declare the "contrary opinion, . . . how then can we depend on them?" Debate demonstrated that the old customs were dear to many, that the mechanics of preventing disease were still unclearly understood, and that the city needed to offer some alternative to those now deprived of a family burial place.[60]

A PUBLIC ALTERNATIVE

During the discussions over the 1823 legislation, an alderman suggested that the grave site should be the place for "those sacred feelings" that bring "tears of affection," and he questioned: "Are our graveyards in the city fit places for feelings like these?" Opponents of in-city graveyards had won a significant victory, and now they needed to design an alternative graveyard. The Committee on Lands and Places soon presented a report on the development of a new city burial ground. Citing the "examples of the cities of Albany and New Haven," the committee suggested a six-acre plot three and one-quarter miles from City Hall, between Fifth and Sixth avenues and between Fortieth and Forty-fifth streets. The site was appropriate because it was "high and pleasant" and had "soil for the Purpose in view."[61]

Although the cemetery failed to attract middle- and upper-class families, New York City's plans represented a significant change in cemetery planning. In keeping with past practices of offering a burial ground for the entire community, the committee initially hoped that the cemetery would accommodate the "different religious congregations," as well as individuals "who may choose to select particular Spots for their families" and the "numerous poor whose necessities in the Solemn business of interment" were the same as those of the middle and upper classes.[62]

Soon after the committee changed its recommendation, stating that the potter's field "not only [ought] to be distinct, but remote from the City Burying Ground." In New Haven in 1796, "Strangers," "Negros," and the poor each had separate sections within the new cemetery. New Yorkers now contemplated a spatial segregation of the affluent and those in the "middling circumstances." Economic standing was put forth as a qualifying criterion of a proprietor and lot-holder, even in a municipally owned cemetery.

New York City's 1823 cemetery never attracted family lot-holders. The city built the wall (topping it with locust posts) and planted two rows of weeping willows and elms within the new cemetery. Yet there is no evidence that middle- or upper-class New Yorkers chose to purchase lots and vaults. The land set aside for the cemetery was used as a potter's field from about 1823 to 1836, when the city opened a new graveyard ten blocks to the north. By 1837 the cemetery was filled with the victims of three "cholera epidemics, the Great Fire of 1835 and the hard times that preceded the panic" of that year, and the city decided to use the spot for the Murray Hill receiving reservoir, part of the new Croton water system.[63]

A PRIVATE ALTERNATIVE

In 1830, confronted with the failure of the public alternative, a group of New Yorkers established the private New York Marble Cemetery, which was followed two years later by the New York City Marble Cemetery. The new cemeteries were organized and supported by many of the same people who had led the 1823 battle to prohibit in-city graves. The second Marble Cemetery was located on land owned by Samuel Cowdrey, an alderman who had played a prominent role in passing the legislation prohibiting interments. Among those who purchased vaults was Mayor Allen. The Marble cemeteries were clearly intended to be alternatives to churchyard and graveyard interment. Their design and management reflected a distrust of innovation and a desire to retain as much as possible the practices of the past.[64]

The Marble cemeteries were owned and managed by separate private and nonsectarian corporations. Both used burial vaults built of Tuckahoe marble. This was another example of the move toward marble and away from slate and the other stones of the colonial period. One reason for this change was that three-dimensional monuments required a more easily shaped material. Renewed interest in classical civilizations further spurred use of a material so closely identified with antiquity.

The two cemeteries offered a combined total of 412 vaults and were located in the area of Second Avenue between Second and Third streets. Developers hoped that this neighborhood would soon become a fashionable residential area. Accordingly, the vault owners were of the highest social status. The most distinguished interment occurred in 1831, when James Monroe, former U.S. president, was entombed in a vault purchased by Samuel Gouverneur. Monroe's funeral was carried out with much pomp and spectacle.

According to contemporary accounts, the two cemeteries were quite attractive. The first allowed no individual or family monuments. Each vault was marked with a marble tablet affixed to its front. The second cemetery permitted family monuments and individual markers, but did not allow them to overwhelm the communal nature of the burial place. The New York City Marble Cemetery was laid out with "long parallel walks between which are narrow strips of ground punctuated by the square marble vault slabs." Their simple tablets and family vaults must have reminded vault owners of the churchyards of the past. They may have reminded visitors of graveyards in New Orleans, France, and southern European countries. Yet the Marble cemeteries represented a distinctive alternative to former practices.[65]

LIMITATIONS OF THE ALTERNATIVES

New York City's public cemetery was the least successful of the three alternatives, and the other two were also failures. The New Haven Burying Ground expanded and grew, but growth did not enhance it. As Dwight noted, at the beginning this cemetery exhibited an "exquisite taste for propriety" by being "reverential, but not ostentatious." The grounds had slowly grown from the original six acres to seventeen. The number of lots had increased to seven hundred.

An 1839 reform committee reported that the grounds were imperfectly enclosed; thus the cemetery had become "a thoroughfare" with paths across private lots and over graves. The openness of the cemetery made it the "resort of the idle, the thoughtless, and the vicious," especially on the Sabbath. Trees, shrubbery, and monuments had suffered during this period, so "a great portion of the ground is entirely destitute of trees, shrubs, or anything whatever to shade the walks, to shelter the grass so as to preserve its verdure in dry season, or to impart a general appearance of care cultivation, and decent ornament."[66]

The New Haven Burying Ground would have to dramatically change if it was going to continue to serve the city's population. The reform committee decided that the cemetery should be almost entirely relandscaped. The committee raised eight thousand dollars for improvements. The committee planned to encircle the grounds with a belt of trees; it would plant new rows of trees along the streets and in the alleys (pathways) within sections. The entire cemetery was to be fenced. A new gateway, with a residence for the keeper, was constructed. The New Haven Burying Ground now became known as the Grove Street Cemetery.

The Marble cemeteries suffered a different, but still demeaning, demise. By the 1870s, they primarily were used as storage vaults for bodies awaiting burial in out-of-town locations; the *New York Times* called the cemeteries a "receiving tomb" for Manhattan. Rural cemeteries in Brooklyn and the Bronx offered all the services of the Marble cemeteries, but in larger, more secluded, and more secure locations. Although sporadic entombments continued until the 1930s, in 1889 a group of lot-holders in the New York City Marble Cemetery urged the removal of the vaults to a more secure environment. Instead, first at the New York City Marble Cemetery and then the New York Marble Cemetery, lot-holders collected a permanent-care fund of approximately twenty-five thousand dollars to maintain the cemeteries in the original locations. Although the Marble cemeteries should be considered precursors of the garden mausoleums that have been popular since the 1970s and as miraculous survivors of an age when city cemeteries were often abandoned, they were too novel to succeed at a time when vault burial and city burial were under attack. Only the elite purchased the vaults, and even they would have preferred the churchyard rather than the marble garden.[67]

A PARTIAL SOLUTION

New Haven Burying Ground, New York City's public cemetery, and the Marble cemeteries left an important legacy. New Haven Burying Ground might not be, as John Brinckerhoff Jackson argued, the nation's most important cemetery historically, but other cities viewed it as a model for new graveyards. In upstate New York, Buffalo's Franklin Square Cemetery (1804), Syracuse's First Ward Cemetery (1819), and Teal-Lodi Cemetery (1834) were located on accessible but pleasing sites outside the built-up portions of the cities. One Buffalo resident stated that Franklin Square, on a site covered "with a growth of bushes and scrub oak," was "one of the most beautiful views I ever put my eyes upon." Americans were more willing to consider the environment in which they buried their dead and were less willing to place the dead in what they knew would be temporary storage in the middle of the city.[68]

The first alternatives to colonial churchyards and domestic burial grounds still lacked many of the desirable aspects of America's emerging culture. David Schuyler believes that the New Haven Burying Ground failed to inspire imitators because it had not yet "cast aside" its "urban heritage." Turn-of-the-century Americans were still uneasy with the separation of burial and church, death and religion. The New Haven Burying Ground was coldly geometric in design and formal in style; New York City's public cemetery was unattractive to socially conscious Americans; and the Marble cemeteries were reminiscent of churchyard communal burial practices of the past. The site of all three hearkened back to the accessibility that earlier urban residents had asked of a burial place.[69]

Americans were searching for a burial place that did not evoke the city's fast pace or commercial life. "Only when cemeteries . . . abandoned traditional urban forms and took on aspects of the country, did they become . . . 'rural.'"[70] Only when Americans embraced mid-nineteenth-century rural values did they discover a new burial place.

CHAPTER THREE

Mount Auburn and the
Rural-Cemetery Movement

MOUNT AUBURN CEMETERY

The rural-cemetery movement began with the establishment of Mount Auburn Cemetery in 1831. Mount Auburn, located just outside Cambridge, Massachusetts, and serving the greater Boston area, was an ornamental cemetery situated far from the densely inhabited sections of the city. Although it reflected French and English gardening and landscaping theories of the previous half-century, and its organizational structure owed a debt to the New Haven Burying Ground, Mount Auburn was an American original.

Mount Auburn was organized as a voluntary association of families and individuals. On strikingly beautiful terrain, the cemetery promised to provide a pleasant botanical tour, a local and national historical museum, and an arboretum, all on grounds that provided space for the burial of generations of area residents. Emily Dickinson noted in 1846 that "it seems as if Nature had formed the spot with a distinct idea of its being a resting place for her children."[1]

Mount Auburn resulted from the same crisis that was occurring throughout the larger American cities. Boston's population tripled between the Revolution and the 1820s. Increased urbanization fouled the city's water and air. The city government of the "walking city" was unprepared to provide adequate services to such a rapidly growing population. Symptomatic of the inability of the city to resolve important urban problems, a danger to its water supply was not solved until 1848, with the opening of piped water from Lake Cochituate.[2]

Bostonians attempted to prohibit in-city interments as a way of partly confronting this chaos. In 1822 Mayor Josiah Quincy proposed legislation to ban such burials. Opposition groups blunted Quincy's campaign, but the public's interest had been directed to alternative burial places. Serious questions arose as to whether vault burial was discriminatory within a democratic society, whether in-city burial was a healthy custom, and whether the city government was capable of providing Bostonians with a safe, appropriate place to bury their dead.

One reason New Englanders were prepared to consider a change in burial practices was the deplorable state of many graveyards. The constant shuffling of locations, vandalism, and the abandonment of graveyards angered residents. The graveyards were no longer the idyllic scenes of times past. A New England writer observed in 1831 that "the burying place continues to be the most neglected spot in all the region, distinguished from other fields only by its leaning stones and the meanness of its enclosures, without a tree or a shrub to take from it the air of utter desolation."[3]

The condition of Boston's burial ground and the political conflict over possible solutions led several private citizens to take action. Jacob Bigelow became the primary force in the effort to establish a new cemetery. Bigelow was a horticulturist, a physician, and an influential friend of the city's elite. Author of one of the most important American books on botany and several landmark articles on health diagnostics and procedures, Bigelow was a respected Harvard professor and a founder of the Massachusetts Horticultural Society. He understood Boston's public-health problems. He also supported the new cultural ideas embodied in Romanticism.

In 1825 Bigelow invited a group of Boston's business and civic leaders to discuss the development of an ornamental cemetery. The group quickly agreed on the need for a new cemetery, but the search for a parcel of land took far longer than anticipated. During the next six years, Bigelow encountered landowners who believed he wanted the land for other purposes than a cemetery and some who did not want a cemetery near their property. Eventually, George W. Brimmer, a friend of Bigelow's, enthusiastically agreed to sell a parcel of land near Cambridge, some ten miles from central Boston. Affectionately known by local residents and Harvard students as Sweet Auburn (after Oliver Goldsmith's poem "Deserted Village"), the land was all that Bigelow envisioned for his garden cemetery.[4]

It is difficult today to understand the experimental nature of the cemetery plan. New Englanders had been burying their dead on town commons for two centuries. The association of meeting house (or church) and graveyard was one of the distinguishing features of New England life. Only the social dislocation caused by the migration westward from New England, the appearance of new religious ideas, the rise of industrial manufacturing, and the other changes rocking the region could have shaken the cultural underpinnings of New England to allow dramatic new burial habits.

Not surprisingly, organizers feared they would be unable to convince people to purchase enough lots to justify the new enterprise. Brimmer's 72-acre Sweet Auburn was much larger than any American burial place. The New Haven Burying Ground, which was 6 acres, was considered large. The founders were committing their association to centuries of burying the dead, but what if the public would not buy?

As one way of limiting their risk, the founders joined with the Massachu-

setts Horticultural Society in developing the new cemetery. The society had
long wished to start an experimental garden. The founders and the society
hoped the combined garden and cemetery "would ultimately offer such an
example of landscape gardening as would be creditable to the Society, and assist
in improving the taste of the public in this highest branch of horticulture."
Bigelow hoped that, by gaining the "co-operation of a young, active, and popular society," the founders could overcome public concerns. Even more important, combining resources with the society served as a symbolic commitment to
achieving a new style of burial place based on European landscape gardening.[5]

Bigelow and many other antebellum Americans were passionately involved with improving the nation's horticulture and agriculture. Agricultural
societies had been among the earliest voluntary associations in the new nation.
The Massachusetts Society for Promoting Agriculture was founded in 1792 by
Judge John Lowell and others interested in agricultural improvement and
agriculture's influence on the society. Similarly minded individuals established
horticultural societies in New York in 1818 and Philadelphia in 1829, beginning
a period of new agricultural and horticultural interest throughout America.[6]

Contemporaries thought that such movements not only demonstrated the
vitality of the new republic but also reinforced society's moral virtue. Agriculture was a virtuous occupation. Learning from English theorists and landscape
gardeners, Americans felt that the moral power of nature was best represented
in the cultivated setting of the farm or the garden.

As America became more urban, domestic horticulture also became a
cherished cultural symbol. Americans closely identified domestic tranquility
with agriculture and horticulture. Gradually, horticulture was distinguished
from agriculture as more people turned to planting orchards, growing flowers,
and building greenhouses, first as hobbies and later as businesses.

It was fitting and natural, then, that the founders of Mount Auburn created a "garden of graves." The enormous success of the cemetery and its imitators throughout the nation grew from the public's acceptance of the physical
isolation of the dead from the living. The public accepted such a change only
within the naturalistic landscape that the founders carefully created from the
hills and valleys of the new cemetery. This landscape offered air and light,
safety and nature, joy and optimism. By redefining "the boundary, beyond
which the living cannot go nor the dead return," Mount Auburn's planners
altered the conventional perspective of the grave and reestablished the cemetery as an important cultural institution within the society.[7]

The primary charm of Mount Auburn was its magnificent grounds, laid
out in the landscape plan of Henry Alexander Scammel Dearborn and Alexander Wadsworth. One commentator wrote that cemeteries should be "in
places lonely, but not deserted, where the beauty of nature is heightened by the
care of man, where the gloom of death cannot sadden the hearts of the living,

Entrance to Mount Auburn Cemetery, Cambridge, Mass., 1834
Mount Auburn was America's first rural cemetery. Its gate popularized the use of Egyptian Revival style in American cemeteries. Although some Christian commentators disliked the use of a "pagan" style to celebrate America's dead, Egyptian Revival monuments and gates proliferated in the antebellum period. (*American Magazine of Useful and Entertaining Knowledge* 1 [1 September 1834]. Courtesy of Dartmouth College Library.)

nor the labor of life stand in too close contrast to the stillness of the dead." In Mount Auburn, all these conditions were met.[8]

The landscape impressed visitors because it contrasted so dramatically with the hustle and bustle of Boston and because it so cleverly forced one into considering nature instead of more worldly thoughts. A Mount Auburn brochure touted that "this tract is beautifully undulating in its surface, containing a number of bold eminences, steep acclivities, and deep shadowy valleys. A remarkable natural ridge with a level surface runs through the ground . . . the principal eminence, called Mount Auburn, . . . is 125 feet above the level of the Charles River. . . . From the foot of this monument will be seen in detail the features of the landscape, as they are successively presented though the different vistas opened among the trees." The visitor plunged into a setting that evoked the emotional atmosphere of nature rather than the logic of urban life.[9]

Dearborn's devotion to the development of the cemetery was a critical ingredient. Dearborn was a politician whose passion was horticulture. Although he had no formal training in engineering, designing, or landscaping, he was a founder and the first president of the Massachusetts Horticultural Society. A strong supporter of the cemetery plan and a participant in the 1825

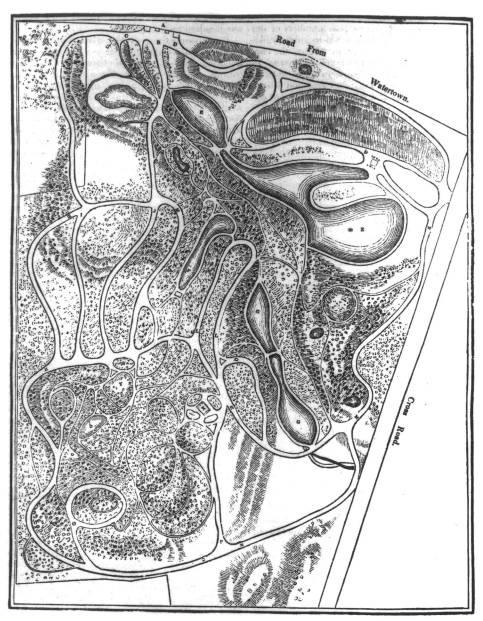

Plan of Mount Auburn Cemetery, Cambridge, Mass., 1834

This plan shows the innovative naturalistic design that helped make the rural-cemetery movement so popular throughout America in the mid-nineteenth century. Note how the roads wind along the terrain's natural levels. Now we take such a design for granted in our suburbs, parks, and cemeteries. Then it was a new idea. (*American Magazine of Useful and Entertaining Knowledge* 1 [10 June 1834]. Courtesy of Dartmouth College Library.)

organizing meeting, he helped in the initial fund-raising and was involved in the planning and planting of the cemetery. In planning the cemetery, he relied on his experiences with planting and farming. Bigelow later wrote that "General Dearborn zealously devoted himself . . . to the examination of the ground, the laying out of roads, and superintending the workmen. He also transplanted from his own nurseries a large collection of healthy young forest trees."[10] Dearborn also became familiar with earlier European cemetery designs, especially that of the world's first garden cemetery, Père Lachaise in Paris.

PÈRE LACHAISE AND THE PICTURESQUE

In 1831 Zebedee Cook, Jr., commented that the Massachusetts Horticultural Society should undertake the "establishment of a public cemetery similar in its design to that of Père Lachaise."[11] Cook's choice of Père Lachaise was not surprising, given the international reputation of the West's first ornamental cemetery. Père Lachaise was established in 1804 by the French government in response to the awful conditions of in-city churchyards, most notably the incredibly crowded situation at the Cimetière des Innocents. The new cemetery was located on the former estate of François d'Aix de La Chaise, who was King Louis XIV's confessor, as well as an avid gardener. The natural beauty of the cemetery, in diametric opposition to its barren, small predecessors, captivated the French bourgeois.

By 1831 Père Lachaise had become a major tourist attraction. Europeans and Americans were charmed. Set on a hilltop overlooking Paris, the cemetery had wonderful natural and scenic vistas. Serpentine roadways wound through the terrain and provided spectacular vistas. Two parallel avenues reached out to the north and south from a grand boulevard leading from the western entrance to a proposed central shrine. One American reported that "it is impossible to visit this vast sanctuary of the dead, where the rose and the cypress encircle each tomb, and the arborvitae and eglantine shade the marble obelisk, without feeling a solemn yet sweet and soothing emotion steal over the senses."[12] Even the Americans who found the monuments contrived and ornate were fascinated by the natural, forestlike setting and the Parisian celebration of the famous, infamous, and unknown dead.

Père Lachaise's landscape applied English æsthetic theories. During the eighteenth century, the English developed a theory of aesthetics embodied in the categories of the sublime, the picturesque, and the beautiful (or pastoral).[13] The sublime was nature in all its wildness, completely outside the control of civilization. The picturesque balanced art and nature. Nature was manipulated in such a way as to allow civilization to be present, but without disturbing the grandeur and power of the natural setting. In the beautiful or pastoral, nature was subordinated to civilization. Art, or the dramatic expression of civilizations, shone in the pastoral setting, and nature served more as a backdrop for the exposition of art.

The picturesque lay between the wildness and irrationality of uncontrolled nature that was the sublime and the formality and artifice that was the beautiful. This balance made the picturesque the "perfect natural landscape" because a person could enter it comfortably, for it did not have the unpredictability of the sublime, and feel a separateness from civilization, a freedom from the artificiality of the beautiful. As Americans learned in the early nineteenth century, untamed nature was a formidable educator about the fallibility of human beings, but only when they were able to comprehend the lesson.[14]

The picturesque offered an opportunity in which nature could be more fully exploited as an instructor about moral and ethical behavior in an increasingly profane and commercial world. The changing seasons reminded visitors of their mortality; the wildness of a thunderstorm, of their vulnerability; and nature's aura, of their insignificance. At the same time, the gentle meadows calmed the aggressive personality, the winding roads diverted the ambitious, and the flowering trees and green shrubs reminded the visitor of a better way of life. At a moment when urbanization and industrialization were isolating people from the forces of nature, the picturesque offered them a view of unhampered nature.

In England, family mausoleums, memorial obelisks, and gilt urns were placed amid the evergreens, flowers, and lakes of great estates, such as Castle Howard, Stowe, and Stourhead. The French were very taken by these examples, as well as others in England and Denmark. Perhaps the most important symbolic rejection of the contemporary visual appearance of the graveyard was the burial of Jean-Jacques Rousseau in 1778 amid the gardens of the estate of the Marquis de Girardin. The French and English were ripe "for a new landscape vision of the cemetery."[15]

Placing the grave in the garden represented a major shift in the European attitude toward death and the dead. Romanticism, with its emphasis on the elegy and the boundary between life and death, found the location of the grave deeply symbolic. Death was transformed from something grotesque into something beautiful. The loss of family members and the private trauma of death became the focus of the death ritual, replacing the more open, public ritual of past centuries. The rural cemetery was a result and an emblem of that transformation. Death became an occasion of solemn celebration.[16]

Père Lachaise was one representation of the new vision. The cemetery soon became a funerary garden, a favorite place for weekend promenades and public displays of monumental taste. The promotion of Père Lachaise provoked one English writer in 1819 to draw a comparison between the cemetery and English customs: "It would hardly happen . . . that we [in England] should have a Guide to the burial-grounds, as a fashionable promenade; that parties would be made to visit them."[17] But within a generation, the establishment of Mount

View of Père Lachaise Cemetery and, in the Distance, Paris, 1854
Père Lachaise was popular partly because it offered a spectacular view of Paris. Even as early as 1854, the cemetery's gardenlike character was rapidly being lost because of the numerous monuments and mausoleums. Some Americans who initially had praised the cemetery later criticized the loss of the naturalistic atmosphere. (Courtesy of Bibliothèque Nationale.)

Auburn, Kensal Green, and their English and American imitators would create a demand throughout both England and America for guidebooks of cemeteries in cities and towns.

AMERICAN ROMANTICISM AND DEATH

Americans were slower than Europeans to accept nature as picturesque. Long after the English embraced the picturesque, Americans continued to conquer uncontrolled wilderness and create a pastoral environment. The majestic forests stretching from coast to coast were barriers to people trying to survive the harsh winters, the conflicts with Native Americans, and often their own ignorance of farming in the New World. Colonists stripped the land of trees and opened wide swathes of pasture land in their battles against nature.[18]

So much of the forest had been cleared by the nineteenth century that commentators began to worry that there would be insufficient firewood to heat American homes. Yet, the father of American Romantic writer Lydia Sigourney could still comment, when planting two apple trees in front of their house, that "it is better to fill the space with something useful than with unproductive shade." Alexis de Tocqueville, who visited America in 1831, the year

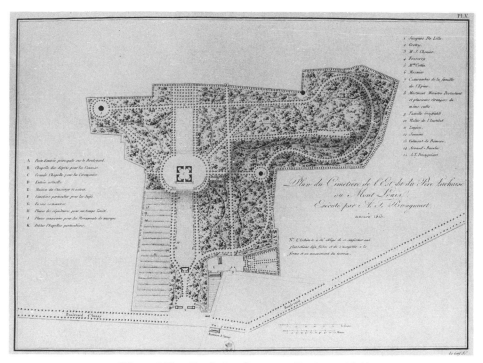

Plan of Père Lachaise Cemetery, Paris, c. 1813

Opened in 1804, Père Lachaise was the world's first garden cemetery. Located in the gardens of the former confessor to Louis XIV, the new cemetery soon became a favorite burial place for Parisian bourgeoisie. The plan shows that the cemetery combined gardenesque and formal styles, in keeping with its transitional quality. Compare its design to Mount Auburn Cemetery's naturalistic one. (Courtesy of Bibliothèque Nationale.)

that Mount Auburn was founded, realized that Europeans misunderstood the American relationship to nature. Europeans talked of the "wilds of America, but Americans themselves never think about them." He concluded that American "eyes are fixed upon another sight, the . . . march across these wilds, draining swamps, turning the course of rivers, peopling solitudes, and subduing nature." Americans simply viewed nature as an obstacle to civilization and domestication.[19]

Such a view of nature had begun to recede by the 1790s, but was nevertheless influential in the planning of New Haven Burying Ground. The straight rows of poplars which divided the burial lots were examples of typical farm geometry. The symmetrical family plots represented a continuation of the formal garden, the victory of art over nature. Nature was welcomed back into the graveyard, but only on limited terms.

Residents now wanted their cities and towns to appear more naturalistic. Those who had worked to clear the land of trees and tree stumps turned to planting trees along the streets. Lydia Sigourney eulogized James Hillhouse in 1832 as the person who had transformed New Haven into "one of the most picturesque spots in New England," with its "fair greens and waving trees."[20] A generation later, homeowners celebrated and created rustic landscapes. William Cullen Bryant and the American Romantic poets furthered the acceptance of the ideas expressed earlier by the poet Thomas Gray and other English elegists and artists. This new attitude toward nature, which was so emblematic of Romanticism, was critical to the spread of the rural-cemetery movement in America.

MOUNT AUBURN AND THE INDIVIDUAL LOT-HOLDER

Dearborn, Wadsworth, Bigelow, and the Mount Auburn corporation created the backdrop; the lot-holders developed the landscape. Mount Auburn was a family-centered institution, which expected that families would decorate the grounds with the finest available plants and memorials. The family lots were three hundred square feet, sufficient for burials over several generations. The serpentine roadways and wide pathways were the access roads through which families drove to lose themselves in the natural setting. The cemetery offered families a stable and secure place of memories.

At Père Lachaise, the French bourgeoisie "constructed their world in the city of the dead as in that of the living." Previously, all the French except royalty had buried their dead in shallow graves, which the family rented for six years. Leases on burials in Père Lachaise were renewable, meaning that the bourgeoisie could use the cemetery as a permanent site for family burials and for their celebration of the family's fortunes. Ornate statues stood atop elaborate family monuments and spacious mausoleums. Such statues echoed the sentiments of Quatremere de Quincy, who stated: "No doubt death equalizes all men, but it is precisely the injustice of this leveling that men should rectify."[21] The monuments in Père Lachaise informed visitors of the family's material success.

Mount Auburn was designed to limit such ostentation. The roadway system provided many more desirable lots than did the central avenues of Père Lachaise. Mount Auburn lot-holders were encouraged to erect a variety of monuments, or to rely on nature as a memorial. Furthermore, a number of craftsmen and artisans, including carpenters, engravers, and sailmakers, purchased family lots soon after the cemetery's opening. Both in their openness to a variety of buyers and in their reluctance to have elaborate monuments, the cemetery founders celebrated the democratic culture and heritage of the new nation.[22]

Despite these actions, social distinctions soon threatened the cemetery's democracy. Families eagerly purchased lots for $60, expecting to enjoy the beauty of the lot long before the need to bury a relative and for generations to come. Proprietors took special pride in the lot's appearance. They began to erect family monuments in the center of their lots. The most prominent monu-

View of Mount Auburn Cemetery, Cambridge, Mass., 1835
The rural cemetery quickly became a popular place to stroll. Its environment, which was naturalistic, contrasted dramatically with that of busy urban streets. Strollers came by the thousands. (*American Magazine of Useful and Entertaining Knowledge* 2 [6 February 1835]. Courtesy of Dartmouth College Library.)

ments were soon noted in newspapers and cemetery guidebooks. Many proprietors also hired gardeners to plant their lots, providing the cemetery with a plethora of beautiful trees and shrubs. Parts of the cemetery resembled a royal British estate.

Many of the bereaved could not afford lots, so the cemetery offered them single graves in a section in the middle of the cemetery, next to the larger lots of the proprietors. Markers were limited by regulation. Single-grave owners were not members of the corporation and had no voting rights. They were outside the decision making about the dead, just as they were often outsiders among the living.

Mount Auburn soon received local, national, and even international praise. Dickinson and Ralph Waldo Emerson, as well as many anonymous magazine and newspaper writers, applauded it. Travelers from Europe came to expect a trip to the cemetery and were amazed by what they saw. Two Polish visitors felt it was "a fine and appropriate resting place for the deceased," with its "beautiful meadows," "shady groves," and "cool recesses."[23] The grounds filled with carriages and pedestrians. Visitors from other American cities came to admire Mount Auburn's magical setting and to plan how to emulate it in their towns and cities.

Forest Pond, Mount Auburn Cemetery, Cambridge, Mass., 1846
The picturesque environment ideally combined flora and fauna, water and shade. Forest Pond achieved this ideal. Small animals lived among the dells, and birds and fish dwelled in the pond. The area was one of the cemetery's most popular spots for visitors and lot-holders. (Cornelia Walter, *Mount Auburn Illustrated,* 1846. Courtesy of Dumbarton Oaks, Trustees for Harvard University.)

THE RURAL-CEMETERY MOVEMENT

Within twenty years, rural cemeteries patterned on Mount Auburn existed from Portland, Maine, to Atlanta, Georgia, and from Worcester, Massachusetts, to Saint Louis, Missouri. Most of these cemeteries were in the emerging cities of the Northeast and Midwest, but new cemeteries in Richmond, Charleston, and Atlanta testified that the concept overcame regional boundaries. Americans changed their burial patterns during this period; they preferred the large cemetery to the small churchyard or the domestic burial ground.

Even the manner in which Americans spoke of the burial place changed. The name *cemetery,* from the Greek word for "sleeping chamber," was for the first time widely embraced. Although used sporadically by Europeans for centuries, the term became the standard one for a burial place in the nineteenth century. Rural cemeteries were different than previous burial places, and their founders believed that they deserved a distinct name. *Cemetery* contained the suggestion of death as sleep, a transition from life to eternal life, which was more in keeping with America's emerging optimistic religion and exuberant nationalism.[24]

"Cemeteries here are all the 'rage,'" wrote the young Englishman Henry

TABLE 3.1
Selected List of American Rural Cemeteries with Their Dates
of Establishment, 1831–1865

Cemetery	Location	Year	Cemetery	Location	Year
Mount Auburn	Cambridge, Mass.	1831	Oakland	Atlanta, Ga.	1850
Laurel Hill	Philadelphia, Pa.	1836	Pittsfield Rural	Pittsfield, Mass.	1850
Greenmount	Baltimore, Md.	1838	Pine Grove	Waterville, Me.	1851
Worcester Rural	Worcester, Mass.	1838	Wildwood	Winchester, Mass.	1851
Harmony Grove	Salem, Mass.	1840	Evergreen	Portland, Me.	1852
Spring Grove	Cincinnati, Ohio	1844	Oakdale	Wilmington, N.C.	1852
Allegheny	Pittsburgh, Pa.	1845	Oak Woods	Chicago, Ill.	1853
Swan Point	Providence, R.I.	1846	Newton	Newton, Mass.	1855
Hollywood	Richmond, Va.	1847	Calvary	Milwaukee, Wisc.	1857
Oak Hill	Washington, D.C.	1848	Mount Olivet	Washington, D.C.	1858
Bellefontaine	St. Louis, Mo.	1849	Calvary	Chicago, Ill.	1859
Elmwood	Detroit, Mich.	1849	Rosehill	Chicago, Ill.	1859
Mountain Grove	Bridgeport, Conn.	1849	Graceland	Chicago, Ill.	1860
Cedar Grove	New London, Conn.	1850	Evergreen	Rutland, Vt.	1861
Forest Home	Milwaukee, Wisc.	1850	Cedar Hill	Hartford, Conn.	1863
New York Bay	Jersey City, N.J.	1850	Marion	Marion, Ohio	1865

Arthur Bright, "people lounge in them and use them (as their tastes are inclined) for walking, making love, weeping, sentimentalizing, and every thing in short." The new cemeteries provided an outlet from the daily routine of city life. As the first planned landscapes generally open to the public in America, rural cemeteries were immensely popular. Visitors came by the thousands, and many people purchased lots for their families, including enough graves for several succeeding generations. Magazine and newspaper articles celebrated new plantings and monuments. Guidebooks provided routes for visitors, information on notable families, and appropriate poetry and stories relating to the melancholy atmosphere of the cemeteries.[25]

The new cemeteries represented an emerging national culture, one created by the new urban citizens of America. The movement was so widespread because the values represented in the new landscapes and lot-holders' monuments were widely accepted as integral to the successful continuation of the republic. Practical concerns such as overcrowded in-city burial grounds provided the catalyst, but Americans were concerned about understanding the history of their communities and nation, strengthening the family, maintaining the virtue of rural life, and encouraging respect for the dead.

NEW YORK STATE'S RURAL CEMETERIES

Mount Auburn spawned imitators throughout the nation, but New York State provides an excellent example of the pervasiveness of the movement. A rural cemetery became an essential element of the new urban culture from New York City throughout its growing urban network. This city's economy and cultural innovations influenced the emerging cities along the Erie Canal—Utica, Syracuse, and Rochester—as well as the established upstate cities of Albany and Buffalo and the booming cities along the Hudson. Rural cemeteries were influential not only in large cities but also in small villages. These villages, such as Cortland, Cooperstown, and Cambridge, represented a significant society within the state. The rural cemetery was a microcosm of the changes occurring throughout America.

The first rural cemeteries in New York State were established in Rochester, Brooklyn, Albany, and Manhattan, where the burial crisis was most urgent and the desire to be culturally progressive strongest. The opening of the Erie Canal in 1825, the tremendous expansion of foreign trade through the port New York City, and the migration of not only New Englanders searching for richer farmland but also Irish and English looking for a better life combined to spur the growth of cities in New York State.

In the cities, commerce replaced agriculture as the primary economic pursuit. In 1815 upstate New York was dominated by farmers who grew market crops and sold grain to New York and the other coastal cities, but by 1840 many upstate residents could no longer depend on wheat, corn, and other grain crops. Farmers in Ohio and other states of the Old Northwest had better land, and new transportation systems shortened their trip to market. The upstate economy gradually changed from an agricultural to a manufacturing and service one. Flowers replaced flour as Rochester's major crop.

New York State's First Rural Cemetery: Mount Hope in Rochester. In the early nineteenth century growth was occurring throughout the state, and Rochester, Albany, Brooklyn, and New York City were particularly influenced by changes. Of these four cities, Rochester was the newest and most volatile.[26] A lonely outpost of less than a thousand people before the coming of the Erie Canal, Rochester had over fourteen thousand people in 1835. As an agricultural center and an important commercial stop for traders between New York City and the Ohio Valley, Rochester had gained a reputation as a tough town full of bars and rough dock workers. However, prosperity and expansion had been accompanied by the development of deep religious ferment and local social-reform activities. Rochester was a city bursting with commercial pride, community conflicts, and energetic individuals.

Rochester was also quickly becoming a center of American horticulture. Rochester was home to the *Genesee Farmer,* one of the pioneer journals in discussing agricultural and horticultural improvements. Nathan Goodsell, its editor, had visited William Prince's Nursery in 1831, returning to Rochester to open the city's first garden nursery, which he did with enthusiasm. In that same year, the journal praised the foundation of Mount Auburn. By the end of the decade,

Rochester would have a thriving nursery and seed industry. Within a decade, the city would become "the nursery center of the continent."[27]

The civic pride and belief in horticulture opened the way for the establishment of New York State's first rural cemetery, Mount Hope. In August 1836, prodded by a group of concerned citizens, the Rochester Common Council formed a committee to purchase a new cemetery site. After some difficulties in finding a location, the city of Rochester bought a 53-acre site south of the city. There the municipal government organized and managed Mount Hope Cemetery in deliberate imitation of Mount Auburn. Reverend Pharcellus Church, the dedication speaker, claimed that "good judges who have visited both [Mount Hope and Mount Auburn] pronounce [Mount Hope's] scenery even more bold and picturesque than that of the celebrated [cemetery] in. . . . Boston."[28]

Reverend Church described Mount Hope's location as perfect: "Rural scenery, undulating surface uniting features both of beauty and sublimity, ponds that may easily be cleared and made to present a smooth and shining expanse as of molten silver, a dry and light soil peculiarly favorable alike to the opening of graves and the preservation of them from intrusion of water, and a location retired and yet sufficiently contiguous to our city." Mount Hope was intersected by several ridges, which created wonderful vistas, "bottom lands," and "abrupt declivities."[29] The terrain was more dramatic than that of Mount Auburn, but did not have its overall beauty. Both proved attractive to visitors.

Although modeled on Mount Auburn, Mount Hope differed from the Massachusetts cemetery in one important way: it was a public cemetery. Eventually, the style of management of the cemetery by the city would be questioned by some dissatisfied with the condition of the cemetery. Other rural-cemetery managers had to answer only to their lot-holders; Mount Hope managers had to answer to the Rochester Common Council, the newspapers, and the public. Only a few other rural cemeteries would be public enterprises.

Green-Wood Cemetery's Shaky Start. As was the case of Mount Hope in Rochester, the first rural cemetery in New York City originated in a public call for change. The 1823 legislation banning burials in lower Manhattan had encouraged discussion and establishment of new sites for new municipal burying grounds. In 1835 Brooklyn businessman Henry Pierrepont urged engineer David B. Douglass to use the opportunity of a well-publicized oration to point out the inadequacy of Manhattan for any new cemetery and to propose that a new cemetery be located in Brooklyn.

Manhattan and Brooklyn, then separate political entities, were considerable rivals for residents and trade. If a new cemetery was successful, it would help Brooklyn and its businesses (such as Pierrepont's Union Ferry Company). Brooklyn boasted a population of about twenty-five thousand, yet boosters of the new cemetery wished to serve the entire New York City area.

Douglass and Pierrepont brought great strengths to the promotion of the new Green-Wood Cemetery.[30] Douglass was well respected because of his engineering experience on the Croton Aqueduct, the recently completed marvel that had temporarily solved New York City's water problems. Pierrepont, a member of a well-known, wealthy Brooklyn family with contacts throughout the metropolitan area, had assumed leadership of the family businesses, concerning himself primarily with land holdings in Brooklyn and upstate New York. He had earlier tried and failed to convince Brooklynites to develop a park for city residents. Pierrepont's interest in a cemetery arose from this experience, from his travels to Boston and Europe, and from his intense commitment to Brooklyn's prosperity.

Pierrepont put together an impressive group as the first directors of Green-Wood Cemetery. The company's subscribers and organizers included Samuel Ward, financier; Charles King, successful merchant and editor; Robert Ray, member of the Prime, Ward, King and Company banking firm; and Pliny Freeman, founder of the original New York Life Insurance Company. William Cullen Bryant and several other prominent newspaper editors publicly believed that the project was important for New York and backed it. Although the cemetery was in Brooklyn, the group's key supporters were from not only Brooklyn but also Manhattan.

Green-Wood was organized in 1838 as a joint-stock company, with the incorporators holding all assets. The initial plan of the organization was to buy land with bonds issued by the stock company. The bonds would be paid off by the sale of lots. Mount Auburn had been organized under a similar plan, but there the Massachusetts Horticultural Society controlled the assets. The Green-Wood plan was reminiscent of the business activities of Pierrepont and his brother-in-law Joseph Perry, another Green-Wood incorporator, in their consolidation of the Union Ferry Company in Brooklyn. The joint-stock company suggested the concept of a private, for-profit burial place.

Although barriers to a commercial cemetery were breaking down, most Americans were not yet ready to support a cemetery as a profit-making venture. The founders responded to the concern over profit motives by changing the joint-stock company to an incorporated trust. They agreed with the critics in their explanation for this change: "The idea of private and individual profit, and . . . the conflicting interest of lot-holders and stock-holders . . . appears not in harmony with an undertaking which, in its nature and aim, is eminently and essentially philanthropic."[31] The new corporation was organized so that no profits could be taken from the cemetery operation, and all expenditures had to serve the lot-holders as owners of the cemetery. Lots could be sold, but not for an individual's gain. The cemetery could prosper for the sole purpose of ensuring that the grounds would always be maintained.

Although Americans refused to allow rural cemeteries to become commercial enterprises, they inevitably became symbols of economic success. Green-

Wood's roads were lined with expensive, elaborate family and individual monuments and markers, which touted the achievements of the age. The public became so interested in the new cemeteries that management developed a route, which they called the "Tour," by which visitors could see the most impressive monuments and finest views. The tour of Green-Wood was marked in a dark line on the maps in guidebooks sold at the cemetery's gates. By midcentury, approximately sixty thousand people visited annually to enjoy the tour.

Such a tour exposed the cemetery's delicate position as a private institution dedicated to a public service. The founders of Forest Hill Cemetery in Utica, New York, asserted that cemeteries should "be regarded as the property of the community." Rural-cemetery directors struggled to balance lot-holders' desire for tranquility and privacy with the cemetery's role as a public place. Lot-holder complaints began within two years of the founding of Mount Auburn, and it was forced within a decade to develop rules governing the presence of the public in the cemetery. Other cemeteries made such rules part of their rules and regulations. Rural-cemetery directors never completely resolved the issue of their responsibility to the community versus their obligation to their lot-holders.[32]

The tours also violated the egalitarian and religious simplicity imbued in the rhetoric of the new cemeteries. The same founders in Utica worried "that no one of us shall be found so wretched that he may not with those of the sons of wealth and honor and luxury, peacefully sleep when life's fitful fever shall be o'er." The elaborately ornamented, expensive monuments at which visitors marveled suggested that there was an economic difference in rural cemeteries. Some seemed more equal than others, their lots prominently placed on the tour, their monuments discussed in guidebooks, their lots carefully maintained by private gardeners. Cemetery rules, such as those of Laurel Hill Cemetery in Philadelphia, which mandated that only lot-holders could ride carriages on the grounds on weekdays, reinforced the distinctions; ownership of a single grave did not make one a lot-holder, only the purchase of a large family lot made one a member of the cemetery corporation.[33]

Churchyard to Cemetery in Manhattan. Four years after the incorporation of Green-Wood, Trinity Church reluctantly accepted the restrictions on the continuation of burials at its site in lower Manhattan and opened a new cemetery in the far reaches of upper Manhattan, which was well beyond any foreseeable growth. Although its directors had considered purchasing a large lot in Green-Wood, Trinity was instead the first American church to establish a new cemetery planned in a naturalistic design. Architect John Renwick completed the plan for the new cemetery in 1842, and the first interments occurred in 1843.[34]

The land on which the cemetery was established had been the site of the Revolutionary War battle of Washington Heights. This area had remained sparsely populated since the Revolution. A few years after Trinity Church

View from Battle Hill, Green-Wood Cemetery, Brooklyn, N.Y., 1846
The view was an important attribute of the new cemeteries, as it was with Père Lachaise. This view of Upper New York Bay was a major promotion point for the cemetery corporation. Note that the section was named after the Battle of Brooklyn, which had occurred near here. Founders strongly believed that rural cemeteries were repositories for the nation's history. (Nehemiah Cleveland, *Green-Wood Illustrated: In Highly Finished Line Drawings Taken on the Spot, by James Smillie,* 1847. Courtesy of Dartmouth College Library.)

Cemetery opened, the Hudson River Railroad established a branch line that swept along the cemetery's boundaries. Prior to that, the quickest ways to reach the new cemetery were by the "Manhattanville line of Stages," which left on the half-hour for the cemetery, or steamboat, which had daily departures at ten in the morning and two in the afternoon.[35]

The establishment of Trinity Church Cemetery was a bold move by the Episcopal diocese of New York City to manage the prohibition against interments in lower Manhattan. The innovation was not the interment of the dead away from the church; Manhattan's churches had long had burial places situated in other, more remote parts of the city. These burial places, though, rarely remained inviolate for more than a generation. Many of them were abandoned and the graves disinterred as land in lower Manhattan became more valuable. The new cemetery was the first of many similarly designed church-owned cemeteries throughout America.

Trinity Church Cemetery represented the diocese's acceptance of the new laws governing interment and its recognition that a new style of cemetery was emerging. Located far up the island of Manhattan, the new cemetery was positioned and planned to last for generations. The grounds were divided into family lots and planted in a picturesque manner. The new cemetery represented a reminder that death was still a spiritual matter and that the dead were in the care of the church. However, though churches owned cemeteries, they had lost some control over the burial process.

The First Imitator: Albany Rural Cemetery. The founding of Albany Rural Cemetery demonstrates the way the rural-cemetery movement spread through the larger cities of the Northeast. In 1840, at the Young Men's Christian Association, a public meeting considered the "propriety and importance of purchasing a plot of ground for a new public Cemetery, on a plan similar to the Cemetery at Mount Auburn." That group resolved to establish a new cemetery that would include extensive, elevated grounds and "facilities that will enable art to remedy whatever nature may have left defective."[36]

The new cemetery was incorporated on 2 April 1841, although the grounds were not consecrated until 1844. Contemporaries felt that the Albany Rural Cemetery was well named. Three ridges, separated by two streams, divided the cemetery, providing varying terrains and startling vistas. Daniel D. Barnard, the dedication speaker, stated: "Yonder city, where . . . the harmonies of society are apt to be broken by petty feuds, by ungentle rivalries, by disturbing jealousies, by party animosities, by religious dissensions, shall . . . send up her multitudinous population to these grounds, and here they shall take their respective places, in amiable proximity to each other, peaceful, harmonious, undisturbed and undisturbing, . . . waiting for the same change and the same resurrection."[37] Supporters of the early rural cemeteries hoped to create a new, secure, permanent, and attractive burial place, which answered the physical and psychological needs of a changing urban culture.

The founders hired Douglass of Green-Wood to plan the cemetery. Thus began a second generation of rural cemeteries which directly imitated the style and design of Mount Auburn and which helped develop a group of professional landscape designers. Mount Auburn and many of the other early rural cemeteries were designed by individuals without any engineering, horticultural, or design training. A few individuals, most notably Douglass, were able to establish reputations for their landscaping of cemeteries, and thus directors turned to them in discussing the establishment of a new cemetery. In addition to designing Green-Wood and Albany Rural, Douglass also made the initial survey of Oakwood Cemetery in Troy, but he died before he could complete it. He was replaced by John Sidney, a Philadelphia engineer who would also plan other cemeteries, including Woodlawn Cemetery in the Bronx.

Douglass was a pioneer who would be followed in the 1840s and 1850s by a growing group of talented individuals, such as Algernon Hotchkiss and Howard Daniels, who would be not only planners of new cemeteries but also pioneers in the design and management of urban parks. The rural-cemetery movement was a critical experience for the professionals who were the forerunners of landscape architecture in America.[38]

The public was actively involved in the rural-cemetery movement throughout America. Urban boosters in cities from Denver to Richmond, dedicated to the improvement and advancement of their cities, apparently viewed the rural cemeteries as one more building block of a successful, prosperous city. In Cincinnati and other cities, boosters also were concerned about the graveyards and churchyards that were dangerous and often dilapidated. They wanted a change.[39]

Few associations successfully organized cemeteries prior to the late 1840s. This was partly due to the high cost of establishing a new cemetery. The purchase of the land was often the largest cost in establishing a rural cemetery, but development of the terrain could also place the association heavily in debt. Nehemiah Cleveland wrote that, between 1839 and 1860, Green-Wood had expenditures of over $1.7 million. The cemetery spent almost $300,000 in purchasing its 318 acres. Another $250,000 had been spent on improving the land. Labor costs were well over $1 million.[40]

Green-Wood could barely afford such large expenditures. The project was almost abandoned in 1842 because the costs of starting the cemetery were not being met by the receipts. A dramatic rise in sales during the last five years of the decade helped to solidify the corporation's finances. Yet by 1860 the cemetery had only received $1,000 more than it had spent. Green-Wood was a lavishly ornamented and carefully maintained cemetery, but such high costs proved large obstacles to the promoters of rural cemeteries in smaller cities. State approval, general societal approbation, and concerted efforts at fundraising were essential requirements for the success of rural cemeteries in the decade prior to the Civil War.

A CIVILIZED RESPONSE

Mount Auburn not only solved Boston's burial crisis but, more importantly, provided the nation with the model for a new sacred space for the dead and a tranquil spot, even a pleasure ground, for the living. Throughout America, rural-cemetery pioneers thanked the Bostonians for their leadership. Each of them imitated Mount Auburn's style and organization. These pioneers tried to adapt the principles of Mount Auburn to local conditions, but there was little need to improve the model. As in Boston, the early rural cemeteries were established in cities that needed to replace crowded existing graveyards. Residents of Philadelphia, New York City, Brooklyn, and Albany also desired an escape from the bustle of the city.

By the end of the 1840s, the rural cemetery had become more than a response to the problems of large cities struggling to expand in a civilized manner. Residents in small cities, large towns, and villages from coast to coast embraced the style and the sentiment of the rural cemetery. They began to organize associations to bury their dead in larger, ornamented cemeteries. Families placed bigger, more artistic monuments on lots. Associations and lot-holders planted trees and bushes. The rural cemetery became the American resting place for the living as well as the dead.

CHAPTER FOUR

An American Resting Place

THE CEMETERY AS A CULTURAL NECESSITY

When Elias W. Leavenworth noted in 1859 that Syracuse's new rural cemetery was the "last great necessity" of a prosperous democratic society, he was referring to more than the need for a healthier, more secure burial place. Syracuse, along with other emerging cities throughout America, had grown, diversified, and prospered. Yet with the happiness of economic prosperity came the uncertainties of a new social order. Residents of the new cities experienced intemperance, poverty, and social isolation. Commentators worried about the influence of commerce on American values and morality. Urban life seemed to isolate residents from their environment and from one another, disrupting the balance between nature and civilization, and between the individual and the community.

The cemetery was intended to be a lesson for the commercial society it mirrored. Mount Auburn provided what David Schuyler has called a "didactic landscape." Visitors were thought to enter the cemetery in a state of anxiety and ambition and to leave calm and contemplative. They would feel a renewed respect for the dead and be reminded of human frailty. They would experience what Edgar Allen Poe called an "interval of tranquility."[1] The cemetery would be an island of peace in the maelstrom of society.

A walk through Mount Auburn, one writer noted in 1848, served "to soften the general tone of feeling, to quench the fire of passion, to moderate the aspirations of ambition, to dispel the illusions of hope, to allay vanity and frivolity, to admonish of the shortness of time and the reality and nearness of eternity."[2] Rural cemeteries were intended to be part of a strong moral and civic culture supportive of daily mercantile life and thus strengthen American society. The cemetery had become a place where Americans could comfortably consider charity, humility, life, and immortality.

IMPACT OF THE 1847 LEGISLATION

Until the late 1840s, the American public remained skeptical of rural cemeteries. As the situation at Green-Wood demonstrated, the financial prospects were daunting. The public was reluctant to separate the cemetery from daily life. Even the legal status of the cemetery was unclear. Rural cemeteries had to receive special state permission to purchase and develop large plots of land.

Massachusetts changed the need for such permission when it passed a general incorporation act for cemeteries in 1841. New York State's 1847 act authorizing the incorporation of rural-cemetery associations and providing general guidelines for the organization and management of the new cemeteries followed the outlines of the Massachusetts legislation.[3] As in similar legislation passed afterward in other states, including California (1859), in the 1847 legislation detailed instructions were given on the number of board members (not less than six), elections (annual), land purchases (not more than two hundred acres), and tax status (exempt as long as the land was used for a cemetery and the corporation was nonprofit). The legislation, which defined corporate limits and powers, acted as a textbook for organizing a new cemetery. The cemetery had become another commercial and social institution, such as a bank and a hospital, protected and overseen by the state through incorporation.

Passage of the 1847 legislation led to the formation of many new cemetery organizations in New York State. Several new rural cemeteries were organized before the end of the 1840s; four of these were in the New York City area and others were in Ogdensburg, Troy, Buffalo, and Johnstown. Small towns, including Niagara Falls, Huntington, Hoosick, Sing Sing (later renamed Ossining), Gloversville, and Rome, added new rural cemeteries by 1855. Niagara Falls was a village of fifteen hundred people when it consecrated Oakwood Cemetery. The rural-cemetery movement was becoming more than an answer to urban overcrowding. The new cemeteries represented a change in custom and culture.

Although much of this chapter discusses the widespread acceptance of the rural cemetery in New York State, events there were not substantially different than in Massachusetts, Ohio, New Hampshire, Pennsylvania, and other states. The elements of the rural cemetery—the family monument, planned landscape, picturesque vistas, rolling roadways, and location outside the city—were imitated throughout much of America. Midwestern and western pioneers latched onto the concepts, as they to did much of what they missed from the East. Southerners, especially rural ones, held to older customs of scrapped graves and individual gravestones. However, rural New Englanders quickly accepted cemetery beautification.

In 1845, in the tiny college town of Hanover, New Hampshire, the new Dartmouth Cemetery Association was formed "to take control of the cemetery," under the state law of 1842. The cemetery had "become crowded and needed enlargement; the fence had become dilapidated; the trees and the grounds greatly needed attention." The cemetery was expanded, a hearse house and receiving tomb were constructed, lots were plotted for families, and new trees were planted to shade the existing gravestones. On three occasions over the next twenty years, local professors delivered addresses to the residents on "the importance of the cemetery." The ideas of the rural cemetery had spread from Boston and other big cities into northern New England.[4]

THE CHANGING GEOGRAPHY OF DEATH
IN NEW YORK CITY

The earliest and greatest impact of the new legislation was felt in large cities, including New York. The 1823 prohibitory legislation started an inexorable removal of the dead from Manhattan and the central areas of Brooklyn and other surrounding cities. In 1844, after years of complaints about the failure of New Yorkers to heed concerns about the dangers of in-city burials, the city inspector, who gathered the annual statistics on interments, added a new category, "Removed," because an increasing number of interments were occurring outside the city. In 1844, 983 out of 8,955 (or 11 percent) of New York City's dead were transported for burial in outlying cemeteries. The next year, the city inspector expressed the "gratifying fact" that "a large proportion to the whole number of deaths" were "removed from the City for interment." The pace of removal grew quickly after 1847, and in 1850 a quarter of the burials occurred outside Manhattan.[5]

In 1853 the city inspector noted that interments "within the city have now nearly ceased."[6] Cemeteries ringed the city. Brooklyn was the main site, with Calvary (1848), Cypress Hills (1848), The "Evergreens" (1849), Salem Fields (1850), and Most Holy Trinity (1852). Other cemeteries, such as St. Michael's (1850), Holy Cross (1849), Dale (1851), and Beechwoods (1854), surrounded New York City. Rockland Cemetery, located in distant Sparkill, was founded in 1847 in hopes of persuading New Yorkers to purchase lots in the Hudson Valley. The city's population was rising rapidly, but not as fast as the number of grave sites available to its dead. By 1860, well over two thousand acres had been set aside for the dead.

Rural cemeteries were also organized in smaller cities. Rose Hill in Syracuse was followed by Oakwood (1859) and St. Agnes (1863). Albany Rural was followed by St. Agnes (1867), which was for Catholics. Typically, Protestant forerunners were joined within a decade by Catholic cemeteries, then perhaps by competing nonsectarian (primarily Protestant) cemeteries. The older town burial grounds and churchyards faced fierce new competition from the popular and scenic rural cemeteries.

The city sexton of Syracuse reported that 297 non-Catholic interments had been made in the city's burial grounds in 1856. Within a decade, Oakwood Cemetery alone had 235 interments annually. The in-city cemeteries did not immediately cease burials; Rose Hill continued to bury for decades. People

TABLE 4.1.
New York City Interment Figures, 1838–1850

Category	1838	1839	1840	1841	1842	1843	1844	1845	1846	1847	1848	1849	1850
African	179	159	164	167	164	157	190	192	263	273	298	268	208
Baptist	165	152	139	153	140	134	139	184	181	171	212	228	162
Dutch Reform	316	278	261	341	260	257	214	278	242	267	231	353	199
Episcopalian	625	370	381	397	397	387	371	341	327	365	496	519	347
Friends	53	56	39	77	55	49	52	53	37	51	46	57	19
German Lutheran	141	166	159	173	220	174	325	380	450	412	535	631	433
Hebrew	25	57	51	75	65	73	60	72	78	122	141	254	176
Marble	181	206	200	221	184	168	143	147	102	132	122	165	117
Methodist	1,190	1,451	1,505	1,619	1,643	1,395	1,409	1,791	1,621	1,679	1,790	2,017	1,471
Presbyterian	979	961	918	1,085	970	861	753	889	741	785	993	1,365	764
Potter's Field	1,514	1,495	1,727	1,692	1,776	1,545	1,248	1,439	1,680	3,662	2,897	5,602	3,023
Removed	—	—	—	—	546	983	1,419	1,602	2,215	4,863	4,760	4,134	—
Roman Catholic	2,685	2,543	2,914	3,088	3,272	2,923	3,043	3,794	3,990	5,646	3,292	7,552	5,925
Others	0	59	16	27	35	24	25	4	4	8	3	2	0
Total	8,053	7,953	8,474	9,115	8,475	8,693	8,955	10,983	11,318	15,788	15,919	23,773	16,978

Source: "Annual Report of Interments of the City and County of New York for the Year," in *Documents of the Board of Aldermen* (New York, 1839–51).

clearly preferred the new cemeteries outside the cities.[7] By the 1870s, residents of small and large towns were much more likely to bury their dead in cemeteries located on the outskirts of the built-up areas than in a central graveyard.

THE PROMOTERS

The new cemeteries were part of a larger civic culture under development in the antebellum period. Urban growth, economic interdependence, and social diversity had disrupted the stability and homogeneity of America's towns and cities.[8] Deprived of the village society dominated by church and family, antebellum city leaders organized associations to reorder and renew their communities. Symbolic links among residents, academies and societies defined community in an increasingly secular and diverse nation.

Rural cemeteries were an integral part of this attempt to re-create community. Most of the men associated with the new cemeteries were, according to Washington Irving, "plain matter-of-fact men," locally important and intensely interested in their communities. Judge Joseph Story, Mount Auburn's first president, was a leading jurist, and Irving was associated with Tarrytown's Sleepy Hollow Cemetery, but most board members were local businessmen.[9]

The first boards of directors of Buffalo's Forest Lawn Cemetery and Syracuse's Oakwood Cemetery were typical of those of other rural cemeteries throughout America.[10] The board members were prosperous men who were well respected in the community for their political, business, social, and volunteer activities. Many had migrated from New England or small communities within New York State. Leavenworth, of Oakwood in Syracuse, came from Great Barrington, Massachusetts. Oakwood board member Robert Wynkoop was a native of small Catskill, New York.

Some of the board members had achieved considerable wealth and notoriety. Lewis Allen of Forest Lawn was a founder of the Buffalo Historical Society, a member of the Board of Health during the 1832 cholera epidemic, president of the New York State Agricultural Society in 1848, and a leading writer on agricultural subjects. Allen was widely known as the coauthor of the *American Farm Book,* the *Short-horn Herd Book* and the *History of the Short-horn Cattle.* Thomas Alvord served as Syracuse's representative to the state legislature for many years and was elected speaker of the State Assembly on four occasions. At the time of his death in 1887, John Crouse, his fellow board member, was reputedly the richest man in the city.

One-quarter of the board members of Oakwood and Forest Lawn were lawyers. The other members were businessmen. For example, Francis H. Root, a director of Forest Lawn, was one of the founders of the Eagle Iron Works in Buffalo. He was also director of the Manufacturer's Bank, the Bank of Buffalo, and the Buffalo Savings Bank. He was also the owner of Root and Keating Tanneries.

The cemeteries' board members shared an intense interest in their cities. Most of them were involved in the local normal school, orphan asylum, and hospital. Members founded and served on the boards of historical societies, public libraries, universities, horticultural and agricultural societies, fraternal groups, and other associations. Charles E. Clarke, the founder of Forest Lawn, devoted time to the Buffalo Female Academy and the General Hospital. Forest Lawn board member Oramus H. Marshall, who also was active with the Buffalo Female Academy, was the second chancellor of Buffalo University and a founding member of the Buffalo Historical Society. Board members took great pride in their cemetery. They worked long hours planning and planting. Many individuals sat on boards of directors for decades and then passed their seats to their sons. If the cemetery had financial difficulty, which many did, board members supported it with loans or gifts. The cemetery was another in the net of associations such men founded and supported in an attempt to build a community in the city.

The important symbolic nature of rural cemeteries assured that they were managed by men. Although American women were having a greater influence over national attitudes toward death and the dead, these board members did not relegate authority over this important cultural and community institution to them. Women influenced the cemetery's landscape through individual artistic works such as monument designs, but the boards of directors, which managed the cemetery corporations, were virtually all male.[11]

Directors of Catholic cemeteries during this period were similar in status and commitment to their counterparts at Oakwood and Forest Lawn. New Catholic cemeteries were established by the church either through the clergy or in concert with a group of interested lay people. Where lay people were involved, such as in St. Agnes in Syracuse and Albany, they were as active in other community activities as their Protestant neighbors. Much of their charitable and volunteer activity was affiliated with their church membership rather than in independent associations such as historical and horticultural societies. The continued influence of church officials in the administration of Catholic cemeteries meant that they were less affected by changing organizational structures, which were so important to the success of the movement among the Protestant elite.[12] Not as influential on institutional structure, the rural-cemetery movement altered the appearance of Catholic cemeteries after 1850.

A FAMILY INSTITUTION

In establishing rural cemeteries, founders were primarily concerned with the burial of their families. Although the cemeteries were designed to heighten cultural consciousness about the past and about salvation, the first order of business of the founders was the establishment of a safe, secure burial place where they could be sure that the remains of their loved ones would not be moved, abandoned, or vandalized. Family lot-holders, who were the cemetery's proprietors, were empowered to select board members and to be involved in the management of the organization. The sections were designed to highlight family lots. The roads, curving and winding through the grounds, were built wide enough to accommodate family carriages. There were enough roads to insure that many family lots were situated right next to the road. The institution was developed to honor, strengthen, and maintain the family.

Many founders of rural cemeteries became involved with them because of concern about their families' future resting places. Just as James Hillhouse had come to the conclusion in 1796 that neither the private burial ground nor the public graveyard would hold the permanently undisturbed remains of his family, John Jay Smith of Philadelphia concluded that a new cemetery was a necessity. In 1835 Smith buried his daughter in a grave of clay, half-filled with water. In 1836 he co-founded Laurel Hill Cemetery, which was along the banks of the Schuylkill River on a hillside that ensured that the soil would drain.[13]

The family plot was the centerpiece of the new rural cemetery, and the individual lot-holder remained in control of the family's lot. Rural-cemetery administrations were not interested in controlling the planting of individual lots. Lot-holders' responsibilities included erecting family monuments and individual markers, contracting for plantings, and maintaining plantings and memorials. The cemetery graded the land, built the roads and pathways, planted a variety of trees and shrubs throughout the grounds, and maintained these parts of the cemetery. A small work force was all that was necessary in the

Valley of Mount Hope Cemetery, Rochester, N.Y., 1982

Rural cemeteries were designed to envelop the visitor. Drawn into the natural landscape by the winding roads, the visitor gradually left behind the worries and concerns of the city. Here the visitor could contemplate the fundamental issues of life and death, nature and civilization. Even if the visitor was not that philosophical, the cemetery's atmosphere was surely a dramatic change from the daily routine.

early years because lot-holders contracted with outside gardeners, florists, and stone carvers to maintain lots.

In 1836 Smith published a set of rules and regulations for Laurel Hill, which, along with that of Mount Auburn, was widely imitated. In Smith's work, Laurel Hill's managers begged "leave to suggest to lot-holders" a set of improvements on previous practices of ornamenting lots. They suggested, among other things, that lot-holders not mound their graves and that they place only a low headstone on the grave, rather than a footstone and headstone. However, the managers assured lot-holders that they had "no wish to interfere with individual taste." They did demand that the superintendent oversee the improvements.[14]

Cemetery managers gradually recognized that this arrangement was defective. Some lot-holders would not maintain their lots, which would produce an uneven, undesirable appearance. As early as 1843, Mount Auburn's board drafted the idea for a trust to serve as a "fund for repairs." The trust limited the cemetery's responsibility and retained the lot-holder's ultimate control over the lot. Cemeteries were particularly unwilling to assume permanent liability for monuments, which were of various materials and styles, so trusts were usually limited to maintaining the lot's appearance.[15]

Other cemeteries followed Mount Auburn's lead very slowly. Prior to the Civil War, few cemeteries established care funds or assumed responsibility for maintaining many lots. In 1859, when Oakwood was founded in Syracuse, there was no mention of care in the initial documents; this situation changed by the 1880s.[16]

A CHANGING VIEW OF DEATH

New religious ideas about death and Resurrection gained great popularity in America in the early nineteenth century. Arminianism, which held that any individual could gain salvation through good works, swept through much of the American Protestant community. Under Arminianism's sway, Protestant Americans repudiated Calvinism, replacing the rigidity of colonial attitudes with a new spirit of hope.

Arminianism lessened the fear of death and brought the world of the dead closer to that of the living. By placing emphasis on the deeds of life and lessening the specter of damnation, evangelicals imparted optimism about eternity to the faithful. Many people felt assured of a happy eternal life. The grave of a loved one became the site of somber celebration. As Reverend Farley of the Church of the Savior in New York City suggested, "I would have [at the grave] words full of hope, and confiding faith, and cloudless trust, and filial submission, and a serene, cheerful piety."

Whether the individual was a Unitarian or an evangelical, the face of death softened and the specter of hell receded. "To those without a divine revelation, the place of the dead has always been a place of gloom," a writer for the *Christian Review* stated, "and whatever may have been done by outward decoration to relieve its deep dreariness, still the thought of it was never pleasant. . . . But Christianity dispels its cold and cheerless horrors. . . . The idea of death, so full in itself of dreariness and terror, is in Scripture, and particularly in the New Testament, softened down into the grateful and peaceful idea of sleep."[17]

Exemplifying this new attitude was a story Reverend John Dowling told at the 1848 dedication of Brooklyn's Cypress Hills Cemetery. A young child stills the tears of a weeping mourner by pointing out that there are no graves in heaven and that the pain of the mourner should be offset by the vision of a tranquil afterlife. Emily Dickinson wrote: "I don't know but [the dead] are the happier, and we who longer stay the more to be sorrowed for."[18] Death had taken on a sentimental, melancholic glow.

The emphasis on children's graves was a manifestation of the precedence of the family and the new conceptions of death. Popular literature of the period celebrated the passing of young innocents, whether in Harriet Beecher Stowe's *Uncle Tom's Cabin* or Lydia Sigourney's stories.[19] The cemeteries were scenes of adoration of dead youth. Charlotte Canda's grave in Green-Wood became a popular shrine primarily because of her death at age seventeen. Commentators touring the cemeteries noted small lambs, the most popular marker for a child's grave.

Such early deaths reinforced Romantic conceptions of death as a moment of celebration. Indeed, the dead were more praiseworthy than the living. William Alcott reminded his readers in 1844 that a Christian mother's child might not be a successful businessman, which would insure "distinction and applause," but he might well be successful if he died young and a Christian, because then he would share "the Throne of universal empire" in heaven. The grave became a symbol of a better life for both young and old, but especially for the young because their noble deaths were so instructive to the rest of society.[20]

The darker side of this cult surrounding the death of innocents was that the American death rate among the young remained relatively high during these years. The continuation of a significant death rate, combined with the social and cultural dislocation associated with the move from rural to urban homes and a lower birth rate, placed a greater emphasis on surviving children. When children died, the family deeply felt the loss.[21]

The rural cemetery would eventually provide a separate section for children. Such a section was favored by young families unable to purchase large lots. These stillborn or young children would be buried in this section, then reinterred when the family was settled or wealthy enough to purchase a family burial lot. Many of these lots were abandoned because families left for new opportunities or avoided reinterment because it would result in further grief.

Rural cemeteries represented a new faith in the salvation of the many instead of the few. These cemeteries, celebrations of life after death, were filled with symbols of hope and immortality. An English visitor, Harriet Martineau, said "there is no gloom about" Mount Auburn.[22] The child's grave was only one symbol of the sad present and the joyful eternal future.

A NEW NATURAL TASTE

New cemeteries not only represented the founders' attempt to renew their communities' sense of unity and their optimism toward salvation but also suggested how important the rural heritage of most Americans was to most Americans' vision of the new city. Most founders shared a passion for horticulture, agriculture, and nature. Buffalo's Lewis Allen, Cincinnati's Robert Buchanan, Philadelphia's John Jay Smith, Syracuse's Elias W. Leavenworth, and Troy's D. Thomas Vail were all active in local horticultural societies, as well as correspondents to journals such as Andrew Jackson Downing's the *Horticulturist*. Horticulture was an important part of their lives. They planted orchards and exotic trees on their estates, argued about the best varieties of fruits and flowers, shared seeds, and exchanged information about a wide assortment of plants.

This reliance on horticulture to help improve society was evident from the first annual report of the Executive Committee of the Albany and Rensselaer

Picturesque Crystal Spring Glen, Rockland Cemetery, Sparkill, N.Y., c. 1881
Located on the Hudson River, Rockland Cemetery was intended to be a rural alternative
to the cemeteries of Brooklyn and the Bronx. The cemetery's rural character was enhanced by illustrators trying to convince urban residents to bury their dead away from
the city. (William Wales, *Rockland Illustrated,* 1881. Courtesy of Dumbarton Oaks, Trustees for Harvard University.)

Horticultural Society in 1848. This group, whose members included several of
the supporters of Albany Rural and Oakwood of Troy, declared that it is
"scarcely . . . necessary to dwell upon the importance of Horticulture. . . . Our
cities and towns are surrounded with beautiful villas and cottages, . . . and we
should be unmindful of our duty if did we not do all in our power to increase
this taste for the beautiful as well as the useful, which adds . . . to the enjoyment
and pleasures of life, which increases our social enjoyments, and adds greatly to
the blessing and comforts of rural life in the cottage of the humble, as well as in
the mansions of the wealthy."[23]

Rural-cemetery promoters viewed the cemetery as an extension of their
efforts in horticulture and gardening. Rochester's garden industry flourished,
and one of its most notable nurseries was Mount Hope Nurseries, originally
located near the cemetery.[24] At Mount Hope Nurseries and the other dis-
seminators of flowers and fruits, the renewed sense of nature which had led
Hillhouse to plant trees along New Haven streets was extended throughout
society; it was a strong motivation for supporting the new scenic cemeteries.

The founders' concern about creating an appropriate, elaborate landscape
for their dead led them to support a growing cadre of landscape gardeners. A
few of the new professionals—Howard Daniels was a prominent example—

succeeded in establishing careers in landscaping. Daniels's career began in 1845, when he was made superintendent of the Cemetery of Spring Grove in Cincinnati. Daniels worked with several board members in redesigning a substantial portion of the original plan submitted by John Notman, architect of Laurel Hill Cemetery. Daniels then opened a landscape gardening firm in New York City. During the 1850s, Daniels designed Oakwood in Syracuse, Spring Forest in Binghamton, and Brookside in Watertown. He claimed in an advertisement in the *Horticulturist* to have laid out fifteen rural cemeteries and "a corresponding number of private grounds."[25] Daniels, Algernon Hotchkiss of Bellefontaine Cemetery in Saint Louis, Adolph Strauch of Spring Grove, and other landscape gardeners represented, along with those in the nursery business, a new professionalism in landscape design and maintenance.

THE LANDSCAPE OF HOPE

The founders' civic concerns, religious liberalism, and horticultural interests resulted in a dramatic new landscape in rural cemeteries. Salvation and the hope of immortality were directly integrated into the landscape through the use of natural and artistic representations. The landscape was also a place of pride for town and family, whose monuments and statues reminded visitors of their successes and their future. The cemetery offered a celebration of life and death, hope for the dead, and repose for the living.

The identity of the cemetery as a place different from the commercial world was established immediately at the cemetery's entrance. Whether directly facing the street or set back along a tree-lined drive, the gates of the cemetery established a boundary between the worlds of the living and the dead. In the first years of the movement, the gates were rarely pretentious. Most cemeteries had simple cast-iron or stone gates of a Gothic or Egyptian motif, which, just as with the family monuments, reflected contemporary styles in architecture. Fences surrounded many cemeteries, which were situated far enough away from the city that its inhabitants often felt insecure about the safety of the grounds, particularly at midcentury, when medical students were still being accused of robbing graves for anatomical study.

The founders intended cemetery visitors to experience something different from their daily life, which was usually dominated by commercialism. The founders hoped that a tour through the picturesque scenery would ease the mourner's grief and evoke the design of nature and the reality of death. Speaking at the dedication of Mount Hope, Pharcellus Church worried that people might misunderstand the cemetery's scenic beauty; thus he warned: "We come here, not merely to look upon . . . the blooming lawn, nor the smooth surface of the pool that mirrors the neighboring landscape, . . . but . . . for the noble purpose of communing with a higher world, and to give scope to those tendencies within which lead us up to immortality."[26] The cemetery was a pleasing retreat, but not a frivolous one. The grave retained its serious purpose as a reminder to the living that death would come. Yet, in the new theology of salvation, one could celebrate death, not fear it.

A landscape that enveloped the visitor conveyed the lesson. Mount Hope's natural ridges constantly offered surprise, with "abrupt declivities, deeply shaded valleys, natural arbors, [and] towering heights."[27] Even in less varied terrain, such as that in the Rural Cemetery in Pittsfield, Massachusetts, the grouping of trees and shrubs and the sweep of the serpentine roadways commanded attention. Designs were intended to draw the visitor as quickly as possible into the new atmosphere. At Oakwood in Troy the road made a sharp turn away from the city into the wildness of the cemetery preserve.

The sense of envelopment in the new cemeteries was heightened by their enormity. Even relatively small communities, such as Poughkeepsie, New York (168 acres), and Newton, Massachusetts (22 acres), purchased far larger parcels than they previously considered necessary. Such large grounds immediately impressed visitors, who were pleased and surprised by the isolation from the noise and atmosphere of town. The grounds immediately became reserves exempt from the economic development that persisted elsewhere. As Washington Irving noted in 1849, the new rural cemetery would keep "a beautiful and umbrageous neighborhood sacred from the anti-poetical and all-leveling axe."[28]

Visitors were constantly turned around by the cemeteries' winding streets. Dearborn's system of roads and pathways in Mount Auburn was widely copied. The roads of Cypress Hills in Brooklyn were designed to "climb every hill, and descend into almost every valley." Winding along several cold-spring lakes, the roads in this 121-acre cemetery were intended to conform with the terrain. Lake Road and Valley Road, which were two of the three major roads, offered views of the "internal scenery" of the cemetery, and Highland Way, the other major road, had commanding views of the ocean and distant landscapes.[29]

Such roads crisscrossed the cemeteries. Because the developers wanted to divert the visitor from the efficiency of the urban grid system of roads and evoke a more contemplative atmosphere, the roads were deliberately twisting. In contrast to graceful curves that allowed carriages to move apace through the grounds, sharp turns slowed the traffic, encouraged looking around, and provided a maximum number of lots with a roadside location. The road system allowed many family lots to be prominently visible, as well as provided a dramatic change from city life.

Often the main road passed by a lake or wound along a stream. Water was an important aspect of the picturesque landscape. In Richmond, Virginia, Hollywood Cemetery was located on a bluff overlooking the James River. Visitors to Mount Hope in Rochester caught glimpses of the Genesee River, which was at its edge, and could stop alongside the artificial pond within the cemetery.

The water not only provided a natural break in the scenery but also encouraged meditation and relaxation.

Rural cemeteries were carefully designed landscapes, not pieces of uncontrolled nature. Plantings were grouped to obstruct wide views of lawns. Vistas were hidden behind plantings to surprise the carriage riders. Various trees and bushes were planted in spots where no monuments were planned. The extravagant natural environment was tamed by the elaborate road and pathway systems. Serpentine pathways provided visitors with many unexpected views and natural surprises, but always led them back to the road and to civilization. The picturesque rural cemetery was balanced between civilized dominance of nature and sublime wilderness.

THE NEW MONUMENTS

The most significant civilized features in the picturesque landscape were family monuments, which emerged from the landscape and stood outlined against the trees. The new monuments represented a shift from an eighteenth-century religious orientation to a more ecumenical, individualistic atmosphere, imbued with nature and hope. The symbols of hope, immortality, and life had long been carved into the markers of America's graveyards, but now they became the prevalent motifs. There were so many that the symbolic language appeared confused, but the central meaning of the ornamentation was inescapable. Statues of Faith, holding anchors of Hope, stood on pedestals decorated with ornaments of ivy (memory), poppy (sleep), oak (immortality), and the acorn (life).

The symbolic language was so complex that writers interpreted their meanings. Edward Fitzgerald's *Hand Book of Albany Rural* includes a list of twenty-six decorations, among them the American eagle (eternal vigilance and universal liberty), the lamb (innocence), and the full-blown rose (prime of life).[30] Americans produced seemingly endless combinations of these natural, mythological, and religious symbols, all reflecting the era of Christian hopefulness and the new attitude toward death.

The Charlotte Canda monument in Green-Wood, one the most celebrated monuments of the period, was illustrative of the hopeful and eclectic symbolism.[31] The monument, designed by the young woman it memorialized, traced her heritage and life. The monument combined marble Gothic arches, fleurs-de-lis, a Grecian urn, carved books of music, and a statue of Canda, flanked by two guardian angels, ascending into heaven.

Contemporary commentators believed that Canda represented innocent feminine childhood and hence referred to her as a "girl." Canda's grave site became one of the most popular tourist sites in Green-Wood, attracting thousands of visitors each year. People were particularly taken by her early and

Monument to Charlotte Canda, Green-Wood Cemetery, Brooklyn, N.Y., 1870
Charlotte Canda's death on her seventeenth birthday in 1845 was a romantic tragedy.
She had designed her own monument, intending it for a recently deceased aunt. The
monument became a favorite spot on the tour of Green-Wood. (Drawing by Thomas
Hogan, in Henry R. Stiles, *A History of the City of Brooklyn,* vol. 3, 1870. Courtesy of
Dartmouth College Library.)

sorrowful death and by the dramatic fact that she had designed the tomb for
her recently deceased aunt but had herself been placed in it. A visit to such a
grave would "make the laughter thoughtful, and strip the tomb of false horrors."[32]

Erected mostly in soft white marble, rather than the darker slates and
limestones favored by past generations, the new cemetery monuments sparkled
with intensity and reassured the mourner of the rewards of faith and good
works. Whether of a small baby or a benevolent angel, whether draped in holly
wreaths or holding an anchor of Hope, the carved figures conveyed comfort,
success, joy, and relief. In this period, sepulchral art, as well as literature and
other art, portrayed death as a heavenly finale to life. Just as deathbed scenes in
popular literature highlighted the innocence of the dying and the sacrificing
selflessness of the faithful, the new monuments celebrated, through the symbolic wreaths and ornaments, a faith in the afterlife.[33]

These monuments brought a new dimension to the cemetery. Earlier gravestones spoke to the visitor and mourner through elaborate epitaphs and flat
carvings. The new monuments were very different. The family monuments in
rural cemeteries were three-dimensional, often combining a complex decora-

tive molding with sentimental statuary.[34] The change was startling. The carvers of the late seventeenth century had placed fancy lettering and death's-heads on gravestones, but the new monuments were created by a generation of American and European sculptors imitating the grand art of the salons. The cemetery was becoming a museum of memories enshrined in monuments spread throughout the grounds.

In 1833 the *New England Magazine* reported that an exhibition of copies of sculptures by the Italian sculptor Antonio Canova had opened in Corinthian Hall in Boston. The magazine suggested that the "monumental marble[s], . . . all chiseled with exquisite skill, and of appropriate design," would make "suitable ornaments to the cemetery at Mount Auburn, which, we hope, is the place of their destination."[35]

Such monuments began to serve as separate attractions by the 1850s. Powerful and popular sculptures—such as Canda's self-designed monument, James Thom's *Old Mortality* in Laurel Hill in Philadelphia, and Ball Hughes's *Nathaniel Bowditch*—received attention in guidebooks and newspaper articles. Works by American sculptors Horatio Greenough, Thomas Crawford, Henry Dexter, and E. A. Brackett adorned the cemeteries. Dexter's memorial to Emily Binney in Mount Auburn became a necessary stop in the tour of cemetery. Guidebooks described the attractions along the tours and provided etchings of popular monuments and maps of the cemetery.[36]

The most popular styles of monuments were widely imitated. Indicative of this was an article in the *Syracuse Journal* in 1879. The author reported on recent monumental additions to Oakwood Cemetery by the firm of A. Schaefer. Schaefer had recently erected a vault for Warren L. Winslow, the design of which was "new to this part of the State, having been copied from Greenwood, New York." An earlier article praised Sidney Stanton's John Crouse monument in the same cemetery, noting it "will vie in elegance and beauty with the finest in Greenwood Cemetery."[37] Gothic vaults, classical urns, and Egyptian obelisks were patterned after monuments whose styles appeared in guidebooks, influencing monuments and mausoleums throughout the land. The development of a national transportation system of railroads made precut, standardized family monuments available; these replaced locally crafted gravestone markers.

RENEWING THE PAST

The new monuments were one way that rural cemeteries celebrated the family and community. Such a celebration was a critical component of the mission of the founders. The founders hoped that the primary experience that the cemetery would convey to the mourner and visitor would be a renewed sense of morality when confronted with the dead in the peacefulness of nature. Founders also wished rural cemeteries to play a role in the development of American art, cultural taste, and historical consciousness. By linking the cemeteries to the past, they would promote the new organizations and provide a community service.

The formation of rural cemeteries coincided with a national movement to reestablish the American past. The generation that came to power in the cities and towns of New York during the antebellum period was the first not to have direct ties to the Revolution. George Washington was an historical icon for them, a legend from their parents and grandparents. The nation was still relatively new, under serious social and political pressures as the Civil War approached, and yet without a sense of its own history.[38]

Rural cemeteries represented society's desire for stability. A prime characteristic of the cemeteries, touted by their boosters as superior to the old graveyards, was their permanence. Speakers at cemetery dedications favorably compared the new cemeteries to Washington's private burial place at Mount Vernon. The first tomb of the president, constructed of wood, had crumbled into ruins by the 1830s. It was replaced by a permanent stone vault, "of the most unpretending description," apparently constructed to Washington's general specifications. Soon after the vault's completion, there had been at least one unsuccessful attempt to steal Washington's bones.[39] The desire to enshrine Washington securely and permanently was part of the same impulse that led communities to found rural cemeteries: to ensure the security of the grave sites for generations.

The creation of a national past was inextricably linked to the establishment of local histories throughout America. Communities searching for a local history used the rural cemetery as a repository and a shrine. Rural-cemetery founders were often the same people involved in researching and writing the histories. These founders studied military history, particularly that of the American Revolution, and identified their cemeteries with the origin and growth of their cities and towns. The cemetery, by definition a place of memories, became a location for the memory of the community.

Cemetery associations took several steps to link the cemetery to the community's memory, the most obvious of which was to bury and honor the nation's war dead or the place that they died. Some cemeteries easily identified their locations and their lot-holders with the American Revolution. Green-Wood and Trinity Church Cemetery in Manhattan, Cypress Hills in Brooklyn, and Woodlawn in the Bronx were located on sites of major strategic battles of the Revolution. The Battle for Brooklyn, in August 1776, raged on the low hills behind Gowanus Bay. Green-Wood's founders named one of the cemetery's sections Battle Hill and situated it on a hillside overlooking Manhattan and the Atlantic Ocean. Battle Hill was reserved for veterans of the Revolutionary War and the War of 1812.

Sleepy Hollow in Tarrytown, Green-Wood, and other cemeteries began the practice of offering veterans a grave site in a separate section. Many of these new sections were the sites of Revolutionary War battles. At Sleepy Hollow,

*Tomb of Héloise and Abelard, Père Lachaise
Cemetery, Paris, c. 1832*

French officials, much like their American counterparts, reinterred the star-crossed lovers, along with other luminaries (including Molière), to establish the cemetery as a place of memories. Families constructed tombs intended to reflect the glory of famous historical figures. (Courtesy of Bibliothèque Nationale.)

Battle Hill was the "territory . . . fortified and stoutly maintained by the patriots . . . many of the old war-worn heroes are buried nearby—still presumably holding vigil over the redoubt which they threw up."[40] Dedicating the land linked the cemetery to the event and its veterans. Veteran sections would become widespread after the Civil War. Such sections originated simultaneously with publicly owned national cemeteries, beginning arguments over government participation in burying America's dead.

Rural cemeteries also celebrated local pioneers. Particularly noteworthy were the grave sites of those families that had founded communities. Public ceremonies and celebrations marked the reinterment of Colonel Nathaniel Rochester in Mount Hope, Ephraim Webster in Oakwood in Syracuse, and Abraham Lansing in Oakwood in Troy. The remains of many heroes and heroines were moved from churchyards and family and town graveyards that

Battle Hill, Sleepy Hollow Cemetery, Tarrytown-on-Hudson, N.Y., 1897
The Revolution was one of the easiest, most popular means of identifying the new rural cemeteries with the national past. Officials of Sleepy Hollow memorialized the hill on which revolutionaries had fought. (Sleepy Hollow Cemetery brochure, 1897.)

had been abandoned or neglected as the cities grew; such conditions reinforced the rural cemeteries' claim of greater permanence.[41]

Several cemeteries made an effort to include Native Americans in their pantheons of historical figures. This inclusion was an offshoot of, as well as a further encouragement for, the study and gathering of artifacts of Native Americans by local historical societies. These developments were spurred by a growing belief in the innocence of Native American life, especially in contrast to the complexity and worldliness of city life. The numerous poems, stories, and novels portraying the Native American, including James Fenimore Cooper's *The Last of the Mohicans,* were evidence of this new attitude.

Both Forest Hill in Utica and Forest Lawn in Buffalo widely publicized the inclusion of the Native American in their cemeteries. Forest Hill appropriated the Oneida stone, the spiritual symbol of the local Iroquois tribe. Later in the century, Forest Lawn celebrated the reinterment of the Senecan political and military leader Red Jacket during an elaborate ceremony attended by hundreds. Native Americans, who had been so scorned, were now welcomed and adopted into the history of the community; these actions furthered Americans' sense of their national identity and past.[42]

The historical monuments and the artistic family monuments eventually violated the simple atmosphere of the landscape. The imposition of tours and historical spots interrupted the peace of the grounds. Rural cemeteries became one of America's early tourist attractions, and the most famous cemeteries drew thousands of visitors annually. It was estimated that 140,000 people visited

Laurel Hill Cemetery in 1860. The rural ambiance so important in the designs of the cemeteries was slowly lost because of the larger crowds and more monuments.[43]

FAMILY LOTS AND SINGLE SECTIONS

Superficially, the rural cemetery was one of the most open and democratic institutions in antebellum America. Family lots were available to members of any religion, economic class, and ethnic group. Some cemeteries were even open to any race. Rural-cemetery founders spoke of equality and community, favorably contrasting their cemeteries with churchyards and churches' exclusive vaults. At Albany Rural's dedication, Daniel D. Barnard encouraged his listeners to remember that the new cemetery, unlike earlier graveyards, was "open to all—to every class, and every complexion in society, and to every sect in religion."

Founders and supporters contrasted their cemeteries' naturalistic, inviting landscapes to the forbidding and socially distinctive burial places of the past. Oakwood in Syracuse allowed only mausoleums in which the "fronts and roofs are below ground." The new cemeteries were meant to represent the American democratic philosophy of equality. "The poor will have a place here as well as the rich; and wherever the dead are laid in these grounds, there will they remain."[44]

Some cemeteries, including Cypress Hills in Brooklyn, encouraged group purchases. Cypress Hills was established as "a fraternal cluster of cemeteries, surrounded by one common enclosure."[45] Whereas many cemeteries relied on family lots, Cypress Hills encouraged "Ecclesiastical, Benevolent, Social, and Humane Societies and Associations" to reserve graves. Discounts were offered to groups. Cypress Hills attracted several church groups, as well as local chapters of the Odd Fellows, Society of St. Andrew, Masons, and Sons of Temperance. Other rural cemeteries also appealed to church and fraternal groups.

Oakwood in Syracuse, Mount Hope, Albany Rural, and apparently many other northeastern cemeteries buried African-Americans. The races were strictly segregated in southern cemeteries. African-Americans were excluded from white cemeteries or allowed burial only in segregated sections in midwestern cemeteries. However, they were buried throughout many northeastern rural cemeteries. Many of New York's rural cemeteries were founded by individuals who, by the 1840s and 1850s, had supported the end of slavery. Elias W. Leavenworth and Horatio Seymour had fought abolitionism in the 1830s, but were antislavery politicians by the 1850s, when they wrote the rules and regulations for the new cemeteries in Syracuse and Utica, respectively.[46]

For whites, the only barrier to owning a plot in most rural cemeteries throughout America was money. In 1846 a family lot in Albany Rural was sixteen by sixteen feet and cost twenty-five dollars. In that same year, a three-hundred-square-foot lot in Green-Wood, the smallest available, cost eighty dollars. Although such large lots offered families security, their price was an overwhelming obstacle to many Americans.

Rural cemeteries offered the alternative of single graves. Single graves were priced differently in each cemetery, but in 1860 Oakwood in Syracuse priced them at eight dollars for an adult and five dollars for a child, which included "opening, closing and sodding the grave."[47]

The single graves were in sections that were visually and physically segregated from the family lots of the middle and upper classes. Situated along the cemetery's edges, the single sections benefited less than the family lots from the natural envelopment so important to the atmosphere of the rural cemetery. Furthermore, because single graves were sold to individuals, not families, poor families were often divided. A mother and a father might be able to reserve side-by-side graves, but their children—in a throwback to the colonial graveyard—had to be satisfied with nearby graves. Few cemeteries allowed holders of single graves to erect monuments. The graves were marked with simple individual markers. Plantings were also limited by deed restrictions. The poor were crowded in sections with fewer trees, paths, and natural embellishments.

Catholic cemeteries more willingly assumed responsibility for the indigent dead. There were almost three thousand burials in the potter's field in New York City, as well as several hundred free burials of poor Catholics in Calvary and the other cemeteries of the Catholic dioceses. Throughout the century, Catholic and other church cemeteries continued to offer free burials to those who were unable to pay.

Other indigent dead were buried in large lots purchased by fraternal groups and charitable associations. As fraternal organizations spread throughout American society, they assumed, as did many fellowship, craft, artisan, and labor organizations, responsibility for burying their dead brothers and sisters. Benefactors of orphans, the homeless, and other marginal members of the community also purchased such lots. For example, a society woman purchased the Syracuse Orphan Asylum lot in Oakwood Cemetery on behalf of the female residents. Overseen by a large female statue, the lot was covered with small individual markers for the girls and women who died at the asylum.

The single sections were an important option to the poorer members of the community. As the rural cemetery became the standard burial place in American cities, a dramatic distinction in burial practices developed. Those who could afford the rural cemetery, with its natural splendor, were buried there. Those who could not afford it relied upon the government to provide a burial place. In Manhattan in 1848, 2,897 interments, 18 percent of the city's total, were in the potter's field. This percentage did not lessen as the number of rural cemeteries in the New York City area expanded.[48]

Such inequality suggested that the founders' vision of community was neither egalitarian nor democratic. This period was one of growing class. Democratic rhetoric was used to mask the erosion of economic equality. Rural cemeteries fit into the larger pattern of middle-class leaders attempting to establish a new urban status quo.

The cemeteries represented the interests, ideals, and philosophies of their promoters, who were middle- and upper-class urban men. Some commentators noted the disparity. Writing in the *New Englander* in 1849, one critic noted that "the poor must stand aloof and seek some less genteel place of burial. This ought not to be." The critic suggested that all new cemeteries should provide "lots at small cost for the poor, as well as lots for the friendless and the strangers."[49] Rural cemeteries rarely institutionalized such Christian benevolence.

The rhetoric of community clashed with the rules and regulations of rural cemeteries. Mount Auburn and virtually all other rural cemeteries initially welcomed all visitors, but soon limited access on Sundays, the most popular day to visit the cemetery, to proprietors with passes. Many rural cemeteries established rules of social conduct (no eating, drinking, or smoking allowed) throughout the week. Rules that limited eating and drinking on the grounds were much more burdensome for the poor, who walked to their lots, than for the wealthier classes, who rode in their carriages.[50] In 1860 the newly established Oakwood Cemetery in Syracuse published its first rules and regulations:

Section. 1. Each Proprietor of a lot will be entitled to a ticket of admission into the Cemetery with a vehicle, under the following regulations, the violations of which, or a loan of the ticket, involves a forfeiture of the privilege.

Sec. 2. No vehicle will be admitted unless accompanied by a proprietor, or a member of his or her household, with his or her ticket, or unless presenting a special ticket or admission obtained at the office of the Cemetery, or of a Trustee.

Sec. 3. On Sundays and holydays the gates will be closed. Proprietors of lots, however, will be admitted, on foot, by applying to the Keeper at the lodge.

Sec. 4. Fast driving will be especially prohibited, and no vehicle will be allowed to pass through the grounds at a rate exceeding three miles an hour.

Sec. 5. No persons or parties having refreshments to sell, will be permitted to come within the grounds, nor will any smoking be allowed.

Sec. 6. No horse may be left by the driver in the grounds unfastened. Hitching posts are provided for that purpose. Any person violating the above rule, or fastening his horse to a tree, will be required by the Superintendent to leave the grounds forthwith.

Sec. 7. All persons are prohibited from writing upon, defacing, or

otherwise injuring any monument, fence, or other structure in or
belonging to the Cemetery, or from picking any flower, either wild or
cultivated, or injuring any tree, shrub or plant.

Sec. 8. Any person disturbing the quiet and good order of the place,
by noise or other improper conduct, will be compelled instantly to
leave the grounds.

Sec. 9. The gates will be opened at sunrise, and closed for entrance
at sunset.

Visitors are reminded that these grounds are appropriated exclusively to the interment of the dead. It is therefore indispensable
that there should be strict observance of all the proprieties due to the
place. The Superintendent, being clothed with the powers of a special
policeman, will be required to arrest disorderly persons.[51]

The rural cemeteries were sacred places constantly used by the public,
which created inevitable conflicts and controversies. The founders of rural
cemeteries perceived them as places of moral purity, in contrast to the impure
commercial world of the cities. Thus it was particularly disturbing when people
filled the cemetery atmosphere with elements of the real world. The *Syracuse
Journal* reported in 1866 that Michael Leyden, an Oakwood Cemetery special
policeman, had arrested Mary Moran, "a subject of easy virtue," and fined her
ten dollars for picking a flower. The policeman had originally stopped Moran
and her "male wretch" because they were "prowling about the cemetery evi-
dently for no good purpose," and he instructed them to leave. Moran picked
the flower in defiance of the order. Because she was penniless, she was jailed for
her offense.

Other newspapers reported concerns about couples holding hands, beggars, vandalism, and theft. Beginning in the 1850s, Rochester's newspapers
continually attacked Mount Hope's managers for their incompetence and ill-
mannered administrations. The newspaper writers were angered at the "thousands" of people who disturbed Sunday funerals by making the cemetery a
"place of recreation." "Drinking saloons are being erected in the vicinity of the
Cemetery and dance houses were expected to soon be seen there. The time will
soon come when painted harlots will revel with freedom in the grounds."

The *Rochester Daily Union and Advertiser* was particularly incensed by the
gatekeeper. The gatekeeper, according to the newspaper, was a child who was
paid by visitors to open and close the gates. "If there is a place where money
should not be called for, even by beggars, it is at the tomb, where the rich and
poor alike may go to pay respect to the memory of the dead." The newspaper
blamed the city commissioners, suggesting that "we do not know much about
the manner in which Mt. Hope is run. It is a sort of closed corporation—the
commissioners doing pretty much as they think best."[52]

First Entrance to Green-Wood Cemetery, Brooklyn, N.Y., 1870

In keeping with the simple naturalism of the picturesque rural cemeteries, the 1845 entrance was a wooden structure with a bell tower. The bells were rung when a funeral procession entered the cemetery. Later, when the cemetery was very popular, the bells were stopped because of neighbors' complaints. (Drawing by Thomas Hogan, in Henry R. Stiles, *A History of the City of Brooklyn,* vol. 3, 1870. Courtesy of Dartmouth College Library.)

PRIVACY AND EXCLUSIVITY IN THE AGE OF DEMOCRACY

The rhetoric of egalitarianism became more difficult to defend as the cemeteries filled with larger, more expensive, and more ornate monuments. Downing was one of the commentators who criticized the tendency of lot-holders of rural cemeteries to overembellish their monuments and to overplant their lots. Downing was "America's arbiter of taste" from the 1840s until his death in 1852.[53] His work as a nurseryman, editor of the *Horticulturist,* and author of several important horticultural and architectural books made him a widely recognized expert on the American domestic landscape.

Throughout his career, Downing lauded horticulture's influence on society. In 1847 he wrote that "horticulture and its kindred arts, tend strongly to fix the habits, and elevate the character, of our whole rural population." He viewed the establishment of rural cemeteries as an extension of this moral elevation. The burial ground had been changed from "that sad and desolate place" to a spot that showed "our people how soothing and benign" was rural beauty's "influence upon the living." Downing hoped that the success of rural cemeteries would convince Americans that pleasure grounds and parks were necessary "to soften and allay some of the feverish unrest of business which seems to have possession of most Americans, body and soul."

Although Downing applauded rural cemeteries, he strenuously objected to the manner in which some Americans were using them as a place to exhibit status and success. "The only drawback to these beautiful and highly kept cemeteries . . . is the gala-day air of recreation they present." Within this atmosphere, people would enjoy themselves, failing to "indulge in any serious recollections or regrets," which Downing felt essential to the mood of the Romantic cemetery.

Downing believed that the regrettable custom of placing fences around lots reduced the solemnity of the atmosphere. He advocated a balance of nature and art in any landscape, but especially one intended to educate through the lessons of natural beauty. By "enclosing" the lots, lot-holders violated this balance and, to Downing's horror and anger, brought the city into the landscape. "The exhibitions of ironmongery, in the shape of vulgar iron railings, posts and chains, balustrades, etc., all belonging properly to the front-door steps and areas of Broadway and Chestnut-street [in Philadelphia], and for the most part barbarous and cockneyish in their forms, are totally out of keeping with the aspect of nature, the repose, and the seclusion of a rural cemetery."[54]

Such dissatisfaction quickly increased as the number of monuments, fences, mausoleums, and ornamental art works proliferated in the cemeteries. Exemplifying the new ostentation was Leavenworth's decision to replace his unpretentious family monument with a Gothic-style open mausoleum. From his small knoll, Leavenworth could look across at the new fifty-foot-tall pyramid of fellow board member Cornelius Longstreet, who had also torn down a monument to build the new edifice. Throughout rural cemeteries, the simple monuments of the early years were quickly being replaced by more grandiose, sophisticated ones.

Imposing gates began to replace the unpretentious entrances of the early years. The most stylish and ostentatious of rural cemeteries, Green-Wood erected a new entrance: "This gate, monumental in form and character, is constructed of the Belleville brown stone, in the middle pointed English Gothic style, from the design of Messrs. Upjohn & Son. . . . The entombment of the Saviour, and his resurrection, the raising of Lazarus, and the restoration of the widow's son, are happily embodied in these well executed groups and life-like forms, wrought in olive tinted sandstone, the designs, as well as the four allegorical figures on the shields of each gable, being conceived and executed by Mr. John Moffit."[55]

The original idea of the rural cemetery, the "rural" atmosphere in a gardenlike setting, was threatened by such an overwhelming intrusion of artificial ornamentation. The *Christian Review* commented in 1848 that "perhaps there is

Second Entrance to Green-Wood Cemetery, Brooklyn, N.Y., 1870
In contrast to the simple entrance shown in the previous figure, the 1860 entrance was a sumptuous affair. Designed by Richard Upjohn, the new entrance was a symbol of the growing ostentation of America's rural cemeteries. More than any other American cemetery, Green-Wood represented the desire of lot-holders to display their wealth through large, grandiose monuments. The new gates, with their intricate reliefs and huge Gothic arches, were a perfect statement of that desire. (Drawing by Thomas Hogan, in Henry R. Stiles, *A History of the City of Brooklyn*, vol. 3, 1870. Courtesy of Dartmouth College Library.)

no one thing more likely to mar the beauty of the many cemeteries . . . than a desire for singularity, and for a display of expense, in monuments."[56]

Born out of repulsion to the gloominess and unattractiveness of the grave-yard, the rural cemetery was the setting for many attempts to display American artistic achievements. In his 1853 suggestions about monuments for Green-Wood, Nehemiah Cleveland had prodded lot-holders to design a variety of monuments which would enhance the beauty of the natural setting. Lot-holders followed his advice, and the rural cemeteries filled with a wide variety of monumental styles and ornamentation. Less than a generation later, critics charged that the monuments added little but confusion to the landscape, hiding the natural setting and opening the cemetery to a competition for those vying to erect the most ostentatious artistic statement.[57]

The monuments also threatened the democratic nature of the rural ceme-tery. In 1841, when Mount Hope in Rochester and Green-Wood in Brooklyn were less than two years old, an article in the *North American Review* expressed concern that expensively ornamented cemeteries were becoming "exclusively private."[58] The enclosure of family lots not only suggested the status people were exhibiting in the cemetery but also barred entry and denoted exclusivity to those who could afford to be part of the enterprise.

Writers noted that the larger and more dramatic monuments were also more costly. "There is . . . greater danger to the real beauty of our cemeteries, from the great and growing love of expense which marks our country, if not our age, in almost all matters upon which money can stamp its image." This statement was followed by warnings that the cemetery was not the place for such displays: "If wealth will seek display, if gold must tell of its place and its possessor in costly and enduring monuments, let [it] not stand in places of the dead, except it be as a people's tribute in honor of great and heroic deeds to one's country, or some distinguished service to the human race." As rural cemeteries filled with family tributes, some critics began to question the taste of the proprietors.[59]

The monuments, the "gala-day" tours, and the exotic trees and shrubs that lot-holders vied to plant all lent an atmosphere of recreation to the cemetery. Frederick Law Olmsted complained in 1861 that "the rural cemetery, which should, above all things, be a place of rest, silence, seclusion, and peace, is too often now made a place not only of the grossest ostentation of the living but a constant resort of mere pleasure seekers, travellers, promenaders, and loungers."[60] Rural cemeteries had been founded to provide a suitable, private, secure grave site for families, many of whom had witnessed the degradation of previous graveyards. The feeling was growing that the families had traded a sense of impermanence for a sense of inappropriate gaiety.

A CEMETERY FOR CITY AND COUNTRY

While critics were concerned about the impact of ostentatious monuments on the natural appearance and atmosphere of rural cemeteries, city after city added new cemeteries. Most surprisingly, small towns and villages, which had suffered few of the problems of the larger cities, began to organize similar projects. The rural cemetery had become the model for burial places; its features were used in even the most isolated of rural churchyards.

Illustrative of this trend was the organization of Woodlands Cemetery in Cambridge, New York.[61] Cambridge, which had a population of about two thousand, was situated northeast of Albany in Washington County. An agricultural economy, based mainly on the production of flax, had led to the prosperity of the community since its founding in 1791.

Cambridge had had several public and church burial places, the largest and oldest being simply referred to as the Old Grave Yard. Cambridge's early graveyards were community-based in the best sense of the phrase. The Old

Rural Cemetery Gates and Fences, c. 1851

Andrew Jackson Downing, America's preeminent landscape gardener in the antebellum period, believed that lot fences and gates ruined the cemetery landscape's appearance. Gates of this period were usually iron, often elaborately designed. Few exist today. Some were removed by superintendents trying to heed Downing and later critics, whereas others were taken for scrap during the world wars. Ironically, fences that were once much maligned now are often prized possessions in cemeteries. (Nehemiah Cleveland, *Green-Wood Illustrated: In Highly Finished Line Drawings Taken on the Spot, by James Smillie,* 1851. Courtesy of Dumbarton Oaks, Trustees for Harvard University.)

Grave Yard was free and open "for the use of all classes," and, at Ash Grove Burying Ground, the settlement's second-oldest graveyard, the first interment was of an African-American. Both graveyards were still extensively used in 1859, when the new rural cemetery opened.

Contemporaries suggested that the prime motivations for the new cemetery were the rapidly filling graveyards, the concern about the resting places of the children of two prominent citizens, and the success of such ventures in larger cities. The death of Andrew Woods, a locally admired young man, deepened the "conviction of the necessity of a new resting place." On the day of his funeral in 1857, a group gathered to discuss the project and formed the Cambridge Valley Rural Cemetery Association. Members of this group traveled to Troy, Albany, Philadelphia, Baltimore, Cincinnati, and Boston to view other rural cemeteries. They then decided to hire John Sidney, a "rural Architect and Civil Engineer" from Philadelphia and later designer of Woodlawn Cemetery in the Bronx, as their landscape gardener.

Woodlands was laid out on fifteen acres north of the village. The grounds were auspicious for their views of the surrounding countryside and the equal division between "plain and elevated" grounds, which were separated by a belt of woods. Sidney and the board members planted trees and shrubs throughout the cemetery. One thousand graves were created amid the grounds, of which 194 were sold in the first year, for the total sale of $3,756.54.

In keeping with the rising cry against ostentatiousness and privacy, the board members discouraged fences and recommended cornerstones or a hedge of arbor vitae. They also feared that old gravestones brought from older burial places would be placed vertically, giving the appearance of "a marble fence and crowded graves." The board members considered this "not always in good taste" and encouraged lot-holders to place gravestones in a horizontal position—flush to the ground. Prohibiting vertical gravestones and stone fences was still something boards of directors of conservative cemeteries were unwilling to do in this age of lot-holder responsibility.

The new country cemeteries, such as Woodlands and those in Niagara Falls and Cortland, imported the concepts of the city cemeteries from New York City, Albany, Buffalo, and Boston. The new country cemeteries were larger than previous ones, even more than was necessary in these small communities. Their designs often imitated popular characteristics of urban counterparts; roads curved through the grounds even when the terrain was only slightly sloping, and plantings were bunched to hide, then open, vistas. Lot-holders raised monuments that imitated designs popular in famous rural cemeteries. For example, the first monument raised in Woodlands was an obelisk of white marble, well in keeping with the standards and styles of the times. The simple individual grave markers that had been the standard in country graveyards for over a century were largely banned from nineteenth-century cemeteries, both in the city and the country.

Even in those towns that retained the old graveyard, the appearance of burial places changed. Marble markers, granite obelisks, and replicated statues replaced slate and sandstone markers. Maples, oaks, and elms were planted along roadways. Paths were left between rows of graves, and shrubs were planted near monuments. Fences and coping were allowed on new family lots.

The graveyard had been based on the community, with graves of family

TABLE 4.2
Selected List of New York State Rural Cemeteries with Their Dates
of Establishment, 1838–1867

Cemetery	Location	Year	Cemetery	Location	Year
Mount Hope	Rochester	1838	Rural	Poughkeepsie	1852
Green-Wood	Brooklyn	1838	Brookside	Watertown	1853
Rural	Albany	1841	Spring Forest	Binghamton	1853
Trinity Church	Manhattan	1842	Beechwoods	New Rochelle	1854
Rockland	Sparkill	1847	Riverside	Oswego	1855
Calvary	Brooklyn	1848	Lakewood	Cooperstown	1856
Oakwood	Troy	1848	Wiltwyck Rural	Kingston	1856
Cypress Hills	Brooklyn	1849	Green Hill	Amsterdam	1858
Rural	Johnstown	1849	Vale	Schnectady	1858
Sleepy Hollow	Tarrytown	1849	Oakwood	Syracuse	1859
Salem Fields	Brooklyn	1850	Woodlawn	Bronx	1863
Dale	Ossining	1851	Dryden Rural	Dryden	1864
Fort Hill	Auburn	1851	Oakland	Yonkers	1866
Rome Rural	Rome	1851	Silver Mount	Staten Island	1866
Oakwood	Niagara Falls	1852	St. Agnes	Albany	1867

Sources: Dates of establishment are primarily from a 1982 survey of New York State cemeteries and from the files of the New York Cemetery Board, Albany and New York City.

members scattered among their neighbors. The new graveyards, town cemeteries, and rural cemeteries in cities of every size had family lots. Sometimes restrictions on space and need kept these lots smaller in graveyards than rural cemeteries, yet they were the basis of the organization of the burial place in America.

The organization and appearance of the burial place had been irrevocably changed in city and country. No longer would Americans who could afford otherwise look to the church and the state to bury them; the family reigned. No longer would the location of the graveyard be based on accessibility; picturesque sites became the rule. And no longer would rows of similar markers line the relatively plant-free grounds; a variety of markers and monuments would be interspersed between shrubs and trees on undulating grounds.

A CEMETERY FOR THE WHOLE NATION

Rural cemeteries were established throughout America by the opening salvo of the Civil War. Remarkably, in this era of political division and social strife, rural cemeteries were organized in Cincinnati, Louisville, Richmond, Atlanta, and Saint Louis. The conditions that citizens abhorred in New York and New England were similar in the South, Midwest, and West. Indeed, cities outside the Northeast often had more virulent epidemics. Yellow fever remained a tragic killer in the South long after it had lost its impact in the Northeast.

Rural cemeteries overcame sectional distinctions because they answered the public's needs and offered agreeable solutions. Romanticism, with its emphasis on nature, and Arminianism, with its optimistic concept of salvation, were as important in the South as in the North. The graveyards of the South were just as crowded, although the strong tradition of gardening had resulted in more attractive churchyards than in the North. The interest in gardening eased the expansion of a designed cemetery into southern cities and towns. Strong European ties reinforced Romanticism and the new English gardening ideas.

Boosterism played an important role in the development of rural cemeteries. Cities such as Cincinnati were competing with not only neighboring towns but also the prestigious cities of the East Coast. Not wishing to be seen as provincial, leaders such as Robert Buchanan and Robert Bowler in Cincinnati attempted to build a civic culture that would be comparable to that of older cities of the East Coast. Rural cemeteries, including Spring Grove, were one more aspect of this civic culture: a service for the residents and an indication of refinement for the visitor.[62]

A RURAL CEMETERY

The establishment of rural cemeteries was part of a larger effort to shape and maintain a middle-class community based on family, volunteer associations, and commonly accepted cultural ideas, such as a newly recognized national history, a new artistic consciousness, a more optimistic vision of the afterlife, and a belief in the moral virtue of picturesque nature. After inconclusive and unsuccessful attempts in the first two decades of the century to ameliorate the condition of contemporary burial places by expanding existing graveyards and experimenting with Hillhouse's innovation, civic leaders were electrified by Mount Auburn.

The *rural cemetery* was not a misnomer. Many historians would call it the *garden cemetery* due to its horticultural orientation; this term misses the cultural significance of city dwellers' growing isolation from rural life and their attempts—through first the *rural cemetery*, then the *rural park*—to reestablish some of the virtues of country life in the cities. The new cemeteries reversed the priorities predominant in urban life. The visitor was immersed in nature and cut off from urban civilization. The cemetery's landscape integrated various aspects of the ideal picturesque landscape: wild scenery, rolling or sharper terrain, and water. Roads and paths were serpentine, to ensure that the "garden of graves" would not remind the mourner and visitor of life in the geometrically ordered city.

Within these picturesque grounds, lot-holders wished to celebrate their heritage and success. Family lots became means through which middle- and upper-class Americans could commemorate their families, their ancestors, their community, and themselves. Large, artistically styled monuments dotted the sections, and smaller, more standardized monuments filled the spaces between. Even as critics complained about the loss of naturalism, the growing ostentation of the monuments, and the crowding of sections, Americans proud of their success continued to erect monuments to their past.

As much as the founders tried to establish rural cemeteries as burial places for the whole community, the institution embraced the values and goals of only part of the diversified urban community. The number of cemeteries grew because Catholic, Jewish, and other religious groups desired their own communal burial places. Eventually, groups within the Protestant majority organized separate burial places and further diminished the centrality of the rural cemetery. Antebellum Protestant leaders had tried to impose their culture on American society. They were successful in altering the burial habits of the community, but not in fostering all their values and symbols.

The rural-cemetery movement had begun to evolve as soon as the first cemetery was organized. By the 1850s, a new generation of landscape designers was experimenting with a simpler and cleaner landscape, and Americans began to retreat from their close relationship with death.

Commercialization of the Cemetery, 1855–1917

By the 1850s, the rural cemetery had displaced the graveyard in the city and was increasingly influencing burial practices in the country. The successful transformation of American burial practices, however, did not come without complaint. Critics argued that rural cemeteries were becoming crowded and cluttered, which was particularly disagreeable because they had been established to serve as counterpoints to the hustle and bustle of the cities.

As a result of this criticism, the cemetery was refashioned, with a more formal, less picturesque design, which mirrored that of the new urban parks and middle-class suburbs. Adolph Strauch—a landscape gardener who worked at the Cemetery of Spring Grove in Cincinnati—designed one of the first pastoral cemeteries in America. Beginning in 1855, Strauch adapted the cemetery according to the "landscape lawn plan." His plan limited marker size, thinned trees and shrubs, and, most importantly, opened up the cemetery landscape.

Strauch's ideas were an immediate success in many new cemeteries, including Forest Lawn in Buffalo, and redesigned ones, including Oak Woods in Chicago. However, his plan was resisted by lot-holders in many cemeteries, who were required to give up much of their authority over the appearance of their lots. Only slowly, in competition with many older-style designs, did the landscape-lawn plan eventually spread throughout America. By 1900, though, Strauch was the acknowledged progenitor of the modern cemetery and a leader in the professionalization of cemetery management.

Professionalization was accepted partly because evolving attitudes toward death had isolated the cemetery from its lot-holders. The secularization of society threatened people's sentimental vision of the afterlife and provoked a greater fear of death. As a means of distancing themselves from the reality of death, Americans increasingly relied on others to tend the dying, care for the dead, and maintain the grave. This trend opened the cemetery to entrepreneurs, who viewed it as a business, as well as a community service. They were active in developing lawn-park cemeteries, some of which were speculative ventures, in many cities.

Many Americans objected to both the professionalism and the commercialism. One vocal group of protesters advocated an abandonment of earth burial and entombment. The protesters hoped to convince Americans to choose cremation.

CHAPTER FIVE

Retreat from Sentimentality

ADOLPH STRAUCH AND THE LANDSCAPE-LAWN PLAN

Criticism of rural cemeteries played a major part in the decision of the board of directors of the Cemetery of Spring Grove in Cincinnati to redesign their cemetery along the lines suggested by Adolph Strauch. Strauch transformed Spring Grove into a garden-park cemetery three years before the success of Frederick Law Olmsted and Calvert Vaux's Greensward plan for Central Park would start a generation of "rural" parks. Using what he termed the "landscape lawn plan," Strauch, the cemetery's new landscape gardener, proclaimed in his design for Spring Grove an age of new professionalism and renewed accessibility, both physical and psychological.[1]

The sections that Strauch laid out, as well as those he redesigned, were simpler, more spacious, and more pastoral landscapes, in which management's control was increasingly extended over monuments and plantings. Lot-holders' responsibility for molding the landscape was restricted. The goal of melding nature and art into a comfortable balance that could be maintained as the cemetery matured was embedded through the entire design and maintenance plan.

In the decades that followed, Strauch influenced generations of cemetery designers and managers, through both his published reports for Spring Grove and his designs for several cemeteries, including Mount Hope in Chicago and Forest Lawn in Buffalo. His philosophy of professional management eventually spread throughout America. Yet the victory of Strauch's simpler, streamlined landscape-lawn was neither universal nor easily won. Many Americans regretted losing their authority over the graves of their dead. Other Americans, many of them foreign-born or the children of immigrants, simply desired to retain the cherished practices of their ancestors. The result was a wide variety of American cemetery types by the end of the century.

TRANSFORMING SPRING GROVE

Strauch began his duties at Spring Grove in 1855, ten years after the cemetery's opening. A German-born, English-trained horticulturist, Strauch had been

stranded in Cincinnati between trains when he became reacquainted with in-
dustrialist Robert Bowler.[2] Bowler asked Strauch to remain in Cincinnati as his
estate gardener. Strauch quickly proved his skill to Bowler and was asked to take
over several other estates.

Strauch transformed these suburban estates in Clifton, Cincinnati's most
prominent suburb, by opening up their grounds to allow more light, more
space, and more lawn. Following the dictates of English landscaping, he removed fences, hedges, and other enclosures that obstructed the view and expanse of the grounds. He created green lawns interspersed with trees, shrubs,
and flower beds. Slowly curving drives brought visitors up through the lawns to
the houses. Statuary and fountains were selectively spread through the
grounds as ornaments, and slopes and ravines were converted into small lakes
and other picturesque settings. Barns and other unsightly outbuildings were
removed or hidden by plantings. The result was a much cleaner, less wild scene,
one that Strauch thought more fitting for a civilized suburb.

Strauch's success with their private estates led Bowler, Robert Buchanan,
and other Spring Grove lot-holders to ask Strauch to take a look at the cemetery,
which was considered attractive, but full of problems. Strauch informed the
group that it was "a pity [that] the beautiful reposing place of the dead was not
. . . developed on a scientific plan." Strauch thought the cemetery was so cluttered with plantings, family monuments, individual markers, and lot fences
that the natural appearance had been lost. He also suggested that there were
too many streets and pathways and that the trees and shrubs had been planted
too close in a vain effort to heighten the picturesque effect. Strauch assured the
group that the cemetery could be the "most beautiful spot of the surrounding
country," and the group convinced him to accept the position of landscape
gardener for the salary of seven hundred dollars a year.[3]

Strauch used the same set of guidelines he had used in the suburban estates
to redesign the cemetery. The directors had originally called on Strauch because of their frustration with an unmanageable marshy area at the front of the
cemetery. This land had been useless because no one had devised a solution to
the wetness, which made the land unattractive for burials. Today, the *swamp*
might have been treasured as a precious *wetlands*. Instead, the very practical
Strauch designed his new sections to carefully avoid the excesses of the past
while solving the problem of the terrain. His guiding principle was that the
"decoration of a rural cemetery should exhibit, in its classic purity, a just medium between too great simplicity and the excessive ornament usually met with."[4]

To limit possible excesses by lot-holders and to highlight the natural simplicity and beauty of the front section, Strauch planned large sections separated
by a series of connected lakes, which also drew off the water and dried out the
marshy sections. The sections were planted less abundantly, the lots were
larger, individual markers were restricted, and the water divided the sections
and allowed the visitor to see deep into the cemetery. Strauch convinced his

Panoramic View of the Cemetery of Spring Grove, Cincinnati, 1858
Panoramic scenes of cemeteries were frequently used in the nineteenth century to promote cemeteries. This view highlights the Strauchian landscape, with its combination of water and pastoral sections. Note the coaches and strollers along the cemetery's main roadway. (Lithograph by Middleton, Strobridge, and Company. Courtesy of the Cincinnati Historical Society.)

wealthy backers to purchase lots in the new sections, providing him with the capital to finish the project, instant credibility with the lot-holders, and large lots to enhance the sense of spaciousness.

Strauch rewarded lot-holders by plotting the sections to allow them to place monuments well back from the road without concern that another monument would block the public's view of their lot. He convinced the lot-holders that, by keeping individual markers close to the ground, less than six inches high—and by avoiding the cost of larger individual markers—the family monument could become a spectacular artistic addition to a unified landscape. Finally, the gradual elevation of the grounds throughout the front sections allowed Strauch to provide lots farther back in the cemetery the same visual access as those closer to the front. By looking over the water and up through the trees, visitors could see the new family monuments along the outer edges of the new development.

The series of lakes running through the sections was the centerpiece of Strauch's design. The lakes provided the sight of running, gleaming water as a counterpoint to the lawns and monuments of the sections. The water was bordered with shady larch and cypress trees, and some laurel, azaleas, holly, and ivy nestled along the shore. Planted sparsely amid the sections were maples, oaks, and occasionally an exotic variety of tree. Strauch used nonnative plants, but refused to allow them undue space because he believed that they

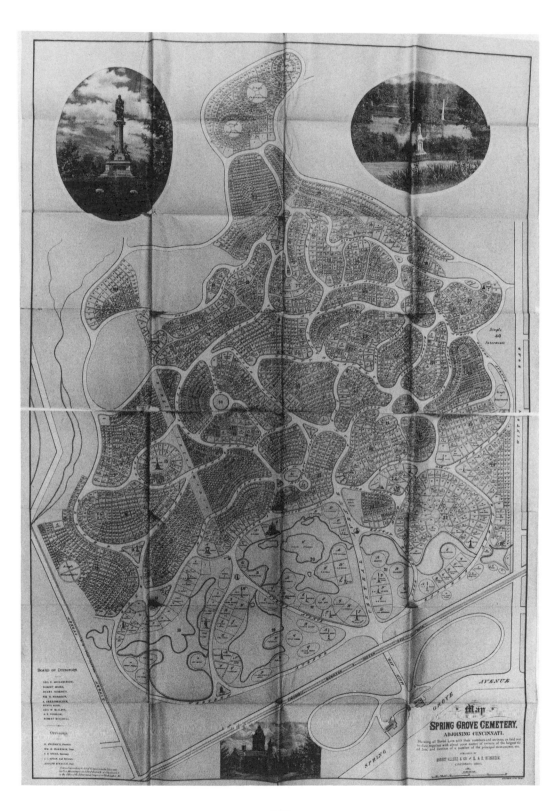

102

would disturb the unity of the landscape. Later, swans enhanced the scene as they swam and flew from section to section, stopping off at the island that Spring Grove's board of directors had presented to Strauch in appreciation of his work. The landscape unified land and water, monument and nature, flora and fauna.

Strauch's work at Spring Grove was indicative of the changing American perspective about nineteenth-century English gardening and landscape techniques. English landscaping had long been acknowledged as the world's finest, and eighteenth-century landscape gardeners, such as Lancelot "Capability" Brown and Humphrey Repton, had strongly influenced the design and planting of the first generation of rural cemeteries.

Strauch's plan turned away from the century-long fascination with the picturesque, instead promoting the simplicity and accessibility of the beautiful. Strauch rejected the "irregularity, abruptly broken contours, and . . . rough and irregular shapes" of rural cemeteries. Instead of diverse settings, individualistic monuments and markers, and abundant plantings—all in the pursuit of the unexpected vista and the immersion into the natural scene—Strauch's landscape "exhibited a preponderance of gently flowing lines, roundness and regularity, balance and symmetry, perfection and repose."[5]

Strauch strove for the unity of art and nature, which had been suppressed in the individualism and naturalism of the picturesque rural cemeteries. Both nature and art had been extravagantly displayed in the earlier cemeteries. The new landscape appeared more sophisticated than the rough terrain of the picturesque. Picturesque scenes, particularly woodlands with running water, were placed alongside the landscape-lawns, but were clearly separate.

Strauch and the designers who imitated him recognized that the clutter of rural cemeteries was an inevitable outcome of the attempt by earlier designers to include too much in the landscape. Monuments, unlike the isolated ruins that had originally inspired interest in the picturesque as a landscape for the dead, were too numerous and too intrusive. The isolated grave of Rousseau had spawned acres of monuments. Status-conscious lot-holders and their forest of obelisks, Gothic-style mausoleums, and other large family monuments diminished, if not destroyed, the unity of art and nature, which was the basis of the rural cemetery.[6]

Map of the Cemetery of Spring Grove, Cincinnati, 1883 (facing page)

This map clearly shows the distinction between Strauch's landscape-lawn plan of cemetery designing and plans of earlier designers. The bottom part of the cemetery, nearest the railroad, was Strauch's masterpiece. Land recovered from a swamp was turned into a section with the finest lots in the cemetery. Wide drives flowed around the large sections and the ponds. The earlier sections of the cemetery, directly above Strauch's new sections, were smaller, with far more roads and paths. Access from carriage to lot was easier, but the grounds were cluttered. (Map by George Moessinger and Frederich Bertsch.)

The landscape-lawn plan accepted that art would vie with nature in the cemetery grounds and that families were unwilling to commemorate their loved ones with trees, landscaped plots, and unassuming small markers. Strauch wished to better control the insertion of monuments and markers into the landscape. His plan severely limited the intrusion of the individual marker and rationalized the placement of the more substantial monument. The earlier cluttered layering of marker and monument, with diverse symbols for eternity, happiness, wisdom, sanctity, and love, was emphatically rejected.

Strauch wanted a simpler, more direct pastoral landscape, interspersed with monuments, which would make a clear statement about society's commitment to the dead and about American artistic achievement. Symptomatic of this desire for strength and simplicity in the scenery was Strauch's promotion of the classical as an appropriate style for cemetery monuments.[7] Classical monuments had the cool sophistication that reinforced the beauty of the natural environment. They also reminded visitors of democratic institutions, such as the Capitol, which Americans had built in a similar style.

The classical style never replaced Egyptian and Gothic motifs, which, along with rural cemeteries, had grown in favor with Americans. The towering presence of the obelisk remained popular throughout the nineteenth century. The obelisk was, however, increasingly joined by columns, pergolas, and other classically styled monuments. There were never enough stylish monuments to satisfy Strauch and other contemporary cemetery superintendents; they consistently argued that their beautifully designed and carefully tended natural landscapes were being desecrated by tasteless stock monuments.

A LANDSCAPE OF UNITY AND BEAUTY

Strauch rapidly installed his vision of Spring Grove throughout the entire cemetery. He reworked parts of the earlier sections, originally designed and created by Howard Daniels in cooperation with the cemetery's founders.[8] The individuality that had been the hallmark of rural cemeteries was severely curtailed. "Gaudiness is often mistaken for splendor," Strauch said, "and capricious strangeness for improvement." Unity and beauty were the twin pillars of the new Spring Grove; Strauch announced that those who conformed with that vision would have the "correct taste."[9]

First, Strauch tore down the cemetery's outer wall, enraging some lot-holders.[10] He wished, as with his work on the new sections, to join the front of the cemetery with the depths of the grounds. He wanted a "complete" landscape from entrance to boundary. He replaced the wall with a gently sloping roadway, bordered by rows of dwarf pines from a Silesian forest. Lot-holders ordered police to stop the work, claiming that rural cemeteries were community institutions whose appearance could not be changed so abruptly without

community or lot-holder approval. Spring Grove's board of directors supported Strauch, and the work was finished.

Second, Strauch gradually restricted private gardeners from working at
Spring Grove so that lot-holders would purchase this service from the cemetery.
A crew of gardeners, working on all the grounds, was critical to Strauch's plan,
because the landscape could retain a unity of appearance only if the entire
terrain was equally maintained. These new activities were expensive, and thus
the cemetery needed to increase the number of lot-holders paying for this
service. Perspective lot-holders were soon offered the option of paying a higher
purchase price and receiving perpetual care or paying a lesser price, supple-
mented with annual-care payments. Those already owning lots were given the
opportunity to join the annual-care program. The care funds rapidly became
important sources of income for all rural cemeteries.

Third, in 1859 A. B. Latta, a lot-holder who claimed to have invented a
refined steam fire engine, purposed to erect a replica of that engine on his
cemetery lot.[11] An iron canopy would be sustained by four high Corinthian
columns, from the soffits of which a miniature steam engine was to be suspended. The cemetery's board of directors upheld Strauch, who strongly objected. Although Latta organized a group to unseat it, the board ultimately
prevailed. This decision was a startling reversal of earlier praise of variety and
the exotic by Cleveland and other rural-cemetery commentators.

Within a remarkably short time, Strauch had successfully placed the cemetery "on a scientific plan." Clutter was reduced, roadways and pathways were
limited, plantings were controlled. As Buchanan, president of Spring Grove,
reported in 1858, individual lots had become part of a "complete landscape"
under the "skillful hands of our superintendent."[12] Spring Grove had been
transformed into a model for the nation.

CHANGING THE MANAGEMENT OF DEATH

Strauch had originally viewed his relationship with Spring Grove as a three-
year project, during which he would revamp the marshy front sections and
offer advice on redesigning the remaining area. He quickly recognized that the
lot-holders would only slowly accept the lawn plan. As he wrote Olmsted in
1875, "they do make considerable opposition at first." Several times during his
early confrontations with lot-holders, he was accused of "Anti-American eccen-
tricities" and "heathen principles." If unity was to be maintained, the manager
had to be able to control the possible excesses of individual lot-holders.[13]

After the front sections opened, the board of directors offered Strauch a
permanent position. He accepted, but only on the condition he be given increased responsibility and authority. He would have been unable to consolidate
his position as superintendent if the board had not expanded his authority.

The creation of such a managerial position was a precedent. Rural cemeteries had always had caretakers, but these individuals had limited authority.
Board members, including Buchanan, Jacob Bigelow, and Henry Pierrepont,
had managed the cemetery. They had been active in its daily financial and
maintenance affairs. Strauch was asking for wider powers: a professionalization of the superintendent's position reminiscent of that of landscape gardeners in Europe.

In January 1859, Spring Grove's board of directors eliminated the position
of landscape gardener, formed the new position of superintendent of the
grounds and landscape gardener, and immediately offered it to Strauch.[14]

The board of directors defined Strauch's enlarged duties to include:

directing "all improvements in the Cemetery, such as grading, planting, prun-
   ing the plants and trees, laying out avenues, and keeping the grounds, lots,
   and avenues in proper order";
employing and having "entire control of the hands and subordinate officers";
having "charge of all horses, carts, and tools";
keeping "a record . . . detailing the number of hands employed and the labor
   performed";
keeping an "account of the various departments under his care," which he
   would report monthly to the board;
allowing him "to improve and keep in order private burial lots, provided the
   owner has paid the amount agreed upon in advance to the Secretary . . .
   and [that] the improvement be in harmony with the system adopted by the
   Board";
keeping a "journal . . . of the weather on the morning of each day, and of the
   time of planting the various trees. . . , their time of flowering";
and being "accountable to the Board of Directors only, for the faithful performance of his duty."

Strauch's new position was an important step in the evolution of the modern cemetery and in the development of the profession of landscape architecture. The partnership of the superintendent with the board of directors represented the recognition by the founders that the cemetery needed more
attention than they could provide it while continuing their primary businesses.
Placing a trained landscape gardener in that position also showed an appreciation for Strauch's skills. Spring Grove's board of directors allowed Strauch to
improve other cemeteries by implementing his landscape-lawn plan and his
ideas on cemetery management.[15]

The new position represented the end of the transition from sexton to
professional and from amateur horticulturist to landscape designer. David
Douglass, Howard Daniels, Horatio Stone, Algernon Hotchkiss, and others
who had pioneered cemetery design did not have Strauch's horticultural train-

ing. Men of diverse talents, their efforts were often only partially successful. Many of Daniels's cemeteries—for example, Oakwood in Syracuse—showed little of the imagination apparent in the new lake sections in Spring Grove. The earlier designers produced grand effects when given a superb site; Strauch created a gleaming set of vistas out of a swamp.

The business of designing a cemetery, an estate, and later an urban park or a residential suburb demanded a sense of engineering, horticulture, aesthetics, and the other forces that combine to make a pleasing landscape. There would continue to be gifted amateurs designing landscapes, but Strauch was the prototype for the future. Few cemeteries in the late nineteenth century would be developed without a landscape architect's detailed plan. Fewer cemeteries would not hire an experienced superintendent to oversee the development of that plan and to maintain the cemetery.

Importantly, Strauch managed the appearance, rather than the institutional image, of the cemetery. Strauch's duties were those of a designer, horticulturist, gardener, and superintendent of a large estate or park. The business of selling lots, managing finances, and burying the dead was continued by the board of directors, and the daily overseeing of interments was the responsibility of another superintendent.

This distinction reflected the importance the founders and board members placed on the cemetery's appearance. Strauch was considered valuable enough to the cemetery that he was paid almost one-third more than the superintendent who oversaw interments. The landscape-lawn plan reasserted the original goal of creating a garden of graves. The economics of the institution still remained a secondary concern. The board's goal was to improve a community institution intended to serve as an arboretum, historical museum, and artistic ornament for Cincinnati.

STRAUCH'S ACHIEVEMENT: THE LAWN-PARK CEMETERY

During the next several decades, many cemetery designers, managers, and lotholders would turn toward Strauch's ideas. In their cemeteries, the pastoral would replace the picturesque. The lawn would expand, and the grouped trees would be thinned. Cemeteries would become more parklike. Monuments would be more formalized and standardized. The artfulness of the landscape would become more obvious and more celebrated.

Strauch's ideas and innovations were central to the development of the lawn-park cemetery and the modern cemetery in general. Jacob Weidenmann, a landscape architect who wrote the first manual of cemetery management and designed several cemeteries, considered Strauch the founder of the modern cemetery. Ossian Cole Simonds, America's most influential cemetery designer at the turn of the twentieth century, called Spring Grove a "Mecca for those

Lake in Oak Woods Cemetery, Chicago, 1898

Strauch's landscape-lawn plan was successfully imitated throughout America, particularly in the Midwest. Oak Woods Cemetery was one of the earliest cemeteries designed using Strauch's ideas. Strauch advised the cemetery company on design. This small lake is typical of the landscape-lawn plan. Water was a critical part of the pastoral landscape, providing a visual break from the lawn sections. (Oak Woods Cemetery booklet, 1898. Courtesy of Oak Woods Cemetery.)

interested in cemeteries." In 1887 the Association of American Cemetery Superintendents (AACS), a professional organization, held its first meeting in Cincinnati as a tribute to Strauch.[16]

Strauch's tenure at Spring Grove established a model of professionalism and practice unequaled in the rest of the nineteenth century. In 1875 Olmsted solicited entries for the landscape competition at the Paris Exposition. The only cemetery he approached was Spring Grove, which he considered "the best from a landscape gardening point of view." When, thirty years later, the AACS organized its hall of fame, Strauch was the only nonactive honoree.[17]

Olmsted's admiration for Strauch's cemetery is not surprising given their similar views on cemetery design. Olmsted was involved in relatively few cemetery projects, believing that the monuments cut up the landscape effects. In his 1865 design for Mountain View Cemetery in Oakland, California, Olmsted thought that the indigenous vegetation was limited enough to rule out any attempt to create the forested park cemeteries of the East. Instead, he insisted on using appropriate local vegetation, designed a straight, tree-lined drive for the level lower grounds, and planned winding roadways for the surrounding hills. This combination of formal and picturesque styles called forth the defense that both natural and synthetic designs were appropriate as long as they had the "single purpose to manifest Christian tenderness and care in the presence of the dead."[18]

Olmsted and Strauch accepted the role of art in the landscape and the cemetery. Both recognized that the cemetery was not a park, a playground, or a garden. Their designs encouraged lot-holders to honor their dead through simple, stylish, and artistic monuments. The designs limited the grandeur of nature, renewed the cemetery's sense of order, and opened up the landscape.

Strauch's ideas marked a major shift in the evolution of the lot-holders' relationship to the cemetery. By placing the cemetery on a more professional basis, Strauch limited the lot-holders' voice in the design and maintenance of the grounds. Monuments had to meet guidelines set by the superintendent. Plantings were agreed to by the superintendent and then planted by the cemetery's crews. Lot-holders could refuse to pay the cemetery the annual maintenance fee that kept the grounds uniformly cared for, but Strauch's victories in the late 1850s set the stage for the emergence of the superintendent as the overseer of the cemetery landscape.

THE RISE OF THE SUPERINTENDENT

Sextons, such as the one appointed to New York City's new public burial ground in 1823, were hired primarily on the basis of their high moral character. Rural and lawn-park cemeteries required a person as well-qualified to manage large groups of manual workers as to plant trees and shrubs and to seed lawns. The diverse responsibilities of the job gradually led to professionalization of the position of superintendent.

The value of the superintendent's role increased as cemetery corporations assumed greater responsibility for the landscape. In 1868 lot-holders formed a corporation and assumed control of Forest Hills Cemetery in Boston. One of their first acts was to sell only lots that included perpetual care of the grass. Forest Hills now had an income from which it could pay the larger labor costs of a general-maintenance crew. As its sources of income grew, the cemetery could consider assuming responsibility for maintaining monuments and plantings, as well as the grass and roads.[19]

By the end of the 1870s, all cemeteries used annual-care fees, bequests, and perpetual-care payments as means of increasing their income. At Mount Auburn, which was one of the first cemeteries to accept bequests and to place all lots under perpetual care, the perpetual-care fund rose dramatically. The cemeteries' "permanent funds" stood at $2,017,078 in 1915, an enormous growth from $32,000 in 1865. By the end of the nineteenth century, much of the information cemeteries were sending their prospective or current lot-holders included requests that they establish a fund to cover the real costs of maintaining the lots.[20]

Technological changes in lawn care helped change cemetery maintenance. The most important improvement was the mechanical lawn mower. This new machine, patented in England in 1830, revolutionized lawn care and the lawn's role in American society. At Regent's Park Zoological Gardens in 1831, the foreman noted that the machine "does as much work as six or eight men with scythes and brooms . . . performing the whole so perfectly as not to leave a mark of any kind behind."[21]

Standards of care rose as equipment became more sophisticated. The use of the lawn mower increased efficiency. The lawns of cemeteries, parks, and even individual houses were easier to maintain. The lawn's appearance was easily changed by different angles of cuts and varied heights of grass. As the century progressed, cemeteries had greater control over the quality of their appearance, especially if they increased the amount of space unencumbered with monuments. (Later superintendents would rue this "advancement" during rainy springs when the grass could not be cut, but high-school students eager for summer jobs would be appreciative.)

Cemetery crews grew as result of the use of the lawn mower. Despite the lawn mower's technological advantages, cemeteries needed more workers. Large cemeteries, such as Woodlawn in the Bronx, employed up to one hundred workers from spring to fall. The crews often included women, who did the labor-intensive jobs of cleaning gutters by hand and trimming ivy-covered graves. Responsible for a large physical plant, the superintendent combined skills as a horticulturist, manager, civil engineer, and mechanic.[22]

As the concept of the lawn-park cemetery spread and the prestige of the position of superintendent rose, a small group of superintendents gathered in 1887 to form the AACS.[23] Superintendents from the most prominent cemeteries in the Northeast and Midwest—including Spring Grove, Green-Wood, Graceland in Chicago, and Mount Auburn—formed the AACS. The association gradually grew, and by 1921 there were 360 members. Most of these members were from Pennsylvania, New York, Ohio, Illinois, Massachusetts, and Michigan. The organization slowly spread throughout the South, Southwest, and West. Representing wealthier cemeteries, the AACS stood for changes that invigorated rural and lawn-park cemeteries.

The main purposes of the organization, as with those organizations formed in the same period by many other professional groups (e.g., historians, engineers, lawyers, doctors), were disseminating information on new and better practices and improving the public perception of the profession.[24] At AACS conventions, as reported by *Park and Cemetery*, members discussed a host of technical and regulatory measures, which the superintendents hoped would improve the appearance of cemeteries and the management of the organization.

Convention participants heard plans for improved record keeping, employee relations, permanent-maintenance funds, and equipment maintenance. There also were speeches on new machinery, tearing out enclosures, lowering grave mounds, and planting shrubs to fit with the landscape. As with other professional groups, the AACS had as its main goals the standardization of rules and regulations and the establishment of minimum professional requirements. The AACS fought for model rules and regulations that would give superintendents greater control over both the maintenance of the landscape and the organization of the cemetery.

In 1890, the AACS produced a set of model rules for adoption by cemeteries:

1. [A] general rule, stating the authority and conditions on which lots are sold and the restrictions on transfers. . .

2. The Trustees desire to leave the improvements of lots, as far as possible to the taste of the owners; but, in justice to all, . . . they reserve the right to exclude or remove from any lot any headstone, monument or other structure, tree, plant or other object whatever which . . . they shall consider injurious to the general appearance of the grounds . . .

3. Lot-owners may have planting or other work done on their lots at their expense, upon application to the Superintendent.

4. No iron- or wire-work, and no seats or vases will be allowed on lots, excepting by permission of the Trustees . . .

5. The Trustees desire to encourage the planting of trees and shrubbery, but, in order to protect the rights of all and to secure the best general results, they require that such planting shall be done only in accordance with the directions of the Superintendent of the cemetery.

6. No coping, nor any kind of enclosure, will be permitted. . . . Corner-stones must not project above the ground and must not be altered nor removed.

7. Mounds over graves should be kept low, not exceeding four inches in height; and stone or other enclosures around graves will not be allowed.

8. Only one monument will be permitted on a family burial lot.

9. (This should be a rule limiting the height of headstones. . . . Even with the lawn is considered best.)

10. All stone- and marble-works, monuments and headstones must be accepted by the Superintendent as being in conformity with the foregoing rules before being taken into the cemetery.

11. No monument, headstone or coping, and no portion of any vault above ground, shall be constructed of other material than cut stone or real bronze. No artificial material will be permitted.

12. The Trustees wish, as far as possible, to discourage the building

of vaults, believing . . . that they are generally injurious to the appearance of the grounds, and . . . are . . . liable to rapid decay, and in the course of time to become unsightly ruins.

13. The Trustees shall have the right to make exceptions from the foregoing rules in favor of designs which they consider exceptionally artistic and ornamental . . .

14. The Superintendent is directed to enforce the above regulations, and to exclude from the cemetery any person willfully violating them.[25]

Although some cemeteries resisted several of the rules, the AACS's goals gradually changed the organization and maintenance of the American cemetery.

The pages of *Park and Cemetery* were filled with new organizational and landscape ideas, but only rarely with articles suggesting innovative sales, investment, and marketing ideas. The main focus of the AACS was the physical maintenance of the cemetery. Superintendents were interested in developing care funds to support their maintenance efforts, especially when the funds allowed them to increase the size of their efforts. They were less concerned with selling lots, which remained the responsibility of the downtown office managers and the board of directors. Furthermore, both rural and older lawn-park cemeteries rarely made strong efforts to sell their "product." They "sold" the cemetery by establishing a good reputation, creating a welcoming atmosphere, and waiting for buyers to come forward.[26]

A CHANGING AMERICA

The concept of the rural cemetery was conceived during a grand period of American expansion and reform. The new cemetery was symbolic of the boosters' pride in the city and their fear of its impact on moral values. The Civil War brought a dramatic halt to reformers' attempt to create a better society, but proved only a small halt in the urbanization of society. Indeed, urban culture was invading the safe confines of the country and even its graveyards.

Some changes in America during the last half of the nineteenth century reinforced and popularized Strauch's landscape-lawn plan, whereas other changes led to the development of communities that attempted to keep out the new ideas embodied in Strauch's plan. Strauch's ideas were increasingly popular among native-born Americans, who felt a great affinity to England, to the countryside of their youth, and to the American past. His ideas—ironically, because he was an immigrant—were less accepted among immigrant communities, which wanted to re-create the less gardenlike burial places of the old country. Their new burial grounds were one way for them to control the remarkable adaptation to American customs that society was demanding.

Native-born Americans and immigrants alike found the city a challenging place in the last decades of the century. After the Civil War, cities underwent sudden increases in population, which stretched the social and political fabric to its limit. Many city dwellers were both frightened and intrigued by urban life. As a result of their rapid expansion, cities became a "fusion of social, political, and technological peril" for their residents—and for American society.[27]

In reaction to the physical expansion and disorderly nature of the city, many Americans embarked on a new crusade of reform. Homeowners and property holders, Alan Tractenberg has written, tried to take "control of urban reality, to define it, shape, and order it according to an evolving urban ideal, a secular Celestial City of shapely boulevards, healthful parks, comfortable and secure private habitations, and elegant public buildings." The promise of the "City Beautiful" entranced designers such as Olmsted and Samuel Parsons, Jr, and architects such as Daniel Burnham and Richard Morris Hunt. This search for order was punctuated by an emphasis on a rational, efficient city, which was beautiful and comfortable for all its residents.[28]

The new order in American cities included bright, shining public buildings in classical styles, large pastoral parks, and other civic improvements. There was also more crime, many poor people, and greater social isolation. Relationships among the living seemed more difficult. Relationships between the living and the dead were also reordered, as the burial process was professionalized. Nurses and doctors cared for the dying, morticians handled the dead, and cemetery superintendents beautified the grave. This was only part of a trend toward specialization throughout the city. Spatially, the city was split into zones of use. Economically, these zones were increasingly under the jurisdiction of a specialist, a professional.

These changes offended, frightened, and horrified immigrant communities, which preferred a closer relationship to death, believed that handling the dead was a family responsibility, and saw many of the new reforms as a means of making them conform to others' conception of what an American was. They resisted the lawns, the new monument styles, and the restrictions on lot-holder involvement. Their cemeteries remained closer to the early ideal of the rural cemetery than to the beautified landscape-lawn of the park.

THE NATIONAL CEMETERIES

Although the Civil War had only an indirect impact on American attitudes toward death, it created a new category of sacred spot: the war battlefield. War memorials, typically depicting an officer on horseback or a single soldier standing with his weapon at ease, dotted the greens and central parks of villages and towns by the 1870s. Larger war memorials, the major battle sites with their vast cemeteries, became among the first of America's historical places. Congress had authorized the first nationally managed cemetery as early as 1862, when former army post cemeteries were rededicated to the use of the rapidly growing Union army. As early as 1863, the battle sites at Gettysburg and Antietam became national cemeteries for the Union dead. Throughout the war, the number of battlefield cemeteries grew. So did concern about their care.[29]

The earliest burials in the military cemeteries were rough and quick, with little attempt at identification and less at sanitary conditions. As the war progressed and the number of causalities escalated, an attempt was made to provide each grave site with a wooden headboard identifying the deceased. Only after the war, during the campaign to reinter all the war dead in appropriate burial spaces, did the War Department finally place white wooden headboards on more than three hundred thousand graves. Marble and granite markers replaced the wooden headboards in the early 1870s, when Congress decided to honor permanently the war dead in the battlefield cemeteries and to extend the privilege of burial to veterans of the war.

America's national cemeteries were striking for their democratic atmosphere. The *Washington Star* noted in 1893 that "all civilized nations have taken pains to inter the bones of their military chiefs and high officers, but to the remains of the common soldier they have been content to allot only the hasty ditch or trench." American battlefield commanders were little different from their European counterparts. As Monro MacCloskey has noted, it was understandable that "military commanders were necessarily inclined to show more concern for the living and the winning of battles than for the burial of those already lost."[30]

Whereas the immediate burial service may have been quick and unorganized, resulting in a large number of unidentified dead and unknown graves, the U.S. government's decision immediately after the war to reinter vast numbers of soldiers who died on battlefields or in hospitals was an original act of a democratic government. Many of the cemeteries were primarily filled with common soldiers. At the national cemetery in Beaufort, South Carolina, the highest-ranking officer was Lieutenant Colonel William N. Reed. The vast majority of soldiers were enlisted men, including many African-Americans.[31]

In 1867 William Saunders reported to the Pennsylvania legislature on his design for the Soldiers National Cemetery at Gettysburg. The cemetery was designed in a semicircle, surrounding a central monument to all the dead. States were given parcels around the semicircle in accordance with the number of dead. Each grave was marked with a nine-inch-high granite headstone. The name, company, and regiment of the deceased was inscribed on each headstone. Saunders hoped that the headstones would secure a "simple and expressive arrangement, [combining] great permanence with durability."[32]

Saunders explicitly designed the grounds to evoke "*simple grandeur.*" Simple, because the eye was led "gradually from one object to another, in easy harmony, avoiding abrupt contrasts and unexpected features." Grand, because the scenery was sublime, composed of a repetition of commonplace objects placed to evoke a solemn atmosphere. "We do not apply [the sublime] to the scanty tricklings of the brook, but rather to the collected waters of the ocean. To produce an expression of grandeur, we must avoid intricacy and great variety of parts, more particularly must we refrain from introducing any intermixture or meretricious display of ornament."[33]

Saunders's desire to keep things simple echoed Olmsted's advice to Quartermaster General Montgomery C. Meigs in 1870. Meigs had asked Olmsted for help on planting in the new cemeteries. In 1870 Congress had appropriated twenty thousand dollars for this purpose. Olmsted suggested that the general design should be "studiously simple; that ambitious efforts of ignorant or half-bred landscape gardeners should be especially guarded against." He reminded Meigs that the "main object should be to establish permanent dignity and tranquility." Olmsted believed that, if everything was done properly now, the national cemeteries would become "sacred groves" in several generations.[34]

As with Olmsted (and Strauch), Saunders wanted scenery that would mature into a quiet and harmonious beauty. Saunders feared that planting more than necessary would "render the whole confused and intricate." He was against a proliferation of roads, which he felt could only be justified by "direct necessity." A few roads and walks were introduced to "secure proper *breadth* of scene." His ideas about the future of the landscape are reminiscent of Strauch's rejection of the clutter of rural cemeteries. Saunders worried that his design would "be impaired or sacrificed to immediate and temporary interest." As Olmsted had found in New York City while creating Central Park, and Strauch and a generation of cemetery designers knew, the public often failed to understand that a landscape was a dynamic design, changing yearly and generationally as plants grew and died.[35]

The decision of the government to mark graves with simple markers set amid the grassy fields heightened the national cemeteries' sense of democracy. Only in Arlington and some other cemeteries, and only for a short time, were individuals allowed to put up privately purchased monuments. Thus, in only one way were the grave sites in national cemeteries dramatically different from the wide variety of family monuments which Americans placed on private lots. Although Americans admired the simple sentiment of the national cemeteries, most did not emulate them. The veterans were joined in a hallowed community, which was distinctly different from that in the secular cemeteries. Not until the twentieth century would some Americans accept a limitation on their right to erect elaborate family monuments.

The national cemeteries reinforced the retreat from Romantic sentimentality, as well as the simplification of the cemetery. Even if Americans were slow to accept identical markers, they did embrace the landscape concepts of the military cemeteries. Simplicity and grandeur were the bases of the new designs.

"PARKOMANIA"

The national cemeteries reinforced pastoral landscape concepts, but the new urban parks brought them to the immediate attention of the entire population. Starting just before the Civil War and extending through the second half of the century, the urban park was a popular subject of discussion and debate in America's cities and towns. Dozens of new parks were ultimately created, and Americans found a new recreational spot to replace the more solemn rural cemetery and adopted new ideas about landscape, which were then applied to new cemeteries.

Strauch believed that a good cemetery blended "the elegance of a park with the pensive beauty of a burial place."[36] At Spring Grove, he applied European concepts of park planning to produce a landscape that joined the artful beauty of the grave site with the soothing peace of the countryside. Strauch's activities fit well with the sudden surge of interest in parks which began in the 1850s and continued into the late nineteenth century.

In 1858, three years after Strauch began his transformation of Spring Grove, Olmsted and Vaux used many of the same European park concepts in their Greensward plan, which was accepted by the New York City Common Council as the design for the new Central Park. After a long struggle, reminiscent of those by rural-cemetery founders to convince the public of a needed change in burial habits, New York City led the nation into a new era of parks. Central Park immediately caught the public's imagination, much as Mount Auburn had a generation before.[37]

Within a decade, Olmsted reported that Philadelphia, Baltimore, Brooklyn, Hartford, and Detroit had begun the process of park development.[38] Druid Hill in Baltimore, Fairmount in Philadelphia, Prospect Park in Brooklyn, and other parks were filled with visitors admiring the landscape and using the facilities. A number of parks were designed by men (such as Daniels) who had begun their landscape gardening careers by planning rural cemeteries. City "rural parks," as John Brinckerhoff Jackson has called them, brought the pensive, soothing charms of the countryside inside the city without the solemn associations of the grave.[39]

The cities were in physical, social, and economic upheaval. They were overcrowded, even though street-railway systems (consisting of both streetcars and omnibuses) allowed development to spread outward from the city core. The contrast between the poor and the rich became more pronounced. In between was the growing middle class of clerks and professionals. Their new homes dotted the streets of the suburbs, and their purchasing provided an ever-larger market for the new department stores. Strikes became commonplace, crime increased, and corruption flourished as government and commerce grew unchecked.[40]

The new parks were an aspect of the struggle by urban residents to control

Footpath in Central Park, New York City, 1869

Olmsted and Vaux's 1859 park received national attention, reminiscent of the reception Mount Auburn Cemetery had received when it was founded in 1831. The park design incorporated many rural-cemetery features, but, from the designers' perspective, fortunately excluded monuments. The new park was much closer than earlier rural cemeteries to the city's population and had the advantage of being a public facility. (Drawing by A. F. Bellows, in Clarence C. Cook, *A Description of the New York Central Park,* 1869.)

their increasingly chaotic environment. Mayor Thomas Swann of Baltimore pointed out that "men cannot labor without relaxation, and the heated atmosphere of a city is not favorable to physical growth and development." Buttressed by statistics and theories gathered by the new social scientists and sanitarians, the arguments of politicians claimed that parks would help ease conflicts and bring the community together. Olmsted evoked these arguments when he wrote that the cities "want a ground to which people may easily go after their day's work is done, and where they may stroll for an hour, seeing, hearing and feeling nothing of the hustle and bustle and jar of the streets."[41]

The new parks epitomized the challenge that urban landscape designers had in balancing nature and use. The first generation of parks combined features of the picturesque, "the apparently wild irregularities of divine creation," with aspects of the beautiful, "the well-regulated precision of human design." Picturesque settings, such as the Ramble in Central Park, were intended to provide startling contrasts to the large lawn areas, which were the central fea-

New Sections in the Cemetery of Spring Grove, Cincinnati, c. 1890
This glass-plate photograph not only demonstrates that Spring Grove remained popular with Cincinnatians throughout the nineteenth century but also highlights the wide drives and parklike scenery of Strauch's front sections. (Courtesy of the Cincinnati Historical Society, gift of Mr. Charles Jenneevein.)

tures of the parks. All the early landscape park planners, especially Olmsted and Vaux, were committed to developing parks as "contacts with nature" where urban dwellers could escape the rigors of daily life and renew themselves.[42]

Strauch, Olmsted, H.W.S. Cleveland, and other landscape designers were the ruralizers of the new cities. Rural cemeteries had been located outside the cities, adjacent to, but removed from, the hustle and bustle of the commercial world. New parks were situated on the edges of old towns, amid the great expansion of the cities. Some of these parks were located adjacent to the older cemeteries. Olmsted designed both Delaware Park and the bucolic grounds of the state asylum on sites next to Forest Lawn Cemetery in Buffalo. The new parks were meant to bring the rural atmosphere into the city. Their designs, which were more accessible and less intricate than those of the cemeteries, reflected that placement and goal.

Yet people wanted more than "scenery" in their parks, more than "a three-dimensional work of art." Rural-cemeteries managers had fought a continuous battle to ensure proper decorum in the cemetery. Now the same fight occurred between designers and users of the rural parks. Olmsted commissioned the Central Park police to maintain order, much as Green-Wood, Oakwood, and other cemeteries had commissioned their own police in an effort to control the activities of visitors. The desire of park users for recreation facilities gradually diminished the peacefulness of the parks and eroded many of the picturesque settings, which were usually the most easily converted to new uses.[43]

The new parks were a huge success and greatly influenced the character of new cemeteries. Thousands continued to visit Mount Auburn, Green-Wood, or Spring Grove, but after the Civil War the popularity of the cemeteries as recreational spots declined. People preferred to use the parks for recreation, promenades, and courting. The parks were closer, publicly owned, and had fewer rules regarding visitors. Away from the dead and the moralistic atmosphere of the cemetery, the park seemed more joyful, a better place for a stroll and a talk.[44]

Not surprisingly, the successes of the parks influenced improvements in cemeteries. Limiting the size and placement of monuments made maintenance easier and diminished the visibility of death. Limiting the number of roadways reduced development costs and made the cemetery less confusing for people who did not wish to be alone among the dead. The entry road to Spring Grove remained a popular place for strollers, partly because the area was so reminiscent of a garden or park.

THE PROFESSIONALIZATION OF THE PROCESS OF DEATH

Death had been an intensely personal experience for survivors in early America. Family members cleaned the body, dug the grave, built the coffin, and sometimes even carved the gravestone. Family control over the process had declined more quickly in the city than in the country. In the city, by the late nineteenth century some people began going to the hospital with the expectation that they would not return home. Funerals continued to be held in the home, but increasingly under the supervision of the undertaker. Cemetery superintendents managed the burial procession, including recording the location of the grave and placing the monument.

A greater percentage of Americans was dying in hospitals than at home by the 1880s. Charles Rosenberg has noted that by World War I "respectable Americans began for the first time to consider hospital care a plausible option when they or members of their families fell ill." Hospitals, which had long been considered places for the poor, had upgraded facilities and increased medical standards in an effort to attract middle- and upper-class clientele. More patients were housed in private rooms and cared for by professional nurses. Most importantly, advances in medicine created an antiseptic environment, where patients had a better chance for recovery. At the end of this period, many people still died at home, but even more died in hospitals.[45]

Regardless of wherever the person died, the wake was most likely in the home. The first funeral homes began to appear in the 1880s, but the vast majority of people resisted removing the wake from the home. Instead, the body was laid out in the parlor by the undertaker. The role of the undertaker was slowly expanding. Undertakers had existed in America for over a century, primarily as providers of the coffin and other funeral paraphernalia. Often, the primary occupation of early undertakers was furniture making or another skilled woodworking trade.

In the last half of the century, undertakers began to exercise greater direction over the entire burial process. First, embalming, which became popular after the Civil War, expanded the undertaker's role. Second, the longer distance from the home to the cemetery necessitated that someone organize the processional. Third, urban life was more crowded than rural life. In cities, more families lived in apartments and small homes, which did not have expansive parlors. Eventually, these families asked undertakers to conduct the viewing and wake in their funeral homes. Fourth, families increasingly looked to the undertaker to handle the dead and to ensure that all the formalities were correct.

Thus the undertaker "moved from [being] a merchant who . . . provided goods needed by the bereaved . . . to a seller of service who actually took part in the preparation of the dead . . . and transport[ed] body and mourners to places of worship and sepulture . . . [to] finally a director who took charge of the body and of the proceedings involved in its ceremonial disposition." The transformation was not completed by the 1880s, or even by 1930. Americans, particularly those in rural areas, resisted professionalizing the process of death. Still, the handing over of the dead to strangers was occurring.[46]

During the general retreat from sentimentality which occurred during this time, the funeral became more formal and mourning rituals were more ritualized. "The house in which the death had struck not only had . . . 'crepe' on the door, but it was not unknown for the bereaved to drape the room in which the dead lay, or possibly, the whole downstairs of the house, in black or deep shades of grey." Veils were hung in doorways, everyone in the household dressed in black, rules on mourning periods were carefully followed, and calling cards edged in black were mandatory from all close friends. Although the color black had been associated with mourning since at least the fifteenth century, the new mourning rites were much stricter.[47]

This formality, identified with Victorian culture in America and England, represented a distancing of the living from the dead. *Parlors* were called *living rooms*. Flowers joined crepe as mourning symbols. Even the language of death began to soften. *Undertakers* evolved into *funeral directors*, and *coffins* into *caskets*. A *dead person* was referred to as the *deceased*. Superficially, the changes suggested a continuing sentimentality toward the dead, but actually the alterations illustrated the formality surrounding the process of death.[48]

THE LAWN-PARK CEMETERY

As a result of the changes wrought by the Civil War, "parkomania," the new attitudes toward death, and the retreat from sentimentality, Americans changed the appearance of the cemetery. The new lawn-park cemetery combined the beauty of the lawn with the artistry of the monument. The goal remained a private, permanent burial place that honored rural values and celebrated lot-holder families. The new landscape reflected the distancing of the living from the dead and the formalization of the burial ritual.

The concept of the lawn-park cemetery slowly spread in the last half of the century. Many of the early attempts to create lawn-park cemeteries failed. Cedar Hill Cemetery in Newburgh, New York, had opened in 1870 as a "park" cemetery. The cemetery emphasized the beauty and harmony of the whole landscape, rather than allowing each owner unrestricted freedom in the decoration of the lot. Charles Downing was active in the development of Cedar Hill and even had the remains of Andrew Jackson Downing, his brother, moved to the cemetery after its opening. Cedar Hill was not a financial success. A director of the cemetery, in explaining its financial failure, suggested that "the public was not yet receptive to the park cemetery."[49]

In other cities, landscape-lawn cemeteries were more successful. In the Ohio cities of Cleveland and Toledo, lawn-park cemeteries succeeded in competition with some established rural cemeteries. West View Cemetery in Atlanta was founded in 1884 as an alternative to the successful, but now crowded, Oakland Cemetery. The new cemetery was located four miles from the city, on a 577-acre site, which included the ground on which the Battle of Ezra Church had been fought in 1864. Edgar P. McBurney, the force behind the cemetery, announced in 1884 that "for years this [cemetery] will be a park. . . . In time there will be a million dollars worth of monuments on this ground." When a newspaper reporter asked which cemetery he planned to pattern West View after, McBurney replied, "Woodlawn, one of the newest, and most beautiful cemeteries in New York." The landscape-lawn idea was becoming a national reality.[50]

Near the end of the century, lawn-park cemeteries became commonplace. New ones were organized north of New York City (Kensico), in Detroit (Woodlawn), in Cleveland (Knollwood), and on Long Island (Pinelawn). Large areas of lawn were dotted with monuments and trees. Few bushes or clusters of trees interrupted the sections. Individual markers did not clutter the lawns. Family mausoleums were highlighted in particularly outstanding settings. Flower beds at the cemetery's entrance and intersections provided splashes of color.

One reason for the public's acceptance of the lawn-park cemeteries was the late-nineteenth-century City Beautiful movement. The movement led to the resurrection in 1889 of Pierre L'Enfant's plan for Washington, D.C. This geometrical masterpiece had originally been prepared at the insistence of George

Washington, but fell into disfavor with Thomas Jefferson and was not implemented. Late-nineteenth-century architects and landscape architects found its planned streets and formal shape a vision of the future.[51]

The movement promoted classical art and architecture forms as the clearest and grandest expressions of art. The 1893 Colombian Exposition in Chicago, which most associate with the movement, was filled with huge temporary structures done in classical motifs. The popularity of the style with exposition visitors led to imitations throughout the nation, as evidenced by courthouses, state houses, and other government buildings.

The new cemeteries paid homage to Strauch, but often ignored his most important principles. Monuments continued to be too large and too ostentatious for the scope of the landscape. The lawn became such a central feature of the more efficient cemeteries that the balance between the natural environment and the civilizing artistry of the monuments was endangered. Flowers in formal garden beds and elaborate character patterns, which Strauch had warned were not desirable, became popular. Artificiality threatened the naturalism that was the basis of the landscape concepts of Strauch and Olmsted.

The emphasis on the lawn heightened the visibility of the monument within the cemetery. Weidenmann cautioned as early as 1888 that a lot-holder erecting a monument on a largely improved section had to take special care. He warned first against grouping monuments. Then he admonished against extravagant expenditure; this was particularly important because so many lot-holders simply copied earlier designs, thus creating rows of similar monuments, which marred the cemetery's appearance.[52]

The similarity was aggravated by the standardization of monument stocks. Because they were readily available, inexpensive, and imitated popular styles, stock monuments sold in large numbers. Monument dealers often purchased stock monuments from the same distributors. Standardization filled cemeteries with stones, which disrupted views and diminished the artistic affect of the truly exceptional monument.

Family mausoleums added to the growing clutter. Mausoleums were much more prevalent in the 1880s and 1890s than previously. Wealthy families used the mausoleum to display their success. Some mausoleums were spectacular, such as the replica of the Parthenon erected in Spring Grove and the copy of Penn Station in Woodlawn in the Bronx.[53]

Mausoleums became more popular after the theft of A. T. Stewart's remains from a Manhattan churchyard in 1878. The thieves eventually settled for twenty thousand dollars in ransom, and the remains were reinterred in the Garden City Cathedral. William H. Vanderbilt responded to the crime by securing a private family cemetery on Staten Island, which he had designed by Olmsted. Others turned to cemeteries such as Woodlawn in the Bronx to protect the remains of their families. The age of the grandiose mausoleum had begun.[54]

PROPOSED GRANITE GATEWAY AND LODGE, JEROME AVENUE ENTRANCE

Proposed Entrance to Woodlawn Cemetery, the Bronx, N.Y., c. 1898
This neoclassical entrance demonstrates the influence of the City Beautiful movement on the architectural features of the American cemetery. Although the entrance was never built, as was true of so many of the grandiose designs of this movement, neoclassical gates, monuments, chapels, and other buildings were constructed throughout the nation. The design lends itself to various modes of transportation, including strolling, open and closed carriages, and the newest rage, bicycling. (Frontispiece of Woodlawn Cemetery annual report, 1898. Courtesy of Woodlawn Cemetery.)

Most mausoleums, though, were as standardized as family monuments. Box-shaped marble houses, often of little architectural or artistic value, appeared in sections. Cemeteries had little understanding of how much mausoleums would cost to maintain, so superintendents demanded minimal perpetual care. If the mausoleums did have problems, superintendents often had to ask the family for more money to cover the costs.[55]

James Scorgie, a former AACS president and the superintendent of Mount Auburn Cemetery, warned in 1920 that the parklike beauty of the lawn-park cemetery was threatened by these "hideous stone structures and garish colors." Superintendents attempted to influence the public's choice by recommending better designs in articles in *Park and Cemetery* and by writing and speaking to local monument dealers about the problem. J. W. Wycoff wrote an article in 1915 in which he railed against the "ocean waves" of the roughly hewed monuments, comparing them unfavorably to the "long, simple decorative lines" of other stones.[56]

Some improved monument designs did appear. A return to classical design and a neocolonial revival produced a generation of better monuments in the

Scene with Mausoleum in Kensico Cemetery, Valhalla, N.Y., 1910
Kensico Cemetery was designed in the style of the landscape-lawn plan. Mausoleums, tall obelisks, and granite neoclassical monuments stood amid small flowering shrubs, evergreens, and the sweeping lawn. There are no visible individual markers, no fences, no boundaries between lots, and no clutter. (Photographs by Kal Khoff Company, in Kensico Cemetery booklet, 1910. Courtesy of Kensico Cemetery and Lawrence Sloane.)

early twentieth century. Doric or Ionic columns set on the base fronted by granite steps or the steles on many family lots were more striking than earlier monuments. As noticeable and as dramatic as earlier Gothic designs, the new monuments better befit lawn-park cemeteries.

DIVERSITY IN THE AMERICAN CEMETERY

While Strauch's design principles gained popularity, a significant number of new cemeteries was designed with a completely different set of principles. Emigrants from Europe organized cemeteries that often drew upon American examples, but adapted them to their culture. Jewish, Russian Orthodox, Greek Orthodox, and other Christian and non-Christian groups that established large enough communities to sustain a separate burial place were just as likely to model their cemeteries on those of Prague, Moscow, or Athens as those of Boston or New York. Catholic diocesan cemeteries were less likely to deviate from the trends in Protestant cemetery practices, but even here the monuments and plantings were different than those in the Protestant cemeteries.

Some immigrant communities established cemeteries that imitated rural cemeteries on sites that were less dramatic and with monuments that were less fancy. Individual lots remained relatively large, although not as large as those in the antebellum period. The roads gently curved through the undulating terrain, and the plantings were mainly evergreens and local deciduous tree varieties. The natural setting, although not as dramatic as that of earlier cemeteries, remained an important part of the design and appearance of these cemeteries.

Lot-holders in immigrant cemeteries continued many of the practices under attack by commentators and forward-thinking superintendents. Family monuments became larger. Large, even huge, obelisks protruded into the sky. Obelisks of twenty, thirty, even forty feet were common. Stone coping surrounded many of the lots. Grave mounds remained essential for many mourners. Although such mounds hampered maintenance, they were regarded as symbols of death and the dead, a perception that made them unseemly to the next generation.

Some immigrant cemeteries were even less naturalistic. The nineteenth-century naturalistic cemetery had little impact on communities of emigrants from eastern and southern Europe. In these cemeteries, the premium was on headstones. Lot-holders retained the European practice of erecting a large gravestone on each grave site, rather than a central family monument with small individual markers. Covering the terrain, the headstones overshadowed the sparse plantings around them. The size, quality, and distinctiveness of the headstones depended on the status and location of the community, but most headstones were standard models with little ornamentation. Headstones bearing a photographic likeness of the deceased were popular. Enameled onto the headstone, the photographic likeness provided the single most important ornament within the cemetery. The photographic likeness was a return to colonial iconography, with a modern touch.

THE CEMETERY IN 1900

By the early twentieth century, there were three broad categories of cemeteries in America.

First, some ethnic, racial, and religious groups opted most often for a cemetery dominated by headstones, individual markers, and family monuments. Much as the French filled the garden of Père Lachaise with monuments, Americans filled these cemeteries with stone records of families, communities, and generations.

Second, other recent immigrants and native-born Americans emulated the design and ideas of the rural-cemetery movement. Many superintendents and some social critics attacked the older practices of stone coping around graves or lots, large and unwieldy individual markers, and an overabundance of plantings, but the cemetery remained basically the same. Markers were visible above the ground; monuments were larger than those of the last generations; and lot-holders purchased from cemeteries or local gardeners (if allowed) smaller shrubs and other adornments for their lots. This was the model in many small-town cemeteries.

Third, the lawn-park cemetery that Strauch had envisioned had become a reality, and, like many suburbs and urban parks, it had a sleek, streamlined landscape. Monuments were almost always granite, for strength, and classically styled, for purity. Family monuments dotted the landscape, and individual markers disappeared. The result was a line of separate, but similar, stones that was reminiscent of a row of individual markers in a colonial graveyard. The irregularity of the picturesque was replaced by the order and gentleness of the pastoral cemetery.

Unfortunately, all of these cemetery designs were confronted with difficult challenges. Rural cemeteries were being closed in by the expanding cities. These cemeteries were often embattled against the very elements that they had been created to end—vandalism, abandonment, and overcrowding. Ethnic and religious cemeteries were increasingly difficult to maintain, even in the closed communities of the large cities. The next generation might bury in the old cemetery or they might choose the grounds of a more progressive synagogue, a more liberal church, or even a nonsectarian lawn-park cemetery.

The lawn-park cemetery balanced formality with naturalism. The large green lawns, with their rows of similar family monuments, lacked diversity and imagination. The superintendents, in their desire for simplicity and ease of maintenance, had helped to strip the cemetery of its emotional strength. The monuments no longer had epitaphs, symbolic carvings, or symbolic statues. The only artistic achievements were the mausoleums, which were of various styles. Architectural styles and fads continued to fascinate and attract wealthy lot-holders, who built mausoleums in every style from Egyptian to Art Nouveau. These architectural triumphs were too often overwhelmed by lines of granite stones.

Volunteer lot-holders managed some of these cemeteries, especially those located in smaller communities and in ethnic neighborhoods within larger cities. Most cemeteries, however, were professionalized. Superintendents were increasingly called upon to oversee the daily operations of the cemeteries as founders withdrew from this responsibility. Americans were rapidly specializing large parts of their lives. For example, general stores were being replaced by grocery stores, department stores, and speciality clothing stores. The complexity of the cemetery was growing. Larger work crews were necessary as the cemetery assumed greater responsibility for the grounds. Lawn mowers, trucks, and other tools of the new technology had to be purchased, serviced, and stored. The business of death was becoming complex.

A RETREAT FROM THE PICTURESQUE AND SENTIMENTAL

Strauch's landscape-lawn design came at a critical time for the American cemetery. Critics of rural cemeteries latched on to many of Strauch's ideas because they were so concerned about the faults they had found in the earlier cemeteries. Furthermore, Strauch's ideas were based on European aesthetic practices that became more acceptable to Americans as urbanization and industrialization changed the city and the countryside. Although many Americans were more comfortable burying their dead either in cemeteries that held the remains of generations of the family or in cemeteries that reminded them of those of their European homelands, other Americans found the lawn-park cemetery more attractive, accessible, and comforting.

The new cemetery, with its less dramatic appearance, was in keeping with the withdrawal of most Americans from a close relationship of death, which had characterized the antebellum period. Sanitarians and medical scientists had jointly lowered the risk of living in the cities. Professionals managed the process of death and burial. Consolation poetry and prose became less prevalent. Death continued to be a powerful social issue, but did not engage the attention of Americans as it had earlier.

Because of all these factors, not only the appearance but also the character of the cemetery changed. Entrepreneurs, who assumed responsibility for so much of the American economy and culture during this period, commercialized the burial ground. Whereas rural cemeteries and ethnic and religious lawn-park cemeteries retained loyal lot-holders, for-profit cemeteries attracted other Americans. Americans began to recognize the commercialization of the cemetery, and such commercialism evoked a storm of anger and ignited a movement of reform, which eventually led to the redesign of the cemetery into the memorial park.

CHAPTER SIX

Commercialism, Cremation, and the Modern Cemetery

ENTREPRENEURIAL EFFICIENCY

Americans have always held a strong belief in business, but in the late nineteenth century that belief reached mythical proportions. Confronted with expanding cities, rising tides of immigration and of migration from rural areas to cities and suburbs, industrialization, labor strife, and all the other problems that summed up their modern industrial society, Americans hoped to reorder and unify it by applying business techniques to many aspects of it. Businessmen such as John D. Rockefeller and Andrew Carnegie seemed to offer examples of ways of resolving the nation's economic, political, and social problems.[1]

Reliance on business strongly influenced the development of the cemetery. Church and government officials were less and less involved with the burial process. Private businesses directed the funerals and buried the dead. In burying the dead, they did a public service, but for a profit. The cemetery, as well as other aspects of the burial process, became an entrepreneurial enterprise. The success of private businesses in selling lots, cutting costs, and providing a wide variety of services led more conservative cemeteries to change their practices. While Adolph Strauch was changing the internal management of the cemetery, entrepreneurs were altering the way the cemetery related to its customers.

There was no national consensus on the appropriateness of the new entrepreneurial cemeteries. Many people questioned the new commercialism in cemeteries and the more important role of the funeral director and superintendent. Some critics were primarily concerned about rising prices and the allocation of precious resources to the dead instead of the poor. Other critics rejected earth burial and mausoleum-entombment, arguing that established customs were unhealthy, undemocratic, and inefficient; they advocated cremation.

THE COMMERCIALIZATION OF THE
AMERICAN CEMETERY

The rural-cemetery movement produced many changes in American burial habits, the most important of which was that motivations for establishing a cemetery were expanded. Prior to rural cemeteries, graveyards were created solely out of need—a settlement experienced its first death or an old graveyard was filled. Rural cemeteries were established partly out of need. Expanding cities and towns needed more burial spaces, especially ones out of the way of economic expansion.

Other reasons began to influence the location, even the very idea, of a new cemetery. First with Hillhouse's New Haven Burying Ground, then Mount Auburn Cemetery and the rural-cemetery movement, aesthetics became an important consideration in the cemetery's location, plotting, management, and relationship to lot-holders. Olmsted wrote in 1865 that the central purpose of a cemetery board was "to prepare a place in which those feelings, sentiments and aspirations which religion and civilization make common to all in [the] presence of the dead, may be expressed." The new, naturalistic landscapes of rural cemeteries created an atmosphere in which appropriate feelings could be expressed.[2]

Increasingly, another reason for establishing new cemeteries was financial gain. John Jay Smith's recollections of his years surrounding the founding of Laurel Hill Cemetery in Philadelphia included noting that the "first sales at Laurel Hill were made this year, and, adding them to my other profits . . . my income was large for those days." He also reported that his family would inherit three hundred shares in Woodlawn Cemetery in the Bronx. Smith was a founding subscriber to the cemetery, and within ten years his stock had an estimated worth nine times that of the original. Although few rural cemeteries offered stock as investments, those that did had created a style of financing which became popular in later decades.[3]

Woodlawn was among the earliest cemeteries that profited investors. When Woodlawn opened in 1863, New York City was already surrounded by cemeteries. The cemetery promoted itself as a special alternative to other rural cemeteries by noting that mourners could reach Woodlawn by the Harlem Railroad, which had placed one of its stops at the cemetery's entrance. Although not the first cemetery located next to a railway, Woodlawn was a prototype of the expansion of cemeteries in the metropolitan areas of America.[4]

Private financing had funded the development of rural cemeteries, but had seldom done so for profit. Rural cemeteries had either borrowed considerable portions of their development money or had held auctions of lots prior to development. Oakwood Cemetery in Syracuse paid $47,100 for 145 acres of land, plus the cost of development and design, for a total of almost $200,000. Organizers attempted to sell lots to subscribers prior to development in order

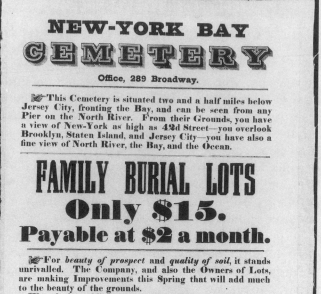

*Advertisement for New-York Bay Cemetery,
Jersey City, N.J., c. 1850s*

This rare mid-nineteenth-century advertisement suggests that the competition among cemeteries in the New York City area had already begun in the early years of the rural-cemetery movement. (Broadside printed by Hart. Courtesy of New-York Historical Society, New York City.)

to pay these initial costs. Oakwood raised almost $22,000 this way in May 1859.[5]

Even with this type of commitment, organizations usually had to borrow money in the form of certificates of indebtedness, which guaranteed that up to 50 percent of lot sales would be used to repay the lenders. The certificates of indebtedness covered the actual cost of the land and developments. When this procedure was used, cemeteries would pay off the certificates as fast as possible, so that future income could be used for further development of the cemetery. The intention of the legislation allowing such borrowing was that the full amount of the money would go toward financing cemetery improvements. By 1881 Oakwood had paid off all its land debts from its $180,000 worth of lot sales.

The private American cemetery had never been free from fears of profiteering. In 1839 Green-Wood Cemetery was forced to redraft its corporate charter, in part because potential lot-holders believed that the cemetery would financially benefit investors. Forest Lawn Cemetery in Buffalo met public apathy from its founding in 1849 until 1864, when it became a nonprofit incorporated trust controlled by lot-holders. In the 1850s, Rochester newspapers expressed concern about the clustering of monument dealers and florists around the entrance to Mount Hope Cemetery.[6]

Later organizers remained concerned about the public's perception, but developed methods of hiding the profitable nature of their investment. In purchasing the land for the cemetery, they gave land-share certificates to the investors, who owned the land. In return, the investors were guaranteed a share of the proceeds of all lots sales on the land for which they had received a certificate. For example, a $10,000 investment in land costing a total of $50,000 to develop could eventually net several hundreds of thousands of dollars for the investors, because lots were priced to cover development costs and maintenance, as well as provide a profit for the investors.

Maple Grove Cemetery in Brooklyn was an example of the possibilities cemetery investment offered.[7] By the time of the founding of this cemetery in 1875, Brooklyn already had several successful cemeteries. Maple Grove was located next to a railway, as close as possible to Brooklyn's residential district to be accessible to the maximum number of residents. Furthermore, the cemetery was designed according to contemporary plans that simplified the road system and the intricacy of the plantings so that it appeared accessible. The founders' purpose was the establishment of a profitable enterprise.

Although state laws, including New York's, forbade a cemetery from using less than 50 percent of the funds generated by lot sales for development and maintenance of the cemetery, half of every lot sale was left as potential profit to be divided among the investors. This could mean an enormous return on a small investment. William Cogswell boasted of starting Maple Grove Cemetery with $10, borrowing the rest from banks and investors, and turning the cemetery into a million-dollar investment. The financing of the American cemetery had emerged as one of the many speculative dealings of the Gilded Age.[8]

CAPITAL CITY CEMETERY AND ENTREPRENEURIAL SPECULATION

Capital City Cemetery Corporation, owner of Albany's New Rural Cemetery, exemplified the potential for speculation in the cemetery. The New Rural, situated one and one-half miles east of Albany on Olcott's Hill, consisted of 116 acres laid out in the modern lawn and park system. Investors were solicited through the Albany Funding Company, self-styled as the only "house that makes a speciality of dealing" in cemetery stocks.[9]

The corporation's prospectus informed potential investors of the enormous returns available from cemeteries that were organized and conducted upon "our plan." The prospectus also noted that most cemeteries sold lots by the square foot, with an average price being 25¢ per square foot. In a parcel of 100 acres, 25 acres would be used for roads, walks, and other institutional needs, leaving the other 75 for burial sections. At 43,560 square feet to an acre, and at 25¢ per square foot, those 75 acres would gross $816,750 in lot sales.

New York State law dictated that half the proceeds, $408,375, be used by the cemetery corporation for the purpose of developing and maintaining the cemetery. The other half was available for shareholders. The prospectus boasted that "no other legitimate business offers such sure and large profit." As the price of land rose, so did profits. Because of inflation and a scarcity of grave sites, returns might be considerably larger. The prospectus noted that other cemetery stocks, notably Kensico in New York's Westchester County and Wood-lawn, had had increases from $20 to $100 per share, with yearly dividends of about $10.

These returns compared favorably with contemporary real-estate investments. Cemetery sections were broken up into smaller lots, potentially sold prior to development. Cemetery promoters also learned to use the sections more efficiently, resulting in more lots per section. Rural cemeteries, with their wide pathways, numerous roads, and ornamental emphasis, provided approximately five hundred graves per acre. The drastic reduction of roads and pathways and limited room for picturesque and ornamental features allowed lawn landscape cemeteries space for about twelve hundred graves per acre.

Prices rose regularly. Green-Wood's price for a grave site went from $25 in 1890 to $51 in 1910. Similarly, services were becoming more expensive. The charge for an *opening* (a cemetery term for digging the grave) at Green-Wood rose from $6 in 1900 to $11 in 1910. There were twelve hundred burials per acre, and thus there was a gross income of about $70,000 an acre over and above the lot sale.[10] While management used these funds to maintain and further develop the cemetery, outsiders handled other services. Markers and monuments were an additional expense; lot-holders usually purchased them from local dealers of monuments, who worked separately from the cemetery.

Although profits were potentially large, they were not guaranteed. The New Rural Cemetery failed to live up to the promises of the prospectus. The stock proved worthless because lot sales lagged and the cemetery eventually drifted into bankruptcy, only to be resurrected in the 1970s by new management working closely with the New York State Cemetery Board.

The New Rural Cemetery was not unusual. Many rural cemeteries had not succeeded financially and were saved only by wealthy lot-holders willing to subsidize the development and prosperity of the institution; commercial cemeteries had no such protection. One notable financial failure was Forest Park

Cemetery in Troy. Organized in 1898, Forest Park was abandoned within twenty years. The mausoleum touted as the cemetery's centerpiece disintegrated when the cemetery was abandoned.

Still, people established new cemeteries primarily because of the potential profits. Between the 1870s and 1920, the number of new cemeteries established nationwide dramatically increased. Whereas many of these cemeteries were organized by emerging immigrant groups needing burial spaces, a significant portion of them were entrepreneurial ventures.[11]

THE NEW ENTREPRENEURS

The new entrepreneurs attempted to apply the latest advances in business and design to create the most efficient and rationally designed cemeteries. They were among the first to apply Strauch's landscape-lawn plan. They adopted innovations developed by Spring Grove, Mount Auburn, and other rural cemeteries, including record-keeping methods and perpetual- and annual-care funds. They developed or adapted new advertising concepts, sales techniques, and additional services. Older cemeteries slowly imitated many of the entrepreneurial innovations.

Although all cemeteries were influenced by the sophistication of business techniques in the late nineteenth century, the entrepreneurial cemeteries embraced them more readily. The administration of the new cemeteries reflected this change in goals. The lines of authority which characterized even antebellum cemeteries became more complex as the cemetery was forced to alter its approach to selling lots. The churchyard had been the responsibility of the sexton, who oversaw the entire process of death, from burial to maintenance. At first, the rural cemetery had a small work force led by an individual who functioned much like a sexton. The founders and lot-holders, who remained responsible for the appearance of the lots, did much of the planning, planting, and other maintenance.

Under the system developed after the midcentury, management began to maintain larger parts of the cemetery. Spring Grove's organization grew to include two superintendents and an expanded work force. The office staff gained responsibility for perpetual-care lots, trust-fund accounts, and revenues from additional services, such as gardening. Gradually, all private cemeteries expanded their staffs.

By 1917 Mount Auburn had a secretary, treasurer, and superintendent, and the office staff and assistant superintendent reported to the superintendent. The assistant superintendent was the immediate supervisor of the ground crew, which included mechanics, laborers, general maintenance personnel, a forester, and the workers who maintained the perpetual-care lots. The office force consisted of a surveyor, bookkeeper, cashier, stenographer, police personnel, and gate keepers. The secretary, treasurer, and superintendent reported to the president and board of directors, who legally represented the proprietors.[12]

As at Spring Grove under Strauch, Mount Auburn's organizational chart included no individual solely responsible for selling burial lots. The office staff, which often worked downtown, away from the cemetery, was responsible for advertising the cemetery and selling lots. The board of directors was a link between the superintendent and financial managers. The cemetery's sales efforts were very limited. The administrators of rural cemeteries relied mostly on people coming to them rather than reaching out to the public.

SELLING THE CEMETERY

Early American cemeteries did not aggressively sell themselves to the public. An eighteenth-century sexton would have been puzzled if someone suggested that the graveyard needed to advertise. Churchyards, domestic graveyards, and public burial grounds did not need to attract lot-holders. Advertising was rudimentary. Handbills announced the latest imports, but certainly not the availability of graves at Trinity churchyard.

Rural cemeteries cautiously approached sales. First, the new, private cemeteries had to guard against violating the taboo of associating the grave with the trades. In 1849 the founders of Hollywood in Richmond had to reassure the public that the cemetery was not exclusively for the wealthy and not a commercial venture before they were awarded a charter.[13] The examples of Green-Wood and Forest Lawn were clear indications of the public's disapproval of commercialism in death. Second, rural cemeteries were founded by men who did not feel that there was any need to sell the cemetery because the community would embrace it, as early American communities had used the local graveyard or churchyard for burials.

Rural cemeteries were still "providing a supply of goods" rather than "creating a demand for their products."[14] As private corporations, rural cemeteries did use newspapers to inform the public of their existence. Small notices of office hours and the hours that visitors were welcome in the grounds were printed in local newspapers, but such notices did not openly promote the cemetery or suggest that lots were for sale. Rural cemeteries expected to attract business through informal networks of elites and the opening of the grounds to visitors. The initial proprietors were usually men of wealth and reputation who convinced their friends and neighbors to support the new endeavor. The parade of people touring the grounds meant that the cemetery was highly visible.

The new generation of cemeteries could not rely solely on the grounds as their advertisement to the community. The development of urban parks, arboretums, community gardens, and other naturally beautiful places both inside and outside cities provided competition for the cemeteries. Rural cemeteries had mature landscapes on large tracts, which would outshine the new cemeteries for a generation at least. The new entrepreneurial cemeteries, founded in inflationary times by less affluent individuals, could not duplicate the large expanses of land. The new lawn-park cemeteries were rarely larger than 100 acres.

Promoters used the smallness and newness of the new cemeteries to their best advantage. Advertisements emphasized that they were more accessible than older, larger, more confusing cemeteries. Landscapes were less cluttered, more parklike, and more open and inviting than those of the previous generation. Riverside Cemetery in Cleveland touted its five miles of drives, 6 acres of lakes spanned by rustic wooden bridges, and the ease with which one could reach the cemetery from downtown. Finally, promoters of new cemeteries such as Riverdale suggested that the numerous acres of the old cemeteries must be expensive to maintain, whereas their own compact cemeteries were designed to cut maintenance costs while still providing a naturalistic atmosphere.[15]

The establishment of a new generation of cemeteries increased the competition for business. Some cemeteries could rely on informal economic, ethnic, racial, or social networks to help sell their lots. Cemeteries institutionally affiliated with a synagogue or church had guaranteed customers. Other cemeteries began to compete more actively for one another's customers. By 1900 the supply of burial lots exceeded the demand. In 1891 *Modern Cemetery* reported that over 3,700 acres around New York City were devoted to cemeteries.[16]

The new competition, combined with the new motivations for starting a cemetery, resulted in a restructured management, which placed increasing emphasis on sales. The new generation of cemetery founders recognized the importance of the landscape and the superintendent, but it was more involved in finances than horticulture. Even where the new cemeteries were not speculative ventures, the managers were primarily interested in expanding the business rather than developing communities through common institutions.

Many of the new managers came from businesses, such as real estate and insurance, that emphasized advertising. Advertising was rapidly becoming a major American industry, having developed from a modest $10 million business in 1865 to a $95 million one in 1900. Cemeteries learned the need for advertising as they struggled to reach an elusive market, but they were still hamstrung by the public's attitude that a cemetery was not a business. The operators had to find ways to inform the public without offending taste. *The Cemetery Hand Book* reminded its readers: "The preparing of advertising matter for a cemetery is a delicate and exacting work, and too great care can not be taken to avoid offense to the sentimental side of humanity."[17]

New cemeteries continued to use their grounds as a selling point. Cemeteries began to publish small booklets of lithographic and photographic views of their grounds. These booklets, which often included the cemeteries' rules and regulations, suggestions for permanent-care funds, and forms for gifts to

HANDSOME CEMETERY ADVERTISING BOOK.

The matter in the two decorative borders and illustrations here and on the next page shows fac-similes of two opposite pages of a handsome twelve-page advertising book recently issued by Mount Tamalpais Cemetery, San Rafael, Cal. The left hand page throughout the book bears a decorative illustration and border and an appropriate quotation just as shown on this page. The right hand page is given to one or two half tones made the proper size to exactly fill the space in the same kind of a decorative border, as shown on the opposite page.

The space occupied by this type is given to a running description of the grounds and general information set in type like this.

Each one of these decorative pages bears a different picture and a quotation appropriate to it. All are just as artistically drawn and as striking as the one shown.

The half tones are of the finest quality and are perfectly printed on the finest enameled paper. They are in every case selected to show beautiful landscape pictures as well as fine views of the grounds. The cover is of pure white, roughly surfaced paper, with the title embossed in well executed lettering in a delicate gray ink. The book shows good taste and the best of printing and illustrating throughout.

"RURAL BEAUTY MIRRORED IN THE CRYSTAL OF THE LAKE."

Advertisement for Mount Tamalpais Cemetery,
San Rafael, Calif., c. 1915

Editors of *The Cemetery Hand Book* used this striking advertisement as an example of excellence in cemetery advertising. The text presented readers with ideas of what they could place in similar advertisements. The illustration and decorative border evoked an atmosphere of rural beauty and tranquility, attributes that virtually all American cemetery managers believed were essential sales points. (*The Cemetery Hand Book*, c. 1921. Courtesy of Woodlawn Cemetery, Syracuse, N.Y.)

the cemetery, were used to both attract new customers and tie lot-holders to the cemetery. Lot-holders were informed of charges for new services, burials, annual and permanent care, and other features of the service-oriented cemetery, while potential customers would be impressed by the business spirit and the beauty of the cemetery. Inserts in the booklets listed prices and the location and hours of the cemetery office.

Most cemeteries continued to be managed through a downtown office, where the treasurer and secretary dealt with the organization's financial aspects. Downtown offices were especially important for the new cemeteries that were situated farther from city centers. Organizers of the earliest rural cemeteries had dramatically changed American burial habits by relocating cemeteries outside town, but now government and local opposition to cemeteries was pushing newer cemeteries ever farther into the suburbs. Lake View in Cleveland was financially unsound for twenty years after its founding in 1869 primarily because it was six miles from downtown. Kensico, north of New York City; Pinelawn, east of the city on Long Island; Greenlawn, west of Syracuse; and Fairmont, west of Buffalo, were all examples of cemeteries that were situated over fifteen miles from their potential markets. Unlike Lake View, they were accessible by railroad.[18]

Cemeteries were also forced to move farther out of town by the scarcity of land and by the public's growing dissatisfaction with nearby cemeteries. Brooklyn and Queens residents were the first to revolt against the rising number of nonprofit cemeteries in their counties. Later, Westchester County and Putnam County residents asked the state for action. One reason the public requested that further cemeteries be prohibited was that large areas of these counties were nontaxable. The other important factor was that the cemeteries were unwelcome; this was a distinct change from the celebrations of cemeteries by antebellum Americans.[19]

Kensico, a typical cemetery located on a railroad line, was founded in 1889.[20] It was located in Westchester County, just above White Plains, on the New York Central and Hudson River Railroad. Established only after a struggle with local opponents who were fearful of another cemetery in the county, Kensico was an aggressive advertiser. In a large-format booklet of photographs published in 1910, Kensico explained how to reach the cemetery by railroad, carriage, or automobile, and it offered timetables and special railroad tickets at the cemetery.

The cemetery also offered special rooms at Grand Central Station in which relatives and the friends of the deceased could hold a quiet reception and "rest with the body in privacy until the departure of the train." When the train left for the cemetery, mourners could request the funeral car "Kensico" or a special train composed of an engine and a funeral car.

These extra services were expensive additions to the costs of burial. In 1910 the special train, which could accommodate thirty-five mourners, cost

*Title Page of Photographic Booklet of Kensico Cemetery,
Valhalla, N.Y., 1914*

Photographic booklets became a popular method of touting the beauties and conveniences of American cemeteries. The photographs often showed manicured lawns, dense landscaping, and isolated mausoleums and monuments. The booklets portrayed an efficiently maintained, expertly designed, clean, and attractive cemetery. (Courtesy of Kensico Cemetery and Lawrence Sloane.)

$60, while an ordinary passenger car attached to a regular train could accommodate forty-five passengers and cost $50. The cemetery also arranged for a family railroad ticket that was good for one year so that the family could visit the grave site. More sophisticated measures of advertising and promotion were essential if the cemetery was to continue to attract new lot-holders.

Older rural cemeteries faced the same need to reach the public and reacted to the new conditions by generating their own publications. Kensico's booklets were matched by those of Oakwood in Syracuse, West Laurel Hill Cemetery in Philadelphia, Newton Cemetery outside Boston, Forest Hill in Utica, and even Mount Auburn. The cemeteries' notices also became more suggestive, noting the availability of the booklets and providing more information about the cemeteries. The cemeteries, whether for-profit or nonprofit, were more aggressive and threatened the delicate balance between financial success and the traditional sacredness of the grave.

WILLIAM H. LOCKE, JR.'S PINELAWN CEMETERY

The ultimate lawn-park entrepreneurial cemetery was located on four square miles of Long Island, almost thirty miles east of Manhattan.[21] Pinelawn Cemetery, founded in 1902 by William H. Locke, Jr., was situated on the land of Greenlawn Cemetery, a defunct cemetery venture. The new cemetery combined an innovative sales program with an intricate landscape design.

Samuel Parsons, Jr., former supervising architect for the Department of Parks in New York City, provided the design.[22] A highly respected, nationally recognized landscape architect, Parsons took this opportunity to develop a "memorial park" that was both beautiful and rational. The design contained a series of concentric circles around a central 72-acre circle permanently reserved as parkland. The cemetery's entire length was bisected with a park drive, ornamented with elms and Norway maples. Locke wanted to preserve the central parkland around Pinelawn's Long Island Railway station, so that mourners and funeral parties would enter the peace of the parkland rather than the monument landscape of the burial sections.

The burial sections were an extension of the cemetery's parklike atmosphere. Wide lawn spaces were irregularly interspersed with elms, Norway maples, and ornamental trees. Family monuments were surrounded by individual markers that were "level with the sod." Shrubbery was planted near the monuments or around the family lots, leaving the flat terrain of Long Island stretched out before the viewer. The landscape was starker and simpler than that of earlier cemeteries and rural parks. The emphasis was on the unity of natural elements into a single scene of pastoral bliss.

Parson's design reflected the ideology and aesthetics of the contemporary City Beautiful movement in city planning and landscape architecture. City Beautiful proponents revered natural beauty within the city. They recognized that, because of the rapid expansion and industrialization of the late nineteenth century, city leaders were unable to retain the unspoiled beauty of an earlier age. "Dirt streets—swirling dust in summer and gluey, sucking mud in spring, redolent with horse droppings"—were the norm in many American cities. These proponents planned to redesign the city: "Well-tended flower gardens, well-done landscape parks, street furniture or straightforward but gracious design, and single or grouped monumental public buildings, all in harmonious relationships, were the basis of civic beauty."[23]

City Beautiful proponents believed that beauty could not be simply decoration; it also had to have a functional utility. Parson's plan combined the beauty of the pastoral into an eminently usable design. The grounds were logically arranged, with the concentric circles providing a classical pattern, which did not confuse the visitor. The monuments, undisturbed by surrounding individual markers, eased the problem of locating a family lot while offering families an opportunity to exhibit their success and taste.

Pinelawn reflected the hope of City Beautiful proponents. If they succeeded in making the city a "locus of harmony, mutual responsibility, and interdependence between classes, mediated by experts," then the city would become a "peaceful and productive place, not a stark contrast to rural scenery." The founders of Pinelawn hoped that it would symbolize such goals. While the design emphasized the harmony between elements, the advertising campaign underlined the need for a cemetery available to everyone.[24]

Pinelawn was a leader in innovative sales promotion. Influenced by cemetery trustees John R. Hegeman and Frederick Ekert, both of whom were leaders of the insurance industry, Pinelawn hired salespeople to sell cemetery lots in their spare time. These salespeople were authorized to offer purchasers a payment plan of 25¢ down and 23¢ weekly until the lot was purchased. Managers and directors of the older rural cemeteries could not understand the policy of selling people graves prior to need on a payment plan.[25]

The innovative style of Pinelawn could succeed only as long as its directors agreed on its goals. In 1913 a fight broke out between the stockholders and management. The stockholders felt they had been deceived by a prominent local politician, Abram De Graw, when he promoted the initial stock offering. The promised high dividends and appreciating stock had failed to materialize, and stockholders brought suit against Pinelawn.[26] Pinelawn was forced to sell off much of its land and to divide the central 72-acre parkland into burial lots to meet the costs of the legal actions. At Pinelawn, Parsons had been able to plan a Strauchian landscape that unified nature and art. But the new cemetery faced still other challenges, which a simple alteration of the landscape could not resolve.

CREMATION AS REFORM

As cemeteries became more commercial after the Civil War, Americans questioned the propriety of profiting from the dead. Some reformers turned contemporary admiration for rational business techniques on their head and advocated the dramatic alternative of cremation as a more efficient and less expensive alternative to burial. Citing the social inequity of the monuments and the potential health concerns surrounding earth burial, the reformers hoped to convince Americans that there was a more scientific and rational approach to the disposal of the dead.[27]

Cremationists also railed against the religious traditions that opposed their reform movement. They had little initial success in converting society away from earth burial and entombment, although they did influence Americans' perception of cemeteries. Their attacks further isolated the cemetery. Stig-

Bird's-eye View of Pinelawn Cemetery, Pinelawn, N.Y., c. 1902
As with Kensico, Woodlawn in Detroit, and other landscape-lawn cemeteries established between 1890 and 1920, Pinelawn Cemetery was strongly influenced by contemporary trends in landscape architecture. The circular sections, taken to an extreme in Samuel Parsons, Jr.'s design of Pinelawn, were a popular feature of the City Beautiful movement's designs for parks and suburbs. Curves represented a formal design, but one in direct contrast to the gridiron style of the city. (Pinelawn Cemetery photographic booklet, c. 1902. Courtesy of Pinelawn Memorial Park.)

matized by opponents as "Radicals, or Socialists, or persons of little or no professed religious views," the reformers laid the groundwork for the later acceptance of cremation as an alternative to traditional burial.[28]

THE EARLY HISTORY OF CREMATION

The only verifiable cremation in America prior to the Civil War occurred in 1792, when the body of Henry Laurens, former president of the Continental Congress and peace commissioner in Paris, was burned on an open-air pyre. Laurens had demanded he be cremated after a near-tragedy involving his granddaughter. The story is that she awoke from a coma just as the family was about to bury her in the family graveyard. Other instances, such as case of a German immigrant farmer in the Midwest whose neighbors stopped him from cremating his wife, demonstrated the strong cultural bias against cremation in American society.[29]

Much religious sentiment strongly opposed cremation, which was viewed as "unnatural." A writer in the *Christian Review* in 1848 assured his readers that "neither the false philosophy, nor the fear of insult from enemies . . . will doubtless ever again impel the human mind to a practice so opposed to all the dictates of refined and tender affection."[30] The religious sentimentalism of the "cult of melancholy" placed great emphasis on the cemetery as the resting place of the body awaiting Judgment Day. The destruction of the body through cremation was said to threaten the hope of Resurrection.

Some antebellum Americans did argue in favor of cremation, primarily because of a fear of disease transmission. In Rochester, a procremation letter to a local newspaper in 1855 suggested that "all fear of contagion, and disease would then vanish, and death would wear a smile, whilst contrasting this earthly body, and its natural decay, with the spirit of the departed." The writer was attempting to find the same spiritual relief from the terrors of death as that promised by rural-cemetery promoters. The cremation of Shelley in 1822 lead to a faddish consideration of the practice in Europe. As long as cremation depended on the open-air pyre, with its "pagan" connections, the practice remained little discussed.[31]

The criticism of earth burial, which propelled the cremation crusade, was an extension of the antebellum medical concerns that had led to the initial removal of the graveyards to the outskirts of town. The dread of cholera helped motivate the rural-cemetery founders, as the horror of miasma had inspired the city councils of the Northeast to pass restrictive legislation in the 1820s. The proliferation of rural cemeteries seemed to solve the health problems posed by decaying corpses buried too close to either water supplies or the surface. Rural cemeteries were large and isolated enough from the city that even surrounding residential neighborhoods did not appear threatened. Later, parks and par-klike cemeteries were praised as the lungs of the cities. The link between the dead and disease seemed broken.

In the last half of the nineteenth century, the problems concerning the graveyard reappeared. In New York City. the death rate rose from 21 per 1,000 people in 1810 to 37 per 1,000 in 1857. People lived in increasingly substandard housing. For example, over 500 people lived in a five-story tenement in New York City. The isolation of rural cemeteries was threatened by the continued expansion of cities, propelled by such new transportation technologies as the electric street railway.[32]

By 1880 Green-Wood Cemetery held the remains of a quarter-million New Yorkers. Brooklyn, which had grown twenty-three times larger since the ceme-tery had opened, engulfed Green-Wood. By the 1880s, Calvary Cemetery, the primary Catholic cemetery in New York City, was interring over 12,000 people annually. Their graves were in addition to the quarter-million graves that al-ready crowded the cemetery's 75 acres.[33]

Although rural cemeteries had been designed to serve their communities for generations, such tremendous numbers of new burials led to new worries

Beginnings of our Street Cleaning Department, 1868

Cleaning New York City's Streets, 1868

During an era of annual epidemics of contagious diseases, the disorganized nature of urban services, such as street cleaning, not only offended but also frightened nineteenth-century Americans. Reformers periodically demanded better service, but they were usually thwarted by the municipal government's corruption and the growing population's extraordinary needs. The lack of services to combat the continuing terrible death rate from contagious disease increased calls for cremation and other public-health measures. (Henry Collins Brown, *Old New York: Yesterday and Today*, 1922. Courtesy of Dartmouth College Library.)

over the safety of the cemeteries. The *Urn: A Monthly Journal Devoted to the Interests of Cremation* reported in 1895 that "Evergreens Cemetery, Brooklyn, has been recently explored by a lynx-eyed N.Y. *World* reporter. He found what, as a direct result of greed, nearly all metropolitan cemeteries will show in common, particularly in their public and poor sections, pieces of half-decayed coffins, rusty metal trimmings and washouts from recent rains, exposing the upper coffin of a tier covered with only eight inches of ground at the top." Such reports, which were intensified in the public's mind by the sporadic suits against established cemeteries, raised again the public's fear for its health and safety.[34]

ORIGINS OF THE MODERN CREMATION MOVEMENT

Similarly overcrowded conditions in European graveyards provoked sanitarians to search for an alternative to earth burial. At the Vienna Exposition of 1873, Ludovico Brunetti, professor of anatomy in Padua, Italy, demonstrated a viable enclosed crematory. His invention led the noted English surgeon Henry

Thompson to write "The Treatment of the Body after Death." Thompson, knighted in 1867 and created a baronet in 1899, was a distinguished member of the English medical community. A member of the Royal College of Surgeons at age thirty, he typified his generation's belief in the potency of the sanitary philosophy of disease prevention. His distress over the unhealthy air and water of English cities led to his promotion of cremation.[35]

Thompson's article articulated the two major thrusts of the cremation movement after the development of a reasonable, safe mechanism for cremation. First, earth burial (or, "inhumation," as he wrote), even in the recently organized garden cemeteries of England and America, was potentially dangerous to all those living near the cemeteries or drawing their water from springs that coursed under the cemeteries' land. Thompson noted that "thousands of human lives have been cut short by the poison of slowly decaying, and often diseased matter." Second, cremation was the least offensive alternative to "inhumation." The body underwent the same process of destruction that it did in the grave, except under scientifically accelerated conditions. Thompson argued that incineration was more scientifically "natural" than the present treatment, which was "artificial." Unlike some other alternatives, including mausoleums, cremation would completely remove a significant depository of decaying matter and a breeding ground of disease.[36]

Thompson's article coincided with Americans' marked increase in interest in cremation. Cremation societies were organized in several large cities, including New York and Philadelphia, and in a few smaller towns, including Lancaster, Pennsylvania. In Lancaster, the central promoter was Miles L. Davis, a surgeon. Davis helped Lancaster develop the country's second crematory in 1884, and then designed crematories in Buffalo, Detroit, and Baltimore. An active participant in the American Medical Association, Davis also patented a garbage incinerator and designed a hospital for contagious diseases. Active professionals, including physicians such as Davis, were often leaders of local cremation societies, which they viewed as extensions of their scientific and social interests.[37]

Cremation societies initially consisted of small groups of professionals. The *New York Times* reported in 1884 that the New Orleans society was "largely composed of physicians, lawyers, and journalists." Later, after the cremation of a popular physician who had treated workers, labor organizers spoke of forming a cremation society for the poor. They argued that cremation was finally becoming financially accessible to workers.[38]

The shortage of crematories throughout the nineteenth century kept the price of cremation high for the consumer. Generally, people accepted that cremation could potentially lower burial costs, but, until the reform was more successful, cremation remained limited to the upper and middle classes. These were the people, whether native- or European-born, who were knowledgeable about European advances in sanitary practices and were willing to consider alternative methods of disposal of the dead.

Many people continued to view cremation as a "pagan" act that violated Christian teachings and possibly ended an individual's hope of Resurrection. As early as the seventh or eighth centuries, when the Catholic church began to allow parishes to establish churchyards and to bury prominent martyrs and churchmen within the churches, cremation became unacceptable to the church.

This attitude was reinforced in 1886 when the Vatican forbade any Catholics to be cremated. One leading American Catholic writer stated that the reform was tainted by "atheists and infidels, professed enemies of God and His revelation." No matter how much cremationists argued that the only difference between the two processes was "sentiment," cremation was identified with anti-church elements in Europe, with liberals and scientists in America, and with an attempt to replace faith in God with belief in science.[39]

NEW ATTITUDES TOWARD THE DEAD

During much of the nineteenth century, the boundary between the living and the dead was unclear. Some even attempted to cross that boundary. The spiritualist movement, very popular first in the 1840s, and again in the 1870s, demonstrated the power of the belief in both the afterlife and the presence of loved ones near enough to communicate with the living. This blurring of the lines was evident by the 1840s and lasted well into the last half of the century, which "may well explain the intensity of grieving during this period."[40]

The rise of science as an important social idea in the last half of the century began to strengthen the boundaries between the living and the dead. Science posited a series of questions and provided a set of answers to important social issues that confronted religion, particularly the sentimental religion of the antebellum period. Darwin's theory of evolution challenged the concept of God as creator and destroyer and thus created doubts about the meaning of life and death. Scientists attempted to demonstrate that thought was an electrochemical discharge. Psychology and biology were creating an intellectual construct that, according to physician William Osler, dispensed "altogether with the soul." If life was an organic reality, then death "was a necessary event in order for new life to survive and for evolution to occur." Death was no longer "a sacred encounter," but a "collective process" for the future of the humanity. The sentimental view of the cemetery as a dormitory sharply contrasted with this materialistic view of the dead as a link to the next generation of living things.[41]

Science continued to diminish God's providence by demonstrating that disease was a result of small microbes, not an individual's sin against an all-powerful being. Earlier, Americans had believed that a moral society was a healthy society, not understanding the links between germs and disease. During the cholera epidemics of 1832, 1849, and 1866, as Charles Rosenberg has demonstrated, physicians and the public recognized that the best way to battle the disease was through proper public-health activities, rather than a clarion call to God to save the worthy.[42]

The moral explanations for cholera which had been popular in 1832 and 1849 were no longer acceptable. Scientific evidence showed that cholera, as well as other infectious diseases, was conquerable by modern medicine. In the 1870s and 1880s, the work of Robert Koch on tuberculosis, Louis Pasteur on anthrax, and others on the diseases that had repeatedly struck nineteenth-century cities reinforced the validity of medical and scientific explanations of various individual and societal problems. As these successes raised the public appreciation of medicine, they diminished religion's influence on daily life.

Thus science raised serious questions about the meaning of death and the reality of the afterlife. One aspect of antebellum thought was that people could envision heaven. Spiritualists attempted to provide proof that the dead were nearby. Their portraits of heaven were accepted as possible representations of the afterlife in which the spirits were living. By teaching that heaven was a beautiful place, that most of those dying would go to heaven, and that the living could stay in touch with those who were gone, the sentimental religion of the day stripped death of much of its horror.

The new theories threatened such portraits. Leslie Stephen warned that "if we admit the difference between men and monkeys is merely a difference of degree, can we continue to hold that monkeys will disappear at their death like a bubble, and that men will rise from their ashes?" Science disturbed people's understanding of salvation and Resurrection, thereby raising anew the fears and confusion people felt when confronted with death.[43]

Society only slowly accepted the scientific theories, as evident in the prolonged discussion among public-health advocates and physicians on the meaning of the work of Pasteur and Koch. Customs such as burial rituals were particularly difficult to question and change, as the advocates of cremation learned. As Elizabeth Phelps wrote in 1886, the new science undermined faith in God and an afterlife: "We have learned that we are not men, but protoplasm. We learned that we were not spirits, but chemical combinations. . . . We learned that the drama of 'Hamlet' and the 'Ode to Immortality' were secretions of the gray matter of the brain." This new view of life would affect American rituals surrounding death.[44]

F. JULIUS LEMOYNE AND AMERICA'S FIRST MODERN CREMATION

The public controversy surrounding the nation's first modern cremation demonstrated the difficulty of convincing the American people about the efficacy of cremation over other types of disposal, as well as the confusing agglomeration of issues surrounding cremation. The early cremation societies were unable to raise enough money to construct a crematory. But in the small town of Washington, Pennsylvania, Dr. F. Julius LeMoyne erected the first crude machine for cremation in 1876, less than two years after Thompson's article was published. At that time, LeMoyne was eighty years old, a survivor of years of reform activities. In the 1840s, he had capped his abolitionist activities by running for the vice-presidency on the Liberty party ticket. He was also a founding trustee of a successful postbellum normal school for African-Americans in Memphis, Tennessee.[45]

LeMoyne patterned his machine on Brunetti's. LeMoyne built the machine primarily for his own cremation, hoping that his cremation would demonstrate that the body was returned to its natural components, exactly as with earth burial. The chief difference between the two methods, he and other cremationists argued, was that decomposition took two hours in an incinerator and at least two years in a grave. Either way, the body decomposed into carbonic acid, water, ammonia, lime, phosphorous, iron, sulfur.

Yet the unusual nature of the first modern cremation obscured the scientific basis for cremation. The first person cremated by LeMoyne was Joseph Henry Louis, Baron de Palm, a penniless, titled follower of the spiritualist religion of theosophy. His funeral in New York City had been presided over by such leading theosophists as Henry S. Olcott and had been, according to the *New York Times,* "a curious mixture of paganism and religion."[46]

The cremation was technically a success, but the lack of any Christian ceremony, coupled with a long speech on spiritualism, overshadowed the scientific discussion. The failure to include religious rites in the second cremation at LeMoyne's crematory led the *New York Times* to conclude that "the entire absence of religious ceremonies at both of these cremations did much toward creating a prejudice against the process, and the people of the town threatened frequently to pull the building down, but did not do it."[47] The first cremation had been judged a circus of infidels, just as the conservatives had predicted.

Cremationists simply worked harder to convince people of the scientific merits of their position. In the early years, the essence of their attack on the cemetery had been their fear of decomposing organic matter, which seeped into the water table and caused intestinal difficulties or worse ones, and of odors emitted by decomposing bodies, which under suitable conditions they felt created conditions for chronic and specific diseases, including the epidemics that were then terrifying the public. The latter fear was a continuation of the miasmatic theory of disease causation, which had helped motivate rural-cemetery founders during the antebellum period.

John Beugless, in support of such considerations, reported that Washington Square in New York City, the potter's field covered up in the 1830s, was a popular spot to send children "every day in search of health!" Yet he pointed out "a dense blue haze several feet deep rests every calm morning over" the square. Frederick Peterson worried that the "scarlatina epidemic of 1873–1874" had reached its greatest mortality in the vicinity of an early nineteenth-century in-city cemetery. As long as sanitarians continued to judge potential health hazards by odor, the smells of the grave were easily perceived as possible threats to the city.[48]

CREMATION CHALLENGED

The sanitarian relationship of the grave to the public's health did not go unchallenged in this age of epidemiology and advances in statistics and health record-keeping. J.F.A. Adams, in *Cremation and Burial: Sixth Annual Report of the Massachusetts State Board of Health* (1875), stated that, after careful study, he found no support for the indictment of cemeteries. "The overcrowded, pestilential graveyards upon which the cremationists build their sanitary argument are a thing of the past," he asserted. "Cremation, therefore, becomes merely a question of sentiment and convenience." As with many researchers, Adams held nothing against the practice of cremation, but simply found no sound medical reason to endorse legislation obligating communities to ban burials. Other investigators in America and Europe supported Adams's findings in their research into the origins of various epidemics and chronic illnesses.[49]

Still, in 1875, the same year as Adams's report, neighbors of the thirty-five-year-old Rose Hill Cemetery in Syracuse petitioned city officials to end burials in the cemetery. A letter to the *Syracuse Journal* stated that "for years its existence has been an increasing source of danger to the public health, and its continued use a folly." Removal of the bodies, suggested by officials planning a park and conservatory, evoked a newspaper article about pauper children in London who died of smallpox after playing with coffin trestles used to bury victims of that disease. The coroner of Newton, New York, the location of Calvary, Mount Olivet, Lutheran, and Cypress Hills cemeteries, charged in 1889 that, "surrounded" by "1,250,000 bodies of slowly decomposing humanity," the residents of Newton had "almost the highest death-rate" in the state. Adams's research did not quiet these fears, which were constantly renewed by cremationist literature.[50]

The belief in the potential for danger from decomposing bodies stemmed partly from doubts about disease causation, which continued to reign through virtually all of the nineteenth century. Koch's successful isolation of the tubercule bacillus in 1882 was the first conclusive proof that the germ theory could be applied to human disease. Even then, uncertainty continued regarding numerous issues, including how viral disease worked, why certain people were carriers, and how devastating diseases such as malaria and yellow fever were spread. "Each infectious disease has its own mode of spread, some undergoing complicated life cycles involving several intermediate hosts. All of this remained obscure in the period immediately after the accomplishments of Koch and Pasteur."[51] Resistance to the new theory was especially strong in America, where the practice of medicine was more conservative and derivative than in Europe. American physicians were slower to establish research facilities to prove such theories clinically.

Such was the confusion surrounding the mechanism of disease that the founder of modern bacteriology, Pasteur, provided cremationists with a powerful new argument through his early work with anthrax. Pasteur discovered that anthrax occurred in animals that were put to pasture in fields where anthrax had not previously appeared. He accounted for the sudden appearance by suggesting that earthworms brought back to the surface anthrax spores from the buried carcasses of the disease-ridden cows. Whenever cows were returned to the field, the disease would recur.

Cremation advocates extrapolated this theory to suggest that dead bodies felled by infectious diseases were repositories and breeding grounds for those diseases. Accepting the new theory that miasmas were not the cause of disease, but that the body was host to germs that somehow spread from person to person, cremationists felt vindicated in their attack on earth burial. Thompson summed up the argument in 1888: "The poisons of scarlet fever, entric fever, smallpox, diphtheria, malignant cholera, are undoubtably transmissible through earth from the buried body by more than one mode. And thus by the act of interment we literally sow broadcast throughout the land innumerable seeds of pestilence; germs which long retain their vitality, etc., many of them destined at some future point to fructify in premature death or ruined health to thousands." If germs were the problem, one physician commented, then "nothing like fire to refine and purify." Indeed, he suggested that "the establishment of the germ theory of disease causation has in many minds given new impetus to the idea of cremation as a means of sanitary reform."[52]

Scientific arguments were countered by many commentators, among them Henry Ward Beecher, who argued: "What is there in science that will help a man in Greenwood? . . . That which makes Greenwood what it is to us is not its science, but those glorious associations that life has treasured up with the names spelled out there."[53] Cremation collided with society's long, close relationship with the grave. Rural cemeteries and the elaboration of the American funeral customs were the result of a commitment to establish a sanctity around the grave and to preserve it for future generations. Any attack on the grave called into question the judgment of society and its cultural leaders.

CREMATIONISTS' SOCIAL CRITIQUE

Cremationists were critical of the contemporary cemetery for more than scientific reasons, although their opponents claimed that other considerations were

TABLE 6.1
Number of Cremations and Sites of Crematories in America, 1876–1901

Site	1876–83	1884–85	1886–87	1888–89	1890–91	1892–93	1894–95	1896–97	1898–99	1900–1901	Total
Washington, Pa.	25	13	2	0	0	0	0	0	0	0	40
Lancaster, Pa.	—	38	21	4	4	8	3	4	4	4	90
Buffalo, N.Y.	—	1	25	39	68	57	72	72	83	117	534
New York, N.Y.	—	9	144	189	347	418	539	661	994	1,256	4,557
Pittsburgh, Pa.	—	—	23	19	22	27	23	30	40	55	239
Cincinnati, Ohio	—	—	11	55	88	76	104	117	115	170	736
Detroit, Mich.	—	—	3	24	45	80	53	73	84	96	458
Los Angeles, Calif.	—	—	7	17	46	78	75	71	110	117	521
Philadelphia, Pa.	—	—	—	42	82	130	162	163	220	238	1,037
St. Louis, Mo.	—	—	—	44	102	136	182	204	237	291	1,196
Baltimore, Md.	—	—	—	3	17	38	26	38	36	38	196
Swinburne Island, N.Y.	—	—	—	4	3	83	4	4	9	7	114
Troy, N.Y.	—	—	—	—	14	29	22	32	33	35	165
Davenport, Iowa	—	—	—	—	6	20	16	32	35	53	162
Boston Mass.	—	—	—	—	—	1	175	295	397	360	1,228
Chicago, Ill.	—	—	—	—	—	6	108	136	257	370	877
San Francisco, Calif. (2)	—	—	—	—	—	42	268	436	776	1,402	2,924
Waterville, N.Y.	—	—	—	—	—	1	5	11	10	11	38
Pasadena, Calif.	—	—	—	—	—	—	4	27	55	72	158
Milwaukee, Wisc.	—	—	—	—	—	—	—	55	83	85	223
Fort Wayne, Ind.	—	—	—	—	—	—	—	5	4	9	18
St. Paul Minn.	—	—	—	—	—	—	—	2	38	36	76
Washington, D.C.	—	—	—	—	—	—	—	25	66	58	149
Cambridge, Mass.	—	—	—	—	—	—	—	—	—	169	169
Cleveland, Ohio	—	—	—	—	—	—	—	—	—	38	38
Portland, Oreg.	—	—	—	—	—	—	—	—	—	20	20
Total	25	61	236	440	844	1,230	1,841	2,493	3,686	5,107	15,963

Source: "Table of Cremations in America Compiled for the Cremation Association of America by E. P. Sampson," Park and Cemetery 24, no. 11, 368.

raised only to buttress the scientific arguments. From the beginning, cremationists stated that they had no wish to disrupt rural cemeteries and that they would eventually make wonderful parks, as well as solemn resting places for cremated ashes. Their criticism of the cemetery centered on wastefulness and expense.

Cremationists claimed that earth burial and, especially, mausoleum interment, increased social tensions because of the elaborate stratification of plots and memorials. Each time a funeral procession of a wealthy person passed, the poor were forced to "look upon the splendid array of its pomp and ceremony, its waving plumes, its long line of glittering carriages." In contrast to this spectacle was "the poor arrangement of the little funeral train wending its way to the potter's field." Beugless argued that the situation was even worse for those in the "lower middle class" who could ill afford the $250–300 to bury a loved one in a rural cemetery.[54]

Cremationists also drew distinctions between the ostentatious mausoleums of the wealthy and the trench graves of the poor. They noted that mausoleums were being erected at an unprecedented rate, that the rich were buried in mahogany caskets with velvet linings, that huge bouquets of flowers decorated tombs. Cremationists cited examples such as the family mausoleum of Charles T. Yerkes, constructed in Green-Wood in 1891. The 50-foot-long, 23-foot-wide, and 20-foot-high mausoleum was styled after the Parthenon, with gables and a frieze, all in Barre granite. Hand-painted windows focused light onto the central sarcophagi of marble and bronze.[55]

In comparison, the "welfare" graves of Calvary Cemetery in New York City were trenches "dug seven foot wide, ten to twelve feet deep, and of indefinite length; in which coffins are stowed tier by tier . . . with not enough earth to hide one from the next." "And this," Beugless cried, "is our vaunted 'Christian burial' in this new country with its myriads of broad acres."[56]

As time passed and cremationists had greater opportunity to present their case, people began to feel less negative about cremation. LeMoyne had been vilified at his death by the *New York Times,* but within a decade that newspaper editorially supported cremation. Prominent Americans, including sanitarian George E. Waring, Jr., anatomist Joseph Leidy, and surgeon Samuel Gross, endorsed the reform. By 1901 crematories were opened across the nation; private associations had established them in New York City, Pittsburgh, Detroit, San Francisco, and other cities. Only in 1924, in Cleveland, was the nation's first municipally owned and operated crematory and mausoleum established.[57]

CREMATION AND THE CEMETERIES

Most cemetery managers were ambivalent about cremation, although all were concerned with the failure of the survivors of the cremated to memorialize them in stone. Cemetery managers noted early on that over half of those cremated were not buried or remembered in stone, and many advocates of the reform attempted to mollify cemetery managers by suggesting that in the future the public would use columbariums (from the Latin for "dovecotes," a *columbarium* is a vault with niches for urns containing ashes) and even earth burials.

Cemetery managers' worries that people practicing cremation would not use the cemetery led Woodmere in Detroit to prohibit the local cremation society from purchasing land within the cemetery to build a crematory. Cremation eventually became a less volatile issue. Cemetery managers then incorporated the practice into their operations. They recognized that cremation was one more service to offer the customer and that the person choosing cremation might be persuaded to purchase a lot or a niche in a columbarium. Cemeteries thus began to cooperate with local cremation societies in building crematories.

As cemeteries offered land on which to place the crematory or even built them at their own expense, cremationists accepted the combination of the cemetery and crematory. In 1889 the family of Gardner Earl presented Oakwood Cemetery, in Troy, New York, with a large trust fund to build and maintain a crematory in the cemetery.[58] The crematory was an ornate structure with an elaborate stone interior to remind visitors of the difference between the beauty of cremation and the drabness of earth burial.

The integration of private crematory and private cemetery was a unique American pattern. Private associations built the earliest European crematories. After 1900 municipal governments owned and operated most European crematories. Because private cemeteries were almost unknown in Europe, Catholic and Protestant churches remained either opposed to or neutral about cremation, the government was the only possible avenue for the establishment of new crematories.

Cremation was available throughout most of western Europe, but only France had more cremations than America in 1900. In Italy, as in France, the anticlerical movement fostered cremation as part of a larger attack on the Catholic church's influence on society. Italy had more crematories than America, but only about 10 percent of its number of cremations. Italy, Germany, England, Sweden, Switzerland, and Denmark combined had two-thirds as many cremations as America, which had about 40 percent as many as France.[59]

The placement of the crematory in the American cemetery was not as contradictory as it might appear at first. Cremationists believed that their supporters wanted to continue to memorialize their dead and that total abandonment of centuries-long customs was impossible. Cremationists believed that the introduction of the crematory into the cemetery symbolized the first of several changes that would eventually rid the cemetery of its health hazards and produce a true memorial park.

James Scorgie, superintendent of Forest Home Cemetery in Milwaukee, who was an advocate of crematories in cemeteries, argued that "the original

Gardner Earl Memorial Chapel and Crematorium, Oakwood Cemetery,
Troy, N.Y., 1902

America's first crematories were private associations rarely associated with cemeteries. By the 1890s, cemetery managers began to incorporate cremation into their growing number of services. The reception room of Oakwood's very ornate crematory had walls of black Siena marble, as well as wainscoting and arches of pink African marble. The crematory was elaborate enough to dissuade anyone who believed that cremation advocates cared little about memorialization. (Frederick S. Hills, comp., *The Gardner Earl Memorial Chapel and Crematorium, Oakwood Cemetery, Troy, N.Y.,* 1902. Courtesy of Oakwood Cemetery.)

function of cemeteries will, in course of time, become obsolete, but in my opinion only in part." Scorgie felt that it was "inconceivable that the cemetery should be utterly abolished." The cemetery would remain "a beautiful place of retreat for meditation and consolation, a place sacred to memory, a place of peculiar historical interest, to be enjoyed by generation after generation for ages to come."[60]

THE NEW PUBLIC-HEALTH MOVEMENT AND CREMATION

Curiously, cremation gained acceptance as the medical justification diminished. Because of the public's acceptance of the bacterial theory for the causation of disease transmission, cremationists were unable to sustain their original medical arguments for cremation. New evidence on the transmission of disease systematically undermined the equation of filth and disease, which had been the basis of the cremation argument. Dramatically, the experiments of Juan Carlos Findlay and Walter Reed in Cuba disproved the theories of sanitarians such as George Waring by showing that a clean city could still have a high incidence of yellow fever. The research proving that the anopheline mosquito carried malaria effectively demonstrated that germ theory was a powerful tool in identifying and combating diseases.[61]

By 1900 the medical profession, particularly a new generation of public-health specialists, was reassessing the general importance of sanitary reforms. Charles V. Chapin and other leaders, in their enthusiasm for the new understanding of contagion, scathingly attacked the believers in the relationship of dirt and disease, as well as the reform movements that had grown out of their beliefs. Concerning health restrictions on mourners attending funerals of individuals who had died of infectious disease, Chapin said that "much greater liberality in the regulation of funerals could safely be permitted . . . and it would teach people that the danger is from the quick and not from the dead."[62] The public-health movement gradually turned away from sanitary concerns and focused on preventive-health programs.

Cremationists resisted this trend. The two most notable physician advocates of cremation after the turn of the century were Dr. Hugo Erichsen and Dr. S. Adolphus Knopf.[63] Knopf, in his 1907 article "A Plea for Cremation in Tuberculosis and Similarly Infectious Diseases," argued that though he had "no evidence that any harm has ever been done by the emanation of obnoxious gases arising from putrefaction, . . . minor disease such as diarrhea and simple dysentery seem . . . to be produced by the suspension in water of earthy and animal organic matter." Knopf warned that decaying corpses buried in the earth held the seeds of disease.

Erichsen, who had his mother cremated in 1885, had long been a leading spokesman for the reform. He was a leader in organizing the Cremation Association of America (which later became the Cremation Association of North America [CANA]), and he used his position as president of the new organization from 1913 to 1916 to convince cemetery managers and the public of the rightness of cremation. He also led the way in collecting a special cremation archive of over eight hundred books, articles, and pamphlets, which was placed at the John Crearer Library in Chicago.

Erichsen and Knopf, as well as other leaders of the cremation movement, recognized that the sanitary argument could not continue to be the central rationale for people to choose cremation. Although they continued to suggest that earth burial was unhealthy and that cemeteries in densely inhabited areas were a mistake, they increasingly focused on the economic differences between the types of disposal. Knopf's 1912 article in the *Journal of the American Medical Association* discussed not only the sanitary advantages of cremation but also the economic ones. Knopf particularly hoped that cremation would be used by "people in moderate means or the really poor."

Soon the cremation movement began shedding its radical image and became less associated with social reform. Although the Catholic church and several other religious groups remained adamantly opposed to cremation, a slowly rising number of Americans chose it. Quincy Dowd reported in 1921 that there were seventy-four crematories in America and that between 1914 and 1918 they had cremated over fifty thousand bodies. Eighteen (almost one-quarter) of the seventy-four crematories were located in California, where the process was becoming most popular. Although it remained a minuscule percentage of the total number of disposals, cremation was gaining acceptance.[64]

John Gebhart's 1921 study of funeral costs, and other analyses of the expensive nature of funerals, mourning rites, and cemetery lots showed that some people, especially the poor, were being left destitute by the cost of burying their dead.[65] Reformers considered cremation, which simplified disposal and left little need for large lots or expensive stones, a possible answer to these expenses. However, the reformers were trying to convince groups most committed to the elaborate funeral.

THE CREMATIONISTS' IMPACT

Using both the early arguments about sanitary advantages and the later economic rationale, cremationists reinforced contemporary criticism of American methods of disposal. The reformers, with their lurid descriptions of the perils posed by the cemetery, undermined the public's faith in it. Cremationists argued that the cemetery, instead of fulfilling the antebellum image of a tranquil, meditative place of repose, was a place of corruption and disease. Cemeteries were "peopleless streets, with coldness and darkness and silent cells, with still inhabitants, and an atmosphere which is the breath of pestilence." The cemetery, which to the last generation had seemed a place of escape, now became a concern to the public.[66]

Cremationists also criticized the cemetery as a waste of space and, even worse, an antidemocratic institution within a republican society. Cremationists were the first group to view the cemetery as a purely wasteful expenditure. The land was unproductive, the monuments were overpriced, the funerals were a drain on life insurance. The whole process was an extravagance whose purpose seemed the glorification of wealth and status in America. The result, LeMoyne warned, was a "custom, the . . . results of which are the division of society into castes or classes."[67]

LeMoyne said that cremation brings "rich and poor to a level in their last homes, [where] the common brotherhood of man may be practically demonstrated, thus avoiding the heartburning and jealousies which the present system entails." The cemetery failed to alleviate the hostilities building between rich and poor in the industrialized and urbanized society of the late nineteenth century. Cremation offered one method of replacing the growing class distinctions with a more democratic vision of the future.

Finally, cremationists argued that the period's burial customs focused attention not on the spiritual future but on the corporeal past. Felix Adler, questioning the appropriateness of prevailing customs, said that "death should be robbed of the blackness, the gloom, with which it is now invested. The only thing of the dead which deserves to be preserved is the heart's affection." The body was too lovingly cared for by the funeral director, the casket too richly ornamented, and the perpetual guardian, the cemetery superintendent, too vigilant. "I want cleanness in death as I do in life," Adler demanded, "I want to get rid of this corruption."[68]

THE TRANSFORMATION OF AMERICAN BURIAL PLACES AND CUSTOMS

In the last half of the nineteenth century, managers and entrepreneurs transformed the cemetery into a business. They simplified the landscape, improved the efficiency of the operation, and elevated the superintendent—all in defense of an increasingly isolated institution. By 1900 the cemetery co-existed with a new set of professionals involved with the dying and the dead. Death was likely to occur in a hospital while a nurse watched and a physician consulted. The funeral director had become the overseer of the funeral process, informing the family of proper and necessary activities and mediating between the family, the hospital, and the cemetery. Throughout the transformation, mourners desired a place of memories where they could meditate on the past.

Cremationists rejected such a view of burial and wished to simplify the entire burial process. They wanted to eliminate the sentimental atmosphere that they felt clouded people's understanding of the impact of the decaying dead on the health of society. Cremationists also wished to limit burial costs, which they believed were based on vanity and guilt rather than on sanctity and honor. Confronted with such views, cemetery managers once again redesigned the cemetery so that people could continue to seek solace on its grounds.

Isolating Death,
1917–1949

In the first half of the twentieth century, Americans became more isolated from death. Medicine offered new, improved treatments and cures for many illnesses that had been fatal a half-century earlier. Cures became available for infectious diseases that had traumatized generations of city-dwellers. The hospital became the primary place for treating the seriously ill. The dead were increasing cared for by professionals who cleaned, preserved, attired, and buried them.

The full development of these trends coincided with the development of the memorial park in America. In 1913 Hubert Eaton arrived in Los Angeles as the new manager of a failed cemetery in a failed suburban development. By 1917 Forest Lawn Memorial-Park emerged as a multiservice business with a redesigned landscape. Within a decade, it was a model for new burial places throughout America.

The central characteristics of the new memorial parks were their familiarity, accessibility, and return to a value-laden atmosphere. The memorial-park movement swept through America in the 1920s and 1930s because it allowed the cemetery to reemerge as a home for art and a repository of American culture and religion. Lot-holders were invited to bury their dead and leave the care and beautification of the burial place to management.

While Americans flocked to buy graves in the new memorial parks, commentators continued to worry about the commercialization of the cemetery. Some commentators believed that modern cemeteries, especially memorial parks, dishonored the sacred nature of the grave. Lots were advertised for sale on the radio and in the press. Forest Lawn was promoted as offering customers all the services necessary for a funeral. After two decades of mounting public criticism of the practices, the attorney general of New York State initiated a campaign to stop cemetery managers from "profiteering from sorrow." The result was the cemetery in crisis.

CHAPTER SEVEN

The Ideal Cemetery: The Memorial Park

FOREST LAWN MEMORIAL-PARK

Beginning in 1913, in Glendale, California, Hubert Eaton restructured the American cemetery. His new memorial park drew upon the experiences of cemetery operators and real-estate developers, as well as on the culture of southern California. Eaton removed most traces of death from the landscape, improved the business operations of the cemetery, and offered lot-holders a safe, secure burial place. He eliminated the family monument, restructured the grounds to expand the lawn, and established a suburbanlike pastoral environment. Eaton streamlined the process of burial by joining the functions of the funeral director, cemetery, and monument dealer within the memorial park. The memorial park became a modern, multifaceted business, which offered a wide variety of services to its customers.[1]

Forest Lawn made startling gains after Eaton's assumption of the general manager's position. In 1917 Eaton began offering financial incentives to lot-holders who agreed to use flush markers. His aggressive sales program was intended to encourage preneed purchases, and in 1918 sales escalated 250 percent. In the 1920s he built the nation's largest mausoleum, modeled after the Campo Santo in Pisa, and installed a large collection of statuary within it. By 1929 Forest Lawn had expanded to 200 acres, had had over 28,000 interments, averaged over $1 million a year in sales, and had assets of $10 million. Each year four hundred employees orchestrated thirty-six hundred interments and nine-hundred weddings and had a half-million visitors. In the 1930s Eaton opened the Forest Lawn Mortuary and Crematory, sold life insurance, and began his collection of large artworks with a stained-glass copy of Leonardo da Vinci's *The Last Supper*.[2]

Forest Lawn captured the attention of the nation unlike any cemetery since Mount Auburn. Other cemetery managers and operators flocked to the new memorial park to view Eaton's methods, see the landscape, and gape at the attractions. Some commentators wrote of Forest Lawn as part of a California culture that was spreading throughout the nation. Others caustically criticized

Forest Lawn as an aberration and extravagance inappropriate to America and insulting to correct sentiment toward the dead.[3]

In the most sincere flattery, imitations of Forest Lawn began to appear immediately in California, then elsewhere on the West Coast and throughout the nation. By 1935 there were over six hundred memorial parks in America. According to the American Cemetery Owners Association (ACOA), Americans purchased $400 million dollars' worth of lots and crypts in memorial parks from 1925 to 1935. Further developments, the ACOA informed the National Recovery Administration in 1934, would lead to expenditures of another $100 million in the next three years. And ACOA President W. L. Halberstadt stated that "the Memorial Park business as yet . . . is only in its infancy."[4]

Forest Lawn's attraction derived from the public's fascination with the new atmosphere that Eaton insisted upon within the memorial park, the artworks that ornamented the grounds, and the open commercialism of the enterprise. Americans were drawn by Eaton's revision of the cemetery and titillated by the mixture of sacred and profane embodied in the land's organization. The memorial park offended so many with its commercialism that many commentators were unable to see that Forest Lawn was actually a conservative American business, in reaction to modernism.

ANTECEDENTS TO THE MEMORIAL PARK

The idea of the memorial park grew out of three factors. First, cemetery operators were discontented with contemporary monument styles and fascinated with the pastoral naturalism of urban parks. Second, American real-estate and insurance industries had developed sales and advertising techniques that Eaton thought were applicable to cemetery lots. Third, Los Angeles provided a unique location to experiment with a new form for the cemetery. Each of these factors influenced the organization and appearance of the memorial park.

Each factor also reflected changes in the broader American culture. The American cemetery, even the new memorial park, was no longer setting trends, but reacting to them. The rejection of Victorian-style monuments, the move away from genteel public relations, and the popularity of another aspect of California culture all represented social influences on the burial place.

The Ideal Cemetery: The Memorial Park. In 1915 J. J. Gordon wrote in the *Cemetery Beautiful* of "The Ideal Cemetery—Memorial Park." His ideal design included a five-acre central park and an ornamental entrance, neither of which had visible monuments or markers. Gordon reminded his readers of the response of Americans to most memorials: "Few but have felt the chill that strikes the heart when standing in the office of some cemetery, even the most beautiful, and seeing the gleaming monuments, silent reminders of the shortness of life. [In the central memorial park] there is no note of sadness. The flowers fling their fragrance far and wide, the fountains tinkle merrily and it is a beautiful park and the onlooker enjoys it."[5]

Gordon's central park section, without monuments and with natural and artistic features, was reminiscent of Samuel Parsons, Jr.'s pioneering design for Pinelawn Cemetery. A section without monuments and with restrictions on plantings remained what the designers planned and the managers desired. Maintenance was easier, the appearance was simpler and cleaner, and the clutter of the graveyard was eliminated. The idea was so appealing that cemetery managers in the Midwest began plotting monument-free sections within their cemeteries, providing lot-holders with a choice between the old and new.

The new designs responded to charges of ostentatiousness and extravagance. The monument-free sections were egalitarian. Rich and poor could have a lot that was not overshadowed by a neighboring obelisk or mausoleum. Simple markers of granite or bronze set at ground level identified the graves. The simpler markers were private family reminders of life rather than public statements.

Gordon's comment about the "silent reminders of the shortness of life" evoking an unwanted sadness also suggested the superintendents' indecision about the purpose and atmosphere of their institutions. Superintendents wanted cemeteries to be places of celebration and joy, but the monuments evoked death. They found it more difficult to believe in the older vision of the cemetery. Superintendents, along with their customers, wanted a new cemetery that could truly be without gloom.

The designs were limited only by the designer's and manager's vision of a cemetery's appearance. Most promoters of lawn-park cemeteries retained some form of the monument. The natural landscape had gradually become a passive backdrop for lot-holders' ideas of artistic (sometimes garish) personal statements in stone. As much as superintendents defended the pristine natural setting, they still allowed survivors to honor the dead and to "do what is right." While the monument restricted the management's ability to shape and then maintain the environment of the cemetery, the monument also marked the cemetery as a sacred space different in atmosphere from the recreational park. Before Eaton's innovations, commentators, managers, and superintendents could not imagine the public accepting a cemetery without monuments.

The Grave as Real Estate. Significantly, Forest Lawn was formed as the last resort of a failed suburban developer who had first tried to establish a more traditional cemetery. Furthermore, many cemetery operators and sales personnel had real-estate experience. The new memorial park reflected the growing power of real-estate subdividers, called "community builders" by Marc Weiss.[6] The methods of early twentieth-century community builders described by Weiss coincided remarkably with the attitudes and actions of Eaton and the memorial-park operators:

—Subdividers took "very large tracts of land and slowly improved them, section by section, for lot sales and home construction." The new memorial parks were developed section by section, using preneed lot sales to offset development costs.

—"Strict long-term deed restrictions were imposed on all lot and home purchasers for lot coverage and building size, minimum housing standards and construction costs, non-Caucasian racial exclusion, and other features." Cemetery lot-holders were carefully restricted as to the size, location, planting, and memorialization allowed. Most American memorial parks included racial-exclusion clauses in their deeds.

—"Extensive landscaping and tree planting were emphasized to accentuate the natural topography and beauty." The memorial park assumed responsibility for ensuring that the grounds were accessible and attractive. The memorial-park administration worked to improve the landscape with trees, shrubs, flower beds, and other attractions. Because the designers had to work with suburban farmland that was usually flat or gently rolling, they were rarely able to create the picturesque visual effects of rural cemeteries.

—"Public thoroughfares included curved streets, cul-de-sacs, and wide boulevards and parkways." Whereas rural cemeteries had intricate road and path systems and lawn-park cemeteries had sweeping drives, memorial parks often had a central boulevard off which short, circular drives extended. Transportation designs were simpler, allowing more intensive use of the land and easier access and greater familiarity by the public.

—"Often special areas were set aside for . . . office buildings, . . . parks and recreation facilities, churches, and schools." Memorial-park operators continued the practice of placing the office at the entrance to facilitate helping visitors who sought information and assistance. Areas were also retained for greenhouses, maintenance buildings, and natural features and artificial features, such as lakes. As in the older cemeteries, the chapel played a significant role as a place where families could hold services and mourn their dead. Several places within the memorial parks were considered public areas, where visitors could view the grounds.

—"Private utilities and public improvements were coordinated as much as possible with present and future plans for subdivision development and expansion." The memorial park was a planned landscape. Unlike earlier cemeteries in which the individual lot-holder played a large role in developing the appearance of the grounds, the memorial park offered lot-holders a choice of sections, each with a separate theme. The memorial park dictated the theme, as well as what was planted or placed on the lot. As individual sections were sold, new ones were designed, each theme carefully considered for its inclusiveness and appropriateness.

Many planned suburbs became merely cluttered subdivisions without charm or grace. Likewise, many memorial parks substituted plaster casts for planned marble statues, never constructed promised chapels, and did not maintain undeveloped, or even some developed, sections. Other memorial parks were creatively constructed and immaculately maintained, but their entrepreneurial quality made them vulnerable to abuse.

Forest Lawn as a Product of Los Angeles. Eaton, like so many Americans who moved to Los Angeles in the early twentieth century, was born in the Midwest. Born in Liberty, Missouri, Eaton, as well as thousands of Midwesterners, came to southern California with hopes for greater opportunity. As Robert Folgelson has pointed out, many migrants at this time were not poor, unemployed, and socially dislocated.[7] They came looking for a golden city with ideal weather and continued economic opportunity. It was a migration of native-born Americans searching for a new life.

And did they come! Between 1880 and 1930, greater Los Angeles grew by over 2 million people. The suburbs that have become Hollywood and television clichés, such as Van Nuys, Beverly Hills, Pasadena, Santa Monica, and Hollywood itself, grew from nothing into crowded communities. The migration was made possible by new water sources, an improved street railway system, and constant promotion. Los Angeles was a city defining itself to the world.[8]

The Los Angeles that appeared after the massive influx was a singularly different city than those of the East Coast. It was a city of single-home dwellings spread over one thousand square miles of plains, hills, and canyons. In 1930 approximately half of the families in New York City, Boston, and Chicago owned a single-family dwelling; over 90 percent of families in Los Angeles owned one. Only Philadelphia, with its long heritage of single-family row houses, had a percentage almost equal to that of Los Angeles.

In Philadelphia people crowded together in the central city, with a population per square mile of over fifteen thousand. In Los Angeles there was not crowding on that scale. Inside the central city, the population per square mile was under three thousand, whereas outside the central city, it was a little over one thousand. The city came close to William Symthe's 1910 wish that cities should "spread until they meet the country, and until beautiful forms of urban life blend almost imperceptibly into beautiful forms of rural life." Reminiscent of nineteenth-century hopes of bringing the country back into the city, the idea was to break down the distinction between city and country entirely by extending suburbia.[9]

A part of the physical expansion of Los Angeles after 1910 was the rapid ascendance of the automobile as a practical competitor to the street railway system. Los Angeles had over one hundred thousand cars by 1920, and another seven hundred thousand by 1930. The street railway system, one of the nation's best, had been critical in the development of the suburbs, but eventually the highway system was given priority by city planners.[10]

By the 1920s, Los Angeles was a special kind of boom town. Filled with transplanted Americans committed to developing and defending their vision of the American dream, Los Angeles was a perfect spot for a new burial place that reflected their needs and dreams.

THE IDEOLOGY OF FOREST LAWN

In the years after he assumed control of Forest Lawn and turned it into the nation's first memorial park, Eaton gradually enunciated his vision. This vision was a remarkable combination of gladsome religion, commercialism, conservative American values, and avoidance of reminders of death. These components of the vision infused the landscape and the policies of Forest Lawn and influenced the memorial parks that imitated Eaton's creation. The ideology of Eaton, like that of Mount Auburn's founders a century before, recognized cultural changes in American society and provided Americans with a more comfortable and acceptable burial place.

In establishing Forest Lawn, Eaton reaffirmed the Protestant Victorian American culture threatened in the early twentieth century by modernism. Daniel Bell has written that, during the first half of the twentieth century, there were American modernists, but not a modernist culture.[11] Modernism influenced American attitudes toward death and burial, but it was more successful initially in creating a reaction than in gaining adherents. Americans flocked to racially segregated memorial parks filled with academic sculpture and explicitly expressed moral values. Few chose cremation, which was associated with a rejection of religion and morality, with science and technology, and with modern rationalism of death. Only after the midcentury were Americans willing to integrate the lessons of modernist art and thought into their burial practices. Even then, Americans were slow to acknowledge the strength of modernist art in expressing the sentiments they associated with the grave.

Instead, Americans praised the establishment of a memorial park that looked both forward and backward. Eaton never stopped proclaiming the newness of Forest Lawn while evoking traditional values. Thus, patriotism and faith, integral components of rural cemeteries, were celebrated and honored in a manner that stripped them of the melancholy of antebellum America. They were presented in a manner that suggested a new vision, a renewed belief.

The basis of Eaton's creation of Forest Lawn was his belief in two concepts of immortality.[12] In designing a burial place for the middle class, Eaton recognized, first, that the acceptance of eternal life was a given in the private and public culture of America, and, second, that individuals memorialized themselves in order to perpetuate their own memory. Eaton strongly believed that the individual was granted immortality by accepting Christ. Death rendered the body inanimate, but the spirit continued for eternity.

Eaton's view of Christian immortality led him to reject the solemn and somber Victorian trappings of death. Forest Lawn evoked the joy that Eaton felt was appropriate to the death of the body and the immortality of the soul.

Bertel Thorvaldsen's Christus, *Forest Lawn Memorial-Park, Glendale, Calif., c. 1980*

This statue, which is a copy of Thorvaldsen's 1821 original (which is in the Church of Our Lady in Copenhagen), is the centerpiece of one of the many burial gardens at Forest Lawn. Typical of the realistic statuary that dots its sections, *Christus* represented Hubert Eaton's attempt to reassert the importance of religious symbolism in Protestant American cemeteries. ("Facts about Funerals," Forest Lawn Mortuary brochure, 1980. Courtesy of Forest Lawn Memorial-Park.)

Indeed, Eaton sought artwork of the smiling Christ, believing that the Son of God could not have been the joyless person so often portrayed in paintings and stories. Although Eaton never found an artwork that satisfied him, much of the art he bought for Forest Lawn conveyed this sense of the rebirth, the glad moments, and the joy of life.

In this search for a joyful Christ, Eaton represented the spirit of the 1920s. Bruce Barton, a successful advertising salesman, wrote an article in 1937 praising Eaton and Forest Lawn. Twelve years earlier, Barton published his influential book *The Man Nobody Knows: A Discovery of the Real Jesus,* which portrayed Jesus as a successful organizer and business leader. Both Barton and Eaton wished to bring Christianity back into the daily lives of people by breaking the shell of invincibility around Jesus. Both felt that in the nineteenth century Jesus had been "feminized" and weakened as a role model for modern society, especially for businessmen. Eaton's memorial park reinforced ideas of Christian sociability by bringing together marriage and death in the same chapel.[13]

Eaton believed that people desired exemption from oblivion through memorialization. People wanted to live on in the memory of those living after them, and this longing prompted the worthiest efforts of the living. This was what Eaton named the "Memorial Impulse" in his book, *The Comemoral: The*

Cemetery of the Future. The Memorial Impulse was the basis for most of the good in society. The "father of art and architecture," the Memorial Impulse had "nourished literature, music, sculpture and painting."[14] It had also influenced the creation of many churches, cathedrals, libraries, parks, colleges, hospitals, orphanages, and museums.

The Memorial Impulse was so important because it drove people to preserve and to create so that their lives would be remembered in the future. Indeed, Eaton believed that most of what we know of the past is derived from the desire of people to be remembered. This is certainly true of the Taj Mahal, the Pyramids, the Parthenon, Westminster Abbey, the Roman catacombs. Eaton argued that 75 percent of the buildings that tourists traveled to see were memorials.[15] The Memorial Impulse could be satisfied through good deeds, but a beautiful memorial was the lasting comfort and shrine to which the living could go to commune with the past and return to society as better citizens.

The primary place for such memorials was the memorial park. Eaton preferred the term *memorial* to those of *monument* and *marker* because the former distinguished his new venture from the morbid, sentimental past. Eaton believed that many salespeople who should have been prompting customers to view their choice of memorial as a statement for the future were unfortunately allowing customers to select stock monuments that offered little aesthetic grandeur to the burial place and nothing to the Memorial Impulse. Salespeople of monuments and markers needed to think beyond the single sale to "the spiritual concepts involved in their work."[16] If the salespeople understood the Memorial Impulse, explained it to the customer, and offered the customer a wide selection of options, the customer would get a better product, the salesperson would earn a better commission, and the memorial park would receive a more pleasant appearance.

FOREST LAWN'S LANDSCAPE

Four characteristics formed the basis for the memorial park's landscape design:

1. Professional management was essential to control the appearance of the landscape and to insure its unity.
2. Nature acted as a passive backdrop to artistic memorials.
3. Memorials emphasized the community of the dead instead of the individual and the family.
4. Memorials were designed to evoke the values of a joyful religion and a united and patriotic community.

Eaton's major contributions to the design history of the American memorial park were his insistence on management's control over every aspect of the burial place and his reappraisal of the memorial park as a sacred recreation space. In a remarkable 1917 statement of the institution's goals, "The Builder's Creed," Eaton enunciated his hopes for the new memorial park:

> I believe in a happy Eternal Life. I believe those of us left behind should be glad in the certain belief that those gone before have entered into that happier Life. I believe, most of all, in a Christ that smiles and loves you and me. I therefore know the cemeteries of today are wrong because they depict an end, not a beginning. They have consequently become unsightly stoneyards, full of inartistic symbols and depressing customs; places that do nothing for humanity save a practical act, and that not well.
>
> I therefore prayerfully resolve on this New Year's Day, 1917, that I shall endeavor to build Forest Lawn as different, as unlike other cemeteries as sunshine is unlike darkness, as Eternal Life is unlike Death. I shall try to build at Forest Lawn a great park, devoid of mis-shapen monuments and other customary signs of earthly Death, but filled with towering trees, sweeping lawns, splashing fountains, singing birds, beautiful statuary, cheerful flowers; noble memorial architecture, with interiors of light and color, and redolent of the world's best history and romances. I believe these things educate and uplift a community.
>
> Forest Lawn shall become a place where lovers new and old shall love to stroll and watch the sunset's glow, planning for the future or reminiscing of the past; a place where artists study and sketch; where school teachers bring happy children to see things they read of in books; where little churches invite, triumphant in the knowledge that from their pulpits only words of Love can be spoken; where memorialization of loved ones in sculptured glass shall be encouraged but controlled by acknowledged artists; a place where the sorrowing will be soothed and strengthened because it will be God's garden. A place that shall be protected by an immense Perpetual Care Fund, the principal of which can never be expended—only the income therefrom used to care for and perpetuate this Garden of Memory.[17]

Eaton took Strauch's "correct taste" to its logical conclusion. He instituted strict rules and regulations that simplified the burial process. Rules prescribed that individual and family memorials must be flush to the ground. The only exception was art inscribed with a family name and approved by the memorial park. The flush markers that identified each grave had to be bronze because they were "more lasting and more artistic." Artificial flowers, popular with lot-holders who did not visit their lots often, were prohibited. Forest Lawn made every effort to eliminate the knickknacks that accumulated on many graves. The memorial park also did all the planting. The landscape was simplified by limiting access to a few spacious (wide enough for automobiles), well-maintained roads.

Many of these rules were not new ideas. Strauch had fought and won power over lot-holders' choice in monuments in the 1850s, late-nineteenth-century managers had advocated that markers be flush or at least close to the ground, most cemetery managers disliked artificial flowers, and many cemeteries planted shrubs, flowers, and trees. The difference was that Eaton combined these ideas within a single burial place, explicitly announcing a new style of cemetery. He stated: "Too many cemeteries do little more than perform the utilitarian function of interment. The resting places of our dead are shrines we visit constantly." The memorial park would be more spacious and accessible, as well as less mysterious and demanding.[18]

Eaton attempted to bring back to the cemetery the vigor of the antebellum period. After the Civil War, recreation places, such as urban parks and amusement parks, diverted people from visiting cemeteries. The burial place returned to its status as a sacred spot outside the daily concourse of the public. People continued to walk through the valleys of the rural cemeteries or to take the train out to Kensico and other suburban cemeteries, but cemetery attendance and public attention to cemeteries was reduced by the end of the century. Guidebooks gave cemeteries less notice, and the public hesitated to enter them.

Eaton's new memorial park was designed to lure back the public. The landscape was accessible, the landmarks were familiar, the scenery was interesting, and the sights were exotic. Eaton balanced a sense of respect for the dead with a public celebration of his Forest Lawn. He continued the long practice of prohibiting picnics, limiting visiting hours, banning smoking and bicycles (and later motorcycles), and warning against vandalism and theft. Yet he established a museum and various sights to attract visitors and went to great lengths to spread knowledge about Forest Lawn. The memorial park was both a private sacred place for burials and a public recreation space intended for the education and enjoyment of the visitors.

Symbols of death were less visible in the memorial park than in any previous burial place. Although there were between thirty and forty funerals each day at Forest Lawn, visitors did not leave the grounds with the mental image of a funeral. The emphasis was on life in the landscape.

The main road began at the cast-iron gates and wound gently around the old monumented sections that preceded Eaton's alterations, around the Great Mausoleum, and upward through rolling hills of green grass dotted sporadically with academic-style white marble sculptures. The road ended at the summit of Forest Lawn, where visitors could look out over the memorial park and Glendale, much as the mount in Cambridge's Sweet Auburn provided views of Boston. The serpentine road system was reminiscent of the tours laid out and specifically marked in the rural cemeteries for the carriage trade of old. The roadways here differed in that they did not have the intricate pathways and secondary roads typical of Albany Rural and Green-Wood. All that was left was the tour.

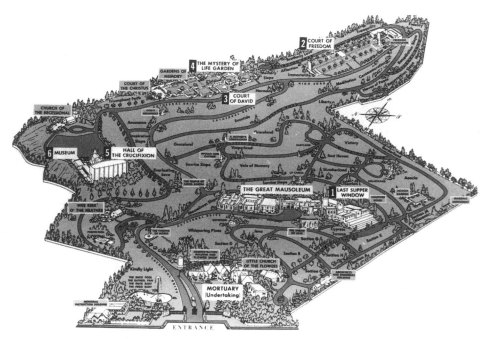

Pictorial Map of Forest Lawn Memorial-Park,
Glendale, Calif., c. 1961

Forest Lawn catered to the casual visitor more than any American burial ground since the advent of the rural-cemetery movement in the 1830s. The memorial park tried to make the visitor's experience as enjoyable as possible, hoping that it would result in a later purchase of services. The white road leading from the entrance was the memorial park's equivalent of the rural cemetery's tour. By following this road for approximately two hours, a visitor could see all of Forest Lawn's treasures. ("The Treasures of Forest Lawn," Forest Lawn Memorial-Park brochure, 1961. Courtesy of Forest Lawn Memorial-Park.)

The Great Mausoleum was a highlight of the tour. It was built in the 1920s to serve those who wanted crypt burial. The Great Mausoleum was a larger, more elaborate version of the nineteenth-century community mausoleum. Forest Lawn ornamented the building with some of its finest statuary, including copies of *The Pietà* and other Michelangelo statues. Eaton charged admission to visitors to see a stained-glass version of *The Last Supper* in the Great Mausoleum. By 1929 the gross sales of vaults in the Great Mausoleum were $3 million.[19]

The burial sections were a mixture of green and white. The carefully maintained lawns, sporadically interrupted by shrubs and trees, swept up the hill. Families were encouraged to purchase a piece of statuary from Forest Lawn's collection to place on their lots. Most sculptures depicted religious figures, such as the Virgin Mary and the Baby Jesus. Eaton believed that the statuary would help to restore the burial place's nineteenth-century role as a repository of American art and aesthetics. The statuary was almost all of white marble; this was a decided change from the preceding generation's preference for granite. Eaton's collection of classical and classically influenced marble sculptures became a symbol of Forest Lawn.

Eaton developed burial sections in which thematic courts depicted religious and patriotic values. Graves clustered around a single sculpture, such as *David*, an exact replica of Michelangelo's statue of the shepherd boy, and a copy of Bertel Thorvaldsen's *The Christus*. Later, Eaton created larger theme courts featuring two or three pieces of art together. The most visually compelling of the courts was the Court of Freedom, with the original statues *Republic* by Daniel Chester French and *George Washington* by John Quincy Adams Ward. These pieces were examples of Eaton's Memorial Impulse. They were offered as a way of joining a private burial with a majestic theme, linking a simple life with a national grandeur.[20]

The statuary gardens were surrounded by sections of lawn where graves were marked only with bronze markers that were flush to the ground. These sections were called Kindly Light, Whispering Pines, Graceland, Eventide, Sunrise Slope, and by similar names suggesting places of light and celebration. The plantings here were limited to ornamental and shade trees placed around the section, as well as a few shrubs surrounding the statuary in the section. Eaton insisted that the trees be evergreens because the loss of leaves reminded visitors of death.[21] The tree-lined avenues provided most of the shade in the memorial park, which was landscaped to emphasize the expanse of lawn and the artistic achievements represented in the individual statuary and in the thematic gardens.

Forest Lawn began to offer the option of locked wall courtyards in the 1930s; the first of these was Acadia Garden. The Gardens of Memory, developed beginning in the 1940s, opened only to a lot-holder's key. The privacy of the gardens appealed to a variety of people, including Humphrey Bogart and other Hollywood stars.[22]

Forest Lawn's managers had a twentieth-century outlook in the manner they presented the memorial park to the public. The new burial place was both a private and a public place. Flush markers were a private manner in which to designate a grave, yet they were set amid gleaming statuary intended to draw crowds of visitors. Private gardens were constructed to keep out intruders, but were promoted and advertised so that visitors could imagine standing in front of Bogart's plaque. The Great Mausoleum offered private vaults, but along long corridors open to the public and amid a plethora of statuary placed to draw visitors. The management promoted a solemn privacy for lot-holders alongside a museum, scheduled tours of artworks for a fee, and bus tours. Forest Lawn introduced a new privacy and created a public spectacle.

In some ways, Forest Lawn was reminiscent of rural cemeteries. As early as the 1920s, thousands of visitors passed through its gates annually. Forest Lawn anticipated and prepared for the public. Eaton proclaimed that he "planned to eradicate gloom and depression" by "substituting cheer, bright colors, depicting galleries of art rather than halls of death."[23] His vision of a cheerful burial place was different from those of Jacob Bigelow, John Jay Smith, or Elias W. Leavenworth, but these founders of the rural cemetery were similarly interested in creating a cemetery of hope and light.

The major difference between Forest Lawn and the rural cemeteries was that the former placed greater restrictions upon lot-holders and allotted management greater freedom. Smaller monuments, such as those that lined the streets of the rural cemeteries, were not welcomed. The new landscape was a realization of management's vision of the most attractive, inviting, and comforting—while least offensive—lawn-park landscape.

MEMORIAL-PARK ART

After World War I, Eaton scoured Europe for sculpture appropriate for Forest Lawn. As his sales revenues allowed, he constructed replicas of notable European chapels. The first was the Little Church of the Flowers. This exact duplicate of the village chapel at Stoke Poges, where Gray had written "Elegy in a Country Churchyard," was intended as an ornament within the landscape and a place for funerals. Eaton did not imagine that a couple would approach the managers for approval to be married in the church, but he certainly knew to capitalize on such a request. The couple made this request in 1923, and, within six years, the memorial park had been the site of twelve hundred weddings.[24]

The Little Church of the Flowers reflected Eaton's beliefs about the type of art that was appropriate for a memorial park. In 1913, the year Eaton moved from Missouri to Los Angeles, the Armory Exhibition in New York City revolutionized the American art scene. European modern art, which had been ignored in America for decades, suddenly was a topic of popular discussion. Many viewers believed that Picasso and other cubists exhibited the most startling paintings in the exhibition, but even the impressionists and their followers shocked Americans used to the realist and academic paintings of the late nineteenth century.[25]

The modernist movement had no place in Forest Lawn. Just as modernists rejected cemetery art in their exhibitions, Eaton considered modern art unworthy of the Memorial Impulse. In the 1950s, memorial-park designer George McClure said that "the cemetery is no place for experimentalization in the use of art objects." Although Eaton wished the memorial park to appear dramatically different from older cemeteries, he purposely chose academic art because that represented art to the middle class. He wanted art that would "reinforce rather than challenge the social traditions from which they originated." The works of Augustus St. Gaudens, Daniel Chester French, and Frederic Remington were well represented among the sculptures of Forest Lawn.[26]

Eaton juxtaposed the works of the academicians with those of the ancients. In his trips abroad, Eaton focused on buying copies of Renaissance and ancient

The Court of David, Forest Lawn Memorial-Park, Glendale, California

Reproduction of Michelangelo's David, *Forest Lawn Memorial-Park, Glendale, Calif., c. 1961*

Hubert Eaton felt that Michelangelo was history's finest artist, the ultimate conveyor of the Memorial Impulse. Eaton gathered together at Forest Lawn reproductions of the artist's greatest sculptures. *David* stands at the memorial park's summit, surrounded by shrubs concealing speakers, from which choral music emanates. *David* originally wore a fig leaf, but the management removed it in the 1970s. (Cover of "Forest Lawn Serves the Living," Forest Lawn Memorial-Park brochure, 1961. Courtesy of Forest Lawn Memorial-Park.)

art. He particularly loved Michelangelo and gathered copies of his greatest sculptures at Forest Lawn. Eaton believed that these sculptures represented the highest expression of the Memorial Impulse. They spoke eloquently to all who flocked to the memorial park, and they held no threat to lot-holders who were unfamiliar and uncomfortable with abstract art. The memorial park hearkened back to the goals of the rural-cemetery founders, except that, instead of promoting innovative American art, Eaton wished to preserve the art of the past.

At the center of the Forest Lawn art collection were the stained-glass reproduction of *The Last Supper,* Jan Styka's *The Crucifixion,* and Robert Clark's *The Resurrection.* These three pieces were strategically placed throughout the grounds in buildings erected to show them in a dramatic manner. As one scholar has noted, "they are not simply exhibited; they are staged."

Beyond the appropriate historical and religious meanings, the pieces also reinforced the central tenets of Eaton's philosophy, as discussed by Barbara

Rubin, Robert Carlton, and Arnold Rubin. *The Last Supper* established "the importance of rational, calm planning to meet the profound crisis death represents." *The Crucifixion* showed "the actual and agonizing moment of crisis—the loss." Finally, *The Resurrection* signified "renewal and the promise of eternal life." The hope of eternal life relieved the pain of death. Almost one hundred years after the founding of Mount Auburn, Forest Lawn was reestablishing the optimism associated with death, even if it was in an entirely different cultural context.[27]

DEATH IN THE MEMORIAL PARK

Eaton's memorial park was not a return to Romantic ideas and attitudes. Philippe Ariès has written that the modern attitude toward death, which he defines as "the interdiction of death in order to preserve happiness," was born in America around the beginning of the twentieth century. This new attitude reminded Ariès of the French Enlightenment attitudes, which gave way to Romanticism in the nineteenth century. The twentieth-century attitude existed as if "the Romantic interval," which softened death and diminished the boundaries between the living and the dead, had not existed.[28]

According to Ariès, Americans refused to suppress everything that reminded them of death and the dead. Americans were willing to mute death's presence, to place the dying in the hands of physicians, to allow funeral directors to orchestrate funerals, and to bury the dead in places that evoked little evidence of death. But, unlike Europeans, who banished death from society, Americans were uneasy with cremation and found memorialization more desirable.

Part of the reason that new attitudes toward the dead developed was that America has had a dramatic drop in the death rate during the twentieth century. Between 1900 and 1954, the mortality rate went from 17.2 per 1,000 population to 9.2. The age at which people died changed even more remarkably. The death rate of infants under the age of one in 1900 was 162.4 per 1,000 population, but by 1966 this had fallen to 23.1 per 1,000. The tragedy of childhood deaths, which had been so common in the nineteenth century, became much rarer in twentieth. The majority of people dying near the middle of the century were older Americans. Although it took time for the mortality changes to be felt by the population, the new attitudes emerging in the early part of the century reflected these changes.[29]

Americans delicately balanced their fear of death with a veneration of the dead. American attitudes toward the funeral director exemplified the balance. For centuries, commentators had criticized funeral costs, but periodically their protests grew louder. One of these periods was the 1870s and 1880s, when funeral directors began to assume greater control over the funeral, embalming gained in popularity, and more wakes were held in the funeral home rather than in the family home. Costs increased substantially as the funeral process became more complex.

Embalming, which America was virtually the only Western nation to practice, represented the new attitudes. Americans began embalming in the antebellum period, but the practice became popular during the Civil War. The numerous battlefield dead were impossible to preserve with ice, as had been the past practice, for the time needed to get them home. Instead, undertakers turned to chemical injection as a means of preserving bodies for the required time. They were led by Thomas Holmes, recognized by authorities as the pioneer embalmer in America. He made national news in 1861 when he successfully embalmed Colonel Elmer Ellsworth, the first ranking officer to die during the war and a close friend of Abraham Lincoln. While viewing the body, Mrs. Lincoln suggested the reason why chemical-injection embalming was spreading so rapidly in the second half of the nineteenth century; she found Ellsworth's face "natural, as though he were sleeping a brief and pleasant sleep." Americans were loathe to accept the decomposition of their loved ones. The American funeral director, who handled the embalming, garnered greater attention than European undertakers.[30]

Embalming contributed to the transformation of the funeral into a celebration of life. Corpses appeared as "sleeping" participants in the funeral, which allowed funeral directors and mourners to focus on the survivors rather than the awful reality of the dead. Such a shift in attention resulted in the funeral, burial, and memorial becoming means of surviving "doing what's right" for the dead. Survivors were surrounded with ritual to support them through their loss. The funeral director eventually offered the survivor the services of a *grief counselor,* who made sure the survivor was contacted after the funeral and that all the necessary insurance and other financial forms were filed.

Because of the reemphasis on an afterlife, the memorial park reasserted the religious character of the burial place. Eaton's guiding rule was to create a landscape that celebrated life, not death; sunshine, not darkness. Eaton ordered that Forest Lawn celebrate happiness and not contain any grotesque figures and painful poses. Eaton insisted that "no bleak tombstone mar its Beauty." "Today," he asserted, "religion is gladsome, radiant, it speaks in terms of the Beatitudes, of joyousness, and the smiling Jesus."[31] Eaton's search for the joyful Christ, as with Barton's portrait of Christ as a business leader, were examples of Eaton's belief that the joy of Christianity had been hidden by centuries of worship by overzealous church members.

Eaton believed that the memorial park was a place to celebrate joyous religion. He stated that "cemeteries are the physical expression of the religious spirit of their time." If the burial place was to survive, it must "not only [give mourners] a safe depository for their beloved dead, but a place that will be spiritually uplifting, physically beautiful, its personnel filled with a sincere desire to serve its fellowman." As a consequence of this philosophy, weddings were permitted in the chapels, tourists were encouraged to walk or drive throughout the grounds, and a huge sunrise service every Easter celebrated the Resurrection.[32]

Eaton believed, as part of this philosophy, that Americans should plan for their death. A sales executive at Forest Lawn in 1929 summed up the rationale behind the preneed program by stating that such sales helped people face death courageously. "Forest Lawn Memorial-Park holds boldly . . . that a rational discussion of death . . . rather than hastening one's death, operates in quite the opposite manner."[33] Residents of Los Angeles should face death, buy a family lot or crypt, make arrangements with the memorial park as they would with an executor, and then move through life without the worry of leaving such details to a grief-stricken survivor.

The funeral and memorial park should comfort, rather than threaten, survivors. Eaton instructed his mausoleum architects that "insofar as possible all evidences of death should be eliminated and that this building should be a creation of art."[34] In their Elizabethan offices, Forest Lawn employees did not discuss death. The memorial park celebrated a joyful religion of reunion without the pain and terror of dying, death, and separation. Forest Lawn's *Pictorial Map and Guide* of the 1950s stated that "to Serve the Living. . . . Such beauty is a constant source of inspiration and comfort, for it affirms unswerving faith in eternal life—a serene confidence that death is not the end, but the beginning."

THE ECONOMICS OF FOREST LAWN

Ariès argued that a prime justification for the new attitudes toward death was the profit earned by the merchants associated with the commercialization of death. Although he remarked that profit-making would not have been tolerated if the funeral and burial rites did not meet a profound need in American society, Ariès justly pointed out the unique American relationship between death and money. The new memorial parks were the culmination of centuries-long developments surrounding the decision of Americans to rely on private enterprise to bury their dead. As John Gebhart pointed out in 1928, cemeteries operating for profit "have come in for bitter attack and criticism, partly because there is a deeply ingrained sentiment against any corporation 'making a profit from the dead' and partly because they are often operated in competition with old, established cemeteries." Gebhart noted that, "from the standpoint of landscape architecture," for-profit cemeteries were some of the finest in the country.[35]

Symptomatic of this ambivalent reliance on private enterprise for the burial of the dead was the small number of publicly owned cemeteries in America. Although Gebhart suggests that municipal cemeteries were quite prevalent in small midwestern cities, the figures he cites demonstrate the strong presence of private cemeteries in America. In the four surveys of publicly owned cemeteries he cites, the largest number of cemeteries was 142, 23 of which had been abandoned. Given that in 1928 New York State alone had more than five thousand burial places and at least one hundred private urban cemeteries, the number of publicly owned burial places was a small percentage nationwide. Furthermore, many Americans identified publicly owned burial places with potter's fields for the poor. Instead of relying on the government, most Americans looked to the Hubert Eatons to offer new services.[36]

Eaton's decisions to expand the services offered by the memorial park was a major innovation in the history of the cemetery. A death in a nineteenth-century city usually meant work for a nurse (washing and preparing the body), a carpenter (making the coffin), a funeral director (supervising the funeral), a grave digger, a florist, and a stone carver (carving the marker or monument). The "full-service" memorial park threatened every link in the chain of service because it prepared the body, sold the casket and vault, arranged the funeral and grave or crypt, sold the flowers, and dictated that a customer place on the grave a bronze marker or statuary purchased through the management.

Such an extension of the business of the memorial park further confused the public perspective of the burial place. Eaton's new services contributed to the redefinition of the burial place away from a communal sacred space toward a private commercial enterprise. This redefinition occurred at a time when American attitudes regarding government regulation were dramatically changing, a development that would eventually threaten the status of the memorial park.

The essence of the new Forest Lawn Memorial-Park was the cemetery-sales program that Eaton had brought with him from the Midwest. Midwesterners had developed a plan to sell lots prior to a death in the family, a concept they termed *preneed*. Eaton, an unemployed engineer, on the advice of a friend in Saint Louis, reluctantly took a quick course in preneed sales from local cemetery-sales managers. A two-week trial in cemetery sales convinced Eaton that the concept worked. Fortuitously, some Californians whose cemetery was failing financially were simultaneously looking for a new sales manager. Eaton accepted their offer to take over the sales program.

Preneed sales were not a new idea. John Pintard, an early nineteenth-century New York City vault owner, had carefully planned where his living relatives would eventually be positioned in their church vault. Rural cemeteries were established with funds solicited from wealthy lot-holders who bought large family lots prior to a death in the family. Graves on the new lots often were used immediately because families reinterred ancestors from dilapidated graveyards in the central city, but many graves were intended for future burials. Some of the largest family lots are still in use today. A family lot in Oakwood Cemetery in Syracuse originally purchased in 1859 was the site of a recent burial.

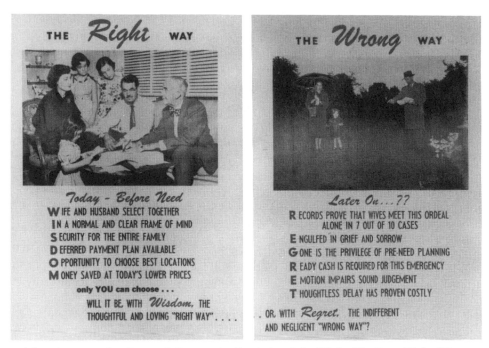

Advertisements for Preneed Programs, Depicting "the Right Way" and "the Wrong Way" to Purchase a Burial Lot, c. 1950s

These advertisements are part of a memorial-park campaign to encourage younger Americans to purchase preneed lots. At left, instead of the grieving widow, the whole family discusses its burial needs with a cemetery representative. Snugly situated in its home, the family can comfortably and rationally decide its needs. Preneed programs in the 1950s and since have focused on in-home sales. Many people prefer not to visit the cemetery to discuss their needs. Some purchasers see their lot for the first time when they bury a relative. At right, a mother is forced by circumstances to confront not only the death of her husband but also the burden of arranging his affairs. (Courtesy of Oakwood Cemeteries.)

In the late-nineteenth-century entrepreneurial cemeteries, the sales manager became an important corporate officer with expanding duties. These cemeteries had more competition and fewer guaranteed customers. They not only offered a product but also actively attempted to sell it. Their sales programs attempted to identify potential customers more efficiently and to use initial sales to build customer bases within ethnic neighborhoods. The lawn-park commercial ownership relied on a sale to one person or a group of people within a neighborhood or an ethnic or religious group to spur further sales.

Essential to the success of lawn-park cemeteries were a more aggressive advertising campaign and a larger, more active sales force. The cemeteries' aggressive sales programs for the first time brought the cemetery to the buyer instead of the buyer to the cemetery. Sales personnel left the cemetery office and went to people's homes. Gaining the confidence and interest of people, sales personnel brought them to the cemetery for the final sale. This method placed greater importance on the cemetery's image and sales materials. The cemetery could not rely on the grounds alone to sell itself.

Midwesterners improved on this sales program by eliminating the trip to the cemetery. For the first time, customers purchased lots without ever viewing the site. The new preneed programs promoted the concept of security. The grave was secondary, and the appearance of the cemetery was important only if it did not detract from the sales pitch.

This sales technique was particularly advantageous in a situation such as that at Forest Lawn, which began as little more than an overgrown hill. Eaton reversed previous California practices by focusing customer attention on the corporate security offered by Forest Lawn. He told his salespeople to advise customers as if they were drawing a will. Eaton used the lessons he had learned from insurance and real estate—that people were interested in advice, not necessarily in a product. Sales at Forest Lawn rose dramatically within a year after Eaton came to work at Forest Lawn.[37]

In order to maximize the financial possibilities inherent in the sales program, Eaton and his associates initiated a new corporate structure for the memorial park. Central to the structure was retaining the memorial park's nonprofit status for the cemetery, thereby ensuring the nontaxable status of the corporation's land. The legal tradition of the private, nonprofit, nontaxed cemetery had been long established in America by 1920. Despite speculation in cemetery stock and community mausoleums during the late nineteenth century, most cemeteries had retained their nonprofit status. By splitting the organizations into a series of interlocking companies, memorial-park owners insured the nonprofit status of the cemetery and still established relatively inexpensive ways of profiting from its sales.[38]

Forest Lawn Memorial-Park consisted of two companies: Forest Lawn Memorial-Park Association, the lot-holders' mutual nonprofit association, was responsible for the memorial park's daily operation; and Forest Lawn Company, a private stock company, which owned the land and the Great Mausoleum and partially developed and built them for the association. Forest Lawn Company sold the mausoleum complex and developed land to the association in return for 50–60 percent of the resulting sales. The company's initial investment resulted in a payback of half of the gross sales of the association. From the remaining 40–50 percent of the sales price, the association completed development and maintained the property in perpetuity. The system insured that the association would never earn any profits, whereas the private-stock corporation would have few long-term costs to consume earnings.

Eaton did not try to hide the profit motive of the memorial park from the public. Adela Rogers St. Johns's biography of Eaton, *First Step toward Heaven,* explained his philosophy of sales in the chapter "Cash and Credit." "That a cemetery must never be separated from religion is one of Hubert Eaton's basic laws," St. Johns reported. "Another is that it can't be separated from being a well-run, efficient, sound operation within the framework of American business and its highest methods."[39] This commercial attitude reflected the entire operation of Forest Lawn and scandalized many people who thought the memorial park should remain a sacred institution.

SYMBOL OF A NEW CULTURE

By the 1930s Forest Lawn had become very successful. It was no longer necessary to convince the public that a monument was unnecessary. Eaton was expanding into life insurance and mortuaries and even beginning to consider opening a second Forest Lawn (after World War II, he would open three additional memorial parks). Success brought public attention, which abetted success. Newspapers wrote about the new memorial park, noting the emphasis on life and the inviting appearance of the landscape. Americans whose vision of cemeteries was of the rural and lawn-park ones with their rows of monuments, large markers, and shady trees were surprised by, and attentive to, the changes.[40]

Other people were less enamored with Forest Lawn. In a scathing satire, Evelyn Waugh lambasted the language and attitudes of Whispering Glades Memorial Park, a thinly disguised substitute for Forest Lawn. His novel *The Loved One* had been preceded several years earlier by Aldous Huxley's novel *After Many a Summer Dies the Swan*, which satirized the immortality that Forest Lawn seemed to preach. Waugh's book was most effective in catching the euphemistic approach to death that Forest Lawn symbolized. The "loved one" took leave and was handled at Whispering Glades by the "mortuary hostess" and the "cosmetician." Death was mentioned by no one and seen nowhere.

Both novels were also critical commentaries on the shallowness of American culture. The protagonist of *The Loved One* is Dennis, a young British poet who has failed in Hollywood. While burying his friend at Whispering Glades, the poet meets a cosmetician, who fascinates him. The book is their love story, set amid the memorial park's glades. In his first visit to Whispering Glades, Dennis contemplates a mortuary hostess who sold him the lot for his friend and arranged the funeral: "She left the room and Dennis at once forgot everything about her. He had seen her before everywhere. American mothers . . . presumably knew their daughters apart . . . but [to him] the Mortuary Hostess was one with all her sisters of the air-liners and the reception desks. . . . She was convenient; but Dennis came of an earlier civilization with sharper needs."[41]

Waugh believed that America's melting pot had destroyed all individual identities. "There is no such thing as an 'American.' They are all exiles uprooted, transplanted & doomed to sterility," he proclaimed in a letter to Cyril Connolly, in response to his question of how *The Loved One* had originated. He suggested that another origin of the book was "memento mori, old style, not specifically Californian." Waugh and Huxley, each for his own reasons, considered the memorial park a harmful illusion, hiding the reality of death and thus abrogating death's purpose in civilization. In his article "Death in Hollywood," Waugh suggested that death should remind "a highly civilized people that beauty [is] skin deep and pomp [is] mortal." He argued that at Forest Lawn "the body does not decay; it lives on, more chic in death than ever before, in its indestructible Class A steel-and-concrete shelf; the soul goes straight from the Slumber Room to Paradise, where it enjoys an endless infancy."[42] Most Americans did not agree with Waugh. They desired the illusion, finding the memorial park's gloomless atmosphere perfectly appropriate for the travail of facing the finality of death. *The Loved One* portrayed the memorial park as a gigantic joke. Americans were not laughing. They were buying lots and visiting the Great Mausoleum.

THE SPREAD OF THE MEMORIAL-PARK CONCEPT

Early twentieth-century Americans did not establish new cemeteries at the same rate as their nineteenth-century counterparts. Only a few groups, such as some ethnic immigrant communities, had compelling reasons for opening a new cemetery. Potential cemetery founders faced competition from cremation advocates and private mausoleum companies, criticism from religious and social commentators, and restrictive zoning legislation prohibiting new cemeteries in cities and towns. For example, between 1903 and 1928 in New York State only eleven large cemeteries were founded, compared with the forty-two new cemeteries in the previous twenty-five years (1877–1902).

Forest Lawn encouraged a boom in new burial places. Most of the six hundred new memorial parks by 1935 were in the West, Midwest, and the South. For example, the Indianapolis area had three memorial parks by 1938. Omaha, Nebraska; Cedar Rapids, Iowa; Youngstown, Ohio; Philadelphia; and Pittsburgh were some of the cities represented by memorial-park representatives at the 1934 ACOA meeting. Not all of the one hundred members of the ACOA prohibited monuments or were privately held investment cemeteries, but all of them were committed to some form of the new concept of the burial place identified with Eaton and Forest Lawn.[43]

Eventually, the concept moved eastward. The presence of large, well-established rural and lawn-park cemeteries limited the need for memorial parks. Because cities were now more closely controlling the location of burial places, the only available land for memorial parks was in the suburbs. Large tracts of about one hundred acres were desirable for the eventual expansion of the memorial parks, and such tracts were to be had only on the outskirts of the city.

Between 1928 and 1945, seventeen memorial parks were established on the outskirts of cities in New York State, all but one of which were nonsectarian. Although this number was considerably fewer than the forty-five rural cemeteries founded in New York State prior to the Civil War, it represented virtually all of the new cemeteries organized in the state after 1920.

Many of the memorial parks, including Forest Lawn in Los Angeles and Memorial Park in Schenectady, New York, were converted lawn-park cemeteries. As land became more difficult to purchase for nonresidential purposes in many of the suburbs, the existing grounds of the lackluster lawn-park cemeteries became very attractive. The older and more established rural cemeteries rarely were taken over. As in Maple Grove Cemetery and Memorial Park, Brooklyn, where an outside sales force reversed the sales figures for a decade, the change could have profound economic implications for the owners.

MEMORIAL-PARK LANDSCAPES

One memorial-park owner stated in 1982 that "the memorial park breaks down the strangeness of the cemetery."[44] Although located far from the center of cities, memorial parks were the most visually accessible cemeteries in a century. They were developed section by section, with each burial section—often called a *garden* instead of a *section*—given a uniqueness by the placement of a sculpture or other artwork at its center. They were usually of familiar themes and done in styles that were attractive to the average customer. Each garden represented a value of the community. Designers planned memorial parks to highlight these artworks, rather than the natural background. The background was also familiar because it was designed to imitate the popular image of the suburban landscape. The strangeness of the Romantic landscape was missing in memorial parks' more accessible and practical arrangement. Memorial parks provided a private, more secular, and comfortable environment for lot-holders and prospective customers.

George McClure, the designer of several memorial parks, reminded memorial-park operators that the natural landscape was important: "A Park does not merely consist of a series of lawns, driveways, and a few scattered trees. Such an area can be referred to as a 'field,' it does not merit the name 'Park.' It is merely a burial area." The landscapes varied little from institution to institution. Memorial parks usually were situated on pasture land, where the topography was flat or gently rolling. A few memorial parks, such as the McClure-designed Vestal Hills in Binghamton, New York, were on steep hillsides. Few trees and shrubs survived bulldozers during the development of memorial parks. Most memorial parks did not contain streams, woodlands, vistas, and other picturesque features, which made most rural and lawn-park cemeteries so aesthetically pleasing.[45]

McClure told memorial-park operators that expense should not limit the landscape, because "it is the Park that we sell—it is the most valuable asset we have." One operator stated that "it is the natural ambition of the engineers and cemetery landscape architects to use the plot of ground which they design in such a manner that after the last interment is made, it will retain its park-like beauty."[46] Memorial parks offered the customer a uniform landscaped garden, which, due to the strict regulations, would remain familiar throughout the years. No lot would disappear behind a statue. The landscaping would never overgrow or overflow another lot.

The spacious lawns were reminiscent of English aristocratic estates, as well as American urban parks and suburban front lawns.[47] The lawns' luxuriance and expanse, suggesting wealth, permanence, and stability, were familiar, easy to maintain, and scenic. The memorial park was neither the "lungs of the city" nor an "outlet for the poor." The memorial park had a natural setting and a pleasing ambiance of hospitality and comfort that reflected American acceptance of the suburb and conquest of the wildness of nature. The lawns were scenic landscapes in which the visitor saw at a glance a flowering tree, a small statue, and other identifying features.

Memorial-park planners did not use nature in the same manner as earlier designers. The natural setting was an integral part of the appearance of both rural and lawn-park cemeteries. Planners expected the memorials to harmonize with the scenery. The natural setting was an important part of the aesthetic philosophy behind the cemetery. In the memorial parks, nature was used exclusively as a backdrop. Even when a focal point was created around a piece of scenery, such as with Vestal Hills's Mirror Lake, with its "two adjoining pools on different levels with [a] bronze fountain in the center of [the] upper pool," nature had been so manipulated as to lose its naïveté.[48]

The role of nature in the memorial parks replicated twentieth-century American attitudes toward the relationship between nature and civilization. Americans were ever more in control of nature, manipulating rivers for power, turning thousands of unirrigated acres into productive farmland, building communities on cliffs, flood plains, wherever people wished to live. Neither the fear of nature, which had influenced colonial society's settlement patterns, nor the feeling of the loss of nature, which accompanied urban growth in the nineteenth century, disappeared, but was greatly muted. Nature was now a canvas on which Americans could record civilization.[49]

Suburban development was indicative of the changes.[50] The early suburbs were influenced by the same Romantic ideas that had led city-dwellers to establish rural cemeteries. Strauch's redesign of Spring Grove was very much in keeping with the aesthetic principles that had guided Olmsted and other nineteenth-century landscape architects in their suburban developments. By the twentieth century, the sense of the suburb as a separate, ruralized community was being lost. Especially in sprawling cities (e.g., Los Angeles), suburbs were no longer isolated and no longer served as a counterpoint to urban values. The suburb had been urbanized, or had lost its unique sense of a bucolic atmosphere.

Memorial parks reflected the suburbanization of the city. White Chapel outside Syracuse, Lakewood outside Jackson, Mississippi, and Sharon outside Boston were not outside the city in the same manner that Boston's Mount Auburn, Brooklyn's Green-Wood, and Chicago's Graceland were in the nineteenth century. The visitor was not torn away from the commercial world and enveloped in a moral and educational experience. Memorial-park designs were twentieth-century suburban, with wide streets, large lawns, and flowering trees. Management attempted to retain a sense of grandeur, solemnity, and graciousness in the memorial park by tastefully designing the grounds and regulating visitors to ensure appropriate behavior, but the atmosphere was familiar—purposefully.

One of the most striking features of the memorial-park landscape was the introduction of the metal memorial as the primary marker. The only markers that Forest Lawn had allowed were bronze; this was part of its attempt to separate itself from past practices. The dramatic reversal of century-long restrictions of metal monuments proved popular with lot-holders and memorial-park operators. Many memorial parks allowed lot-holders to purchase either stone or bronze markers, but bronze was preferred by management and apparently by customers, who purchased it in growing numbers, because of its durability, flexibility, lightness, and strength.

Bronze had been used in cemeteries for decades, but only for statues. Hugh Ball's bronze statue of Nathaniel Bowditch in Mount Auburn was one of the earliest and finest examples of bronze statuary in a cemetery. By the end of the nineteenth century, many of America's finest sculptors made bronze statues for the nation's cemeteries. Particularly notable was the stunning monumental bronze that Augustus St. Gaudens sculpted for the grave site of Henry Adams's beloved wife. During the twentieth century, this tradition would continue, as memorial parks placed many bronze sculptures among their grounds as central features for individual garden sections.[51] The first large court in Forest Lawn, the Court of Freedom, includes Ward's *George Washington*.

Whereas bronze statuary was acceptable, metal statuary was controversial. Symptomatic of this controversy was the attempt in the late nineteenth century of a few companies to sell white bronze monuments as alternatives to marble and granite ones. White bronze monuments were actually made of zinc, but, because they usually took on a bluish-gray color when exposed to air, manufacturers renamed them white bronze, "an attractive, elegant trade name." Hundreds of these monuments in dozens of styles were sold throughout America before 1914. However, many cemeteries, including Mount Auburn and Spring Grove, prohibited them, categorizing them (as well as cast-iron fences) as inappropriate. Although durable, inexpensive, and novel, white bronze did not have stone's reputation for endurance, was perceived as cheap, and was perhaps too unusual for most Americans, fearful of placing a faddish monument on an eternal resting place.[52]

Individual bronze markers that were flush to the ground helped many

twentieth-century Americans overcome their reservations. The new markers
were invisible until you approached the grave site, which increased the lot-
holder's privacy. Made of high-quality bronze, these plaques gradually assumed
a greenish patina, which further melded them with the green lawns of the
memorial parks. The average size of lots being purchased was smaller, but the
markers gave individual lots and entire burial sections a less cluttered, more
natural, and more inviting appearance.[53]

There was opposition to the bronze monopoly, as well as to the severe
restrictions on monuments. In 1955 Eric Marmorek, a noted cemetery-sales
consultant and at the time executive vice-president of Sharon Memorial Park in
Boston, spoke at the National Cemetery Association meeting on the "art of
persuasion." He noted that Sharon Memorial Park was a predominantly Jewish
burial place. In trying to sell the concept of the memorial park to the Jewish
community of Boston, the park's management found that the idea of the flush
bronze marker was resisted because of the biblical story of Jacob setting a pillar
on Rachel's grave. "To counteract this," said Marmorek, "we 'reconditioned' our
prospects by showing them pictures of the oldest cemetery in the world, the
Mount of Olives, in Jerusalem, where flat stone slabs are often set flush with the
ground [and] . . . of the oldest cemetery in this hemisphere, Curaçao [Nether-
lands Antilles], where this same system has been used. Thus, the new becomes
acceptable by associating it with the old."[54]

Bronze markers provided memorial parks with a new source of income.
The markers were cast by founders who had little connection with established
stone dealers. Memorial parks wished to offer their customers a complete
burial package, which included the memorial. Stone dealers fought this decision with every means available to them, including lawsuits. Using bronze markers allowed memorial-park operators to limit their dealings with monument
dealers and the stone quarries; many of the latter owned or had close connections with the nation's monument and marker businesses.[55]

MEMORY GARDENS ASSOCIATION AND THE *FEATURE*

Eaton's display of a variety of statuary demonstrated that a landscape of lawns
and simple markers was unthinkable to memorial-park operators. McClure
stated that the "elimination of the monument" could have produced a memorial park that "too much resembled the public park." The memorial park, struggling to distinguish itself from the lawn-park cemetery, could not allow its
landscape to be even less spiritually and aesthetically interesting. "To remedy
this defect," McClure wrote, "architectural and sculptural features have been
introduced to give the Memorial Park a sense of its real purpose and to differentiate it from the typical old-time cemetery."[56]

Many of the nation's memorial parks were not immediate financial successes. They lacked the funds to imitate Forest Lawn's treasure trove of art. For

THE EVOLUTION OF CEMETERIES

THE OLD WAY—IMPRACTICAL

THE PARK LAWN TYPE—DESTROYS SENTIMENT

INDIVIDUALIZED GARDEN—THE MODERN WAY

"The Evolution of Cemeteries," Advertisement for Memorial Parks, c. 1950s
Memorial parks used comparisons with monumented cemeteries effectively in their
sales campaigns. The evolution shown here was intended to persuade buyers that
memorial parks were not only more practical but also filled with greater sentiment.
(Courtesy of Oakwood Cemeteries.)

example, Fort Hill Memorial Park in Lynchburg, Virginia, opened in 1929, but
floundered for decades before establishing a stable, secure ownership that
turned around its finances. Many early memorial parks had grandiose plans for
features, which were cut short by the Depression. White Chapel in Buffalo and
White Haven in Rochester proposed, but never built, elaborate chapels. White
Chapel's was modeled on the chapel in Alexandria, Virginia, where George
Washington sometimes attended services. White Haven's would have been part
of an enormous Renaissance-style gate, which proved far more expensive than
the operation could afford.[57]

In the late 1930s, Edward L. Williams, a midwestern real-estate developer,
created Memory Gardens Association (MGA) to exploit the new concept of the
garden feature.[58] The garden feature was usually located at the center of the new

burial section, or *garden*. The features ranged from a concentric arrangement of flags to a bronze statue of George Washington to an artificial landscape effect. Garden-style sections with these central features divided the burial place into manageable parts, which could appeal to different segments of the community.

The features in a memorial park were often loosely connected symbolically. A Masonic section could be adjacent to a veterans' section, which could be adjacent to a Jewish section. The Masonic chair might stand within sight of a statue of Christ, a howitzer, and a star of David, and the landscaping and topography could be developed to accentuate the presence of these features. The individual feature provided an identifying symbol for the lot-holder, a representation that met with the survivors' approval. In this way, memory gardens could be designed and sold as funds became available.

MGA eventually managed over 125 memorial gardens throughout America. Most of MGA's properties were in the Midwest and the South, with particular emphasis on the expanding cities of the Mississippi Valley region. Memory Gardens in Albany and White Chapel Memory Gardens in Syracuse at one time were managed by MGA, and Acacia-Resthaven in Tonawanda, New York, has long been managed by a person trained by MGA. Williams assembled well-trained salespeople from the real-estate and insurance businesses, taught them a sophisticated direct-sales technique, and loosely managed the individual operations. Memorial parks could be even more efficiently and profitably developed if they used the garden plan.

Memorial-park design reflected the differentiation of twentieth-century America. Rural-cemetery landscapes were intended for the entire community, designed and developed by boards of directors responsible to their communities. Even late-nineteenth-century entrepreneurs, who were appealing to smaller segments of the community, were still developing cemeteries in which anyone would feel safe and secure. Memorial parks presumed instead that lot-holders wished to be buried with those neighbors with whom they had some cultural or religious affinity. Sections were identified by ethnic and religious symbols; each section would attract similar people. If the community had a small Jewish population, there would be no star of David, but in almost all places the veterans and the Masons would each have a section appealing to their members.

Gardens were built around symbols of Christian ideals of brotherhood, faith, and meditation. White Chapel Memorial Park in Detroit advertised a series of such gardens in 1966. Among the eighteen gardens were the Garden of Prophets, with a central feature of the three prophets David, Jeremiah, and Isaiah, and the Garden of Religious Awakening, with a feature celebrating the resurgence of religion in the eighteenth century. The Garden of the Last Supper, a popular topic for many memorial parks, included a marble statue of the famous event. The artistic features were often exhibited on a pedestal, with a reassuring biblical quote engraved on the pedestal.[59]

EQUALITY AND EXCLUSIVITY

Differentiation led to exclusion. Founders and managers of memorial parks struggled with a central American paradox that had long troubled cemeteries. Americans believe in democracy and equality, but go to extremes to differentiate themselves from others in housing, clothing, lifestyles, and even in death.

Superficially, the memorial-park landscape solved the long-discussed problem of social distinctions in the cemetery. No longer did the middle-class lot-holder face "a wide range of cost of monuments [fixing] the financial status of each individual family more or less permanently." No longer would "the difference between a $100 headstone and a family mausoleum costing perhaps $10,000 [give] obvious though gruesome evidence of financial standing."[60] No longer would nouveau riche families reinter their ancestors in new, gleaming mausoleums or below new, larger, more sophisticated monuments. The individual garden section was the property of all the lot-holders, for it symbolized all their graves.

Yet social distinction remained important. One memorial-park owner experimented in the early 1950s with a small feature section, nothing more than a circle surrounding a small birdbath worth less than $500. He priced this section's lots differentially, with the highest priced lots closest to the birdbath, the lowest farthest away. The highest priced lots sold first. After that, this memorial park's sections were all differentiated circles surrounding increasingly sophisticated features.[61] This practice was typical of the pricing structure in most memorial parks.

Such social distinctions were flexible, but attitudes toward racial integration were rigid. Memorial parks enforced rules similar to the one at Forest Lawn that stated "no interment of any body or the ashes of any body other than that of a human body of the Caucasian race shall be permitted." In 1926 the Forest Lawn exclusionary clause was upheld in a lawsuit in which the memorial park sought to cancel the contract of an African-American whose race was not revealed at the time of purchase. In that lawsuit, Forest Lawn argued that the burial of an African-American would "cause great and irreparable damage . . . by depreciating the same and causing the owners of lots of land . . . to cancel their said contracts."[62] Such an attitude was not surprising given the racial-exclusion clauses in many real-estate contracts, as well as the racism of many citizens. A resident of Los Angeles suggested that the minorities made up "a dirty, vile, degraded, unredeemable humanity that sits idly in the shade and suffers the rich gifts of climate and soil to go to waste unused and not even appreciated."[63]

Such exclusionary practices had not always been true in American cemeteries. Rural cemeteries did not have exclusionary clauses in their lot deeds, nor
apparently did lawn-park cemeteries. Many midwestern and some eastern
rural cemeteries spatially segregated African-Americans. In all the cemeteries
of Chicago, for instance, African-Americans and whites have always been separated. The discrimination was not formal in other cities. In Cleveland, African-
Americans were expected to purchase lots in the less prestigious Harvard
Grove Cemetery and leave Woodland to the whites, but there were no overt
prohibitions.[64]

In New Jersey in 1884, an African-American sexton was refused burial by
a cemetery and the *New York Times* supported the indignant response of the
state's governor. This incident occurred in a time of deteriorating race relations
and the opening phases of the southern Jim Crow legislation, which discrimi-
nated against African-Americans and established a "separate but equal" society.
By 1917 *Park and Cemetery* could inform a questioner that "it is now a fairly
settled rule of law that a cemetery company or association may refuse a lot or a
grave for the interment of a colored person." By 1930 memorial parks had
exclusionary clauses to protect themselves and their lot-holders.[65]

Racial segregation in burial places was not legally challenged until well
after World War II. If names have symbolic meaning, memorial parks could not
have been clearer in their message to nonwhites. White Haven and the two
White Chapels were the first cemeteries in New York State history to be so
designated in any town or city that itself did not include "White" in its name.
This was a nationwide trend. Rural cemeteries and some segregated cemeteries
retained the patronage of African-Americans and other minorities.[66]

THE FAMILY AND THE MEMORIAL PARK

Memorial parks excluded nonwhites because they were trying to attract the
white, Christian family that Eaton and the other middle-class founders and
operators of memorial parks viewed as the building block of America. The
landscape was carefully designed to meet the wishes and reflect the attitudes of
customers and to be inclusive rather than exclusive. The religion was ecumenical, a heroic nation was praised, the family was celebrated, and death was
muted, if not entirely eliminated from the landscape. The landscape, like the
sales approach of the institution, invited the consumer to join a community of
familiar values by purchasing a lot.

Symbols of Christianity were used throughout as features within sections.
Gardens in White Chapel in Detroit held statues of praying hands and of
Christ. Cedar Lawns Memorial Park, outside Seattle, Washington, had only one
garden in 1975, a statue of Christ. Values traditionally related to Christian
behavior, such as peace, love, and harmony, served as names for gardens in
many memorial parks. Each of these gardens was representative of the Ameri-

Court of Freedom, Forest Lawn Memorial-Park, Glendale, Calif., 1982
Patriotism has long played an important part in the landscape of the American cemetery. In the aftermath of World War II, veterans' sections became particularly popular.
Forest Lawn had introduced patriotic motifs into its gardens even before the war.
Bronze markers provide memorials for the individual, and the community can contemplate John Quincy Ward's statue of George Washington. Thus the Court of Freedom intends to achieve the dual attributes of privacy and public display.

can belief in a religion with a "Supreme Being whose appeal was inter-
denominational and whose guidance could be ritually invoked on all public
occasions."[67]

Memorial-park developers appropriated American history, much as the
post-Revolutionary generation had used rural cemeteries to promote a new
local and national heritage. National historical figures and icons were appropriated as the basis for the commemoration of the dead. Acacia-Resthaven developed a Masonic garden around a bronze statue of Washington, himself an early
Mason. In its three new memorial parks, Forest Lawn built large burial courts
around themes such as liberty, the battle for which was depicted on a 162-by–
28-foot mosaic in Hollywood Hills. This mosaic was a composite of twenty-five
"famous American paintings and art works. . . . Its subjects span the time from
the First Legislative Assembly in the New World to the first prayer in Congress."[68]

A powerful bond for many middle-class people, especially after World War
II, was their military experience. Veterans' sections, festooned with flags and
antique weaponry, were common. Changing regulations for U.S. government
veterans' cemeteries, particularly those allowing spouses of veterans the priv-

189

ilege of burial, made them serious competitors with private ones. So memorial parks, along with other cemeteries, attempted to demonstrate that the veterans would receive as much honor in their grounds as in those of publicly owned cemetery.

The landscape of the memorial park appealed to the American white middle-class. Many of the religious statues and quotations were ecumenical enough that, if Greek Orthodox or Catholics wished to purchase a lot, the memorial park could easily find them a place. Indeed, as the concept of the garden spread, memorial-park operators offered separate sections to customers of diverse ethnic and religious backgrounds. Each garden became a community cemetery where the lot-holders shared some explicit or implicit assumptions and values. Only race or lack of funds kept an individual from purchasing a lot in a memorial park.

CONSERVATISM AND COMMERCIALISM

Ironically, in their charges that memorial parks were commercial organizations, commentators failed to recognize the conservative nature of the new burial places. Twentieth-century Americans did not want the close relationship with the cemetery that their nineteenth-century counterparts had craved. Memorial parks represented a distancing of the grave site from the mourner. They offered lot-holders a total-service package by which the institution accepted responsibility for maintaining the lot. The landscape of memorial parks reaffirmed the values of religion, patriotism, and the family.

By strongly emphasizing the sales program, by competitively advertising and presenting that advertising in people's homes, and by becoming for-profit organizations, memorial parks threatened the long tradition of nonprofit, noncommercial burial places. Consumers and communities looked to government to respond to the threat of commercialism. In one nationally significant instance, the attorney general of New York State responded by investigating specific cemeteries and, in 1949, proposing sweeping state legislation to regulate the industry and to restrict cemeteries from "profiteering in sorrow."

CHAPTER EIGHT

The Cemetery in Crisis

THE CHANGING RELATIONSHIP BETWEEN THE CEMETERY AND THE GOVERNMENT

In 1839 the Massachusetts legislature passed the first of many state rural-cemetery acts regulating the organization and management of cemeteries. These acts were primarily guides to the proper, legal steps in forming and maintaining a private corporation dedicated to the management of a cemetery. The acts ensured that organizations established under them would remain nonprofit and nontaxable. Instead of limiting the creation of cemeteries, the legislation was intended to promote their organization. The legislation encouraged rather than proscribed.

Such legislation reflected contemporary beliefs about the government's role in the encouragement and regulation of corporations. The most influential opinion of what was an appropriate relationship between a private corporation and the government was expressed by the U.S. Supreme Court in the case of the *Trustees of Dartmouth College* v. *Woodward* in 1819. Justice John Marshall stated that a group of private citizens had applied to the government for a charter so that they might execute some "beneficent object" at their own, rather than the public's, expense. Through granting them incorporation, the government provided them with the "capacity" to achieve their objective. The government asked nothing more in return, including no payment of taxes, than the group's benefit to the public. The government also did not ask the "right to exercise over this artificial being a power which changes its nature, and touches the fund, for the security and application of which it was created." The government empowered, but the corporation acted independently.[1]

During the century after that decision, the status of the corporation in America changed dramatically. Private corporations expanded their role in the nation's commerce and industry. They also grew in size and political power. National, then international, corporations offered goods and services beyond a locality or region, eventually extending through the whole nation, then to the world. Especially in the areas of transportation and basic industries, such as steel, the private corporation came to have a major impact on the economic life of all Americans.

As the definition of the corporation changed, some Americans worried that the government should do more than simply encourage corporate activities. As railroads expanded across the nation, utilizing land gifts all the way across, farmers and small merchants were ambivalent about their presence. They desperately wanted to use the railroads to reach larger markets for their goods, but they did not want to be subject to the arbitrary decisions of businessmen who had never visited their small towns. Partly out of their frustrations grew a series of reform movements which historians term Populism and Progressivism.

The reform movements had a significant impact on American life. Lifestyles, relationships between workers and management, and political parties were all affected by the new ideas. Progressivism was particularly important in cities. Progressive interest in neoclassical architecture, as expressed in the City Beautiful movement, strongly influenced the buildings and monuments of early twentieth-century cemeteries. At the same time, attacks on corporate greed, as well as the atmosphere of muckraking, probably were partly responsible for this generation of industrialists ordering fewer elaborate monuments and mausoleums than the past one.

Faced with huge private corporations created for private gain rather than public good, Populist and Progressive reformers convinced the government to establish new rules regulating their activities. Legislation passed that limited the portion of the market any enterprise could control and created quality-control mechanisms in areas of public concern, such as child labor.

Reformers such as Robert LaFollette of Wisconsin viewed the successful businessman as a model for America, and the legislation was not intended to eliminate private capital or the corporation. Indeed, businessmen were often integrally involved in the new regulatory legislation. Progressives hoped that such legislation would weed out incompetent and dishonest competitors. Although the cemetery industry was not directly affected by the reforms, early twentieth-century legislation pointed the way toward a more active stance by the government by midcentury.[2]

During the New Deal of the 1930s, government regulation was once again expanded. Prior to this decade, Americans envisioned the government's regulatory role as essentially negative, stopping harmful activities. The New Deal suggested that government could act as both inhibitor and helper, through Social Security, work relief, and other direct-aid programs. The American people had decided to use the government to protect them from corruption, dishonesty, and immoral behavior. This was a remarkable turnaround from most Americans' skepticism toward government action in the previous century.

"PROFITEERING FROM SORROW"

During 1948 and 1949, New York State Attorney General Nathaniel Goldstein campaigned to halt what he termed "profiteering from sorrow."[3] Reflecting growing national concerns about the manner in which cemeteries operated, the national atmosphere of business reform instituted by the New Deal, and societal confusion regarding the cemetery's role, Goldstein's campaign was an attempt to restrict the cemetery's commercialization and corruption. Previously, informal community opinions were believed to have limited such developments. Now the legal forces of the state government had to bring these developments under control. The guiding legislation of 1847 was replaced with binding regulation in 1949.

Goldstein's campaign was the last act of a decade-long drama in which New York State public officials increasingly criticized the state's cemeteries. As early as 1930, some reformers agitated for regulation of Jewish burial societies, which controlled Jewish funeral homes, cemeteries, and even some monument dealerships. Buttressed by these consumer complaints, state legislators spoke out against the practices and profits of the entire cemetery industry. In 1947 Nathan Lashin spoke at the state cemetery convention, warning members that the state had permitted cemeteries to become virtual monopolies and that cemeteries needed a "proper regulatory body" to protect the public. He declared that the state had not passed legislation allowing cemeteries tax-exempt status so that "high salaries and indirect bonuses to high priced sales representatives . . . [would] be used to siphon off surplus moneys . . . for private use."[4]

In 1948 Goldstein announced that his office had received a series of complaints from citizens that cemetery operators had defrauded customers. By October 1949 Goldstein found enough evidence of problems to issue the first of seven suits against some New York State cemeteries. He charged that, over the previous seven years, Cedar Grove and Mount Hebron cemeteries had paid out over $2 million to the six stockholders and three officers who Goldstein believed controlled both cemeteries. Goldstein accused the managers and owners of pricing items 100 percent above cost, establishing an insufficient fund for permanent maintenance, and neglecting care of the cemetery. Goldstein warned that "there is no question in my mind that cemeteries should be controlled like public utilities."[5]

During the remainder of 1948 and the early months of 1949, Goldstein first sued more New York State cemeteries, then attempted to solve the general problem by convincing the state legislature to establish a regulatory board to oversee the activities of cemeteries. Goldstein's revelations about the profits made at some cemeteries fueled a public demand for the legislation. Perhaps most damaging was the case of Maple Grove Cemetery and Memorial Park in Brooklyn.[6] Maple Grove had been founded as a lawn-park cemetery in 1875 by the entrepreneur Colonel William Sterling Cogswell. Cogswell convinced a group of Brooklyn landowners to allow him to develop Maple Grove Cemetery on their land, in return for which they would receive a share of future lot sales.

Because of the cemetery's high expenses, only a small portion of each sale was placed in a permanent-care fund. In 1949, after five years of intense selling and seventy-five years of existence, Maple Grove had a permanent maintenance fund of approximately $100,000. Knowledgeable cemetery managers agreed that the investment income from a fund of that size could not support the maintenance of a 62-acre cemetery. Lot-holders who had purchased perpetual care would find that the management had only enough money for minimal care.

In 1942, seven years after the death of William Cogswell, his son George reached an agreement with a group who wished to transform Maple Grove's remaining land into a memorial park. Although Maple Grove had been prosperous since 1875, it was no longer successfully competing with other Brooklyn cemeteries. There were considerable financial advantages associated with the memorial-park concept. The group formed a separate sales corporation, which purchased lots at discount prices and sold them to the public at considerable profit. As with Forest Lawn Memorial-Park's two separate corporations, the two separate Maple Grove corporations ensured that the cemetery retained its nonprofit status and that the for-profit sales corporation had few direct costs.

Goldstein was particularly upset by Maple Grove's tactics to sell lots. "High pressure methods mark the sales operation. A battery of three to seven telephone solicitors work full shifts making blind calls through the directories to reach potential buyers. Trained salesmen—sometimes twenty are in the field at a time—follow up the leads with kits of color pictures, testimonials and other literature. An easy payment installment plan, plus six percent interest, is offered prospects."[7] In January 1949, Goldstein charged that customers bought over four thousand lots at almost 100 percent mark-up, earning the memorial-park corporation over $3 million in a seven-year period. Goldstein attacked state regulation of cemeteries as inadequate and weak, given the profits flowing to these ostensibly nonprofit organizations.

Other suits portrayed the operators' apparent lack of compassion for the dead or the survivors. Goldstein related that in January 1949 a family informed an unidentified cemetery that the body of a son who had been killed in Germany during the war was being brought back to America for burial. The family was informed that the service could not proceed until it paid $14 in back assessments for perpetual care. The grief of the family was extended as it struggled to pay the assessments. One lot-holder was charged with the costs for three years of trimming a hedge that had been removed by a cemetery. Goldstein believed that the cemetery business had lost an understanding of its purpose. The "last great necessity" had become nothing more than a profitable opportunity.[8]

In February 1949, Goldstein concluded his investigation by presenting Governor Thomas Dewey with proposed legislation to regulate the state's nonprofit, nonsectarian cemeteries. Goldstein stated that "inasmuch as the service [the cemeteries] are supposed to render is an essential one, the cemetery corporations may well be regarded, in the exact sense, as public utilities." The state had intended since 1847 that the cemetery corporations would operate "without profit and for the mutual benefit of those persons who purchase burial space. . . . There is, however, a shocking disparity between theory and actuality."[9]

Citing Maple Grove, Cedar Grove, and other cemetery operations he had filed suit against as examples, Goldstein concluded that "a large number—probably larger than is known—have been and continue to be run as lucrative commercial ventures." He noted that the "trend toward profiteering with reckless disregard of public interest" had become apparent "some 40 or so years ago. This trend intensified in the decades following the first world war and is now in full tide."[10] Goldstein was underestimating the extent and the history of commercialism, which had existed as early as the 1860s, as the active trading of stock in Woodlawn in the Bronx demonstrated.

The most important aspect of the newly rewritten Cemetery Act of 1949 was the creation of a Cemetery Board, managed by the office of the secretary of state and consisting of representatives of the secretary of state, the attorney general, and the commissioner of health. The board was to administer the new law, acting to ensure that cemeteries "comply with the law or any rule or regulation adopted by the board, or to refrain from doing any act in violation thereof."[11]

The act limited the corporate powers of the incorporated nonsectarian cemeteries by regulating prices and permanent-maintenance funds, prohibiting the resale of lots by any person, firm, or corporation, banning any outside sales organization from receiving commissions on the sale of cemetery lots, and placing under state supervision the purchase of any additional cemetery land and the issuance of certificates of indebtedness. The act passed with a minimum of debate, and Governor Dewey signed it on 12 April 1949.

The act was limited in several respects. Most importantly, the legislation only covered nonsectarian incorporated cemeteries. Religious cemeteries were not covered, despite public complaints aimed at private burial societies associated with Jewish cemeteries.[12] Cemeteries founded prior to the legislation were allowed to keep their corporate structures, with some exceptions. Those cemeteries that were found to have defrauded their customers and exploited their funds were forced by the state to change their corporate and institutional activities. Other cemeteries, including Pinelawn, were not mandated to become nonprofit subscription corporations. Individual shareholders and certificate owners continued to own and manage cemeteries throughout the state.

Many cemetery operators publicly supported the legislation. In March

1949, at a meeting of ninety-five cemetery owners, managers, and superintendents, Alfred Locke of Pinelawn Cemetery argued that the majority of those present opposed the legislation, but there is little evidence that he was correct. Superintendents, cemetery managers, and owners did little to stop it. Crawford Perkinson, president of the New York Association of Cemeteries, argued that "some of our members . . . do not understand certain parts of the bill, but when these matters are explained properly they realize the benefit that this law will be ultimately to the responsible, legitimate, cemeterians in the State."[13] (Beginning in the twentieth century, professionals in the business used *cemeterian* to describe themselves. One reason for the term was that the superintendent was no longer the only executive due to the cemetery's diverse management. Also, *cemeterian* is another of the euphemistic terms popular in the business.)

The new legislation was important as much for how it reflected the cemetery's changing role in American society as for its direct impact on New York State cemeteries. The new law suggested that the government had now accepted responsibility for overseeing that the dead were treated fairly and equitably. Unlike the 1847 legislation, in which the state provided a mechanism for the voluntary associations to establish their cemeteries independent of controls, the 1949 legislation placed cemeteries under the state's direct supervision.

One reason for this changing relationship was that community groups rarely organized new cemeteries. At Elmlawn, outside Buffalo, not one of the founding board of trustees was buried in the cemetery. Individual entrepreneurs or small groups of businessmen had spearheaded the organization, often establishing cemeteries in growing suburbs. Not all of these cemeteries were founded for the purpose of personal gain, but many were intended by their founders to offer their communities a service in return for a profit. Long before the creation of memorial parks, state legislation had been manipulated to allow such cemeteries to exist.

Goldstein's campaign, as well as the general attack on cemeteries of which it was a part, signaled an attempt to limit abuses. This campaign directed that cemeterians acknowledge that the nineteenth-century paradigm was still the appropriate and acceptable vision of the cemetery. Goldstein wanted to abolish cruel hoaxes perpetuated on the investor, particularly practices such as investment selling—whereby purchasers were encouraged to buy a number of lots with the expectation that, because of inflation and a scarcity of grave sites, the lots would increase in value and be available for resale. Investment lots almost never increased in value; most decreased because there were so few avenues open to sell them.

Goldstein's attack on investment lots, overspending by cemeteries, and high-pressure sales techniques was widely applauded, but rarely emulated. The public was not interested in returning to the lot-holder-maintained cemetery of the last century. Lot-holders were not as involved in the operation of the cemetery, but only interested in the graves of their family. American culture had left the dead to the ministrations of professionals, and mourning had become a personal, private custom.

The best that the society seemed capable of was regulating the worst aspects of the business. California did have a series of hearings, and other states established cemetery boards, often controlled by cemeterians and funeral directors, to oversee the limited regulation passed by state legislatures. In general, though, states did not strictly restrict advertising, aggressive sales campaigns, the spread of the memorial parks, and the consolidation of the burial process. Americans wanted only the limiting of abuses.

CRITICISM OF THE TWENTIETH-CENTURY CEMETERY

The new legislation was part of a decade-long attack on the contemporary American funeral. Articles in the *Christian Century*, the *Nation*, the *American Mercury*, and other magazines exemplified the public anger over two aspects of the modern funeral. First, funerals lacked Christian dignity and were characterized by "pagan" practices not yet exorcised from Christian customs. Second, funerals were still too expensive, and, more importantly, the expense seemed due to funeral directors and cemetery operators intent on profiting from the tragedy of death. Each of these criticisms was related to the changes in American funeral customs brought about by new societal attitudes toward death and the dead.[14]

In 1934 Marian Castle wrote the article "Decent Christian Burial" for the *Forum*.[15] She stated that a "'decent Christian burial'" was seldom either "decent or Christian." The funeral retained too many features of "pagan" practices to be Christian. The embalming of the body, "our funeral flower fetish," the emphasis on an ornate casket, and perpetual care in cemeteries focused attention on the body rather than on the spirit, and on the loss of the individual rather than on the celebration of the soul's ascension to heaven. Castle admitted she did not have a reform that would suit everyone, for "that which would seem humane to some would be agonizing to others." She suggested that the body be unobtrusively and quickly disposed of by the funeral director and that then a memorial service be held, which would consist of "whatever was most comforting to those who were left. . . . The entire emphasis would be on the spirit and not on the body."

Castle's suggestions were in keeping with the questioning of some Protestant Americans of the value of an elaborate funeral, mourning, an ornate monument, and even of a cemetery plot. Articles argued against all of these practices, hoping that Americans would plant "memorial trees" and "abandon funerals." In 1929 Roy Burkhart suggested that families declare that they would approach the burial process not "in weakness, but in strength; not to be morbid, but to be victorious, not [as] a funeral service, but to an intimate meeting of the family with its close and loving friends."[16] Twentieth-century

commentators who were uncomfortable with the melancholy and sentimentalism of the nineteenth-century funeral reconsidered each aspect of the
ceremony.

Attacks on the funeral stemmed from alienation from death, concern
about privacy, worries about Christianity's role within American society, and
legitimate anger about the rising cost of funerals. Hubert Eaton wished that
Americans could find a gladsome feeling in the memorial park, but it was more
likely that they felt alienated, isolated, and afraid. They began to challenge
death rather than accept it as a part of life. Overall, they were increasingly
unable to place death in a comfortable context, and thus the funeral became a
painful and self-conscious experience.

As part of this reaction to the discomfort of a funeral, authors complained
that the funeral was a public spectacle rather than a private affair intended to
give solace to the survivors. They particularly railed against Victorian mourning rituals, which elongated the burial process and made the funeral more
public. An article in the *Christian Century* reminded its readers that "the display
of grief in public, either by mourning garments worn by women or by the
donning of conspicuous armbands by men, savors of the paganism from which
civilization has emerged in part, and which it wishes to forget." The article
praised those who wore customary clothing because of the challenge such
clothing offered death and "all the gloom and pageantry of sorrow which is too
frequently associated with funerals."[17]

Such concerns about the public nature of funerals were behind the desire
to remove the body from the funeral. As early as 1917, a writer in the *Congregationalist* suggested that the "presence of the body at a funeral-service is pagan
superstition."[18] Castle's suggestion that the body be quickly removed and that
the funeral be a memorial service was widely praised. Others suggested a
speedy cremation so that the body would be completely disposed of prior to the
funeral. Arguments similar to these were also used by twentieth-century cremation advocates. All of the ideas focused attention on the survivors and the spirit
rather than on the dead and the bodily remains.

The emphasis on the survivor was a startling revision of past practices.
Since the Middle Ages, the dying person had held center stage in the burial
process. The deathbed scene had been followed by tender care and honoring of
the dead body. Presumably, these actions were not only to prepare the body for
eternity but also to demonstrate the love that the survivors felt for the deceased.
The actions of twentieth-century Americans seemed to suggest that the best
way to honor the dead was to bolster the spirits of the living. Their actions
implied that the dead no longer needed the ministrations of the living.[19]

Most of the calls for a new funeral came from Christian publications or
ministers writing for more popular publications. The articles suggested that
the concern was as much for the state of Christianity as it was about the cost or
public nature of the funeral. In 1938 a group of ministers in Middletown, New

Modern Appearance of Grave-Site Service,
Morningside Cemetery, Syracuse, N.Y., c. 1950

The introduction of several conveniences has changed grave-site services in cemeteries. Caskets are now lowered into the ground using a mechanical device, mourners
are protected by a tent, the immediate family rests in chairs, and mats are placed
around the grave for cleanliness. Artificial greens surround the grave, and the dirt pile
is placed to its side. The entire appearance diminishes the presence of death, and
mourners are spared the harsh finality of dirt covering the casket or urn. (Morningside
Cemetery photographic booklet, c. 1950. Courtesy of Oakwood Cemeteries.)

York, attempted to regain a semblance of control over the funeral by defining a
"decent Christian burial," as opposed to contemporary practices, in a pamphlet. The group proposed that the body be disposed of as quickly as convenient;
that the casket be closed during the service; that only a trusted friend of the
family accompany the body to the cemetery; and that the "false set of values
which causes people to make lavish outlays for caskets, huge floral displays, new
clothes for the corpse, and expensive grave-markers" were not a show of respect for the dead.[20]

The ministers were surprised by the hostile reaction to their pamphlet.
Supporters of the funeral directors and the florists wrote letters to local newspapers reminding readers that, unlike these ministers, the local business people
"were not newcomers" and knew "their professions and adhere to them." The
suggestion was plain that the ministers had overstepped their role in society by
publicly endorsing a simpler funeral. One commentator stated: "Why don't
these young men preach the gospel and leave other people's business alone?"[21]
Funeral directors reacted by using out-of-town clergy as often as possible. Ironically, funeral directors were furthering their own isolation by reminding people that death was, after all, just another business in America.

The incident surrounding the ministers' pamphlet suggests how little the
clergy had to do with the modern American funeral. Clergy had always served
the family and had never been in control of the funeral, but by the twentieth
century the clergy were little more than hired workers. As the Middletown

ministers noted, "when the family and the undertaker had arranged everything, they asked if we could 'officiate' at the funeral."[22]

The ministers felt that religious concerns were among the last to be considered and that the funeral needed to fit first into the plans of the mourners,
the funeral director, and the cemetery superintendent. Their criticisms were
directed most clearly at the public nature of the burial and the hodge-podge of
rituals, which diminished the importance of the service as a religious ceremony.
The ministers declared that the clear Christian message of eternal hope and
possible salvation was hidden beneath the casket and flowers, the monument
and statue, the mourning clothes and perfunctory black armbands.

THE BURIAL OF THE POOR

Some Americans could not afford the rising costs of burying the dead. Private
burial was expensive, beyond their savings or even their small life-insurance
benefits. These people turned to the government for burial. The government
had long provided burial sites for indigents. In the eighteenth century,
churches had often interred their indigents, but, as burial was privatized in the
nineteenth century, the government assumed a larger role. Distinctions among
burial places were magnified, as virtually everyone who could afford to do so
purchased a burial site in a private cemetery, and publicly owned cemeteries
took on the image of potter's fields. In some smaller cities, indigent burial
sections were alongside middle- and upper-class ones in publicly owned cemeteries. In most cities, though, the funerals of indigents occurred in a separate
burial place and were performed as efficiently and cost-effectively as possible.

In 1931 New York City buried approximately 8,000 dead, about 500 of
whom were unidentified, in its potter's field on Hart's Island, raising the total
burials there to over 330,000.[23] This potter's field contained people of every
race, religion, and national origin, most of whom had either no one to pay for
their burial or no one who could afford their burial. All of the caskets were
carefully numbered because about six a week were reclaimed by mourners who
could now afford to remove their dead from the anonymous pauper burial
ground to the private cemeteries surrounding Manhattan. The dead were
interred without ceremony in Hart's Island, though a Catholic priest went there
twice a week to administer an en masse blessing to the recent dead. The only
public celebration of the dead took place annually when a veterans' group
honored the indigent dead of the Civil War.

The relatively consistent presence of a large number of pauper dead partly
motivated commentators' anger about the cost of an elaborate American funeral. Articles such as "Thrown in with the City's Dead" appeared, castigating cities
for their poor treatment of the pauper and viewing potter's fields as symbols of
the failure of American society to achieve democracy in death as well as life.
Although the ratio of pauper dead decreased from the nineteenth to the twen-

tieth century, the number remained a significant portion of the nation's dead. Commentators dramatically distinguished the grand mausoleums and $5,000 bronze caskets from the cloth-covered caskets buried anonymously in every city.[24]

THE CHANGING BUSINESS OF DEATH

Americans spent a significant sum in privately interring their dead. The Department of Commerce reported that during 1942 Americans spent $560 million on funerals, cemeteries, cremations, and monuments.[25] Two-thirds of this amount, about $337 million, went toward the funeral and burial service and presumably included such costs as embalming and flowers. Americans reportedly spent $163 million on cemeteries and crematories. And $60 million was spent on tombstones and monuments.

Costs rose even though the number of dead was relatively constant. Except for unusual events such as the great influenza epidemic of 1919, the death rate declined steadily after 1900. By the 1930s, the death rate stayed consistently about 10 per 1,000, or approximately 1.5 million deaths a year. In 1927 the average funeral cost about $250, according to a study funded by Metropolitan Life. The average increased to about $350 in 1938 and $400 in 1942. This average included a very wide range of costs because in 1942 indigents could be buried for $18 in Los Angeles, whereas a wealthy family might spend over $10,000 on a funeral and more for a cemetery monument.[26]

The funeral director received the largest portion of these expenditures, in return for a wide variety of merchandise and services. Perhaps as much as two-thirds of the total cost of the funeral would be paid to the funeral director, who would be responsible for the embalming, casket, funeral service, and personal services. A much smaller portion would go to the cemetery, although wealthier individuals spent more than others on the grave site. Wealthier families spent over a third of the cost of the funeral on "extra" charges related to the cemetery, whereas the family of a deceased member whose estate was under $5,000 spent only about 6 percent on monuments, cemetery plots, and other things beyond the funeral itself.[27]

The market for services was growing at a much slower pace than the number of businesses wishing to provide the services. Between 1900 and 1935, the number of funeral directors significantly rose. In 1900, there were 1,400,000 deaths in a population of about 75 million. The funerals were overseen by 8,000 undertakers. By 1946 the population had almost doubled since 1900, the number of deaths had fallen to 1,330,000, and there were 26,000 funeral directors.[28] The large majority of them oversaw only two funerals a month. Their expenses and any profits had to derive from payments from those two funerals. It is not surprising that critics wondered if the price of the funeral was related to the amount of business available to the undertaker.

Twentieth-century American funeral directors were making every effort to shed their image as nineteenth-century undertakers. Distressed by the unprofessional associations of the term *undertaker,* they experimented with alternatives, such as *funeral director* and *mortician,* a particularly scientific-sounding appellation. Their critics rarely discussed the American business of death without castigating them for their semantic games. One critic noted in 1931 that, though "pride of profession has made them 'morticians,' the damp of cemeteries is in their hands."[29] Gradually, undertakers abandoned their hope of becoming scientists and accepted the term *funeral director.*

The funeral director orchestrated the death rites for most deceased Americans by the mid-twentieth century. Survivors would contact the funeral director to arrange to pick up the body from the hospital or home, embalm the deceased, hold visiting hours at the funeral home, and contact the cemetery and the minister, priest, or rabbi to coordinate the funeral. If the family had a prearranged burial site, it would often not visit the cemetery until the funeral itself, relying upon the funeral director to bill the cemetery charges with the rest of the arrangements. If it needed a grave, the family would visit the cemetery, sometimes accompanied by the funeral director, and select a lot and pay for it directly.

The funeral director's orchestration of the procedure was threatened by Eaton's opening of a mortuary as part of Forest Lawn Memorial-Park in 1934. Eaton had prophesied in 1929 that "God forbid that I shall be compelled to enter the undertaking business, but . . . the memorial park of tomorrow will demand sweeping reforms on the part of the undertaking craft or . . . will build . . . establishments of their own."[30] Within five years, through its mortuary, Forest Lawn dealt directly with the customer rather than through the funeral director. Furthermore, if the family chose the mortuary it would presumably also purchase a lot, a bronze marker, and other services, such as flowers, all from Forest Lawn Memorial-Park.

The potential advantage of the memorial park was even greater because it had a trained sales staff. The sale of the funeral was an simple addition to that system. Funeral directors relied on repeat business, family referrals, and community visibility to draw customers. Very few funeral directors aggressively advertised, and small funeral directors could by no means compete with the sales forces of memorial parks. Advertising for customers became much more acceptable and customary as the century progressed and the competition increased.

Other cemeteries were slow to follow Forest Lawn's lead because of the large capital investment in starting a new funeral home, the possible conflicts between a cemetery funeral home and funeral directors, and state and local regulatory and zoning legislation. More likely than the cemeteries entering into the funeral business was the consolidation of funeral homes under a central corporation. The new competition would eventually lead not only to cooperation between funeral directors but also to national chains of funeral homes.

A similar situation prevailed with the monument dealers, who were even more threatened than funeral directors by the full-service package of memorial parks. Throughout the last century, monument dealerships had congregated around cemeteries, providing lot-holders with monuments and individual markers and duplicate markers for future burials on the lots. The dealers geared their business and their stock to the economic level of the lot-holders in their neighboring cemetery, and they fought all attempts by cemeteries to enter the business.

The monument industry suffered first from the advent of the memorial parks, then from the Depression. Memorial parks offered prospective lot-holders a lot and a marker for each grave as a package deal. Many followed Eaton's example and prohibited granite and marble monuments that were not statuary. The Depression deepened the shock by lowering all revenues surrounding death. People simply could not afford the cost of an average funeral.

Although the Depression diminished revenues in all aspects of the industry, only monument dealers failed to recover to 1929 levels by 1942.[31] Monument dealers continued to offer commodities rather than services to their customers. Monument businesses generally remained small and family-owned and were little versed in advertising or sales. Many monument dealerships situated close to cemeteries had been criticized in earlier years for commercializing the area immediately outside the cemetery. Now they were on the outside more than ever.

The monument dealers and funeral directors represented a long American tradition of self-employed artisans plying their crafts. Neither group efficiently provided its services in twentieth-century terms. Both groups relied upon personal relationships, individual workmanship, and continued adherence to traditions for their business. As the cities were restructured in the midcentury, with the development and proliferation of suburbs, many funeral directors and monument dealers found their businesses located in declining neighborhoods. Their clientele was moving into residential suburbs that rarely allowed funeral homes or, especially, monument dealerships. Twentieth-century urban patterns were affecting their business as much as that of memorial parks.

THE PLIGHT OF THE MONUMENTED CEMETERIES

For some of the same reasons, many monumented cemeteries found themselves in financial trouble by midcentury. The costs of doing business were escalating for cemeteries confronting higher per-grave maintenance expenses, as well as sales prices that failed to cover their management and maintenance expenses.

Much of the discussion in state association meetings of the 1930s focused on perpetual care because many cemeteries were beginning to worry about long-term maintenance.[32] Cemeteries depended on four sources of income to meet their expenses: general funds accumulated through lot sales, burials, and other services; annual-care funds to which lot-holders paid a small annual bill for the purpose of maintaining their lot; perpetual-care funds, which were usually created by placing a percentage of the lot sale in a trust fund, from which the cemetery used the interest to pay for general maintenance; and special-care funds, which lot-holders paid for special services, such as cleaning the monument or the periodic planting of flowers. Special-care funds were available only for the maintenance of specified lots, not for the general maintenance of the cemetery.

By the mid-twentieth century, rural cemeteries had sold thousands of lots for which they had promised perpetual care. Many of these had sold for under $100 a lot and had provided only $10–15 to perpetual-care funds. Therefore, some cemeteries had perpetual-care funds of only $20,000 to cover the expenses of perhaps a 100-acre cemetery.[33] Realizing that such funds would allow only a minimum of maintenance, superintendents started to campaign for larger funds.

Other cemeteries depended on a small annual-care payment. It often stopped when a widow died or a family moved to another city. Even when a family continued payments, cemeteries often asked for smaller amounts than were needed to maintain the lot. Superintendents argued whether 30¢ or 50¢ a square foot was appropriate. They could not even agree whether perpetual and annual care covered the repair of broken monuments. By the end of the 1940s, such small funds became pitifully inadequate because technological changes, postwar inflation, and labor unionization forced higher costs.

Methods of cemetery maintenance had changed little in one hundred years. Superintendents depended on manual labor for many jobs within the cemetery. Lawn mowers had been mechanized since 1897, but only in the 1940s were modern rotary mowers available in America. The cemeteries had large seasonal employment despite rotary mowers. The tedious jobs of weeding and trimming around gravestones and cleaning road gutters were helped by the invention of the still-unwieldy power weeder and the advent of powerful insecticides, respectively.[34]

Improvements in the technology of grave-digging, which would have reduced the expense of managing a cemetery, were slow. In 1949 an angry letter writer complained that "nobody has enough brains to invent a machine that will dig a square hole in the ground."[35] The lack of a mechanical gravedigger forced cemeteries to maintain large labor forces at a time when wages were rising and personnel issues were becoming more complex.

After World War II, fewer large lots were sold. Because families were smaller and children often lived in other states, there was less need for a large family lot. Many people had large lots left from past generations. Cemeteries

ENTRANCE TO A CEMETERY LOT SHOWING LANDSCAPE TREATMENT

Elaborately Landscaped Lot, Swan Point Cemetery, Providence, R.I., 1934
Although Swan Point Cemetery was prosperous and was able to maintain an elaborately landscaped lot, by midcentury many other monumented cemeteries could not do so on the income generated from the perpetual care originally paid by the purchasers. (Swan Point Cemetery annual report, 1934. Courtesy of Swan Point Cemetery).

had to sell a larger number of two-, three-, and four-grave lots. Such lots were problematic for monumented cemeteries. The large family monument celebrated in their grounds was less intrusive when widely spaced. This was the lesson of Strauch's landscape-lawn plan. The two-, three-, and four-grave lots were not widely spaced. Even small monuments soon looked like a line of teeth rising from the green of the cemetery. Small monuments were also less artistic than large statues or mausoleums. Memorial-park salesmen effectively used photographs of these lots crowded with stock monuments of little distinction to argue that traditional cemeteries were old-fashioned and lent less dignity to the dead.

Many cemeteries were unable to increase their permanent-care funds because they used all available income to cover their costs. In 1946 Clare Buck, superintendent of Spring Forest Cemetery in Binghampton, New York, reminded his colleagues that many "cemeteries of the medium or smaller size . . . are not in too good a financial condition." He suggested that the main reasons for the financial problems were low interest rates and "the small charge the cemetery has for perpetual care." The costs of maintaining a cemetery had

Landscape-Lawn Section, Swan Point Cemetery, Providence, R.I., 1934
Although memorial-park operators tried to persuade customers that garden sections
were designed the "modern way," many Americans continued to want monuments on
their family lots. Granite monuments lined the newer sections of Swan Point and other
cemeteries. Although monuments were often similar in shape and style, some were
distinguished by their imaginative scrolling, lettering, and other decorative features.
(Swan Point Cemetery annual report, 1934. Courtesy of Swan Point Cemetery.)

grown beyond the amounts provided by the interest on the small sums cemeteries placed in permanent-care funds at the time of the lot sale. Buck suggested
raising the amount "several times" the current charge so that cemeteries could
provide "better roads, fences, new buildings, new water lines, along with many
other items which enter into the picture of a well-maintained cemetery."[36]

Other cemeteries attempted capital-fund drives during the next decade,
both to increase the number of lots under perpetual care and to gain enough
funds to maintain their grounds despite inflation. Rural cemeteries were only
partly helped by such drives. They had long depended on the income provided
by wealthy lot-holders purchasing large lots.

Financial problems might have been a motivation for some cemeterians to
support regulatory legislation. By ridding their industry of corruption and
raising the public's perception of their institutions, cemeterians could more
easily establish fund-raising drives to replace diminished capital funds. The
closure of cut-rate speculative industries could result in the older monumented cemeteries not only ridding themselves of competition but also improving the industry's image.

206

THE SUPERINTENDENT IN 1949

Confronted by a growing fiscal crisis, many cemetery superintendents continued to view their profession much as their predecessors did a century before. Annual conventions of state associations primarily consisted of talks on record-keeping, pesticides, landscaping techniques, tree diseases, new trees, and new equipment. Superintendents discussed new techniques and technologies in a framework that would have been comfortable for Strauch or any of the other leading superintendents in 1870.

One reason for the focus of the superintendents was their training and orientation. There was an increasing emphasis on training, as demonstrated by the career of Sam Stueve of Spring Grove. A graduate of the University of Cincinnati in horticulture, Stueve gradually worked his way to the position of superintendent, then president, of Spring Grove. Many superintendents were the sons and grandsons of superintendents, who trained them on the job. In 1937 William Lee assumed the position of superintendent at Fort Hill Cemetery in Auburn, New York, continuing his family's role, which had begun in 1854. Jack Sloane was superintendent and then executive director at Oakwood Cemetery in Syracuse; his father, Fred, had been superintendent at Tod Homestead in Youngstown, Ohio; and his grandfather Nathan had been superintendent at Ironton Cemetery in Ironton, Ohio. A selective survey of the death notices in the *Modern Cemetery* and *American Cemetery* suggests that this phenomenon occurred in every region of the nation.

In 1947 Floyd Gallagher, superintendent of Cortland Rural Cemetery in central New York, recounted the changes since its establishment in 1854. His grandfather had become its sexton in 1878, and his father had been its superintendent. "The work of the sexton [in the early days of the cemetery]," Gallagher pointed out, "was to dig the graves, mow the cemetery with a scythe about twice a year, hoe and weed the roads, paths and gutters, and to lawn mow several lots for which annual care was paid and some that were in perpetual care."[37]

The superintendent's responsibilities at Cortland Rural Cemetery gradually changed. The cemetery built a new receiving vault and began to accumulate equipment, lower grave mounds, and assume responsibility for mowing all lots and putting in all foundations. By 1947 the cemetery had a light truck, a dump truck, trailers, an air compressor, power mowers, electric trimmers, and a repair shop. The superintendent's job changed to meet these new requirements, but the sense of the position—that of maintaining the grounds and enhancing the beauty of the cemetery—never changed.

Fathers and grandfathers trained their sons and grandsons in the intricacies of the business. Superintendents in the post–World War II era acquired enormous knowledge about horticulture, small engines, record-keeping, and personal relations. Few of them had any experience in advertising, public relations, business systems, or investments. Naturally, they were interested in the areas of their expertise. They were also convinced that the appearance of the cemetery was its best possible advertisement. The superintendents believed that their actions continued a century-old tradition of offering a community service. Thus they were not offended, but instead agreed, when a speaker started an 1948 talk on preneed sales by saying that he knew that 99 out of 100 of the superintendents in the room were not interested in the topic.[38]

A growing loss of control was evident in the topics and meetings of the cemetery superintendents' discussion in the 1930s. Labor problems were rising, financial concerns seemed endless, competition with memorial parks was a constant threat, maintenance was a drain on energy and resources. A superintendent of a nineteenth-century cemetery had been a practical professional with a knowledge of civil engineering, landscape architecture, and ministering to those in despair, attributes that did not necessarily fit a sales manager of a twentieth-century memorial park.

MANAGING THE CEMETERY

The cemetery business was changing. In 1944 a colleague reminded cemeterians that the burial of the dead was a business: "We are manufacturers. Instead of coke, slag, pig-iron, etc., we take ground, fertilizer, seed, shrubs, trees, flowers, water, stones, top dressing, etc. and with equipment and men we manufacture a 'product' known as a cemetery. Then we divide this product into individual lots—'packages'—and there you have it."[39] Labor relations, installment sales, even preneed sales and legislation were new topics at state cemetery conventions in the 1940s.

Although the fundamental concerns of many superintendents had stayed the same, the business had changed tremendously since the nineteenth century. One cemeterian noted that superintendents in the "golden age" (as usual, an undefined historical era) "of the cemetery profession in America" had made certain assumptions about care, customs, and lot size which no longer applied to the contemporary cemetery. "Lots had to be priced higher and higher," after the "golden age," "the auto and railroad scattered the families all over the country, and there were 'hard times' when people had to buy as little cemetery space as they could get." Thus, instead of large lots and beautiful monuments, there were six monuments where one was intended, which led to "the graveyard or stoneyard" and eventually "to the cemetery with no monuments at all."[40]

The changing business affected the relationship of employees to management, lot-holders to the cemetery, and even superintendents to their profession. Perhaps the greatest challenge to the twentieth century superintendent was the evolving labor situation. Often trained to consider the cemetery a family enterprise, superintendents were unprepared when unions began organizing cemetery workers. Superintendents felt betrayed by workers, some of whom had been with the cemetery for years, sometimes decades. Unable to understand why workers felt any need to organize, superintendents blamed unions on "subversive outsiders" unfamiliar with the cemetery.

A public example of this strain occurred in 1949 when the Food, Tobacco, and Agricultural Workers Union of the Congress of Industrial Organizations went on strike against the Catholic diocesan cemeteries of New York City. Angered by the diocese's refusal to agree to a five-day, forty-hour week at the pay of $59.40 with time and a half for overtime, the workers went on strike on 13 January 1949. Cardinal Francis J. Spellman charged that this union was Communist-dominated. The strikers' leaders responded by denouncing Communism, disaffiliating, and joining the Cemetery Workers Local, Building Service Employees International, of the American Federation of Labor.[41]

When redbaiting did not end the strike, Cardinal Spellman appealed to the strikers as Christians to return to their jobs, arguing that the church looked "upon their work as a religious service, not just an industry." Angry at their refusal, he called the strike an "outrage" and "an anti-American, anti-Christian evil."[42] He finally said that the church had a responsibility to bury the dead with or without the workers. Gathering together seminary students, priests, and cemetery managers, he led his force into Calvary Cemetery on 3 March to begin burying the dead.

By then there were over one thousand bodies awaiting burial. Graves at Calvary were usually dug to nine feet so that three bodies could be buried in each grave. The volunteers were allowed to dig only to four and one-half feet, so as to avoid injuries to themselves. They buried approximately thirty-four bodies the first day and increased their productivity to seventy-nine the following day. Although they were able to bury the dead from that day's funerals and to begin working on the backlog, the volunteers were no replacement for the 240 striking employees of the New York City diocese.

The strikers stayed off work for eight weeks until 11 March, when a settlement was reached whereby they would receive an 8 1/3 percent pay increase and the issue of the forty-hour week would be handed over to a mediation board. The church did not publicly agree to accept the striking workers back as a group, saying that each would be considered as an individual applying for a job. Under strong public pressure to settle, the Building Service Employees International announced that the strike would never have happened "if there had been responsible union leadership." Union leader David Sullivan promised Cardinal Spellman that such a "strike will never again occur under my leadership."

Other cemeteries, including nonsectarian ones in metropolitan New York, were confronted with similar union pressures during the next few years. Unlike their upstate counterparts, who faced little union action for another decade, New York City cemeterians attempted to confront the issue as a united front. Although cemeteries were unionized individually, by the early 1950s the Metropolitan Cemetery Association was able to convince Building Service Employees International negotiators to have almost all of the contracts expire on 31 December of each year. The cemeteries then negotiated as a group, with management and worker representatives of nonsectarian, Jewish, and Catholic cemeteries. Gradually, the wages of cemetery workers rose and such innovations as the forty-hour week, holiday pay, and mandatory paid vacation were instituted.[43]

Cemetery work was primarily unskilled manual labor. Workers, like superintendents, tended to work at a cemetery for long periods. Workers were often lifelong employees. Although workers' seeking a public solution to their demands for higher wages was a nationwide trend that had been occurring for decades, the cemetery industry had been isolated from labor conflict. The seemingly sudden decision by cemetery workers in the 1940s to unionize angered and alienated superintendents unused to personnel issues. Societal trends forced the cemetery to formalize its internal labor relations, but this was not the only area where relationships were changing.

THE NEW STYLE OF SALES

During the mid–1940s, cemeterians attending cemetery conventions heard several important speeches on the subjects of advertising and preneed sales. The role of the superintendent was clearly changing, as dropping "Superintendent" from the New York State Association of Cemeteries' name in 1934 made evident. Many cemeterians only slowly accepted the new emphasis on aggressive sales techniques, as indicated by the existence of two national organizations: the American Cemetery Association, representing most of the older, more traditional cemeteries that had been founded in the nineteenth century; and the National Cemetery Association, evolving from the American Cemetery Owners Association, which had been formed in the 1920s by memorial parks and entrepreneurial owners who were more interested in sales and operations than maintenance.

The older cemeteries affiliated with the American Cemetery Association attempted to deny that they were in competition with the newer, sales-oriented, nonmonumented cemeteries. In 1935 one cemeterian asked at his state association meeting what a cemetery should do if a nearby memorial park started offering lots for $5 down and $5-a-month payments, with the cost of burial subsidized by the management. An older, more experienced cemeterian answered that the "minute you try [to compete] you are starting competition and that is what you want to avoid." A colleague agreed and then said that the best way to compete was to make your cemetery "a little more attractive so as to create some interest in your community."[44] Cemeterians continued to believe that the grounds sold the cemetery to the customers. The older cemeteries continued to offer a product rather than a line of services.

Map of Hillcrest Memorial Park, DeWitt, N.Y., c. 1935

Because many sales were made in the home rather than in the memorial park, a map was a critical sales tool. Hillcrest Memorial Park is shown here as a fully developed project, with a pond and a "Musical Tower of Memories." As with so many attractions planned for numerous other Depression-era memorial parks, the pond and tower were never completed. Instead, a white plaster sculpture was placed as a central feature on each burial section of the renamed White Chapel Memorial Park. ("Dedicated to Cherished Memories," Hillcrest Memorial Park brochure, 1935. Courtesy of Oakwood Cemeteries.)

In 1944 and 1947, though, speakers at the New York State cemetery convention suggested that cemeteries needed to sell lots by using direct mail, radio, suggestion cards with bills, and other techniques borrowed from the real-estate business. The speakers approached their subjects warily, noting that they were not suggesting that cemeteries violate their principles and become too aggressive. Nor did they believe that every cemetery needed a phone bank and twenty salespeople.[45]

The speakers tried to convince a determinedly uninterested audience that the cemetery could no longer wait for customers to come to it. The speakers attempted to turn the cemeterians' attention away from the mechanical care of the grounds to the spiritual and psychological care of the deceased's survivors. The dead certainly could not care if death was spoken of openly, but advertising experts warned convention audiences that one "passed away" or "moved on toward heaven." The turn from the dead to the living was implicit in the sales of preneed lots, which were sold on the theory that survivors would have less to worry about at the time of the death.

THE LOT-HOLDER

Although cemeterians worked that much harder to convince the public to purchase lots in their cemeteries, they did not define what the lot-holder's relationship to the cemetery should be. Cemeterians rarely discussed the role of the lot-holder in the modern cemetery. Lot-holders were sold lots and told of restrictions on planting and monuments, but they were not told what they could do for the cemetery, except through purchases and gifts.

This reflected cemeterians' remoteness from considerations of the tastes and actions of the lot-holders. Monuments were criticized, plantings were pulled up, maintenance was removed from the lot-holders' responsibility, and special services were offered to those who did not have time to bring flowers on Easter or a wreath at Christmas. The lot-holder had little to do within the cemetery, for the cemeterian now controlled the lot.

Many Americans willingly acceded to a limited role in maintaining the lot, and perpetual care was part of the purchase price. Special-care funds were plentiful at many cemeteries. The days of large crowds visiting cemeteries simply for enjoyment were gone. Not only were the neighborhoods of many cemeteries increasingly undesirable, but Americans felt uneasy within the cemetery itself. Locke's remark that the memorial park removed the "strangeness of the cemetery" reflected both the accessibility of the newer memorial park and the labyrinth of the older cemetery. No longer did people wish to get lost in the cemetery, either figuratively or literally. People visited the cemetery only on Memorial Day or other days of "historical ritual." Their duty done, their obligation served, they retreated from the cemetery.[46]

CONCLUSION

Just as cemeteries were learning to do business in the twentieth century, they faced strict new regulations mandated by state legislatures. Compelled by competition, increasing disinterest among lot-holders and the general public, and by rising costs, cemeterians began exploiting new advertising and sales techniques. The modern, multiservice cemetery had arrived, operating a crematory, offering monuments, planting flowers, selling concrete vaults, building mausoleums—and continuing to bury the dead.

The change had indeed been significant. Many cemeterians alive in 1950 could remember the days of a simple horse-drawn coach carrying a wooden box and accompanied by a small family group in carriages. Now cemeteries allowed cars to roam the tight roadways, automobile hearses and lines of cars formed the procession, and wooden boxes were for the indigent only.

Basic maintenance of the grounds had changed little. The grass needed to be mowed, the trees pruned, the flowers planted, the shrubs clipped. The management of the cemetery as an institution was different. The cemetery confronted a society that feared its presence, distrusted its motives, complained about its activities, and mourned its "golden age." Fewer people visited. Even fewer publicly admitted any allegiance. The cemetery was isolated from the community, forced by the public's avoidance to try to hide its function beneath a green-and-white veneer.

PART

4

The American Way of Death, 1950–1990

Since 1950 many of the same issues have confronted cemetery designers, managers, and customers. How big a lot is sufficient? How much privacy is necessary? What social, economic, and class distinctions should be allowed? What should be the relationship between the government and the private, nonprofit, nonsectarian cemetery? Should managers or those who purchase graves manage? Finally, what role should the cemetery play in society's relationship to the dead and to each individual's inevitable death?

Social commentators have continued to wonder about the worth of the cemetery. In 1962 such sentiments provoked a major public debate after the publication of Ruth Mulvey Harmer's *The High Cost of Dying* and Jessica Mitford's *The American Way of Death*. Both authors rejected the need for a traditional funeral, believing that such a funeral fulfilled little purpose, cost far too much, and existed primarily because of the guilt felt by survivors.

Perhaps remarkably, most Americans have continued to bury their dead in traditional style. Yet, the rise of cremation, the isolation of the cemetery, the restructured family, and a continuing—even increasing—alienation from death have dictated that the grave has less cultural importance than it did a century ago. The next century may witness a substantial readaptation of the American way of death.

CHAPTER NINE

Serving the Living

PINELAWN MEMORIAL PARK

Alfred Locke, operator and part-owner of Pinelawn Cemetery on Long Island, faced a difficult decision in 1949.[1] Since the death of his father, William, in 1922, the cemetery had fallen into serious financial trouble. The grand lawn-park cemetery, established in 1902, was broke. Few people were interested in purchasing lots—either at the time of a relative's death or preneed. Locke greatly admired his father's ideas and was committed to rescuing the enterprise. He realized that the only way to save the cemetery was to make fundamental commercial and aesthetic changes in it.

Locke created a new cemetery, Pinelawn Memorial Park, out of the old one. Only Maple Grove Memorial Park, also created from the financial ruins of a lawn-park cemetery, stood in competition to Pinelawn, east of New York City. Ferncliff and other cemeteries that would experiment with memorial-park sections in the future were still focused on selling mausoleum spaces and monumented burial lots.

Much like Hubert Eaton did at Forest Lawn, Locke quickly turned around the financial situation. Locke used inventive advertising, direct mail, and door-to-door approaches. He gradually improved Pinelawn's appearance by creating a series of gardens around unusual and interesting pieces of art and architecture. From the remains of the grandiose 1902 design emerged a modern memorial park, which offered customers a range of services and merchandise.

The parklike section in the center was all that Locke retained of the original grandiose design. Because of its financial difficulties after a 1915 suit, Pinelawn was forced to sell approximately half of the enormous land holdings accumulated by William Locke. By 1949 the memorial park consisted of approximately 832 acres, most of which were undeveloped. The tracks of the Long Island Railroad split Pinelawn's central reserved park section in half. On the southern side of the tracks were the main burial sections of William Locke's lawn-park cemetery. Starting in 1949, Alfred Locke used the northern side of the tracks for his memorial park.

At first, Alfred Locke, following his father's rules and regulations, allowed lot-holders to raise family monuments. In 1951 he directed that only bronze markers would be used in the new sections. During the 1960s, Pinelawn built intimate gardens with simple features, such as the Garden of the Sanctuary and the Garden of Companions. The memorial park also began mausoleum construction. The first mausoleum was within a burial section, but later mausoleums were constructed across the street from the main burial section. Pinelawn, as part of an increasingly popular trend, built a cluster of "garden mausoleums" that offered crypt burial to a wider range of people. Individual mausoleums were not built within the memorial-park grounds, although some did exist in the older lawn-park sections. This isolation of the mausoleum complex provided Pinelawn with an opportunity to expand it. A single building had been joined by four others by 1989.

Pinelawn was well maintained, using all the latest technologies in tree, lawn, and landscape care. The superintendent even used technology to further alleviate the age-old problem of the sunken or mounded grave. Pinelawn offered underground burial vaults of concrete and steel, which withstood the settling of the grave and kept the surface as smooth as a putting green. These vaults were reminiscent of the brick graves offered as early as the 1830s by Laurel Hill Cemetery in Philadelphia. In a modern touch, Pinelawn instituted the practice of forced settling of graves by spraying a jet of water as the dirt filled the grave. By the next day, a mourner could visit a grave covered with green sod, a representative flower arrangement, and a temporary marker. The protruding muddy grave mound covered with wilting flowers no longer provided a visitor's only identification of a recent burial.

By the 1970s, Pinelawn had become one of the New York City area's most successful burial places. On the advice of architect Ismar David, Locke began developing more elaborate garden sections. Stone blocks engraved with biblical phrases and the words of John Donne and Henry Stimson were centrally located in larger burial sections extending out from the main boulevard. In the far northeastern corner of the developed section of the memorial park were the new Garden of Normandie and the Garden of Peace, which were the most ambitious gardens. The Garden of Normandie included the enormous statue *Peaceful Normandie,* which once had a place of honor in the main dining room of the French luxury liner *Normandie.* After the liner's destruction during World War II, the statue disappeared, only to reappear forty years later in Pinelawn.[2]

AMERICAN CEMETERIES SINCE 1949

As the restructured Pinelawn suggests, the business of death has continued to increase since midcentury. Social and economic distinctions were muted, but did not disappear in the differentiated pricing of the garden sections. Part of the reason for the muted distinctions was the unease families felt regarding the public spectacle surrounding death. Funerals and cemeteries continued to be personal affairs. Professionals were needed to manage the complex tech-

Garden of Normandie, Pinelawn Memorial Park,
Pinelawn, N.Y., 1983

Peaceful Normandie by Dejean was the pride of the ocean liner *Normandie*. It sank in New York Harbor during World War II. The statue was taken to a church in nearby New York City for safckeeping, where it remained until Pinelawn purchased it. The statue provides the dramatic central feature for a large garden section. Indicative of the continuing attempt by designers of memorial parks and cemeteries to incorporate art into them, the statue is reminiscent of the nineteenth-century statues that adorned many family lots. (Courtesy of Pinelawn Memorial Park.)

nologies used to maintain the bucolic appearance of the grounds. The family was less visible and smaller than ever before, but mausoleums, markers, private gardens, and double flush bronze markers noted the continuing hold that family ties had on survivors. Although the cemetery was brighter and more cheerful, death remained its business; this was at best a paradox for cemeterians.

The more cheerful burial place was not the only paradoxical situation.

Privacy was desirable, but mausoleum complexes became the rage of the industry. Americans continued to spend billions on funerals, but the percentage of deceased who were cremated steadily and inexorably increased. The cemetery remained under the watchful eye of the government, but continued to grow more sophisticated in its marketing techniques. More Americans than ever seemed to have a similar vision of the cemetery, but fewer wanted to visit that cemetery or even be buried in it. Americans began to violate the taboo against talking about death, but continued to draw themselves away from the funeral and the grave site, society's traditional places for expressing grief.

THE MAUSOLEUM

The most remarkable changes in the American cemetery industry in the last forty years have been the resurgence of entombment as an important method of disposal and the steady, recently spectacular, rise of cremation. Each method of disposal has a long history, reaching back to antiquity. Each represents an alternative to the usual custom of earth burial, although cremation has been and remains the more radical practice. The increases in entombment and cremation reflect other concerns—questions regarding the necessity of funerals, the costs associated with burial, and the need for memorialization.

The practice of entombing the dead has a long, remarkable history.[3] The first structure termed a mausoleum, one of the Seven Wonders of the World, was built in approximately 1350 B.C. at Halicarnassus for the wife of Mausolus, king of Caria in Asia Minor. By then, large stone structures erected for the disposal of the dead had existed for centuries, most notably in Egypt. Since the days of the kings and pharaohs of Asia and Africa, the tomb often has been a last resting place for the wealthy and powerful. European monarchs and merchant princes imitated such earlier practices, vying with one another to build the most elaborate and ostentatious mausoleum. The Campo Santo in Pisa, one of the world's most magnificent cemeteries, was filled with beautiful monuments, vaults, and mausoleums in the centuries after the central building was completed, which was no later than 1350.

In the eighteenth and nineteenth centuries, when concern about the health risks associated with the decomposition of the dead reached its height, entombment remained popular in Europe. Large private mausoleums were featured on the tour of Père Lachaise in Paris and other European garden cemeteries. The Italians, French, and Spanish brought the practice of entombment to the New World. Whereas earth burial was used by the poor throughout America, the wealthy and middle classes in South America and in enclaves of European influence in North America (e.g., New Orleans) continued the practice of entombment. Even as yellow fever raged in New Orleans in the nineteenth century, the dead were entombed in cemeteries consisting of vaults.[4]

Health considerations led rural-cemetery founders in antebellum America

Fleischman Mausoleum, Cemetery of Spring Grove,
Cincinnati, 1985

A replica of the Parthenon (completed c. 438 B.C.), this early-twentieth-century mausoleum represents not only the continuing American fascination with classical architecture but also Spring Grove's retention of the fundamental concepts of Strauch's landscape-lawn plan. The mausoleum is located off the road, isolated amid the green lawn and shrubs.

to criticize the practice. Vault burial underneath churches was a popular practice in many of the cities where debates raged on the risks posed by the decomposition of the dead. Rural-cemetery founders discovered that they could restrict, but not prohibit, the practice. Hillside and free-standing mausoleums were constructed in most American cemeteries. Grand, elaborate mausoleums dotted the landscapes of particularly wealthy cemeteries, including Green-Wood in Brooklyn. Some of the nation's best examples of the Egyptian Revival style are the mausoleums of rural cemeteries. Built in a variety of styles and shapes, the mausoleums closely followed architectural trends.[5]

Mausoleums were particularly popular in non-Protestant cemeteries. Catholics did not agree with the restrictions on tomb burial. Catholic cemeteries were dotted with small and large mausoleums built by prosperous members of the community. Prominent Jewish cemeteries, such as Salem Fields in Brooklyn, were filled with private mausoleums of various dimensions.[6]

After 1875, the great new industrial wealth financed a wave of mausoleums. Lawn-park cemeteries were most often the sites of the largess of the nouveau riche. Often, huge cathedral-like or château-like structures were constructed to memorialize the families of the Rockefellers, Vanderbilts, and local industrial barons. Some cemetery patrons lent their names to cemetery chapels and entrances; most bought Tiffany stained-glass windows for their family mausoleum.

Admirers of mausoleums viewed them as symbols of the greatness of America, icons to material and social success. Newspaper articles noted their size and expense, much as they described that of the estates and city homes of the wealthy. Richard Morris Hunt, James Renwick, John Russell Pope, and other leading architects designed mausoleums for their favorite clients. Frederick Law Olmsted, who refused most commissions to design cemeteries, accepted the Vanderbilts' request that he landscape the grounds surrounding their mausoleum. Woodlawn in the Bronx, Oak Hill in Washington, D.C., and Graceland in Chicago were among the cemeteries filled with ornate mausoleums.[7]

Some Americans criticized mausoleums as elitist and provocative. As long ago as the 1830s, the Marble cemeteries in lower Manhattan were perceived as elite burial places partly because they consisted entirely of vaults. Later, the 50-foot pyramid of the Longstreet family in Oakwood Cemetery of Syracuse, New York, or the Gothic cathedral of the Dexter family in the Cemetery of Spring Grove in Cincinnati left little doubt about the cost needed to leave such a mark on the landscape. Families left little doubt as to who had built the mausoleums, for family names were prominently displayed on their fronts. As with the new department stores, mausoleums advertised with large signs above the doors.

In the 1870s, superintendents responded to public interest in entombment by widening the opportunity for vault entombment through *community mausoleums*.[8] These were buildings owned by the cemetery, which offered spaces for sale. The first ones were simple buildings with a practical design and little decoration. Designers interspersed small private vault rooms along the marble corridors. These rooms provided customers with a choice, if they could afford it. They could purchase one or more vaults along the corridor or one of the small rooms, which were usually fronted with locked iron gates, upon which the family name was engraved. Huge flower arrangements and Chinese vases ornamented the corridors. Although the later community mausoleums were expensive, they were targeted to the middle class.

Many community mausoleums were constructed and sold by speculative companies, such as the Eastern Mausoleum Company, which was very active throughout the East after 1900. These companies offered to build a community mausoleum for a cemetery. They persuaded the cemetery that the profits would be enormous if it would allow them to build the mausoleum and sell crypts to the community. The speculative companies would deduct the cost of the building plus a set percentage of the purchase price, then the cemetery could collect the rest. The buildings were often shoddily built, and not only the cemetery but also the customers were defrauded. The Association of American Cemetery Superintendents quickly urged its members to discourage boards of directors from entering contracts with these companies.[9]

The association's advice did not stop speculative companies from making ambitious plans to build new mausoleums. A remarkable piece of promotional material was the *Temples of Peace, or the Endowed Community Mausoleum vs. Earth-Burial and Cremation,* published by the Northwestern Mausoleum Company in

Ferncliff Mausoleum, Ferncliff Cemetery, Hartsdale, N.Y., c. 1960
This is a magnificent example of the large community mausoleums built in the early twentieth century. Unlike many community mausoleums, Ferncliff Mausoleum was expertly constructed and sold under a plan that ensured maintenance. The crypts were expensive, and the furnishings were elaborate. Sales were rapid. (Ferncliff Memorial Park brochure. Courtesy of Ferncliff Cemetery.)

about 1916.[10] This pamphlet contained photographs of a funeral held in a heavy snow, quotes from prominent Europeans and Americans who had chosen entombment, descriptions of the "evils" of earth burial, and accounts of cremationists' "mis-representations" as arguments for purchasing a vault in the community mausoleum to be constructed in the reader's area. Many photographs rendered classically styled large buildings, which represented strength. The mausoleum was associated with style and stability, permanency and privacy. Unfortunately for the speculative companies, many of their plans were stopped by communities fearful of fraud.

One cemetery that built an elaborate mausoleum was Ferncliff in suburban Hartsdale, north of New York City. Started in 1903 as a lawn-park cemetery, Ferncliff was converted into a memorial park in 1925. The centerpiece of the new memorial park was the Cathedral of Memories, built by the James Baird Construction Company, contractors for the Tomb of the Unknown Soldier and other landmarks. The new building held 8,800 crypts, with 250 private family rooms. Each private vault room had a one-of-a-kind stained-glass window, selected by the customer, as the rooms were sold unfinished. The mausoleum included an eighty-seat chapel available to families entombing or burying their dead at Ferncliff.[11]

Memorial parks seldom allowed personal mausoleums, but Forest Lawn did build the Great Mausoleum. The Great Mausoleum reminded cemeterians that a cemetery could make money and have a building that was an artistic addition to the grounds. Such mausoleums attracted public attention and customers. Few memorial parks, especially those established during the Depression, could erect an imitation of Eaton's Great Mausoleum. But some memorial parks built structures that could serve as both chapels and mausoleums.

Elaborate mausoleums such as those in Ferncliff or Forest Lawn were period pieces; costs of construction escalated rapidly after the 1960s. Such mausoleums became too expensive to build and were increasingly costly to heat and maintain. Ferncliff added nine wings to its original mausoleum, Cathedral of Memories, but soon realized that many people could not afford a crypt in it. In 1968 the cost of a double crypt at Ferncliff was $3,500. Other memorial parks and cemeteries wrestled with the question of how to provide crypts at affordable costs without building mausoleums that would deteriorate and become maintenance nightmares.[12]

In 1949 two speakers at the National Association of Cemeteries meeting described the new *garden crypts* being developed in three California memorial parks. One memorial park had constructed hundreds of crypts underground, covered only by individual bronze markers. Another had constructed a series of above-ground, low-level crypts, which served as the boundary of the memorial park. The final memorial park had built a series of above-ground crypts, surrounding them with a concrete sidewalk and forgoing the expense of closing and heating the surrounding area. Out of these three ideas grew the concept of the *garden mausoleum,* pioneered first in California, then adopted by cemeteries and memorial parks throughout America.[13]

The garden mausoleum solved the cost problem and offered cemeteries and memorial parks an opportunity to add inexpensive and attractive crypts. They were similar to the 1831 innovation of Perkins Nichols and the founders of the Marble cemeteries. The buildings placed crypts back to back, facing out onto small courtyards. The crypts were not enclosed in a structure and thus required no heating. The price of construction was lower because the concrete frame was covered with a veneer of granite and marble. Finally, the improved concrete and other building materials offered durability to both customers and managers fearful of maintenance costs.

The complex of mausoleums in Elmlawn Cemetery in Buffalo is typical of many around the country. The mausoleums surround an enclosed and heated central mausoleum, which is used as a chapel for services. Concrete arches line the building's front, shading the crypt fronts and creating a passageway for visitors. The mausoleums are designed as a complex, but built one at a time. As one sells, others are constructed.

The garden mausoleum is a more efficient use of available land than earth burial because a greater number of interments can be placed in a small acreage. By building mausoleums, the cemetery also can gain even greater control over the burial process. The vaults act as a permanent grave liner, awaiting a casket.

Garden Mausoleum Complex, Elmlawn Cemetery, Kenmore, N.Y., c. 1985
In the 1970s, cemeteries could no longer afford to build large, heated community mausoleums such as the one in Ferncliff Cemetery. *Garden mausoleums,* consisting of unenclosed stacked crypts, replaced community mausoleums. The least expensive way to construct garden mausoleums is to group buildings. The complex included a central enclosed mausoleum, which also served as a chapel. (Elmlawn Cemetery brochure, c. 1985. Courtesy of Elmlawn Cemetery.)

The marker is directly fixed to the face of the vault and is usually purchased with it. The service can be held in the cemetery's chapel or in other space provided near the mausoleum. Crypt, vault, marker, cemetery service, and maintenance can all be purchased as a package payable in installments prior to the burial.

Garden mausoleums have been a profitable investment. Estimates of the land price, the cost of building the crypts, and the service charges indicate that many cemeterics make a large profit on mausoleums. The cemetery offers perpetual maintenance and care. The building fund needs to be large enough to ensure that future expenses can be covered. Many cemeteries have faced serious financial problems because of vandalized individual mausoleums, and cemeteries are cautious in assessing their needs.

THE RETURN OF THE PRIVATE MAUSOLEUM

The golden age of the private mausoleum was from 1880 to 1920, when firms such as Presby-Leland of New York City erected hundreds of stylish mausoleums across America. Imitations of a variety of architectural motifs, built mainly of granite and various shades of marble, they stood as icons to America's industrial wealth. Less affluent Americans soon purchased smaller, less ornate mausoleums, which copied the largest mausoleums. These smaller

"You've Earned the Prestige," Advertisement for
Memory Hill Gardens, Tuscaloosa, Ala., 1990

Memory Hills Gardens is one of numerous memorial parks in the South and West. The advertisement is using prestige to appeal to Americans committed to economic success as a barometer of achievement. After working for a lifetime to afford the "good life," why settle for less during an eternity? (Courtesy of Cold Spring Granite Private Estate Mausoleums and Memory Hill Gardens.)

mausoleums often were located side by side, creating a area separated from the more densely populated monumented sections.

The popularity of the private mausoleum diminished after 1920 because of its rapidly escalating price, the popularity of the garden mausoleum, and the increase in cremation among wealthy Anglo-Saxon Protestants. Private mausoleums were still built, but they were fewer and had less decoration. There were generally more private mausoleums in cemeteries catering to ethnic groups, Catholics, and Jews than in Protestant nonsectarian cemeteries.

In the 1980s, the mausoleum regained popularity.[11] St. Michael's Cemetery in Queens, a Protestant nonsectarian cemetery, built seven new mausoleums between 1985 and 1988. More people can afford mausoleums because of the increase in disposable and retirement income. Social differences and symbols of economic distinction were more accepted in the 1980s than they had been in decades. As a result, people once again built elaborate monuments to their dead.

The reappearance of the mausoleum coincided with the decision of more Americans to buy monuments. Bronze markers, which continue to be used in memorial parks, slowly appeared in the burial sections of monumented cemeteries. Small individual markers and marble, granite, and bronze flush markers became popular methods of marking graves. Throughout the 1960s and 1970s, granite and marble quarries, as well as monument dealerships, attempted to provide cemeteries with new designs that incorporated monuments, even if they were smaller and less ornamented than in the past. The quarries and monument dealerships were most successful in ethnic, Catholic, and Jewish cemeteries.

In the 1980s, monument lots increased in popularity. It appeared that a wide range of upper- and middle-class Americans purchased monuments. Although a two-grave lot where no monuments are allowed was as much as $600 less than a two-grave lot with monument space, lots permitting monuments sold.

CREMATION TODAY

Growing numbers of Americans are turning away from the customs of burial and memorialization, despite the continuing attraction of private and garden mausoleums. The Cremation Association of North America reported the following 1988 statistics. Of 2,169,773 who had died in America, there were 332,183 (15.31 percent) cremations. The nation had 954 crematories. A third of them were in the Pacific states of Alaska, California, Hawaii, Oregon, and Washington; in these states, over 38 percent of those who had died were cremated. In a region in the South (Alabama, Kentucky, Mississippi, and Tennessee), less than 3 percent of those who had died were cremated.[15]

After the medically driven reform activities of late-nineteenth-century cremationists diminished with the verification of the germ theory and the emergence of the new science of public health, cremation became less of a reform movement. This change probably enhanced the long-term advance of the practice, because the reform had been "tainted" with atheism and other unpopular ideologies. The antagonism of many clerical and conservative commentators toward cremation slowly diminished. Since 1963 the Catholic church has modified its position against cremation, but it still prefers earth burial.[16]

Cremation has remained a distinct alternative to mainstream customs. Cremation has been promoted as an inexpensive alternative to the increasingly expensive funeral and cemetery lot. Clerical and social critics of the funeral process suggested cremation as one option for those who could accept it theologically. Articles on pauper burial in the cities advocated cremation as less

TABLE 9.1
The Rise in Cremation, 1959–1988

Year	Cremations	Deaths in Millions	%	Year	Cremations	Deaths in Millions	%	Year	Cremations	Deaths in Millions	%
1959	59,376	1.657	3.58	1969	85,683	1.922	4.46	1979	179,393	1.905	9.42
1960	60,987	1.712	3.56	1970	88,096	1.921	4.58	1980	193,343	1.985	9.74
1961	61,595	1.702	3.62	1971	92,251	1.928	4.78	1981	217,770	1.988	10.96
1962	63,435	1.757	3.61	1972	97,067	1.964	4.94	1982	232,789	1.985	11.73
1963	67,330	1.814	3.71	1973	112,298	1.973	5.69	1983	249,182	2.019	12.40
1964	67,658	1.798	3.76	1974	119,480	1.934	6.18	1984	266,441	2.040	13.02
1965	70,796	1.828	3.87	1975	123,918	1.893	6.55	1985	289,091	2.084	13.81
1966	73,339	1.863	3.94	1976	140,052	1.910	7.33	1986	300,587	2.099	14.32
1967	77,375	1.851	4.18	1977	145,733	1.902	7.66	1987	323,371	2.127	15.21
1968	83,977	1.930	4.35	1978	163,260	1.924	8.49	1988	332,183	2.170	15.31

Sources: "CANA (Cremation Association of North America) News Report: Cremation Historical Figures: 1876-On," *Cremationist* 19, no. 2 (April–June 1983); "North American Cremation Statistics, 1983–85," *Cremationist* 22, no. 2 (April–June 1986); and "North American Cremation Statistics, 1986–88," *Cremationist* 25, no. 2 (April–June 1989). The cremation numbers are voluntarily submitted by crematories responding to CANA's annual survey, so the numbers are probably slightly underreported.

expensive than typical earth burial and more dignified than pit burial or burial in the potter's field.[17]

Both cemeteries and funeral homes own crematories. Crematories are now much more cost-efficient, compact, and longer-lasting due to improvements in engineering and heat sources. The first cremation in the LeMoyne crematory took four hours to cremate the body, and over forty-eight hours to preheat and cool-down the crematory. Today, a gas-fired crematory cremates a body within one-half hour, requires virtually no preheating, and needs an hour of cooling between cremations.

Cremation is legally considered the final disposition of the body in most states, meaning that the cremated remains do not necessarily have to be buried or entombed. To guard against public-health problems and misuse of the crematory by criminals, most states prohibit a cremation without the involvement of a licensed funeral director. Some advocates of less expensive funerals have argued that this requirement forces people wishing to have the simplest possible funeral to abide by the sometimes arbitrary rules of individual funeral directors.

Cremains (the industry term for cremated remains) often are not buried or entombed in cemeteries and memorial parks. Figures vary and evidence is elusive, but most people in the cemetery trade agree that at least 50 percent of all cremains are not placed in a columbarium *niche* (a small stone vault in which a cremation urn is entombed), a mausoleum, or a family grave. Cremains may be left with the crematory for permanent storage, spread by survivors, or even kept in the family home.

Interestingly, most Americans are not shocked by the failure of many survivors to memorialize the cremated dead. Few Americans complain that a heritage is being lost or state that the dead deserve permanent remembrance. Nineteenth-century Americans created rural cemeteries to ensure that their dead would be permanently interred and remembered. Twentieth-century practitioners of cremation believe that the dead can be memorialized in other ways or live in the hearts and memories of those who knew them.

One explanation for the failure of Americans to react to this disregard for custom is the privacy that increasingly surrounds the contemporary American funeral. Death has become an intensely private matter, which is a reversal of the public expression of death in the last century. Cremation, with its mechanical disposition witnessed by none of the family, incorporates the desire for privacy and efficiency. Cremation is the final disposition, which means that the survivors are free to choose the ritual of burial if they wish. This freedom of choice has led to the popular folk story of Father or Mother placing Grandmother's cremains in the car at Christmas for the trip home. The family can reclaim control over the burial of the dead through cremation.

Recently, the terrible epidemic of AIDS, with its high toll among younger gay men, has demonstrated how disaffected some Americans feel from the traditions surrounding death. Many AIDS stories end with friends of the deceased going to the favorite beach, vista, or park of the deceased and scattering the cremains. A memorial service in which the body of a person who has died of AIDS, cancer, or the other traumatic diseases is not present seems much more humane to those struggling with deep feelings of grief.[18]

The rising number of cremations also reflects the continuing alienation many Americans feel toward death. Americans have recently begun speaking more openly about death and disease, most prominently cancer. Patients have been attempting to gain more control over the process of dying and death, as manifested in the new popularity of hospices and living wills and in the sometimes gruesome court cases in which dying people demand from society the right to die. Yet death remains a terrifying presence. Cremation may have become more popular with people alienated from traditional rituals surrounding death, but many Americans with strong ethnic, racial, and religious ties continue to rely on older, more defined relationships to death.

Few Americans, especially the young, have little sense of how to understand death when someone around them dies. Part of this is simply the infrequency of the occurrence. Except for those in the health-care and funeral professions, few Americans have to acknowledge death on a regular basis. Part of this failure to understand death is the strong American belief that death can be challenged, even beaten, if one does everything right. One story tells of a nurse reassuring herself and a friend of a deceased man that "he's really not dead," as if she could separate the dead body from the living being. The American funeral, with its embalmed corpse and accentuation on the survivors, reinforces the belief that Americans do not have to accept the inevitability of death, so it is not surprising that it is so difficult for the young to understand death.[19]

Such attitudes directly confront the relationship between the dead and the living in American society. By disposing of the dead without displaying a permanent marker to their memory in a cemetery or a memorial park, some Americans are stating that they no longer accept the grave's role in society. Unlike lot-holders, many of whom rarely visit the grave or visit only on such occasions as Memorial Day, cremationists refuse to allow the cemeterians and funeral industry to direct the manner in which they mourn. This refusal threatens the cemetery.

"THE AMERICAN WAY OF DEATH"

The concern about the issue of the relationship of death and private enterprise intensified in the 1960s, with the publication of Mitford's *The American Way of Death* and Harmer's *The High Cost of Dying*, both attacks on America's burial places, especially California's memorial parks. These two authors particularly attacked new, expensive mausoleums and promoted the inexpensive alternative of cremation.

Mitford's book was the more widely read and acclaimed. It assembled a mass of evidence about the commercialism of death in America. Mitford was forthright about her view of American funeral directors. Her "Foreword" states: "This would normally be the place to say . . . 'I am not, of course, speaking of the vast majority of ethical undertakers.' But the vast majority of ethical undertakers is precisely the subject of this book. To be 'ethical' merely means to adhere to a prevailing code of morality, in this case one devised over the years by the undertakers themselves for their own purposes."[20]

Mitford argued that a new mythology "essential to the twentieth-century American funeral rite" had been "built up step by step" to bolster the obligation of Americans to have an elaborate ceremony directed by a funeral director and including many unnecessary services.[21] She believed that the new funeral was a creation of twentieth-century funeral directors. They were making huge, outrageous profits from this funeral—with its expensive embalming, costly caskets, and extravagant flowers—and foisted it on the public. Mitford also rejected the psychological justification for the ornate funeral, stating that, although "authentic-sounding," it was merely a rationalization for high costs.

Mitford mercilessly revealed the depths of commercialism in the funeral industry. She discussed the method funeral directors took to steer mourners toward the more expensive caskets. She highlighted the all-too-numerous hidden service costs, which dramatically increased funeral bills. She discussed in detail the phone banks and direct-mail campaigns of the cemeteries. She probed each aspect of the funeral and displayed it for a shocked America.

Mitford proposed, as an alternative to existing choices, the formation of memorial societies that would offer Americans simple and inexpensive funerals. Noting that in 1961 the average funeral cost $708 before the expenses of the burial vault, flowers, clothing, honorariums to clergy and musicians, and cemetery charges, which probably brought the total to about $1,450, Mitford made a strenuous plea for memorial societies that would greatly limit the costs.[22] Successors to workers' burial societies of the nineteenth century and co-operative funeral societies of the 1930s, memorial societies would offer the public an alternative to the usual procedures that followed a death in the family.

Mitford's argument was influenced by the rational view of burial current in England at the time.[23] English funerals had become simple indeed because most of the dead were cremated. Geoffrey Gorer had written in 1955 that death was denied completely in England; immediate family members were encouraged to forego the funeral entirely and to continue on as if nothing had happened. Unlike Americans who refused to accept such restrictions, the English turned the business of death into a public service.

Mitford applied the lessons of England to America. She argued first that the family should retain control over the funeral rather than giving it to the funeral director. To retain control meant understanding the procedures surrounding death and burial, so Mitford wanted people to educate themselves about prices, customs, and "products." Memorial societies would offer great assistance here, because they would arrange prepaid inexpensive funerals and provide information on other aspects of the interment or disposal process. Then the public would no longer stand for the unbridled greed of the funeral directors and change the American way of death.

Mitford wondered on her book's last page if even memorial societies would go far enough. She suggested that some individuals might want do-it-yourself funerals; others, to follow the French system of several classes of funerals directly purchased from the government; and still others, the Swiss method, in which a grave, coffin, hearse, and state funeral were all considered the right of every citizen and, regardless of his or her financial status, were provided free by the government.[24]

Mitford's declaration of the American way of death, while a deft description of the commercialization of the burial process, indicated the continuing inability of commentators to differentiate Americans' desire for private control over the burial from their willingness to pay for that right. Memorial societies, like co-operative burial societies and workers' funeral societies, primarily attracted people committed to an ideology critical of the marketplace or forced by economic problems to seek alternatives to popular contemporary practice. Mitford conceded that memorial societies would have little support outside the "more sophisticated" academic and intellectual communities, which found the commercialism of American society distasteful.[25]

A PUBLIC ALTERNATIVE FOR VETERANS

A 1974 congressional report on veterans' cemeteries opened with the statement that "death is preeminently a family matter—the ensuing family loss, funeral and cemetery arrangements, and economic adjustment are in a highly personal domain which Americans have preferred to keep beyond government scrutiny."[26] Yet, just as memorial societies provided an alternative to the traditional funeral, veterans' cemeteries were an alternative to the private cemetery for a growing number of Americans in the post–World War II era. By 1990 the National Cemetery System, which had begun because of the pressing needs of the Civil War, was under the supervision of the Veterans Administration and encompassed 113 cemeteries. Furthermore, the army managed Arlington National Cemetery, near Washington, D.C., and the American Battle Monuments Commission was responsible for 24 overseas military cemeteries and 18 separate battle monuments, 14 of which were abroad. Finally, starting in the 1970s, the federal government joined with state governments in creating a system of state-owned and -maintained veterans' cemeteries, with the hope that the state system would lessen the pressure on the national one and eventually result in a veterans' cemetery in every state.

The Department of War established the original national cemeteries to inter soldiers who had died on Civil War battlefields. These cemeteries were an emergency measure when the war suddenly resulted in thousands of casualties. In the decade after the war, America decided to retain the cemeteries, making them hallowed shrines to the tragedy of the war. The national cemeteries were retained partly because the number of the unidentified dead was so large that it would have been impossible to have returned all of the corpses to families.

In 1872 Congress "extended the right to burial [in national cemeteries] to honorably discharged soldiers in a destitute condition."[27] Furthermore, cemeteries were established for the deceased who had resided in the National Homes for Disabled Volunteer Soldiers. Between 1872 and 1948, the two systems gradually liberalized the regulations regarding who could be buried in national cemeteries. The two most important modifications were that the requirement of destitution was gradually ignored and that, starting in 1890, spouses (and later all minor children and unmarried adult daughters) of veterans were also allowed interment. The national cemeteries' impact on other burial places was negligible, though, as long as Americans retained their loyalty to local cemeteries, the number of national cemeteries was limited, and the number of veterans remained relatively low in proportion to that of the remaining population.

In the twentieth century, there were more national cemeteries because more veterans were eligible for burial. Twenty million American veterans had survived the world wars. Beginning in 1929, veterans' groups attempted to expand the National Cemetery System. Plans for a veterans' cemetery in every state and territory, a total of 79 of them, were proposed in 1944. Cemetery and memorial-park organizations successfully stalled the legislation until the post–World War II period, when Congress was more economy-minded. Indeed, until the 1970s, there was virtually no growth in the system of veterans' cemeteries that had existed in the 1940s.

One reason the system did not expand as fast as some veterans' organizations wished was that most twentieth-century veterans, like their nineteenth-century counterparts, chose to be interred in private cemeteries rather than in national ones. Private cemeteries that dated from the nineteenth-century, as well as the government, recognized veterans' special status in American society. Sleepy Hollow in Tarrytown, N.Y., and other older cemeteries not only designated memorials to veterans, but also reserved burial sections for veterans and their families. Some cemeteries provided free graves for those who had combat casualties. These sections are easily recognizable today because of cannons of the eras of the Civil War and Spanish-American War, which typically stand watch over the rows of the upright marble markers. Private cemeteries with such sections were able to retain the business of approximately 85 percent of American veterans.

Through its free marker program, the government explicitly supported the right of private cemeteries to veterans' business. Beginning in 1879, the government guaranteed a free marker for every veteran's grave, whether it was in a public or private burial place. The design of the marker underwent some modifications, particularly in 1922, when an alternative design for all World War I veterans was accepted. The new "general" headstone that was adopted was the upright slab one, which marks most graves of twentieth-century veterans. The advent of memorial parks forced the government to further adapt the marker, resulting in a Department of War design for a flush marker available in marble, granite, or bronze. Whereas veterans' cemeteries, with a few exceptions, have retained the "general" headstone, private cemeteries and memorial parks have usually chosen the flush marker, especially of bronze and granite, because it is more durable and requires less maintenance. In 1987 the government shipped over 250,000 markers to private, religious, and municipal cemeteries as a part of this program.

The National Cemetery System expanded in the 1970s as the Veterans Administration was given responsibility for it and the number of potential users skyrocketed. Because the majority of existing cemeteries will be full by 2020, veterans' groups have strenuously lobbied for the opening of new cemeteries throughout America. Their goal has been to locate a cemetery within one hundred miles of each veteran, because the number of veterans who will choose to be buried in a national cemetery plummets when it is farther than that distance. The government has refused to accede to this objective, instead creating ten large regional areas and guaranteeing that a veterans' cemetery burial site in each area will be available for any veteran. The Veterans Administration hopes that state veterans' cemeteries will supplement these national ones.

The American Cemetery Association and other industry groups have long lobbied to limit the impact of veterans' cemeteries on private ones. In 1988 the Monument Builders of North America enunciated the concerns of the funeral and burial industries: "The private cemetery industry and the private memorial industry of this country have demonstrated their ability to fully and completely meet the burial needs of the citizens of this country, whether veterans or non-veterans, and at no burden to the taxpayers. . . . Efforts to expand the national veterans cemetery program fly in the face of national trends, national experience, and national need."[28] Charging that the government would better serve veterans' wishes and America's economic needs by providing a one-time subsidy of burials in private cemeteries than in maintaining national ones, the association worried that new cemeteries would be created only because government administrators wanted to perpetuate their positions. Although the system has expanded by three cemeteries in recent years, the association's position has gained the considerable sympathy of Republican administrations, which have been pressured by a huge budget deficit.

The National Cemetery System is the single most visible publicly owned cemetery system in America. Although many cities and counties own burial grounds for the destitute, this system has outgrown its original designation as a program for needy veterans. Burial grounds are available to all honorably discharged veterans, their spouses, and some children; the system provides a striking alternative to the custom of private burial and to the American way of death. In 1987, over 55,000 Americans were interred in Arlington National Cemetery and in cemeteries in the National Cemetery System. Even though that number represented approximately 14 percent of the veteran deaths of 1987, cemeterians have long seen the system as a threat to private cemeteries and as an unusual intrusion of the government into the American customs surrounding death.

INCREASING REGULATION

Partly in response to the immense controversy evoked by Mitford's book, the federal government held hearings on the funeral industry in 1964. These hearings began the federal government's sporadic involvement in the public examination of the funeral business. Funeral directors continue to be primarily regulated by state boards that monitor licensing and public-health conditions. Prior to the 1960s, the government did little to regulate prices.[29]

In the 1960s and again in the 1970s, the federal government claimed that the consumer had the right to know more about the funeral industry's practices and prices. This claim forced the funeral industry to discuss prices with customers and to acknowledge the private, commercial nature of the burial process. Increased regulation, most importantly the 1970s legislation calling for itemized bills, has been resisted by the funeral industry, which worries that such restrictions will reinforce the public's distrust of it.

Cemeteries have rarely been the focus of federal hearings. The funeral director's large role in arranging the burial has brought most of the public attention. At hearings, cemetery fees usually were discussed as add-on prices to the funeral. In the 1980s, the public's concern about prepaid funerals and the expansion of cemetery conglomerates, and monument dealers' concerns about competition, resulted in a closer look at cemeteries. The federal government has done little to restrict practices further.

THE CONSOLIDATION OF THE CEMETERY

The cemeteries have faced, instead of greater federal control, increased competition and mounting pressures to expand in order to maintain their market position. Managing the cemetery has become more challenging primarily because of personnel pressures, as well as economic ones, including new, expensive marketing techniques and costly garden mausoleums. The superintendent who focused on the grounds and knew little about advertising, raising funds, managing personnel, and purchasing appropriate equipment became an anachronism. A new generation of college-educated, sales-oriented managers began to replace the horticulturists of the earlier years, or a corporation that specialized in management took over the cemetery itself.

Although most cemeteries remain independently operated organizations, the cemetery has entered a period of consolidation. Nationally, several corporations are buying cemeteries and funeral homes in order to develop networks of services. Locally, financially strong and commercially aggressive cemeteries are offering management services to weaker, less commercially viable cemeteries. In each instance, the cemetery has begun to apply modern financial methods to an industry that had been operating as if it were 1930, or even 1830.

In 1986 *Business Week* reported on the rapid expansion of Service Corporation International (SCI), the nation's largest holding company of funeral homes and cemeteries.[30] Founded in the 1960s, SCI had acquired 316 funeral homes and 80 cemeteries by 1986. Robert Waltrip, chairman of SCI, told the magazine he was attempting to turn the company into "the True-Value hardware of the funeral-service industry." Sales in 1985 were $263.9 million, with a pending acquisition about to add another $190 million. That adds up to about $450 million, which was approximately the amount that Americans spent on all crematories, cemeteries, funerals, and related services in 1942. In 1985 SCI's profits were $40.9 million. Death has indeed become a big business.

SCI's success was only one more chapter in the maturation of the cemetery industry. In the 1940s, Edward "Doc" Williams had developed the first cemetery empire, Memory Gardens Association. This association demonstrated that consolidation offered tremendous opportunities to cemetery and memorial-

park operators. Williams had developed an empire of over one hundred memorial parks, but it collapsed amid various court cases and personal rivalries.
Few followed his lead before the 1960s, apparently because of the industry's
decentralized nature.

The local orientation of the cemetery slowed consolidation. Cemeteries'
strong tradition of local boards of directors and local involvement in decision-
making made it difficult to work cooperatively with other cemeteries. Directors
rarely see the cemetery primarily as a business. They care more about their lots
than the cemetery's overall profit, although that is changing because greater
numbers of cemeteries face severe financial difficulties.

Interestingly, when Memory Gardens Association or other speculative
memorial-park operations decided to open a new memorial park in an area,
they recognized and profited from the local character of the burial place. Often, a group of local business people and civic leaders would originally an-
nounce a new memorial park. Only later, when various town and city boards
approved the project, or only after the memorial park went into operation,
would a manager arrive from the home operation. Local business people and
civic leaders were lured into participation through offers of free lots, in some
cases through offers of a share in the profits, and in many cases through
excellent sales pitches that lead them to believe that they were doing a public
service.[31]

The first consolidations were of funeral homes. Consolidators easily convinced funeral homes, which were usually small businesses that had high over-
heads and faced significant competition, that working together could improve
performance and profits. In 1986 in America there were 22,000 funeral homes
and two million deaths. Many funeral homes cannot compete with the large-
volume businesses that SCI and its competitors are adding to their growing
networks.

On a local level there has also been consolidation, through the development of cooperative relationships based on a management contract. In Syracuse, Oakwood Cemetery entered a management contract with a neighboring
lawn-park cemetery, Morningside Cemetery, as early as the 1960s.[32] Later,
Oakwood Cemetery merged with Morningside and its crematory to create a
single corporation, Oakwood-Morningside Cemetery, which in turn established contracts with White Chapel Memorial Park, Valley Cemetery, and
Greenlawn Cemetery. (The corporation had temporary relationships with two
smaller country cemeteries and the Jewish synagogue cemeteries, but has with-
drawn from them.) Oakwood Cemeteries, as it is now called, competes with
Jewish synagogue cemeteries, Catholic diocesan cemeteries, an independent
Catholic cemetery, a municipally owned cemetery, and the other nonsectarian,
nonprofit cemetery in the area, Woodlawn.

Oakwood's expansion resulted from the inability of small, poorly financed
cemeteries and memorial parks to maintain community interest. Each had been

a successful organization at some time in the past, but was now sustained only by old relationships, previous sales, and its trust funds. Oakwood offered each organization quality maintenance, a central office staff to audit funds and keep records, and other services at a price that the individual organization could not match. Oakwood is unusual, but other cemeteries and memorial parks have inquired about how consolidation would benefit them.

Consolidation has accelerated changes in the managerial hierarchy in the cemetery industry. Superintendents and sales directors have become middle managers as financial matters have become more complex. Although many cemeteries still retain the structure that was created in the late nineteenth century on the model pioneered by Adolph Strauch, others have become part of a larger corporation, and managers therefore do not have the total control that their predecessors did.

This change has confused the issue of professionalism within the industry. Cemeterians have long viewed themselves as professionals, specialists in their work. The areas of expertise are losing definition as superintendents become grounds managers, sales executives imitate wider business practices, and the industry loses its uniqueness. Today more than ever, a cemeterian need not have mowed lawns, fixed engines, designed sections, overseen construction— all of which were the marks of the nineteenth-century superintendent. It is questionable whether *cemeterian* is actually a separate professional designation.

SELLING THE CEMETERY TODAY

Pressure to produce sales has pushed cemetery executives to broaden their concepts of advertising and sales techniques. Precluded by public ambivalence toward the cemetery and competition from simply offering itself as a community resource as a rural cemetery did 150 years ago, a cemetery has to sell lots if it is to survive financially. If a cemetery is to sell lots, it must either have a large part of the community closely identified with it or reach out to those without affiliation and persuade them to purchase lots. As a result, many cemeteries necessarily have become much more up to date in their public-relations, advertising, and sales programs.

Some cemeteries and memorial parks now send direct mail to households in neighborhoods selected by ethnicity, income, and other factors. Applicants for sales positions are screened with psychological tests to judge how they match a profile of a successful salesperson. Subtle television advertising has been added to radio and newspaper spots. Cemeteries and memorial parks offer brochures on estate planning, wills, and spiritual matters to potential customers.

The appropriateness of bold advertising is still debated. In 1978 Trinity Church Cemetery, the only active burial place in Manhattan, ran a series of controversial advertisements. One was titled "Sex and Death." In this advertisement, Trinity challenged the taboo surrounding death, noting that people who once refused to talk of sex were now surrounded by it in the media. Trinity noted that death was "not the most pleasant of subjects," but argued, as Eaton had several decades earlier, that the "refusal to talk about it or even think about it is unwise." The advertisement offered a free "Personal Request Folder" containing information on advance planning for wills, burial, insurance.[33]

A New York cemeterian wrote to Trinity charging that the advertisement had "a cheap provocative, sensational, and pulpy trashful headline." He declared that "most of us have devoted a lot of time trying to convince people of the fact that most cemetery people and those who care for the dead are men of good will and worthy of trust, and confidence." He finished by stating that "your headline sullies and besmirches this concept."[34]

This complaint highlighted the continuing controversy over the role of the cemetery as a business. Psychologists and sociologists view death as a powerful taboo. Harmer and other commentators still refuse to accept the cemetery as a business enterprise. Those in the cemetery business cannot agree on how aggressively a cemetery should confront the taboo of death and display its "products" to the public. If Trinity's advertisement had appeared in 1878, it would have shocked both superintendents and the public; in 1978, it seemed to receive criticism only from cemeterians.

NEW TECHNOLOGIES

In many ways the cemetery is no different today than in the 1870s. Although changes have occurred in the management hierarchy of larger, more aggressive cemeteries, the obstacles to consolidation remain substantial. The cemetery industry continues to consist primarily of thousands of discrete operations, most having little contact with competitors. The typical small cemetery continues to function much as it has for decades, retaining a sufficient level of business to maintain its grounds and slowly build its care funds. Few cemeterians are interested in the rapid growth of the cemetery or its becoming part of a larger corporation. The majority of Americans continue to bury their dead in a manner similar to that of their parents and grandparents, and the majority of cemeterians manage their operations much as their predecessors did.

These traditional cemeterians continue to assert that the major problem facing cemetery management is the care of the grounds. If the grounds look bad, lots are difficult to sell. If the grounds look good, they support the sales program. Technology has offered superintendents better ways to maintain the landscape, but has also proved a double-edged sword because lot-holders have come to expect a suburban manicure on grounds that which were often planned for a more picturesque appearance.

For the cemetery industry, the most important technological innovation since 1949 was the mechanical backhoe. The mechanical gravedigger became a reality in the 1950s. By the 1980s, every medium- to large-size cemetery owned at least one backhoe. Digging a grave by hand takes between three and eight hours, depending on conditions, whereas digging one with a mechanical grav-edigger takes about twenty minutes, allowing cemeteries to decrease their full-time staff dramatically. For example, Woodlawn in the Bronx digs between twenty to thirty graves a day and now operates with three backhoes (mechanical gravediggers) instead of between ten to twenty men digging by hand. Ceme-teries that once had to stop burying in the winter can now operate year round.

Lawn care has also improved. Older superintendents had long hoped for a mechanical trimmer to use around their markers and monuments, this work having been done previously by hand, which was expensive. The 1940s marked the innovation of the first gas-generated trimmers. They were bulky and ex-pensive, and their sharp mowerlike blades scraped monuments unless opera-tors were extremely careful.[35] Only with the invention of the weed-eater was a lighter, easily maneuverable trimmer available to cemeteries. Although their strings damaged trees and stones, weed-eaters did less damage and were more efficient than trimmers.

Technology has also posed other major challenges. The foremost chal-lenge for many older cemeteries is how to accommodate the numerous auto-mobiles that now routinely travel their roads. The winding roadways of Mount Auburn in Boston, Oak Hill in Washington, D.C., and other rural cemeteries were developed for the horse and carriage, which was a much slower means of transportation. Later, cemeteries were designed for pedestrians and the small carriages provided by the cemetery, because most people arrived at the ceme-tery gates by public transportation.

The advent of the automobile age forced cemeteries to redesign their roadways and to reconsider their rules. As early as the 1910s, cemeteries were debating the advisability of allowing cars. Because the older roadways were so narrow and the curves were so sharp, at first many cemeteries limited access. Spring Grove opened its grounds to cars in April 1911, but restricted their access to certain hours of the week and to the afternoon of Memorial Day. Later, cemeteries were forced to close roads that could not accommodate cars. Memo-rial parks, designed in the automobile age, were clearly more accessible and appeared more fashionable because their roads were much wider and their roadway systems were much simpler.[36]

Twentieth-century changes in maintenance and design have been expen-sive for older cemeteries. The increased cost of sophisticated equipment, the need for better-skilled employees, and an aging physical infrastructure have dramatically raised the expenses of such cemeteries. The early rural cemeteries are now over 150 years old. Many were financially devastated during the infla-tionary cycles of the 1960s and 1970s. Road and water systems are no longer completely maintained. In some cases, older sections are mowed less fre-quently, and monuments that fall or are vandalized are repaired only if the family is willing to pay for the work. Dependent on allied industries, such as funeral homes and monument dealerships, for referrals, less aggressive commercially than their neighboring cemeteries and memorial parks, or simply running out of new burial spaces, some antebellum cemeteries are gradually assuming an abandoned appearance.

The situation of older graveyards is even more precarious. In towns and cities throughout America, especially in the East, gravestones that have existed for two to three centuries are in danger of falling apart due to dirt, acid rain, vandalism, and aging. Many states have passed legislation mandating that municipalities assume responsibility for the maintenance of these old graveyards, but that only sometimes includes more than minimum care. Family graveyards, distrusted by James Hillhouse in the 1790s, today face an even more uncertain future. Some are on isolated knolls surrounded by suburban developments; others are lost among the growth as nature takes over the landscape. Work by local, state, and national cemetery associations, including the Association for Gravestone Studies, has raised public awareness, but the task of maintaining the old graveyards is enormous.

THE CONTEMPORARY CEMETERY LANDSCAPE

Cemeterians are taking greater risks in order to draw attention to their "products"; their actions are the result of the threats of competition, the improvements in technology, the attacks of critics, and the pressures on sales. In the 1980s, both Mount Auburn and Spring Grove added abstract sculptures, which are different from anything else on their grounds, as major features. The ethereal sculptures highlight Spring Grove's new area of ground crypts (below-ground individual vaults) and are not near the more traditional burial sections. The sculptures suggest a new vision of the interaction of art and nature within the landscape. Cemeteries may once again be sites for contemporary sculpture.

Memorial parks have generally been less willing to take such risks to draw attention to their "products." At Pinelawn, the Garden of Normandie and the Garden of Peace are suggestive of the direction in American landscape design. Both are more dramatic and imaginative than past efforts, such as the use of Masonic tablets and elaborate bird baths as central features. In the Garden of Normandie, the statue *Peaceful Normandie* stands thirteen feet tall, providing a bright golden spot in the green landscape of lawn which surrounds it. More interesting is the Garden of Peace, where eight Corinthian columns, which were originally part of the Federal Reserve Bank in Atlanta, surround a flowing bronze fountain. The columns reassert classical themes, but in a less formal, more abstract manner than the Beaux-Arts buildings of the early twentieth century.[37]

The new art in Mount Auburn, Spring Grove, and Pinelawn reflects the most important development in cemetery design: the perceived necessity to

Modern Sculpture, Mount Auburn Cemetery, Cambridge, Mass., 1989
The older rural cemeteries long resisted abstract modern art within their grounds and considered academic and realistic art more solemn and appropriate. By Richard Duca, this untitled 1981 sculpture is the central feature of a memorial-park section in Mount Auburn. This sculpture and others around the country represent the gradual inclusion of abstract art in modern American culture.

focus the landscape around an art object. Burial sections lined with lots consisting of two, three, or four graves continue to be designed in many cemeteries, but such lots are among several of the choices offered to customers. In Spring Grove, Oakwood, and Elmlawn, new burial sections were planned around a statue of Johnny Appleseed, a bronze Bible open to the Lord's Prayer, and a granite relief map of Vietnam honoring America's participants, respectively.

The landscape has been miniaturized in an attempt to provide familiarity, ease the expense of expanding a cemetery, and attract customers. An art object is easy to put on the front of a brochure or film for a commercial. A view of a green landscape provides little to attract the many Americans living in the suburbs and vacationing in Yosemite.

CONCLUSION

Take a walk in a cemetery during the first week in June. Are there flowers on the graves? Do American flags fly above the graves of veterans? Is the grass mowed and are the bushes clipped? Are there fresh mounds of dirt, a yard of new sod, or other signs of new graves? Americans tend to think of the cemetery as a static

"Cremation Has Many Alternatives,"
Advertisement for Kyger and Trobaugh
Funeral Home, Inc., and Crematory, 1990

In America, cremation began as a self-conscious alternative to earth burial and entombment. By the 1990s, however, cremation had become part of the American way of death. Whereas some crematories advertised the cost savings of cremation in order to do a high volume of cremations, other crematories hoped to transform the public's perception of cremation as an inexpensive method of disposal into a prestigious and valued alternative to the traditional funeral. (Harrisonburg, Va., *Daily News-Record*, 12 May 1990.)

institution, one that has existed, and will exist, forever. But the cemetery is dynamic. Cemeteries, like farms, cities, suburbs, theaters, businesses, and people, are born, live, and die. Anyone who has ever walked through the high grass and broken stones of a country graveyard or urban cemetery knows this.

The American cemetery is far from extinct. During the 1970s, a rebirth of interest in Victorian culture brought one of that period's finest creations, the rural cemetery, back into the public eye. Historical societies organized guided tours of Mount Auburn, Spring Grove, and other rural cemeteries. Supporters in Philadelphia; Rochester, New York; Mobile, Alabama; Atlanta; and other cities formed friends' organizations to help finance improvements in cemeteries. Books boasted of cemeteries' sculpture and landscape artistry.

The business of death has never been as big as it is today. Government estimates reported that in 1979 Americans spent over $7 billion on their dead, of which the nation's cemeteries and memorial parks received somewhat less than $2 billion. Cemeteries and memorial parks survive, buttressed with new sales programs, more efficient maintenance programs, and price increases.[38]

As the twenty-first century dawns, however, the cemetery remains in crisis. Americans are more willing to discuss death today than before, but they are also more willing to cremate the dead, scatter their cremains, and memorialize them with a poem or a tree. The public uses the cemetery more today than any time since the antebellum period, but the use does not translate into respect for the dead or the cemetery. Vandalism increases yearly, as do strange incidents of the occult.

Alternatives flourish. As late as the 1960s, there were virtually no memorial societies offering simple funerals. Today there are hundreds of such societies. They form a national network offering help and information to new societies and to the public. Protestants, who once viewed cremation as a stigma, now widely choose it. Even Catholics and Jews, who just a quarter-century ago virtually never practiced cremation, have turned to it in ever-increasing numbers.

The most significant issue concerning the cemetery is the public's crisis of confidence about it. Afraid of death or uncomforted by faith, many Americans have little understanding of the cemetery. Reinforced by Mitford, Harmer, and other critics of the funeral industry, the views of many Americans appear hostile. New cemeteries are usually unwelcome in the neighborhoods of America. In the nineteenth century, residents gathered in the thousands to celebrate the formation of a new cemetery. Today protesters lobby legislators to forbid their creation or expansion.

Vandalism, which has become a major issue for many American cemeteries, is symptomatic of Americans' crisis of confidence. Vandalism has always existed. Rural-cemetery founders organized their new cemeteries partly because of urban vandalism, then asked cities to deputize their workers. The rampage of youngsters through a cemetery was a rare, but not unknown, occurrence in the nineteenth century. The violence to gravestones, mausoleums, flowers, and other objects in today's cemetery has become endemic. The *American Cemetery* has published a column of short notices for several decades. In some years, issue after issue, the notices are almost all incidents of vandalism.

Society sometimes reacts almost nonchalantly to such incidents. In 1988 a mausoleum was broken open and a body decapitated. A public furor reigned.

A local college student was discovered to have stolen the head for use in an art project. His instructor told the court that his action should be viewed as "nothing more than a prank." A local newspaper editorial wondered what precautions the cemetery had taken to keep this from happening. The culprit was suspended from school, but freed of criminal charges.[39]

The response of society to the incident suggests its distance from the cemetery. The private character of the American cemetery has long been celebrated by founders and managers, but, conversely, the private corporation is viewed as responsible for incidents. The public's tie to the cemetery has been loosened. Because death has become such a private ritual and a less frequent occurrence in everyday life, the cemetery no longer has cultural significance for much of society.

Leavenworth argued that the public's obligation mandated the cemetery as the city's "last great necessity." As the twentieth century ends, the social and cultural mandate that he assumed his audience accepted can no longer be taken for granted. Two million Americans die a year, but fewer and fewer Americans view the cemetery as the "last great necessity" and as the meaningful institution it once was in their society.

NOTES

PROLOGUE. THE LAST GREAT NECESSITY

1. Elias W. Leavenworth, *The History and Incorporation, Rules and Regulations of Oakwood Cemetery, at Syracuse, N.Y., Together with the Dedication Odes and Addresses, with Other Papers,* 2d ed. (Syracuse, 1881); for quotes below, see 23–24.

2. I thank R. Gregory Sloane, executive director of Oakwood Cemeteries, for this information. *Monumented cemetery* includes all burial places founded after 1831 which have two- and three-dimensional family and individual monuments as major features. *Memorial park* includes all burial places established after 1917 which prohibited or dramatically limited the use of family and individual memorials that were not flush to the ground.

CHAPTER ONE. AN AMERICAN MOSAIC OF DEATH

1. There is no summary volume of American death customs, but the best overviews are in Robert W. Habenstein and William M. Lamars, *The History of American Funeral Directing* (Milwaukee, 1981); John R. Stilgoe, *Common Landscape of America, 1580–1845* (New Haven, 1982); and William Lloyd Warner, *The Living and the Dead: A Study in the Symbolic Life of Americans* (New Haven, 1959). European burial practices are summarized in Robert Habenstein and William Lamers, *Funeral Practices the World Over* (Milwaukee, 1960), and are best analyzed in Philippe Ariès, *The Hour of Our Death,* trans. Helen Weaver (New York, 1981); Michel Ragon, *The Space of Death: A Study of Funerary Architecture, Decoration, and Urbanism* (Charlottesville, Va., 1983); and Richard Etlin, *The Architecture of Death: The Transformation of the Cemetery in Eighteenth-Century France* (Cambridge, Mass., 1984).

2. Discussion with Dr. Claus Harmsen, Paris, 28 August 1989.

3. Philippe Ariès, *Western Attitudes toward Death: From the Middle Ages to the Present,* trans. Patricia M. Ranum (Baltimore, 1974).

4. Charles Rosenberg, *The Care of Strangers: Rise of the Modern American Hospital* (New York, 1987).

CHAPTER TWO. DISPLACING THE DEAD

1. "A Rustic Cemetery," *Literary Magazine and American Register* 4, no. 128 (August 1805):22–27.

2. John R. Stilgoe, *Common Landscape of America, 1580–1845* (New Haven, 1982), 219–31. I do not discuss the burial practices of Native Americans. Their graveyards provide fascinating insights into their culture, but they had little influence on colonial practices. Furthermore, I am primarily interested in the change from pioneer burial practices to the cemetery. Native American cemeteries had no discernible influence on the cemeteries of later Americans.

3. W. Clayton, *History of Onondaga County, New York, with Illustrations and Biographical Sketches of Some of Its Prominent Men and Pioneers* (Syracuse, 1878), 144. Webster's journal is quoted in *Memorial History of Syracuse, N.Y., from Its Settlement to the Present Time,* ed.

Dwight Bruce (Syracuse, 1891), 297. Colonial New York gravestones are discussed in Richard Welch, "Colonial and Federal New York and New Jersey Gravestones," *Journal of Long Island History* 17, no. 1 (Winter 1981):23–34.

4. Harriet Martineau, *Retrospect of Western Travel,* 2 vols. (London and New York, 1838), 2:228.

5. James Stevens Curl, "The Design of the Early British Cemeteries," *Journal of Garden History* 4, no. 3 (July-September 1984):223–53; the quote is on 223; and Philippe Ariès, *The Hour of Our Death,* trans. Helen Weaver (New York, 1981), 33–40.

6. On Washington and southern domestic burial grounds, see Stilgoe, *Common Landscape of America,* 228–31, and Blanche Linden-Ward, *Silent City on a Hill: Landscape of Memory and Boston's Mount Auburn Cemetery* (Columbus, Ohio, 1989), 100–113. On slave and free African-American burials, see John Blassingame, *The Slave Community: Plantation Life in the Antebellum South* (New York, 1972), 17–18 and 33–34; Eugene Genovese, *Roll, Jordan, Roll: The World the Slaves Made* (New York, 1974), 194–202; and Angelika Krüger-Kahloula, "Tributes in Stone and Lapidary Lapses: Commemorating Black People in Eighteenth- and Nineteenth-Century America," *Markers: The Annual Journal of the Association for Gravestone Studies* 4 (1989):33–102.

7. Susan Cooper, *Rural Hours* (New York, 1851), 280. For more information on colonial and antebellum burial places, see Beatrix Rumford, "The Role of Death as Reflected in the Art and Folkways of the Northeast in the Eighteenth and Nineteenth Centuries" (Ph.D. diss., State University of New York at Oneonta, Cooperstown Graduate Program, 1965).

8. Ariès, *The Hour of Our Death,* 29–33. See also the quotes in the next two paragraphs.

9. Committee on Laws, "Report on Interments to the New York City Common Council" (9 June 1825), in *Minutes of the Common Council of the City of New York, 1784–1831* (hereafter cited as *MCC*) (New York, 1917), 14:574–634; Ariès, *The Hour of Our Death,* 32–33; and Stilgoe, *Common Landscape of America,* 221–22.

10. Stilgoe, *Common Landscape of America,* 221–22; see also Clare Gittings, *Death, Burial and the Individual in Early Modern England* (London, 1984), 139–40.

11. Curl, "The Design of the Early British Cemeteries," 223. For a remarkable view of British churchyards, see Mrs. Basil Holmes, *The London Burial Grounds: Notes on Their History from the Earliest Times to the Present Day* (New York, 1896).

12. Information on Trinity churchyard is in Morgan Dix, *A History of the Parish of Trinity Church in the City of New York,* 4 vols. (New York, 1905); and Trinity Church, *Churchyards of Trinity Church in the City of New York* (n.p., 1969). Traveler William Blane noted that in America "some of the churchyards have become so full, that they are raised several feet above the . . . street" (Blane, *An Excursion through the United States and Canada during the Years 1822–23, by an English Gentleman* [London, 1824], 12). As Curl notes in "The Design of the Early British Cemeteries," this was not unusual. Because the use of charnel houses was discouraged in Great Britain, "churchyards had to rise in level to accommodate the dead" (223).

13. "Reports of the Committee of the City Council of Charleston, upon Interments within the City and the Memorial from Churches and Citizens" (Charleston, 1859), 22–23.

14. Ira Rosenwaike, *Population History of New York City* (Syracuse, 1972), 27 and 53. For information on the increase of Catholics throughout New York, see Frederick Zwierlein, *The Life and Letters of Bishop McQuaid,* 3 vols. (Rochester, 1927), 14; and Most Reverend Michael Augustine, "The Catholic Cemeteries of New York," *United States Catholic Historical Society, Historical Records and Studies* 1, no. 2 (January 1900):369–78.

Figures on burials in New York City are reported in City Inspector, "Annual Report of the Interments in the City of New York for the Year 1839," in *Documents of the Board of Alderman*, doc. no. 48 (New York, 1840).

15. Stilgoe, *Common Landscape of America*, 220–30. For an example of well-meaning reordering, see Oliver Wendell Holmes, *The Autocrat of the of Breakfast Table*, vol. 2 of *The Works of Oliver Wendell Holmes*, Standard Library Edition (1858; reprint, Boston, 1892), 239–40.

16. Stilgoe, *Common Landscape of America*, 220–30; Syracuse Public Library, *Three Old Syracuse Cemeteries: First Ward, Franklin Park, and Rose Hill* (Syracuse, 1967); Rumford, "The Role of Death as Reflected in the Art of the Northeast;" and "Aaron Hampton's Diary: Notes on a Journey from Kingwood in New Jersey to Lake Erie in the Year 1813," *New York History* 21, no. 3 (July 1940):333–34.

17. Diana Williams Comb, *Early Gravestone Art in Georgia and South Carolina* (Athens, Ga., 1986); Francis Y. Duval and Ivan B. Rigby, *Early American Gravestone Art in Photographs* (New York, 1978), esp. vii–ix; Peter Benes, *Masks of Orthodoxy: Old Gravestone Carvings in Plymouth County, 1689–1805* (Amherst, Mass., 1977); Welch, "Colonial and Federal New York and New Jersey Gravestones," 23–34; Harriette Forbes, *Gravestones of Early New England and the Men Who Made Them, 1653–1800* (Boston, 1927); Edwin Dethlefsen and James Deetz, "Death's Heads, Cherubs, and Willow Trees: Experimental Archaeology in Colonial Cemeteries," *American Antiquity* 31. no. 4 (April 1966):502–10; and Blanche M. G. Linden, "The Willow Tree and Urn Motif," *Markers: The Annual Journal of the Association for Gravestone Studies* 1 (1979–80):149–56.

18. Comb, *Early Gravestone Art in Georgia and South Carolina*, 6–7.

19. *Diary of William Bentley, D., Pastor of the East Church, Salem, Massachusetts*, 4 vols. (Salem, Mass., 1905), 2:442–43; and Linden, "The Willow Tree and Urn Motif," 149–56.

20. Sheppard Knapp, *A History of the Brick Presbyterian Church in the City of New York* (New York, 1909), 141–43 and 262.

21. "Report on Interments" (9 June 1825), in *MCC* 14:633.

22. John Pintard to Eliza Noel Pintard Davidson, 25 November 1820, *Letters from John Pintard*, ed. Dorothy C. Barch, 4 vols. to date (New York: New-York Historical Society, 1937–40), 1:348–49.

23. Knapp, *A History of the Brick Presbyterian Church*, 136.

24. "Reference Report on Early Chicago Cemeteries, 3 March 1971," file in Chicago Historical Society; Robert Hendre Kelby, "Notes on Pottersfield" (miscellaneous paper at New-York Historical Society, with notes from Furman's notebook); and Margaret F. O'Connell, "Potter's Field Has Found a Resting Place at Last," *New York Times*, 31 August 1975.

25. Material on Charleston: "Report of Committee upon Interments," 27; on Chicago: "Reference Report on Early Chicago Cemeteries;" and on New Haven: a copy of Josiah Meigs's 1797 map of New Haven Burying Ground, in the collection of New Haven Colony Historical Society, clearly shows the area. See figure on p. OO below.

26. Rumford, "Death as Reflected in the Art of the Northeast," chaps. 3 and 4; Margaret Coffin, *Death in Early America: The History and Folklore of Customs and Superstitions of Early Medicine, Burial and Mourning* (New York, 1976), chaps. 4 and 5; and Sarah Orne Jewett, *The Country Doctor* (Boston, 1884), 36–41; the quote is on 38.

27. Rumford, "Death as Reflected in the Art of the Northeast," 59.

28. Charles Allen Shively, "A History of the Conception of Death in America, 1650–1850" (Ph.D. diss., Harvard University, 1968), 129 and 149.

29. Kenneth Scott, "Funeral Customs in Colonial New York," *New York Folklore Quarterly* 15, no. 4 (Winter 1959):274–82.

30. Stilgoe, *Common Landscape of America*, 228–30. Rumford, "Death Reflecting the Art of the Northeast," tells of Hugh Gaine's complaint in 1755 that no matter how poor the deceased, "he cannot be buried, without their *[sic]* being at the Expence of 18s. to some Person . . . to invite People to the Funeral" (41).

31. John Pintard to Eliza Noel Pintard Davidson, 1 September 1829, *Letters from John Pintard*, 3:92–93.

32. Note that the notice calls for the presence of friends and acquaintances of the family. Other notices invited friends and neighbors of the living relatives rather than those of the dead person. These notices suggest both a recognition that the funeral was a part of a larger process of grief and separation and that the funeral process was now focused on the survivor.

33. John Pintard to Eliza Noel Pintard Davidson, 5 November 1819, *Letters from John Pintard*, 1:244; and Rumford, "Death Reflecting the Art of the Northeast," 56 and 63–64.

34. "Cemeteries and Catacombs of Paris," *Quarterly Review* 21, no. 42 (January-April 1819):359–97.

35. Ibid.; the quote is on 382; and Richard Etlin, *The Architecture of Death: The Transformation of the Cemetery in Eighteenth-Century Paris* (Cambridge, Mass., 1984), 12–13.

36. "Cemeteries and Catacombs of Paris," 379.

37. Peter Goldman, "Liberal Myths, Middle-Class Mentalities and Social History in Enlightenment Spain: The Struggle to Establish Municipal Cemeteries" (1983). I would like to thank Professor Goldman for sharing this paper and helping me better understand the relationship between European and American burial practices.

38. Etlin, *The Architecture of Death*, 3–39.

39. Timothy Dwight, *A Statistical Account of the City of New Haven* (New Haven, 1811), 63 and 81: The diseases were "dysentery" and "Yellow fever," but 1795 also was a bad year for "Angina maligna" and "measles," which would have added to the total number of deaths. Henry T. Blake, *Chronicles of the New Haven Green from 1638–1862* (New Haven, 1898), 272, puts the figure at 930 illnesses and 139 deaths out of a population of 5,000.

40. Charles C. Smith, "Manuscript Journal of Reverend John Pierce," in *Proceedings of the Massachusetts Historical Society*, 2d ser. (Boston, 1886), 3:48; and Timothy Dwight, *Travels in New England and New York*, 4 vols. (1821–22; reprint, Cambridge, Mass., 1969), letter no. 15, 1:136–37.

41. Rollin Osterweis, *Three Centuries of New Haven, 1638–1938* (New Haven, 1953), 191–94; the quote is on 194.

42. Rudy J. Favretti, "The Ornamentation of New England Towns, 1750–1850," *Journal of Garden History* 2, no. 4 (October-December 1982):325–42.

43. *Dictionary of American Biography*, s.v. "Hillhouse, James"; and Leonard Bacon, "Sketch of the Life and Character of the Hon. James Hillhouse," *Quarterly Christian Spectator* 5, no. 2 (June 1833):238–47.

44. Bacon, "Sketch of the Life and Character of the Hon. James Hillhouse;" Henry H. Townsend, "The Grove Street Cemetery" (Paper delivered at New Haven Colony Historical Society, New Haven, Conn., 27 October 1947), 7; and "Report of the Committee, Appointed to Inquire into the Condition of the New Haven Burying Ground, and to Propose a Plan for Its Improvement" (New Haven, 1839), 4. For general information on voluntary associations, see Richard D. Brown, "The Emergence of Voluntary Associa-

tions in Massachusetts, 1760–1830," *Journal of Voluntary Action Research* 2 (1973):64–73.

45. Townsend, "The Grove Street Cemetery," 11–12; T. R. Bacon, "Lessons from a City's Life," in *The Hundredth Anniversary of the City of New Haven* ed. F. B. Dexter (New Haven, 1885), 30.

46. Dwight, *Statistical Account of the City of New Haven,* 55.

47. Dwight, *Travels in New England and New York,* letter no. 15, 2:137.

48. Dwight, *Statistical Account of the City of New Haven,* 55; and William Tudor, *Letters on the Eastern States* (Boston, 1821), 25–26.

49. (31 March 1823), in *MCC* 12:810–12. The following discussion is primarily based on *MCC,* as reported in compilations of the Common Council debate in the *New-York Evening Post* and *New-York Spectator.* Also helpful were John Duffy, *A History of Public Health in New York City, 1625–1865* (New York, 1968), 218–21; and Hendrick Hartog, *Public Property and Private Power: The Corporation of the City of New York in American Law, 1730–1870* (Chapel Hill, N.C., 1983), 71–81.

50. Duffy, *History of Public Health,* 97–270. An excellent description of yellow fever, including its epidemiology in Europe, is in William Coleman, *Yellow Fever in the North: The Methods of Early Epidemiology* (Madison, Wisc., 1987), 3–25.

51. The debate is discussed in Erwin Ackerneckt, "Anticontagionism between 1821 and 1867," *Bulletin of the History of Medicine* 22 (September-October 1948):562–93; and Duffy, *History of Public Health,* 97–270.

52. Committee on Laws, "Report on Internments" (9 June 1825), in *MCC* 14:593.

53. Duffy, *History of Public Health,* 219.

54. Ibid., 220.

55. Francis Allen, *Documents and Facts Showing the Fatal Effects of Interments in Populous Cities* (New York, 1822).

56. Daniel Walters, "Diary of the Occurrences of the first month of the Yellow Fever which prevailed in the city of New-York in 1822, with facts and observations relative to the nature and character of the disease," *New-York Medical and Physical Journal* 1, no. 4 (October-December 1822):469–502.

57. *New-York Spectator,* 4 April 1823.

58. "The Memoirs of Stephen Allen," ed. John C. Trowis (1927), 102, in the collection of New-York Historical Society.

59. *New-York Spectator,* 14 April 1823.

60. *New-York Spectator,* 30 May 1823.

61. Ibid. See also J. B. Jackson, "The Vanishing Epitaph: From Monument to Place," *Landscape* 17, no. 2 (Winter 1967–68):22–23; and Committee on Lands and Places, "Report on Public Burying Ground" (9 June 1823), in *MCC* 14:116–18.

62. *New-York Spectator,* 30 May 1823; and Committee on Lands and Places, "Report on the Subject of the City Burial Ground" (20 December 1824), in *MCC* 14:209–11.

63. *New York Times,* 31 August 1975.

64. Material on the New York City Marble cemeteries is from *New York Times,* 30 March 1886; for evidence assembled for the purpose of designating these cemeteries as historic landmarks, see "New York City Marble Cemetery," New York City Landmarks Preservation Commission, March 1969, nos. 4 and 5, LP–0464 and LP–0466; John Summer, executive vice president of Green-Wood Cemetery in Brooklyn provided copies of these works. Information on these cemeteries is also in the New-York Historical Society. See also St. Clair McKelway, "The Marble Cemeteries," *The New Yorker* 10, no. 25 (4 August 1934):29–32.

65. In 1857 Virginians began a successful campaign to return the remains of

Monroe to his native state. He was reinterred in Richmond. See "New York City Marble Cemetery."

66. Dwight, *Travels in New England and New York,* letter no. 15, 138; and "Condition of the New Haven Burying Ground," 15.

67. "The Homes of the Dead," *New York Times,* 30 March 1866; and McKelway, "The Marble Cemeteries," 29–32.

68. William Hodge, "Buffalo's Cemeteries," in *Publications of the Buffalo Historical Society* (Buffalo, N.Y., 1879), 1:51; and Jackson, "The Vanishing Epitaph," 22–23.

69. David Schuyler, *The New Urban Landscape: The Redefinition of City Form in Nineteenth-Century America* (Baltimore, 1986), 41.

70. Ibid.

CHAPTER THREE. MOUNT AUBURN AND THE RURAL-CEMETERY MOVEMENT

1. Emily Dickinson to Abiah Root, 8 September 1846, *Letters of Emily Dickinson,* ed. Thomas H. Johnson and Theodora Ward, 3 vols. (Cambridge, Mass., 1958), 1:36–37. Mount Auburn has received considerable attention from historians; the most impressive discussion is Blanche Linden-Ward, *Silent City on a Hill: Landscape of Memory and Boston's Mount Auburn Cemetery* (Columbus, Ohio, 1989). See also Barbara Rotundo, "Mount Auburn Cemetery: A Proper Boston Institution," *Harvard Library Bulletin* 22, no. 3 (July 1974):268–79; Barbara Rotundo, "Mount Auburn: Fortunate Coincidences and an Ideal Solution," *Journal of Garden History* 4, no. 3 (July-September 1984):255–67; and Stanley French, "The Cemetery as Cultural Institution: The Establishment of Mount Auburn and the 'Rural Cemetery' Movement," *American Quarterly* 26, no. 1 (March 1974):37–59.

2. Anne Whiston Spirn, *The Granite Garden: Urban Nature and Human Design* (New York, 1984), 23. Boston history is discussed in Walter M. Whitehill, *Boston: A Topographical History* (Cambridge, Mass., 1959).

3. William O. Peabody, "Mount Auburn Cemetery: Report of the Massachusetts Horticultural Society upon the Establishment of an Experimental Garden and Rural Cemetery," *North American Review* 33, no. 73 (October 1831):405.

4. *Dictionary of American Biography,* s.v. "Bigelow, Jacob"; and Linden-Ward, *Silent City on a Hill,* 168–70. Early efforts to establish Mount Auburn are discussed in Jacob Bigelow, *A History of the Cemetery of Mount Auburn* (Boston, 1860), 1–2.

5. David Schuyler, *The New Urban Landscape: The Redefinition of City Form in Nineteenth-Century America* (Baltimore, 1986), 42–43.

6. Robert Manning, ed., *History of the Massachusetts Horticultural Society, 1829–1878* (Boston, 1880). On the development and importance of horticulture and agriculture, see Rudy J. Favretti, "The Ornamentation of New England Towns, 1750–1850," *Journal of Garden History* 2, no. 4 (October-December 1982):325–42; Stevenson Whitcomb Fletcher, *Pennsylvania Agriculture and Country Life, 1640–1840* (Harrisburg, Pa., 1950); and U. P. Hedrick, *A History of Horticulture in America to 1860* (New York, 1950).

7. Peabody, "Mount Auburn Cemetery," 398–99.

8. Ibid., 400.

9. The quote is from a Massachusetts Horticultural Society circular advertising the new cemetery project, quoted in *American Magazine of Useful and Entertaining Knowledge* 1, no. 1 (September 1834):9.

10. Bigelow, *History of the Cemetery of Mount Auburn,* 20; and *Dictionary of American Biography,* s.v. "Dearborn, Henry Alexander Scammell."

11. The quote is in Schuyler, *New Urban Landscape,* 42. Père Lachaise is discussed by Linden-Ward, *Silent City on a Hill,* 90–104; Richard Etlin, *The Architecture of Death: The Transformation of the Cemetery in Eighteenth-Century Paris* (Cambridge, Mass., 1984); Frederick Brown, *Père la Chaise: Elysium as Real Estate* (New York, 1973); and by a nineteenth-century commentator, G. W. Wallerston, "Ornamental Graveyards," *Knickerbocker* 7, no. 4 (April 1836):376.

12. Wallerston, "Ornamental Graveyards," 376. An opposing view was expressed in "Cemeteries and Monuments: A Review of *The Rural Cemeteries in New England,*" *New Englander* 7, no. 28 (November 1849):495.

13. Changing aesthetic tastes are discussed by Neil Harris, *The Artist in American Society: The Formative Years, 1790–1860* (New York, 1966); Hans Huth, *Nature and the American: Three Centuries of Changing Attitudes* (Berkeley, 1957); and George Tatum, "The Beautiful and the Picturesque," *American Quarterly* 3, no. 1 (Spring 1951):36–51.

14. David Schuyler, "The Evolution of the Anglo-American Rural Cemetery: Landscape Architecture as Social and Cultural History," *Journal of Garden History* 4, no. 3 (July-September 1984):291–304.

15. Richard Etlin, "Père Lachaise and the Garden Cemetery," *Journal of Garden History,* 4, no. 3 (July-September 1984):217.

16. Philippe Ariès, *The Hour of Our Death,* trans. Helen Weaver (New York, 1981), 410–74, esp. 442.

17. Richard Etlin, "Landscapes of Eternity: Funerary Architecture and the Cemetery, 1793–1881," *Oppositions: A Journal for Ideas and Criticism in Architecture* 8 (Spring 1977):22. See also "Cemeteries and Catacombs of Paris," *Quarterly Review* 21, no. 42 (January-April 1819):391.

18. A new, provocative discussion of the process of conquering the frontier is in Terry G. Jordan and Matti Kaups, *The American Backwoods Frontier: An Ethnic and Ecological Interpretation* (Baltimore, 1989).

19. Favretti, "Ornamentation of New England Towns," 325–26; and Alexis De Tocqueville, *Democracy in America,* quoted in Roderick Nash, *Wilderness and the American Mind* (New Haven, 1982), 23.

20. Favretti, "Ornamentation of New England Towns," 342.

21. Etlin, "Landscapes of Eternity," 22.

22. Rotundo, "Mount Auburn: Fortunate Coincidences and an Ideal Solution," 259.

23. Francis Pulszky and Theresa Pulszky, *White, Red, Black: Sketches of American Society,* 2 vols. (New York, 1853), 2:185.

24. Barbara Rotundo, "The Rural Cemetery Movement," *Essex Institute Historical Collections* 109, no. 3 (July 1973):231. Charles O. Jackson, "Death in American Life," in *Passing: The Vision of Death in America,* ed. Jackson (Westport, Conn., 1977), 229–32. One example of the relationship between the living and the dead which was a foundation of the rural-cemetery movement is in Reverend G. W. Hoyt, "The Graves of the Innocents," *Mount Auburn Memorial* 1, no. 27 (14 December 1859):211. Hoyt encourages his readers to visit Green-Wood Cemetery in Brooklyn and view the section reserved for infant children, the truly innocent, who "opened their eyes upon this sinful world, passed a few days, sickened, died, and their spirits were taken home to heaven." Hoyt reminded his readers that the children would rise again, so "while, therefore, you weep, be resigned."

25. Blanche Linden-Ward, "Strange but Genteel Pleasure Grounds: Tourist and Leisure Uses of Nineteenth-Century Rural Cemeteries," in *Cemeteries and Gravemarkers: Voices of American Culture,* ed. Richard E. Meyer (Ann Arbor, 1989), 305. An example

of a guidebook to a local cemetery is R. A. Smith, *Smith's Illustrated Guide to and through Laurel Hill Cemetery* (Philadelphia, 1852).

26. James Henretta, "Families and Farms: *Mentalité* in Pre-Industrial America," *William and Mary Quarterly*, 3rd ser., 35, no. 1 (January 1978):3–31; Dan Parks, "The Cultivation of the Flower City," *Rochester History* 45, nos. 3–4 (1983):25–45; Paul Johnson, *A Shopkeeper's Millennium: Society and Revivals in Rochester, New York, 1815–1837* (New York, 1978); and Blake McKelvey, *Rochester, the Water Power City, 1812–1854* (Cambridge, Mass., 1945), 204–323.

27. Park, "Cultivation of the Flower City," 27–32; McKelvey, *Rochester;* and the quotation is from Ulysses Prentiss Hedrick, *A History of Agriculture in the State of New York* (New York, 1933), 387.

28. Reverend P. Church, *An Address Delivered at the Dedication of Mount Hope Cemetery, Rochester, 2 October 1838* (Rochester, 1839), 16–17; and William F. Peck, *Landmarks of Monroe County, New York* (Boston, 1895), 138.

29. Church, *Address Delivered at the Dedication,* 16–17.

30. Henry R. Stiles, *A History of the City of Brooklyn,* 3 vols. (Brooklyn, 1867–70), 3:622–30; Nehemiah Cleveland, *Green-Wood Illustrated: In Highly Finished Line Drawings Taken on the Spot, by James Smillie* (New York, 1847); Nehemiah Cleveland, *Green-Wood: A History of the Institution from 1838 to 1864* (New York, 1866). See also David B. Douglass, *Exposition of the Plan and Objects of the Green-Wood Cemetery* (New York, 1839); *Dictionary of American Biography,* s.v. "Douglass, David Bates"; "Henry E. Pierrepont," in Henry R. Stiles, ed.-in-chief, *The Civil, Political, Professional, and Ecclesiastical History, and Commercial and Industrial Record of the County of Kings and the City of Brooklyn, N.Y., from 1683 to 1884* (New York, 1884), 443–44; and *In Memoriam: Henry Evelyn Pierrepont of Brooklyn* (New York, 1888).

31. Douglass, *Exposition,* 15–16.

32. The figure is from Edward F. Bergman, *Woodlawn Remembers: Cemetery of American History* (Utica, N.Y., 1989), 6. Green-Wood's "Tour" is described in Stiles, *A History of the City of Brooklyn,* 3:627. See also Linden-Ward, "Strange but Genteel Pleasure Grounds," 317.

33. Bergman, *Woodlawn Remembers,* 4; the quotation is from M. M. Bagg, *Historical Sketch of Forest Hill Cemetery, Utica, N.Y.* (Utica, N.Y., 1895), 16. See also *Regulations of the Laurel Hill Cemetery* (Philadelphia, 1837), 3–4; and Linden-Ward, "Strange but Genteel Pleasure Grounds," 312–22.

34. "Audubon Park and Trinity Cemetery," *Eighteenth Annual Report, 1913, of the American Scenic and Historic Preservation Society* (Albany, 1913), 464.

35. Ibid., 463–66.

36. Albany Rural Cemetery, *Rules and Regulations, with an Appendix* (Albany, 1846), 2–6.

37. H. P. Phelps, *The Albany Hand-Book: A Strangers' Guide and Residents' Manual* (Albany, 1884), 137 and 67.

38. The role of the rural cemetery in the origins of the profession of landscape architecture has been touched on by several authors, but no one has fully developed the subject. *Dictionary of American Biography,* s.v. "Douglass, David Bates," places more emphasis on his experience with the Croton Aqueduct than his planning of cemeteries. His activity in Troy is discussed in Dewitt Clinton, ed., and Frederick S. Hills, comp., *Picturesque Oakwood . . . Its . . . Past and Present Associations* (Troy, N.Y., 1897), 13–38. Hotchkiss is discussed by Ruth Bohan, "A Home away from Home: Bellefontaine Cemetery, St. Louis, and the Rural Cemetery Movement," *Prospects: An Annual of*

American Cultural Studies 13 (1988):136–37; Daniels is discussed by Schuyler, *New Urban Landscape,* 110–14.

39. Blanche Linden-Ward and David Sloane, "Spring Grove: The Founding of Cincinnati's Rural Cemetery, 1845–1855," *Queen City Heritage* 43, no. 1 (Spring 1985):17–32.

40. Cleveland, *Green-Wood: A History,* 212.

CHAPTER FOUR. AN AMERICAN RESTING PLACE

1. David Schuyler, *The New Urban Landscape: The Redefinition of City Form in Nineteenth-Century America* (Baltimore, 1986). The quote is in Joan Burbick, "'Intervals of Tranquility': The Language of Health in Antebellum America," *Prospects: An Annual of American Cultural Studies* 12 (1987):175.

2. "Thoughts Connected with Rural Cemeteries," *Christian Review* 13, no. 46 (March 1848):11.

3. *Laws of the State of New York, Passed at the First Meeting of the Seventieth Session of the Legislature, Begun and Held the Fifth Day of January, 1847, at the City of Albany* (Albany, 1847), 125–29. The California Rural Cemetery Act of 1859 is mentioned in Gunther Barth, "Mountain View: Nature and Culture in an American Park Cemetery," in *The Mirror of History: Essays in Honor of Fritz Fellner,* ed. Solomon Wank, Heidrun Maschl, Brigitte Mazohl-Wallnig, and Reinhold Wagnleiitner (Santa Barbara, Calif., 1988), 163.

4. The rural-cemetery movement has received a great deal of attention from historians. Although they have focused on the large, visible cemeteries of Boston, New York City, Atlanta, and Philadelphia, we are just beginning to see how pervasive was American acceptance of the ideas of the rural cemetery. Hanover material is in John King Lord, *A History of the Town of Hanover, N.H.* (Hanover, 1928), 298–99.

5. City Inspector, "Annual Report of the Internments in the City and County of New York for the Year 1844," in *Documents of the Board of Alderman,* doc. no. 63 (New York, 1845). See also "A Law for Procuring a Regular Bill of Mortality in the City of New York," passed on 26 October 1801 by the New York City Common Council, as reported in *Minutes of the Common Council of the City of New York, 1784–1831* (New York, 1917), 3:43–44. The law ordered that "every Corpse buried in such buryial places" be accounted for, or the sexton fined $10." Ira Rosenwaike, *Population History of New York City* (Syracuse, 1972), 176, provides a summary of the number of deaths in New York City during the antebellum period.

6. Thomas Downing, "Annual Report of the City Inspector, of the Number of Interments in the City of New York, for the Year 1853," in *Documents of the Board of Alderman,* doc. no. 2 (New York, 1854). Downing noted that in 1851 the city prohibited burials in the area below Eighty-sixth Street, except in private vaults and private graves.

7. *Syracuse Standard,* 8 January 1857. Information on Oakwood Cemetery interments is in Elias W. Leavenworth, *The History and Incorporation, Rules and Regulations of Oakwood Cemetery, at Syracuse, N.Y., Together with the Dedication Odes and Addresses, with Other Papers,* 2d ed. (Syracuse, 1881), 116–17.

8. Mary Ryan, *The Cradle of the Middle Class: The Family in Oneida, N.Y., 1790–1865* (Cambridge, 1981), chaps. 2 and 3. On the development of voluntary associations in America, see Richard D. Brown, "The Emergence of Voluntary Associations in Massachusetts, 1760–1830," *Journal of Voluntary Action Research* 2 (1973):64–73.

9. *Sleepy Hollow Cemetery at Tarrytown-on-Hudson* (New York, 1897), 4.

10. Forest Lawn Cemetery was founded in 1849, but was restructured in 1855; the board of directors discussed below is the first under the new corporation. Oakwood Cemetery was established in 1859. Information on its board members is from a variety of sources, including local directories and histories. Information on Root, Clarke, and Marshall is from a variety of primary sources in "Cemeteries of Buffalo," file in Buffalo Public Library. Marshall's career is capsulized in H. Perry Smith, *History of the City of Buffalo and Erie County* (Syracuse, 1884), 53. In 1838 Lewis Allen had dinner with the visiting H.A.S. Dearborn, as described in Frank H. Severance, ed., "Journals of Henry A. S. Dearborn," in *Publications of the Buffalo Historical Society* (Buffalo, N.Y., 1904), 7:201 and 207. Information on Alvord and Crouse is in Annie C. Maltbie, *Picturesque Oakwood: Its Past and Present* (Syracuse, 1894), 36 and 60.

11. The male control of cemetery boards of directors was representative of the public/private split in American public life in the nineteenth century, but the lack of female influence raises interesting questions about the "feminization of American culture" as proposed by Ann Douglas, *The Feminization of American Culture* (New York, 1977).

12. The decision on lay representation seemed a result of the original advocacy of the cemetery. In Syracuse, lay community members urged the creation of St. Agnes and controlled the board of directors when it was formed, whereas the new Long Island cemeteries were the idea of the clergy and remained under its management. See *Syracuse Journal*, 22 May 1873, 7 June 1875, and 11 October 1873; and John K. Sharp, *History of the Diocese of Brooklyn, 1853–1953: The Catholic Church on Long Island*, 2 vols. (New York, 1954), 2:132–33.

13. "Laurel Hill," *Godey's Lady's Book* 28, no. 10 (March 1844):108.

14. *Regulations of the Laurel Hill Cemetery* (Philadelphia, 1837), 9–11.

15. "At a meeting of the Trustees of the Proprietors of the Cemetery of Mount Auburn, on Saturday the fifteenth day of July 1843," in Mount Auburn Cemetery Archives. My thanks to Barbara Rotundo for relaying this and other valuable information to me.

16. Leavenworth, *History . . . of Oakwood Cemetery* (1860 and 1881). This booklet, which contains Oakwood's rules and regulations, history, and financial status, was first published in 1860. The second edition was published in conjunction with the completion of the Oakwood chapel in 1881. Many cemeteries periodically reprinted such booklets to give to their lot-holders and to use them as sales aids.

17. Farley is quoted in Nehemiah Cleveland, *Green-Wood Illustrated: In Highly Finished Line Drawings Taken on the Spot, by James Smillie* (New York, 1847); 71; "Thoughts Connected with Rural Cemeteries," 20; and Michael McDowell, "American Attitudes toward Death, 1825–1865" (Ph.D. diss., Harvard University, 1978), 18–19.

18. *The Cemetery of Cypress Hills* (New York, 1851), 15–16; and McDowell, "American Attitudes," 23.

19. *Visitor's Guide to Calvary Cemetery* (New York, 1876); Lydia Sigourney, *The Western Home and Other Poems* (Philadelphia, 1854); Mary Ryan, *Cradle of the Middle Class*; Douglas, *Feminization of American Culture*; and Isabelle White, "The Uses of Death in *Uncle Tom's Cabin*," *American Studies* 36, no. 1 (Spring 1985):5–17.

20. Samuel Pickering, Jr., "The Grave Leads but to Paths of Glory: Deathbed Scenes in American Children's Books, 1800–1860," *Dalhousie Review* 59, no. 3 (Autumn 1979):462.

21. Ann Douglas, "Heaven Our Home: Consolation Literature in the Northern United States, 1830–1880," in *Death in America*, ed. David E. Stannard (Philadelphia, 1975), 49–67.

22. Harriet Martineau, *Retrospect of Western Travel*, 2 vols. (London and New York, 1838), 2:231.

23. On the development and importance of horticulture and agriculture, see Rudy J. Favretti, "The Ornamentation of New England Towns, 1750–1850," *Journal of Garden History* 2, no. 4 (October-December 1982):325–42; and U. P. Hedrick, *A History of Horticulture in America to 1860* (New York, 1950). The quote is in the 1848 report of the Albany and Rensselaer Horticultural Society (n.p., c. 1848?).

24. Dan Parks, "The Cultivation of the Flower City," *Rochester History* 45, nos. 3–4 (1983):25–45.

25. On Daniels, see Schuyler, *New Urban Landscape*, 110 and 214n.26; on his experiences at Spring Grove, see Blanche Linden-Ward and David Sloane, "Spring Grove: The Founding of Cincinnati's Rural Cemetery, 1845–1855," *Queen City Heritage* 43, no. 1 (Spring 1985):17–32.

26. Reverend P. Church, *An Address Delivered at the Dedication of Mount Hope Cemetery, Rochester, October 2, 1838* (Rochester, 1839), 16–17.

27. Ibid.

28. *Sleepy Hollow Cemetery at Tarrytown-on-Hudson* (New York, 1897), 4. Newton later enlarged the cemetery to 115 acres; see *The Newton Cemetery, Newton Massachusetts* (Boston, 1923), 4–5.

29. *The Cemetery of Cypress Hills*, 8–10.

30. Edward Fitzgerald, *A Hand-Book for the Albany Rural Cemetery, with an Appendix on Emblems* (Albany, 1871), 126–27.

31. The story of Charlotte Canda is told in J. G. Wilson, "Green-Wood Cemetery," *Hours at Home* 7, no. 4 (August 1868):362. The Canda monument remained a popular tourist attraction well into the late nineteenth century, as evident in Willard Glazier, *Peculiarities of American Cities* (Philadelphia, 1885), 82.

32. "Review of the Poems of William Cullen Byrant," *American Monthly Review* 1, no. 3 (April 1832):302.

33. Pickering, "The Grave Leads but to Paths of Glory," 452–64.

34. Blanche M. G. Linden, "The Willow Tree and Urn Motif," *Markers: The Annual Journal of the Association for Gravestone Studies* 1 (1979–80):149–56; Kenneth Ames, "Ideologies in Stone: Meanings in Victorian Gravestones," *Journal of Popular Culture* 14, no. 4 (Spring 1981):641–56; Edmund Gillon, Jr., *Victorian Cemetery Art* (New York, 1972); and Fitzgerald, *A Hand-Book for the Albany Rural Cemetery*, 126–27.

35. "Sculpture," *New England Magazine* 5 (December 1833):480. See also Blanche Linden-Ward, "Putting the Past under Grass: History as Death and Cemetery Commemoration," *Prospects: An Annual of American Cultural Studies* 10 (1985):279–314.

36. The finest guidebook to Green-Wood was Nehemiah Cleveland, *Green-Wood Illustrated*. For the list of sculptors whose work is in Mount Auburn, see Edward F. Bergman, *Woodlawn Remembers: Cemetery of American History* (Utica, N.Y., 1989), 4. See also Frederic A. Sharf, "The Garden Cemetery and American Sculpture: Mount Auburn," *Art Quarterly* 24, no. 1 (Spring 1961):80–88.

37. *Syracuse Journal*, 11 July 1879; and *Syracuse Standard*, 20 June 1859.

38. Daniel Boorstin, *The National Experience* (New York, 1965), 356–73; David O. Van Tassel, *Recording America's Past* (Chicago, 1960), 66–76 and 87–102; Linden-Ward, "Putting the Past under Grass," 279–314; and Henry Shapiro, "Putting the Past under Glass: Preservation and the Idea of History in the Mid-Nineteenth Century," *Prospects: An Annual of American Cultural Studies* 10 (1985):243–78.

39. "Mount Vernon Thirty Years Ago," *Mount Auburn Memorial* 1, no. 9 (10 July 1859):66.

40. "Greenwood Cemetery," *Mount Auburn Memorial* 1, no. 46 (9 May 1860):381; and "Historic Sleepy Hollow Cemetery," *Park and Cemetery* 28, no. 3 (May 1918):56.

41. For one fascinating example of rural-cemetery ceremonies promoting national history, see Henry O'Reilly, *Notices of Sullivan's Campaign or the Revolutionary Warfare in Western New York: Embodied in the Addresses and Documents Connected with the Funeral Honors Rendered to Those Who Fell with the Gallant Boyd in the Genesee Valley, including the Remarks of Governor Seward at Mount Hope* (Rochester, 1892).

42. "Red Jacket," in *Transactions of the Buffalo Historical Society* (Buffalo, N.Y., 1885), 3:1–111, and M. M. Bagg, *Historical Sketch of Forest Hill, Utica, N.Y.* (Utica, N.Y., 1895).

43. Blanche Linden-Ward, "Strange but Genteel Pleasure Grounds: Tourist and Leisure Uses of Nineteenth-Century Rural Cemeteries," in *Cemeteries and Gravemarkers: Voices of American Culture,* ed. Richard E. Meyer (Ann Arbor, 1989), 322–24; and Schuyler, *New Urban Landscape,* 77–100.

44. D. D. Barnard is quoted in H. P. Phelps, *The Albany Rural Cemetery: Its Beauties and Its Memories* (Albany, 1893), 66. Oakwood Cemetery's rules on mausoleums are noted in Leavenworth, *History . . . of Oakwood Cemetery* (1860).

45. *The Cemetery of Cypress Hills,* 8–9; and Henry R. Stiles, *A History of the City of Brooklyn,* 3 vols. (Brooklyn, 1867–70), 3:630–32.

46. On exclusionary practices, see William D. Patton, "The Cemeteries of Chicago: A Phase of Land Utilization," *Annals of American Geographers* 45, no. 3 (September 1955):245–57; other information on exclusionary practices is from a conversation with Samuel Steuve, former superintendent of Spring Grove. *The Ninth United States Census, 1870,* vol. 1 (Washington, D.C., 1872), reported that Syracuse, Rochester, Buffalo, and Utica had less than one thousand African-American residents. On Seymour, see Leonard L. Richards, *"Gentlemen of Property and Standing": Anti-Abolition Mobs of Jacksonian America* (New York, 1970). Henry R. Stiles, ed.-in-chief, *The Civil, Political, Professional, and Ecclesiastical History, and Commercial and Industrial Record of the County of Kings and the City of Brooklyn, N.Y., from 1683 to 1884* (New York, 1884), 608, discusses the Citizen Union Cemetery, noting that it was founded in 1851 by "the colored people, who were at that time debarred from most of the other cemeteries." Little evidence of overt discrimination exists. Robert Wells reported that Vale Cemetery in Schenectady had a separate section for African-Americans in "In Memoriam: Marking the Loss of a Family Member" (Paper delivered at the conference on New York State History, Tarrytown, N.Y., 3 June 1989).

47. Leavenworth, *History . . . of Oakwood Cemetery* (1860), 49; and Albany Rural Cemetery, *Rules and Regulations, with an Appendix* (Albany, 1846).

48. D. T. Valentine, *Manual of the Corporation of the City of New York, for the Year 1850* (New York, 1850), 327.

49. T. D. Woolsey, "Cemeteries and Monuments," *New Englander* 7, no. 28 (November 1849):495; and Edward Pessen, *Jacksonian America: Society, Personality, and Politics* (Homewood, Ill., 1978).

50. One controversy about picnics is recounted in *Rochester Daily Union and Advertiser,* 2 July 1861. Rules and regulations for visitors were included in almost all cemetery publications and in many guidebooks; for example, see *Regulations of Laurel Hill Cemetery,* 5. Linden-Ward, "Strange but Genteel Pleasure Grounds," 318, reports that cemeterians' attempts to limit Sunday attendance to those with tickets failed.

51. Leavenworth, *History . . . of Oakwood Cemetery* (1860), 42–44.

52. Articles are, respectively, in *Rochester Daily Union and Advertiser,* 30 May 1864, 6 June 1861, 2 July 1861, and 3 June 1856.

53. George B. Tatum, "Andrew Jackson Downing: Arbiter of American Taste, 1815–1852" (Ph.D. diss., Princeton University, 1950).

54. Andrew Jackson Downing, "Review: *Green-Wood Illustrated,*" *Horticulturist* 1, no. 5 (November 1846):229–30.

55. Stiles, *A History of the City of Brooklyn,* 628.

56. "Thoughts Connected with Rural Cemeteries," 18.

57. Cleveland's advice was published in several works, including *Green-Wood Illustrated,* 42–60.

58. J. Brazar, "Rural Cemeteries," *North American Review* 53, no. 113 (October 1841):396.

59. "Cemeteries and Monuments," 492, 497, and 499; and "Thoughts Connected with Rural Cemeteries," 18.

60. *Creating Central Park, 1857–1861,* ed. Charles E. Beveridge and David Schuyler, vol. 3 of *The Papers of Frederick Law Olmsted,* ed. Charles Capen McLauglin, 5 vols. to date (Baltimore, 1983), 357. The quote is from Olmsted's article "Parks at Home and Abroad," published in 1861.

61. Information on Cambridge is from John H. French, *Gazeteer of the State of New York* (Syracuse, 1860), 680. Information on Woodlands, including the quotes that follow, is from *The Woodlands Cemetery at Cambridge, N.Y., with Historical Sketches, and an Address of Rev. A. D. Gillette, D.D., Delivered at the Dedication, June 2, 1858* (Troy, N.Y., 1859).

62. Linden-Ward and Sloane, "Spring Grove," 17–32.

CHAPTER FIVE. RETREAT FROM SENTIMENTALITY

1. Material on Spring Grove is in Adolph Strauch, *Spring Grove Cemetery: Its History and Improvements with Observations on Ancient and Modern Places of Sepulture* (Cincinnati, 1869); H. A. Ratterman, "Spring Grove Cemetery and Its Creator" (Speech of 4 March 1905 to Cincinnati Literary Club, in "Spring Grove," file in Cincinnati Historical Society); John McLean, *Cemetery of Spring Grove: Its Charter, Rules and Regulations, Also an Address Delivered at the Consecration, August 20th, 1845, by the Hon. John McLean and a Catalogue of the Proprietors on the 1st Day of May, 1849* (Cincinnati, 1849); "Spring Grove: The Pioneer Lawn Cemetery," *Park and Cemetery* 29, no. 7 (September 1919):170–73; Blanche Linden-Ward and David Sloane, "Spring Grove: The Founding of Cincinnati's Rural Cemetery, 1845–1855," *Queen City Heritage* 43, no. 1 (Spring 1985):17–32; James J. Farrell, *Inventing the American Way of Death* (Philadelphia, 1980), 113–38; and Ray F. Wyrick, "Pilgrimage to the Home of the Lawn Plan: Spring Grove Cemetery, Cincinnati," *Modern Cemetery* 45, no. 4 (June 1935):306–8.

2. Ratterman, "Spring Grove Cemetery and Its Creator," 15–17. See entry on Adolph Strauch in *Biographical Encyclopedia of Ohio of the Nineteenth Century* (Cincinnati, 1876), 39–40.

3. Ratterman, "Spring Grove Cemetery and Its Creator," 6.

4. Strauch, *Spring Grove Cemetery,* 7. The issue of American wetlands has become increasingly important, as evidenced in William Robbins, "For Farmers, Wetlands Mean a Legal Quagmire," *New York Times,* 24 April 1990. Robbins reports that between the arrival of the first Europeans and 1900, developers had converted over half of the wetlands into tillable agricultural lands or residential housing. Strauch's shifting of the ground water into lakes was a typical nineteenth-century solution for a converted wetlands.

5. George Tatum, "The Beautiful and the Picturesque," *American Quarterly* 3, no. 1 (Spring 1951):42.

6. Richard Etlin, "Landscapes of Eternity: Funerary Architecture and the Cemetery, 1793–1881," *Oppositions: A Journal for Ideas and Criticism in Architecture,* no. 8 (Spring 1977):28.

7. Strauch, *Spring Grove Cemetery,* 7 and 23.

8. In the late 1840s, Howard Daniels and John Notman quarreled over the credit for originally designing Spring Grove; see *Cincinnati Atlas,* 18 March 1846, and *Cincinnati Morning Herald,* 17 March 1846 and 27 March 1846; see also Minutes of the Board of Directors of Cemetery of Spring Grove, 14 March 1846, 12 February 1846, and 2 April 1846, in the collection of Cemetery of Spring Grove, Cincinnati, Ohio.

9. Strauch, *Spring Grove Cemetery,* 9 and 12.

10. Ibid., 11.

11. The quotes are in Ratterman, "Spring Grove Cemetery and Its Creator," 14. The Latta controversy can be followed in Minutes of the Board of Directors of Cemetery of Spring Grove, 5 and 13 April 1860, in the collection of Cemetery of Spring Grove, Cincinnati, Ohio. In the cemetery's bound newspaper clippings is Latta's flyer, "To the Lotholders of Spring Grove Cemetery."

12. Taken from the 1858 Cemetery of Spring Grove annual report, quoted in Ratterman, "Spring Grove Cemetery and Its Creator," 11.

13. Adolph Strauch to Frederick Law Olmsted, 17 March 1875, in Frederick Law Olmsted Papers, Olmsted Associates Papers, Library of Congress. See also Ratterman, "Spring Grove Cemetery and Its Creator," 11.

14. Minutes of the Board of Directors of Cemetery of Spring Grove, 6 January 1859, in the collection of Cemetery of Spring Grove, Cincinnati, Ohio.

15. Information on the agreement to let Strauch accept other design projects is from Minutes of the Board of Directors of Cemetery of Spring Grove, 6 November 1860, in the collection of Cemetery of Spring Grove, Cincinnati, Ohio.

16. Jacob Weidenmann, *Modern Cemeteries: An Essay upon the Improvement and Proper Management of Rural Cemeteries* (Chicago, 1888); Ossian Cole Simonds, "Progress of the Rural Cemetery," *Park and Cemetery* 33, no. 9 (November 1923):234–36; and R. J. Haight, "Changing Aspects of Cemetery Progress," *Park and Cemetery* 42, no. 7 (September 1932):194.

17. Frank Eurich, "Life of Adolph Strauch," in *The Fourth Proceedings of the AACS* (n.p., 1890), 9. The original remark is in Frederick Law Olmsted to Adolph Strauch, 12 March 1875, in the Olmsted Associate Papers, Library of Congress. Olmsted asked Strauch for material on the lawn plan for the use of William Robinson, an English writer who used lithographs of Spring Grove and quotes from Strauch in *God's Acre Beautiful, or the Cemeteries of the Future* (London, 1880).

18. Gunther Barth, "Mountain View: Nature and Culture in an American Park Cemetery," in *The Mirror of History: Essays in Honor of Fritz Fellner,* ed. Solomon Wank, Heidrun Maschl, Brigitte Mazohl-Wallnig, and Reinhold Wagnleiitner (Santa Barbara, Calif., 1988), 163.

19. Henry Adams, "Care of Lots Not under Perpetual Care" (Paper delivered at New England Cemetery Association), in *The Cemetery Hand Book: A Manual of Useful Information on Cemetery Development and Management* (Chicago, 1921), 438.

20. On Mount Auburn, see James C. Scorgie, "Perpetual Care of Monuments and Mausoleums" (Paper delivered at Association of American Cemetery Superintendents meeting, 1916), in *The Cemetery Hand Book.* The chart of the perpetual-care fund is on 436. Scorgie stated that perpetual care was included in the price of Mount Auburn lots only after 1876 (427). General descriptions of the various funds that were used by cemeteries, although the names might be slightly different, are found in most early-

twentieth-century cemetery pamphlets. Farrell, *Inventing the American Way of Death*, 136–138, discusses the rise of perpetual care.

21. David G. Halford, *Old Lawn Mowers* (Aylesbury, Eng., 1982), 4.

22. Matthew P. Brazill, "Lot Enclosures," in *The Third Proceedings of the AACS* (n.p., 1889), 86–88, reported that one hundred employees took care of the grass in Green-Wood and that "a small force of men and horse drawn mowers" took care of Spring Grove.

23. *The First Proceedings of the AACS* (n.p., 1887), 37–38, has a list of the inaugural members. See also Farrell, *Inventing the American Way of Death*, 112–45; and the periodicals the *Modern Cemetery*, the *Cemetery Beautiful*, and *Park and Cemetery*.

24. Farrell, *Inventing the American Way of Death*, 112–45. See also Burton Bledstein, *The Culture of Professionalism: The Middle Class and the Development of Higher Education in America* (New York, 1976).

25. Association of American Cemetery Superintendents, *Modern Cemeteries: A Selection of Papers Read before the Annual Meetings of the AACS, 1887–1987* (Chicago, 1898).

26. Examples of the interests of Association of American Cemetery Superintendents members are in *The Cemetery Hand Book*. Although "Advertising the Modern Cemetery" is a short essay, the section "Trees and Shrubs" extends over eighty pages.

27. Alan Tractenberg, *The Incorporation of America: Culture and Society in the Gilded Age* (New York 1982), 104.

28. Ibid., 104–5. See also Robert H. Wiebe, *The Search for Order, 1877–1920* (New York, 1967); and William H. Wilson, *The City Beautiful Movement* (Baltimore, 1989).

29. Monro MacCloskey, *Hallowed Ground: Our National Cemeteries* (New York, 1968), 17–36; and Charles Cowley, "Our National Cemeteries," *Bay State Monthly* 2, no. 1 (October 1894):58–60.

30. MacCloskey, *Hallowed Ground*, 23; and "National Cemeteries," *Public Opinion* 15, no. 9 (3 June 1893):201.

31. Cowley, "Our National Cemeteries," 59.

32. *Revised Report Made to the Legislature of Pennsylvania, Relative to the Soldiers National Cemetery at Gettysburg* (Harrisburg, Pa., 1867), 158–59.

33. Ibid., 159.

34. Frederick Law Olmsted to General M. C. Meigs, 2 August 1870, forthcoming in vol. 6, ed. Charles Beveridge and David Schuyler, of *The Papers of Frederick Law Olmsted*, ed. Charles Capen McLaughlin, 5 vols. to date. I thank David Schuyler for giving me a copy of the letter.

35. *Revised Report Made to the Legislature of Pennsylvania*, 159–60.

36. Strauch, *Spring Grove Cemetery*, 11. Andrew Jackson Downing coined "Parkomania" in "Notes on the Progress of Gardening in the United States during the Year 1840," *Gardener's Magazine* 16 (December 1840):642–45.

37. Indeed, both Olmsted and Downing felt that the success of cemeteries was important to the public promotion of urban parks. See David Schuyler, *The New Urban Landscape: The Redefinition of City Form in Nineteenth-Century America* (Baltimore, 1986), 55. For further information on parks, see Thomas Bender, *Towards an Urban Vision* (Lexington, Ky., 1975); and J. B. Jackson, "The American Public Space," *Public Interest* 74 (Winter 1984):52–61.

38. Schuyler, *New Urban Landscape*, 101.

39. Jackson, "The American Public Space," 59.

40. Kenneth T. Jackson, *Crabgrass Frontier: The Suburbanization of the United States* (New York, 1985), 103–38; Tractenberg, *The Incorporation of America*, 104–39; and Wiebe, *The Search for Order*, 44–165.

41. The Swann quote is in Schuyler, *New Urban Landscape,* 101; and the Olmsted quote is in Tractenberg, *The Incorporation of America,* 109–10.

42. These definitions were used by Strauch, *Spring Grove Cemetery,* 7–8. See also Jackson, "The American Public Space," 62.

43. Jackson, "The American Public Space," 60.

44. Blanche Linden-Ward, "Strange but Genteel Pleasure Grounds: Tourist and Leisure Uses of Nineteenth-Century Rural Cemeteries," in *Cemeteries and Gravemarkers: Voices of American Culture,* ed. Richard E. Meyer (Ann Arbor, 1989), 317–18.

45. Charles Rosenberg, *The Care of Strangers: Rise of the Modern American Hospital* (New York, 1987), 244.

46. Robert W. Habenstein and William M. Lamars, *The History of American Funeral Directing* (Milwaukee, 1981), 257–85, esp. 284–85.

47. Ibid., 271; and Philippe Ariès, *The Hour of Our Death,* trans. Helen Weaver (New York, 1981).

48. Ibid., 274 and 182; and Farrell, *Inventing the American Way of Death,* 160 and 173–76.

49. Minutes of the Board of Directors of Cedar Hill Cemetery, 25 June 1920, in the collection of Cedar Hill Cemetery, Newburgh, N.Y. The cemetery was severely damaged by the early death of its founder, Enoch Carter. Material on Cedar Hill Cemetery is primarily from "Cedar Hill Cemetery Association, Newburgh, Orange County, New York" (n.p., n.d.). Cedar Hill is notable as the resting place of Andrew Jackson Dowling, whose brother Charles was active in the planting of the cemetery.

50. Franklin M. Garrett, *Atlanta and Environs: A Chronicle of Its People and Events* (Augusta, Ga., 1954), 71.

51. Norman Newton, *Design on the Land: The Development of Landscape Architecture* (Cambridge, Mass., 1971), 267–427; William H. Wilson, "The Ideology, Aesthetic and Politics of the City Beautiful Movement," in *The Rise of Modern Urban Planning, 1800–1914,* ed. Anthony Sutcliffe (New York, 1980); and Wilson, *The City Beautiful Movement.*

52. Weidenmann, *Modern Cemeteries,* 64–67.

53. These are the Fleischman and Huntington mausoleums, respectively.

54. Edward F. Bergman, *Woodlawn Remembers: Cemetery of American History* (Utica, N.Y., 1989), 10.

55. Examples of twentieth-century stock monuments and small mausoleums are in *Commemoration: The Book of Presbrey-Leland Memorials* (New York, 1950). Although *Commemoration* is from a later date than the period discussed in this chapter, it provides a wide range of monument styles. Presbrey-Leland was the leading dealership of small mausoleums and fine monuments in the East during the first half of the twentieth century.

56. James C. Scorgie, "The Control of Stonework in Cemeteries," *Park and Cemetery* 30, no. 8 (October 1920):213; and J. W. Wycoff, "Some Stock Monument Forms Redesigned," *Park and Cemetery* 25, no. 9 (November 1915):276–78. See also *Park and Cemetery* for its yearly examples of the best monuments of the year; for example, "Best Monuments of 1916," 26, no. 11 (January 1917):331–33.

CHAPTER SIX. COMMERCIALISM, CREMATION, AND THE MODERN CEMETERY

1. Alan Tractenberg, *The Incorporation of America: Culture and Society in the Gilded Age* (New York 1982); and Robert H. Wiebe, *The Search for Order, 1877–1920* (New York, 1967).

2. Frederick Law Olmsted, "Preface to the Plan for Mountain View Cemetery, Oakland, California," May 1865, in *The California Frontier, 1863–1865*, ed. Victoria Post Ranney, Gerard J. Rauluk, and Carolyn F. Hoffman, vol. 5 of *The Papers of Frederick Law Olmsted*, ed. Charles Capen McLaughlin, 5 vols. to date (Baltimore, 1990).

3. John Jay Smith, *Recollections* (Philadelphia, 1892), 101 and 291.

4. Albany Funding Company, "Prospectus for Capital City Cemetery Corporation Stock" (n.p., 1900), 1.

5. Elias W. Leavenworth, *The History and Incorporation, Rules and Regulations of Oakwood Cemetery, at Syracuse, N.Y., Together with the Dedication Odes and Addresses, with Other Papers*, 2d ed. (Syracuse, 1881), 116–20.

6. The Green-Wood situation is discussed in chap. 3 above; *Forest Lawn: Its History, Dedications, Progress, Regulations, Names of Lot Holders, Etc.* (Buffalo, N.Y., 1867); and, for example, "Mount Hope—Is Its Natural Beauty to be Sacrificed to Profit and Utility?" *Rochester Daily Union Advertiser,* 6 December 1864.

7. The information on Maple Grove Cemetery is from "Maple Grove Cemetery and Memorial Park," file in New York State Division of Cemeteries, New York City, which was the source of most of the financial evidence, and from material in the cemetery's office files.

8. This information is from the cemetery's short biography of William S. Cogswell.

9. Howard Carr, New York State Division of Cemeteries, Albany, kindly lent me his personal copy of Capital City Cemetery Corporation's original "Prospectus" and development pamphlet, *New Rural Cemetery, General Summary, the By-Laws and the First Annual Report of the Controller* (Troy, N.Y., n.d.); the quote is on 1.

10. Quincy L. Dowd, *Funeral Management and Costs: A World-Survey of Burial and Cremation* (Chicago, 1921). See also the *Urn: A Monthly Journal Devoted to the Interests of Cremation,* 1892–95.

11. A sampling of the news items in any *Park and Cemetery* or *Modern Cemetery* for the 1890s illustrates the increase in cemeteries.

12. A chart illustrating Mount Auburn's organizational hierarchy appears in John Peterson, Assistant Superintendent, Mount Auburn Cemetery, "The Execution of Perpetual Care Contracts," in *The Cemetery Hand Book: A Manual of Useful Information on Cemetery Development and Management* (Chicago, 1921), 407.

13. W. Ashbury Christian, *Richmond: Her Past and Present* (Richmond, Va., 1912), 163–65.

14. Keith L. Bryant and Henry C. Dethloff, *A History of American Business* (Englewood Cliffs, N.J., 1983), 185.

15. "Riverside Cemetery," in *The Encyclopedia of Cleveland History*, ed. David D. Van Tassel and John J. Grabowski (Bloomington, Ind., 1987), 835.

16. "Cemetery Notes," *Modern Cemetery* 1, no. 4 (June 1891 and July 1891).

17. Bryant and Dethloff, *A History of American Business*, 185; and "Advertising the Modern Cemetery," in *The Cemetery Hand Book,* 100. General trends in advertising are discussed in Roland Marchand, *Advertising the American Dream: Making Way for Modernity, 1920–1940* (Berkeley, 1985); and T. J. Jackson Lears, "From Salvation to Self-Realization: Advertising and the Therapeutic Roots of the Consumer Culture, 1880–1930," in *Culture of Consumption: Critical Essays in American History, 1880–1980,* ed. Richard Wrightman Fox and T. J. Jackson Lears (New York, 1983).

18. "Lake View," in *The Encyclopedia of Cleveland History,* 610.

19. "Cemetery Notes," *Park and Cemetery* 40, no. 11 (January 1931):284.

20. The following information is primarily from the photographic booklet *Kensico* (New York, 1910).

21. The following information is from my interviews with Alfred Locke, Steven Locke, and Louis Natalie, Pinelawn Memorial Park, Pinelawn, N.Y.

22. Parsons wrote extensively on landscape gardening and planning, including Calvert Vaux and Samuel Parsons, Jr., *Concerning Lawn Planting* (New York, 1881). Parsons's life is described in Mabel Parsons, ed., *Memories of Samuel Parsons: Landscape Architect of the Department of Public Parks, New York* (New York, 1926,) esp. 290–306.

23. William H. Wilson, *The City Beautiful Movement* (Baltimore, 1989), 9–99, esp. 78–79. See also Jon A. Peterson, "The City Beautiful Movement: Forgotten Origins and Lost Meanings," *Journal of Urban History* 2, no. 4 (August 1976):15–34; Thomas S. Hines, *Burnham of Chicago: Architect and Planner* (New York, 1974); and Peter J. Schmitt, *Back to Nature: The Arcadian Myth in Urban America* (New York, 1969).

24. Wilson, *The City Beautiful Movement,* 86.

25. Changes in the insurance business are discussed in Edward A. Woods, *The Sociology of Life Insurance* (New York, 1928), and Morton Keller, *The Life Insurance Enterprise, 1885–1910: A Study in the Limits of Corporate Power* (Cambridge, Mass., 1963).

26. Based on "Cemetery Notes," *Park and Cemetery* 23, no. 1 (March 1913):19, and 23, no. 6 (August 1913):107.

27. There is no adequate history of cremation in America, but details can be found in Paul Irion, *Cremation* (Philadelphia, 1968); James J. Farrell, *Inventing the American Way of Death* (Philadelphia, 1980), 164–69; George B. Catlin, "Cremation in Michigan," *Michigan History Magazine* 14, no. 1 (Winter 1930):38–59; and John Storer Cobb, *A Quartercentury of Cremation in North America: Being a Report of Progress in the United States and Canada* (Boston, 1901). For an extensive, though now outdated and incomplete, bibliography of the worldwide cremation movement, see H. E. Mose, ed., *A List of Books, Pamphlets and Articles on Cremation; including the Collection of the Cremation Association of America at the John Crerar Library* (Chicago, 1940).

28. Mrs. Basil Holmes, *The London Burial Grounds: Notes on Their History from the Earliest Times to the Present Day* (New York, 1896), 270.

29. For a discussion of the early history of cremation, see Dr. Hugo Erichsen, *The Cremation of the Dead Considered from an Aesthetic, Sanitary, Religious, Historical, Medico-legal, and Economic Standpoint* (Detroit, 1887); and Augustus G. Cobb, *Earth-Burial and Cremation: The History of Earth-Burial with Its Attendant Evils, and the Advantages Offered by Cremation* (New York, 1892).

30. "Thoughts Connected to Rural Cemeteries," *Christian Review* 13 (March 1848):15.

31. "Burning and Burying," *Eclectic Magazine of Foreign Literature, Science, and Art* 42–43, no. 1 (September 1857):536–38; and *Rochester Daily Union,* 14 November 1855.

32. Robert P. Hudson, *Disease and Its Control: The Shaping of Modern Thought* (New York, 1983), 176.

33. Cobb, *Earth-Burial and Cremation,* 24–25.

34. *Urn: A Monthly Journal Devoted to the Interests of Cremation* 4, no. 6 (June 1895):7.

35. Henry Thompson, "The Treatment of the Body after Death," *Contemporary Review* 23 (January 1874):319–28. The reference to the Vienna Exposition is on 327. The technology necessary for an enclosed crematory is discussed in "Cremation and Crematories," *American Architect and Building News* 12, no. 341 (8 July 1882):22.

36. Thompson, "The Treatment of the Body," 321. *Dictionary of National Biography,* s.v. "Thompson, Sir Henry." See also Lloyd G. Stevenson, "Science down the Drain: The Hostility of Certain Sanitarians to Animal Experimentation, Bacteriology and Immunology," *Bulletin of the History of Medicine* 29, no. 1 (January-February 1955):1–10.

37. Lancaster Cremation and Funeral Reform Society, *Cremation: History of the Move-*

ment in Lancaster, Pennsylvania, with an Account of the Building, Furnace, Other Apparatus and the Process (Lancaster, Pa., 1886). Information on Dr. Miles Davis is in John W. W. Loose, "The Lancaster Crematorium: First in the USA," *Journal of the Lancaster County Historical Society* 89. no. 2 (1985):46–52.

38. *New York Times*, 1 January 1884. The United States Cremation Company, the New York City cremation society, noted in its 1888 annual report that merchants, physicians, and journalists were the people most likely to choose cremation; see *New York Times*, 8 May 1888. See also *New York Times*, 14 April 1890.

39. Reverend H. A. Bran, "Christian Burial and Cremation," *American Catholic Quarterly Review* 10, no. 40 (October 1884):678. Right Reverend James A. Corcoran, "The Church and Cremation," *American Catholic Quarterly Review* 11, no. 42 (April 1886):361. See also James P. Murphy, "The Cremation Movement Is Anti-Catholic," *Catholic World* 73, no. 436 (July 1901):453–62.

40. John S. Stephenson, *Death, Grief, and Mourning: Individual and Social Realities* (New York, 1985), 25.

41. Paul Carter, "If a Man Die, Shall He Live Again?" in *Passing: The Vision of Death in America*, ed. Charles O. Jackson (Westport, Conn., 1977), 115.

42. Charles E. Rosenberg, *The Cholera Years* (Chicago, 1962).

43. Carter, "If a Man Die, Shall He Live Again?" 125.

44. Ibid., 115. See also Elizabeth Stuart Phelps, *The Gates Ajar* (Boston, 1869).

45. Biographical material on LeMoyne is in Margaret McCulloch, *Fearless Advocate of the Right: The Life of Francis Julius LeMoyne, M.D., 1798–1879* (Boston, 1941); *Dictionary of American Biography*, s.v. "LeMoyne, Francis Julius"; and *New York Times* editorial "The End of Cremation," 17 October 1879.

46. *New York Times*, 7 December 1876. An elaborate description of Palm's funeral and cremation is in Henry Steel Olcott, *Inside the Occult: The True Story of Madame H. P. Blavatsky* (originally entitled *Old Diary Leaves*) (Philadelphia, 1975), 147–84. A medical perspective is in "The Cremation of Baron Palm," *Boston Medical and Surgical Journal* 95, no. 24 (14 December 1876):710–12.

47. *New York Times*, 17 October 1879.

48. John D. Beugless, "Incineration," *Princeton Review* 59, no. 2 (September 1883):147; and Frederick Peterson, M.D., "Cremation," *Buffalo Medical and Surgical Journal* 20, no. 9 (April 1881):386.

49. J.F.A. Adams, *Cremation and Burial: Sixth Annual Report of the Massachusetts State Board of Health, Public Document 30, January 1875* (Boston, 1875). The quote appears in a letter by Adams in "The Sanitary Aspect of Cremation," *Boston Medical and Surgical Journal* 95, no. 24 (14 December 1876):715–16.

50. *Syracuse Journal*, 19 April 1875 and 28 July 1876; and Cobb, *Earth-Burial and Cremation*, 23–46.

51. Hudson, *Disease and Its Control*, 165.

52. A. K. Stone, "The Hygienic Argument for Cremation Considered from a Bacteriological Standpoint," *Boston Medical and Surgical Journal* 129, no. 18 (2 November 1893):433–34; Henry Thompson, "The Progress of Cremation," *Nineteenth Century* 23, no. 131 (January 1888):10; and Dr. Pattengill, "Cremation," *Urn: A Monthly Journal Devoted to the Interests of Cremation* 4, no. 12 (December 1895):10.

53. *New York Times*, 7 July 1884.

54. Francis Julius LeMoyne, *Cremation: An Argument to Prove That Cremation Is Preferable to Inhumation of Dead Bodies* (Pittsburgh, 1878), 15; and Beugless, "Incineration," 153.

55. "Cemetery Notes," *Park and Cemetery* (November 1891):106.

56. Beugless, "Incineration," 148.

57. *New York Times,* 17 October 1879 and 3 October 1887. See also *New York Times,* 20 November 1885. Waring is noted in *Urn: A Monthly Journal Devoted to the Interests of Cremation* 2, no. 9 (September 1893):3; Leidy, in *New York Times,* 20 May 1884; and *The Autobiography of Samuel B. Gross,* ed. Samuel W. Gross and Albert H. Gross, 2 vols. (Philadelphia, 1887), 2—209–11. See also Cobb, *Quartercentury of Cremation,* 117–18. Because of the continuing social stigma attached to cremation, not all of those who professed support for the idea were themselves cremated. See Mary Deal, "Cemeteries," in *The Encyclopedia of Cleveland History,* 165.

58. Frederick S. Hills, comp., *The Gardner Earl Memorial Chapel and Crematorium, Oakwood Cemetery, Troy, N.Y.* (Albany, 1902).

59. James C. Chadwick, "Cremation of the Dead," *Journal of Social Sciences* 43 (September 1905):82–84. Cremation in Europe is discussed in Cobb, *Quartercentury of Cremation.*

60. James Scorgie, "The Crematory in the Modern Cemetery," in *The Cemetery Hand Book,* 278.

61. James Cassedy, "The Flamboyant Colonel Waring: An Anticontagionist Holds the American Stage in the Age of Pasteur and Koch," *Bulletin of the History of Medicine* 36, no. 2 (March-April 1962):163–76.

62. Clarence L. Scammon, *Papers of Charles V. Chapin, M.D.* (New York, 1934), 20ff.

63. S. A. Knopf, M.D., "A Plea for Cremation in Tuberculosis and Similar Infectious Diseases," *Journal of the American Medical Association* 48, no. 4 (26 January 1907):300–304; S. A. Knopf, M.D., "Cremation Versus Burial—A Plea for More Sanitary and More Economical Disposition of Our Dead," *American Journal of Public Health* 12, no. 5 (May 1922):389–99; Hugo Erichsen, *Via Lucis (The Way of Light): A Symposium of Opinions on Cremation* (n.p., 1917); and Hugo Erichsen, "Cremation in America," *Park and Cemetery* 36, no. 8 (October 1926):210–11.

64. Dowd, *Funeral Management and Costs,* 242–44.

65. John Gebhart, *Funeral Costs* (New York, 1928), xix.

66. Peterson, "Cremation," 397.

67. LeMoyne, *Cremation,* 14.

68. "In Favor of Cremation," *New York Times,* 18 May 1883.

CHAPTER SEVEN. THE IDEAL CEMETERY: THE MEMORIAL PARK

1. The information on Forest Lawn is quite extensive. The most important works are Barbara Rubin, Robert Carlton, and Arnold Rubin, *L.A. in Installments: Forest Lawn* (Santa Monica, Calif., 1979); Adela Rodgers St. Johns, *First Step Up toward Heaven: Hubert Eaton and Forest Lawn* (Englewood Cliffs, N.J., 1959); Ralph Hancock, *The Forest Lawn Story* (Los Angeles, 1964); Bruce Barton, "A Cemetery without Gloom," *Reader's Digest* 31, no. 184 (August 1937):73–76. Also important are brochures, as well as the following books, published by Forest Lawn Memorial-Park Association: *Forest Lawn Interpretation: A Guide Book to Forest Lawn Memorial Park* (Los Angeles, 1927); *Among the Hills* (Los Angeles, 1917); and *Art Guide of Forest Lawn* (n.p., c. 1941).

2. These figures are from St. Johns, *First Step Up toward Heaven,* 90–96; H. Eaton, "Creation of Forest Lawn" (Paper delivered at Association of American Cemetery Superintendents meeting, Los Angeles, 1929), as reprinted in *Park and Cemetery* 29, no. 7 (September 1929):209–10; and Rubin, Carlton, and Rubin, *L.A. in Installments,* 11–19.

3. Eaton, "Creation of Forest Lawn." Mitford devoted an entire chapter, "Shroudland Revisited," to Forest Lawn, her symbol of cemetery perfidy, in *The American Way of*

Death (New York, 1963), 119–28. See also Evelyn Waugh, *The Loved One* (New York, 1948); and Aldous Huxley, *After Many a Summer Dies the Swan* (New York and London, 1939).

4. "National Memorial Parks Association," *Modern Cemetery* 44, no. 5 (July 1934):88. There are no scholarly studies of the memorial park. In his compilation of articles on death in America, *Passing: The Vision of Death in America* (Westport, Conn., 1977), Charles O. Jackson included a brief 1917 article by Herbert Blaney, "The Modern Park Cemetery," 115. The best information on memorial parks is derived from my interviews with managers and other memorial-park officials, site visits, cemetery magazines, sales literature, and popular exposés, such as Mitford, *The American Way of Death*. The American Cemetery Owners Association was an outgrowth of the Memorial Park Association, which was founded in 1933. In 1957 the former assumed the name National Cemetery Association, under which it existed until its merger with the American Cemetery Association in the mid–1980s.

5. J. J. Gordon, "The Ideal Cemetery—Memorial Park," *Cemetery Beautiful* (1915):14.

6. Marc Weiss, *The Rise of the Community Builders: The American Real Estate Industry and Urban Land Planning* (New York, 1987), 45.

7. The discussion of Los Angeles is primarily from Robert Fogelson, *The Fragmented Metropolis: Los Angeles, 1850–1930* (Cambridge, Mass., 1967).

8. Ibid., 56, 78–79, and 164–85.

9. Ibid., 143 and 146; the quote is on 137.

10. Ibid., 92.

11. Daniel Bell, "Modernism Mummified," *American Quarterly* 39, no. 1 (Spring 1987):125.

12. Hubert Eaton expressed his views on both ideas of immortality in his short booklet *The Comemoral: The Cemetery of the Future* (Los Angeles, c. 1954).

13. Eaton's vision of the smiling Christ is discussed in "Creation of Forest Lawn," 209–10. See also Bruce Barton, *The Man Nobody Knows: A Discovery of the Real Jesus* (Indianapolis, 1925); Bruce Barton, "A Cemetery without Gloom," 73–76; and Leo P. Ribuffo, "Jesus Christ as Business Spokesman: Bruce Barton and the Selling of Corporate Capitalism," *American Quarterly* 33, no. 2 (Summer 1981):206–31.

14. Eaton, *Comemoral*, 17, 19, and 20.

15. Ibid., 25.

16. Ibid., 35.

17. Eaton, "Creation of Forest Lawn," 209–10.

18. Ibid. See also Ralph Hancock, *The Forest Lawn Story* (Los Angeles, 1964), 89.

19. Eaton, "Creation of Forest Lawn," 210–11; Harry A. Earnshaw, "Advertising a Cemetery (Forest Lawn)," *Park and Cemetery* 39, no. 7 (September 1929):212–15.

20. See Forest Lawn Memorial-Park Association, *Art Guide of Forest Lawn*, as well as sales brochures for the four Forest Lawn locations.

21. Eaton, "Creation of Forest Lawn," 210.

22. John Wheeler, director of public relations for Forest Lawn, provided these dates. A survivor of Bogart, probably Lauren Bacall, most likely chose his crypt, so perhaps it would be more precise to say the site appealed to her.

23. Eaton, "Creation of Forest Lawn," 209.

24. St. Johns, *First Step Up toward Heaven*, 165–76; "California Cemetery Convention," *Park and Cemetery* 39, no. 7 (September 1929):207.

25. Daniel Joseph Singal, "Towards a Definition of American Modernism," *Modernist Culture in America*, ed. Singal, special issue of *American Quarterly* 39, no. 1 (Spring

1987):7–26. The 1913 Armory Show is discussed in Milton W. Brown, *The Story of the Armory Show,* 2d ed. (New York, 1988).

26. Edward F. Bergman, *Woodlawn Remembers: Cemetery of American History* (Utica, N.Y., 1989), notes that cemetery art was explicitly excluded from the later 1930 art exposition in New York City. See also George McClure, "A Beautiful Memorial Park: The Best Friend of the Salesmen," in *The National Cemetery Association, 1955–1956 Cemetery Yearbook* (n.p., 1956), 108; and William Hubbard, "A Meaning for Monuments," *Public Interest* 74 (Winter 1984):17–30. There is one abstract sculpture at Forest Lawn today. The former vice-president of American Airlines was given permission to place a memorial in the shape of the company's logo. The last quote is from Rubin, Carlton, and Rubin, *L.A. in Installments,* 40.

27. Rubin, Carlton, and Rubin, *L.A. in Installments,* 34–37; the quote is on 35.

28. Philippe Ariès, "Forbidden Death," in *Death: Current Perspectives,* ed. Edwin S. Shniedman (Palo Alto, Calif., 1976), 77–78.

29. Monroe Lerner, "When, Why, and Where People Die," in *Death: Current Perspectives,* ed. Shniedman, 145. Although America's infant mortality rate has declined consistently during the twentieth century, it remains an important health problem. America has a higher rate than many other developed nations. See Margaret W. Pratt and Vince L. Hutchins, *Infant Mortality and Perinatal Mortality Rates by Age and Race: United States, 1976–1985* (Vienna, Va., 1988), i–xxv.

30. Robert Habenstein and William Lamers, *The History of American Funeral Directing* (Milwaukee, 1981), 207. For European attitudes toward embalming, see Ariès, "Forbidden Death," 79. The reliance of Americans upon funeral directors is discussed in Mark Lino, "Consumer Decisions, Expenditures, and Knowledge Regarding Funerals," *Family Economic Review* 2, no. 4 (1989):2–6.

31. Eaton, "Creation of Forest Lawn," 211.

32. Ibid.

33. Earnshaw, "Advertising a Cemetery," 213.

34. Forest Lawn Memorial-Park, *Among the Hills.*

35. Ariès, "Forbidden Death," 79–80; and John Gebhart, *Funeral Costs* (New York, 1928), 50–51.

36. Gebhart, *Funeral Costs,* 51–52

37. St. Johns, *First Step Up toward Heaven,* 90–96; and Eaton, "Creation of Forest Lawn," 209–10.

38. The corporate structure is discussed in Eaton, "Creation of Forest Lawn," and St. Johns, *One Step Up toward Heaven,* 112–19; the corporate tactics used by memorial parks are discussed in Nathaniel Goldstein, *Report of the Attorney General on the Subject of Cemeteries,* legislative doc. no. 7, State of New York (Albany, 1949), 5.

39. St. Johns, *First Step Up toward Heaven,* 141.

40. "Forest Lawn," *Travel* 123, no. 1 (January 1965):41–43.

41. Waugh, *The Loved One,* 65–66.

42. Evelyn Waugh to Cyril Connolly, 2 January 1928, *The Letters of Evelyn Waugh,* ed. Mark Anthony (New Haven, 1980), 259–60. Waugh's comment on Forest Lawn is from "Death in Hollywood," *Life,* 29 September 1947; quoted in Jeffrey Heath, *The Picturesque Person: Evelyn Waugh and His Writing* (Montreal, 1982), 193.

43. William A. Hoefgen, "The Fallacy of Investment Selling," *American Cemetery Owners Association Handbook and Buyer's Guide* (n.p., 1938), 158; and "National Memorial Parks Association Holds Convention at Pittsburgh," *Modern Cemetery* 44, no. 5 (July 1934):88–94. At this convention the members voted to rename their organization the

American Cemetery Owners Association in order to relieve the confusion surrounding the term *memorial park.*

44. From my interview with Alfred Locke, Pinelawn Memorial Park, Pinelawn, N.Y.

45. McClure, "A Beautiful Memorial Park," 106.

46. Ibid., 107.

47. Kenneth T. Jackson, *Crabgrass Frontier: The Suburbanization of the United States* (New York, 1985): Anselm Strauss, "Changing Imagery of American City and Suburb," *Sociological Quarterly* 1, no. 1 (January 1960):15–24; and David Schuyler, *The New Urban Landscape: The Redefinition of City Form in Nineteenth-Century America* (Baltimore, 1986).

48. "Vestal Hills Memorial Park Map and Visitor's Guide," available at the office.

49. Peter J. Schmitt, *Back to Nature: The Arcadian Myth in Urban America* (New York, 1969).

50. Jackson, *Crabgrass Frontier.*

51. Very little has been published about the remarkable treasure trove of art objects in America's cemeteries. Art historians have ignored the grounds, presumably seeing cemeteries as repositories of popular rather than fine art. Historians of material culture are beginning to note the incredible range of markers and monuments. For discussions of the subject, see Frederic A. Sharf, "The Garden Cemetery and American Sculpture: Mount Auburn," *Art Quarterly* 24, no. 1 (Spring 1961):80–88; Edmund V. Gillon, Jr., *Victorian Cemetery Art* (New York, 1972); Bergman, *Woodlawn Remembers;* James Hijiya, "American Gravestones and Attitudes toward Death: A Brief History," *Proceedings of the American Philosophical Society* 127, no. 5 (1983):339–63; and Richard E. Meyer, ed., *Cemeteries and Gravemarkers: Voices of American Culture* (Ann Arbor, 1989). A specialized study shows the possibilities such monuments possess for scholars; see Michael Wilson Panhorst, "Lest We Forget: Monuments and Memorial Sculpture in National Military Parks on Civil War Battlefields, 1861–1917" (Ph.D. dissertation, University of Delaware, 1988).

52. Barbara Rotundo, "Monumental Bronze: A Representative Company," in *Cemeteries and Gravemarkers,* 263–92; the quote is from 263.

53. I have had difficulty locating the origins of the custom of placing bronze plaques flush to the ground. Plaques attached to granite backs and placed on buildings might have been a source of the inspiration. Several companies, including Matthews Bronze of Pittsburgh, seem to have rapidly spread the custom.

54. Eric S. Marmorek, "Tools and Methods of Persuasion," in National Cemetery Association, *1955–1956 Cemetery Yearbook,* 39.

55. In the 1930s, discussions of flush markers fill professional journals for monument dealers. See George E. Wemhoff, "Attack on Memorials Answered," *Granite, Marble and Bronze: A Monthly Magazine for Every Monument Man* 42, no. 12 (December 1932):11–13 and 22.

56. McClure, "A Beautiful Memorial Park," 107–8.

57. "Fort Hill: Now Prospering, after a Dramatic Turnaround," *American Cemetery* 56, no. 2 (February 1974):16–17; "Vestal Hills Memorial Park Map and Visitor's Guide"; "1949–1950 Rules and Regulations of White Chapel Memorial Park," in "White Chapel," file in New York State Division of Cemeteries, Albany; and my interview with Clint Adams, White Haven Memorial Park, Rochester.

58. Information on Williams is from my interviews with A. John Hansen, Acacia-Resthaven Memory Gardens, Buffalo; Robert Bruce, Vestal Hills Memorial Park, Binghampton, N.Y.; Jack Sloane, retired executive director, Oakwood Cemeteries (which now manages White Chapel Memory Gardens), Syracuse; and Donald Hurlburt, Schenectady Memorial Park, Schenectady. See also "The Legacy of 'Doc' Williams," *PIAA*

Ideas: A Sales Bulletin (publication of the Pre-Arrangement Interment Association of America, Inc.) (September-October 1974):1 and 4–5.

59. Material on White Chapel Memorial Park in Detroit is from the newspaper insert "Where Memory Lives in Beauty: White Chapel Memorial Cemetery," 1966.

60. Myron West, "Developing Memorial Parks with Monumented Areas," *Modern Cemetery* 45, no. 4 (June 1935):313, in the collection of Oakwood Cemeteries, Syracuse, N.Y.

61. From my interview with Alfred Locke, Pinelawn Memorial Park, Pinelawn, N.Y.

62. "Racial Distinction Upheld," *Park and Cemetery* 36, no. 12 (February 1927):305. Earlier developments in racial distinction are discussed in "The Color Line at the Grave," *Park and Cemetery* 27, no. 3 (May 1917):71–72.

63. Quoted in Fogelson, *The Fragmented Metropolis*, 188.

64. William Pattison, "The Cemeteries of Chicago: A Phase of Land Utilization," *Annals of American Geographers* 45, no. 3 (1955):245–57; and Mary Deal, "Cemeteries," in *The Encyclopedia of Cleveland History*, ed. David D. Van Tassel and John J. Grabowski (Bloomington, Ind., 1987), 166.

65. "The Colored Sexton's Burial," *New York Times*, 29 January 1884; "The Color Line at the Grave," *Park and Cemetery* 27, no. 3 (May 1917):71. In 1935, according to "Modern Development of Negro Cemeteries: National Organization Formed," *Modern Cemetery* 43, no. 3 (May 1933):54–55, there were enough African-American cemeteries to establish the National Negro Cemetery Association.

66. The first African-American burial in White Chapel Memory Gardens in Syracuse occurred in 1981. White Haven Memorial Park in Rochester had fewer than a dozen black lot-holders in 1982, Clint Adams said in my interview with him there. During the mid–1960s, public pressure forced White Haven to sell a lot to an African-American. White Chapel in Syracuse first buried an African-American after merging with Oakwood Cemeteries, a traditional place of African-American burial. A typical racial exclusionary clause can be found in the contracts of the 1950s of White Chapel Memory Gardens, located in the Corporation and Historical Papers of Oakwood Cemeteries, Syracuse. As Barbara Rotundo reminded me in a letter of May 1989, the exclusionary clauses were aimed at not only African-Americans but also other minorities, because Orientals and Hispanics would have been a greater "problem" than African-Americans in some cities, including Los Angeles.

67. D. H. Meyer, "American Intellectuals and the Victorian Crisis of Faith," *American Quarterly* 27, no. 5 (December 1975):593. See also Robert N. Bellah, *Beyond Belief: Essays on Religion in a Post-Traditional World* (New York, 1970), esp. his seminal essay "Civil Religion in America."

68. Quote taken from the postcard "The Birth of Liberty," Forest-Lawn Memorial-Park (n.d.).

CHAPTER EIGHT. THE CEMETERY IN CRISIS

1. Hendrick Hartog, *Public Property and Private Power: The Corporation of the City of New York in American Law, 1730–1870* (Chapel Hill, N.C., 1983), 194–95; the quote is on 194.

2. Robert Wiebe, *Businessmen and Reform: A Study of the Progressive Movement* (Cambridge, Mass., 1962); Gabriel Kolko, *Triumph of Conservatism* (New York, 1963); and Gabriel Kolko, *Railroads and Regulation, 1877–1916* (Princeton, 1965).

3. The campaign can be followed in *New York Times*: 25 May 1948, 19 October 1949, 5 January 1949, 15 January 1949, 25 March 1949, 12 April 1949, and 20 July 1949. The

quote is from an article of the last date. See also the Nathaniel Goldstein Papers, Syracuse University.

4. The Honorable Nathan A. Lashin, "The Legislator Looks Forward," in *Proceedings of the Nineteenth Annual Convention of the New York State Association of Cemeteries, Incorporated, 1947* (n.p., 1947), 70–74. These proceedings are in a series that will hereafter be cited by date in the Notes; for example, *NYSAC Nineteenth Proceedings, 1947*, 70–74. On Jewish burial societies, see A. F. Florence, "A Jewish Mausoleum," *American Cemetery* 39, no. 11 (January 1930):18.

5. *New York Times,* 19 October 1949.

6. The best place to trace Maple Grove Cemetery's finances is "Maple Grove," file in New York State Division of Cemeteries, New York City. Maple Grove's current administration was very helpful in explaining past dealings; see also *New York Times,* 5 January 1949.

7. *New York Times,* 5 January 1949.

8. Nathaniel Goldstein, *Report of the Attorney General on the Subject of Cemeteries, 1949* (Albany, 1949), legislative doc. no. 7, 11–15, provides other examples.

9. Ibid., 5.

10. Ibid., 6.

11. Ibid., 16–17.

12. Edward Zeltner, "Over the River," New York *Sunday Mirror,* 5 June 1949, quoted in *Broadcaster* (monthly publication of New York State Association of Cemeteries), July 1949.

13. Letters to legislators which relate to the Feinberg-Mailler Bill, which became the New York State Cemetery Act of 1949, are collected in "Bill Jacket 533," Legislative Archives, New York State. Two letters are particularly helpful: letter from Frederich Martyn, "Memorandum by the Evergreens Cemetery Relating to the Feinberg-Mailler Bill Pertaining to Cemeteries," 1 April 1949, and that from Crawford T. Perkinson, president of the New York State Association of Cemeteries, 25 February 1949.

14. Examples of the articles are Robert E. Glass, "A Team of Tactful Men," *New Republic* 116, no. 16 (21 April 1947):26–28; Paul Blanshard, "It Costs Money to Die," *Nation* 127, no. 3311 (19 December 1928):682–86; Philip McKee, "The High Cost of Dying," *American Mercury* 42, no. 167 (November 1937):307–12; Morris Markey, "Requisat in Pace," *Reader's Digest* (reprinted from *The New Yorker*) 30, no. 181 (May 1937):89–90; and Hugh Stevenson Tigner, "Decent Christian Burial?" *Reader's Digest* (reprinted from *Christian Century*) 39, no. 189 (January 1938):72–74. Co-operatives are discussed in Ellis Cawling, "Churchmen and the Co-Operatives," *Christian Century* 53, no. 50 (9 December 1936):1651–52.

15. Marian Castle, "Decent Christian Burial," *Forum and Century* 91, no. 4 (April 1934):253–55.

16. Roy Burkhart, "Let Us Abandon Funerals," *American Mercury* 39, no. 7 (September 1929):105.

17. H.L.W., "The Question Box," *Christian Century* 53, no. 53 (30 December 1936):1755.

18. "The Unseemliness of Funerals," *Literary Digest* (reprinted from *Congregationalist* [Boston]) 59, no. 16 (21 April 1917):1170.

19. Philippe Ariès, *The Hour of Our Death* (New York, 1981), trans. Helen Weaver, is the best source for discussions of these long-term trends.

20. Tigner, "Decent Christian Burial?" 73.

21. Ibid.

22. Ibid., 72.

23. Markey, "Requisat in Pace," 90.

24. See, for example, Boyden Sparkes, "But I'd Hate to Die There," *Saturday Evening Post* 209, no. 43 (24 April 1937):20–26.

25. William Shaw, "Consumption Expenditures, 1929–43," *Survey of Current Business* 24, no. 6 (June 1944):10.

26. John Gebhart, *Funeral Costs* (New York, 1928), 67–128; "Death Is Big Business," *Current History* 49, no. 2 (October 1938):36; and The Officiating Clergyman, "Of Weddings and Funerals," *Harper's* 191, no. 1147 (December 1945):499.

27. Gebhart, *Funeral Costs*, 78–79; LeRoy Bowman, *The American Funeral: A Study in Guilt, Extravagance, and Sublimity* (Washington, D.C., 1959); and Vanderlyn Pine, *Caretaker of the Dead: The American Funeral Director* (New York, 1975).

28. Glass, "A Team of Tactful Men," 26; and Charles M. Brown, "Reducing the High Cost of Dying," *Christian Century* 53, no. 43 (21 October 1936):1391.

29. Samuel Harkness, "No More Funerals," *Scribner's* 9, no. 4 (October 1931):395.

30. H. Eaton, "Creation of Forest Lawn" (Paper delivered at Association of American Cemetery Superintendents meeting, Los Angles, 1929), as reprinted in *Park and Cemetery* 29, no. 7 (September 1929):211.

31. Shaw, "Consumption Expenditures," 10.

32. Typical of the discussions was "Perpetual Care" by Leon Rains of Washington Cemetery in New York City, in *NYSAC Eighth Proceedings, 1936*, 45–50.

33. J. W. Eldridge, "Question 3," in *NYSAC Second Proceedings, 1930*, 11–12.

34. L. E. Leader, "New Labor and Time Saving Equipment," *Broadcaster* (September 1948)19–24.

35. Letter writer quoted in "Drastic Action by Cardinal Ends Strike in Calvary," *American Cemetery* 21, no. 3 (March 1949):27. The issues surrounding the lack of a mechanical gravedigger are discussed in Leader, "New Labor and Time Saving Equipment."

36. Clare Buck, "How to Increase Income of Small Cemeteries," in *NYSAC Eighteenth Proceedings, 1946*, 107–8.

37. Floyd B. Gallagher, "Our Cemetery of Yesterday and Today," in *NYSAC Nineteenth Proceedings, 1947*, 12.

38. Crawford T. Perkinson, "Better Pre-Need Selling" (Paper delivered at New York State Association of Cemeteries meeting, 1948), quoted in *Broadcaster*, no. 12 (December 1948):15.

39. Thomas Rankin, "Pre-Need Selling," in *NYSAC Sixteenth Proceedings, 1944*, 65.

40. Ray F. Wyrich, "The Golden Age in American Cemeteries," in *NYSAC Seventeenth Proceedings, 1945*, 34–35.

41. Cardinal Spellman's were summarized in "Drastic Action by Cardinal Ends Strike," 25–27. The practice of blaming the evils of America on communists was not lost on C. T. Perkinson, a leading New York cemeterian, who was quoted in 1947 as saying: "If we should ever lose our symbolism and sentimentality in burying our dead, progress will cease. . . . We have to protect ourselves from communism. The best way . . . is to steadfastly maintain our own traditions of burying the dead, . . . our most effective weapon against communism IS the sentiment of traditional burial rites." Quoted in Glass, "A Team of Tactful Men," 27.

42. "Drastic Action by Cardinal Ends Strike," 26.

43. C. T. Perkinson, "Union Labor Relations and Pension Plans," in *NYSAC Twenty fifth Proceedings, 1953*, 20–21.

44. Charles Benisch, "Co-Operation with Allied Industries," in *NYSAC Seventh Proceedings, 1935*.

45. Rankin, "Pre-Need Selling"; and Clarence Nelson, "Advantages of Advertising for Small Cemeteries," *NYSAC Nineteenth Proceedings, 1947,* 14–19.

46. William Lloyd Warner, *The Living and the Dead: A Study of the Symbolic Life of Americans* (New Haven, 1959), 320.

CHAPTER NINE. SERVING THE LIVING

1. Most of the material on Pinelawn Memorial Park and Alfred Locke is derived from my interviews with Alfred Locke, Steven Locke, and Louis Natalie, Pinelawn Memorial Park, Pinelawn, N.Y. See also the brochures, pamphlets, and other records of Pinelawn at its office.

2. According to Locke, the statue had been stored in a New York City church, from which he purchased it.

3. Little has been written about the history of entombment and mausoleums. See Michael Ragon, *The Space of Death: A Study of Funerary Architecture, Decoration, and Urbanism,* trans. Alan Sheridan (Charlottesville, Va., 1983); and Quincy Dowd, *Funeral Management and Costs: A World-Survey of Burial and Cremation* (Chicago, 1921).

4. *Vault interment* and *entombment* are used interchangeably here. In the nineteenth century, *vault internment* typically meant earth burial in a grave lined with bricks or stones, whereas *entombment* was interment in a stone building. Today, cemeterians once again offer underground burial in preprepared concrete vaults known as *ground crypts.*

5. Edmund Gillon, Jr., *Victorian Cemetery Art* (New York, 1972). John Vinci, "Graceland: The Nineteenth-Century Garden Cemetery," *Chicago History* 6, no. 2 (1977):86–98, describes several of the mausoleums of Graceland.

6. Meyer Stern, *Rise and Progress of Judaism* (n.p, 1935) 201–5, plus several pages of photographs.

7. Examples of Woodlawn's mausoleums are in Edward F. Bergman, *Woodlawn Remembers: Cemetery of American History* (Utica, N..Y., 1989).

8. Dowd, *Funeral Management and Costs,* 134–38.

9. The American Association of Cemetery Superintendents, Report of Committee on Community Mausoleums is in "Cemetery Opinion on Community Mausoleums," in *The Cemetery Hand Book: A Manual of Useful Information on Cemetery Development and Management* (Chicago, 1921), 396–98.

10. Franklin Edson Belden, *Temples of Peace, or the Endowed Community Mausoleum vs. Earth-Burial and Cremation,* (Seattle, 1916).

11. "Ferncliff," *American Cemetery* 41, no. 10 (October 1968):22–24.

12. Ibid.; the price of a crypt in Ferncliff is cited on 23.

13. William Mershon and Carl Linge, "Garden Crypts and Mausoleum Sales—Pro and Con," in the *NCA Cemetery Yearbook, 1948–49* (n.p., 1949), 105–6.

14. The following discussion of mausoleums and monuments is based on my interview with Lawrence Sloane, L. F. Sloane Consulting Group, Albany, as well as talks with various cemeterians over the last decade. For an insight into earlier practices, see "Commemoration: The Book of Presbrey-Leland Memorials" (New York, c. 1950).

15. "Nineteen Eighty-Six, 1987, 1988 Cremation Statistics," *Cremationist* 25, no. 2 (1989):9.

16. Pope Paul VII approved cremation for Roman Catholics on 5 July 1963, but warned that "every care be taken so as to respect the Christian burial." By 1970 eight million Catholics had been cremated worldwide. Quoted from William S. Cook, "Cremation: From Ancient Cultures to Modern Usage," *Casket and Sunnyside* 103, no. 1 (January 1973).

17. Cook, "Cremation: From Ancient Cultures to Modern Usage." Cook noted that the average costs in 1973 for a grave and opening were $120–500, a crypt was $350–600, and a cremation was $35–100. He did mention that niches in a columbarium could raise the price of cremation to $750 and that urns cost $50–250.

18. Randy Shilts, *And the Band Played On: Politics, People, and the AIDS Epidemic* (New York, 1987), 140.

19. Ibid., 605. On cancer and American society, see James T. Patterson, *The Dread Disease: Cancer and Modern American Culture* (Cambridge, Mass., 1987).

20. Jessica Mitford, *The American Way of Death* (New York, 1963), viii.

21. Ibid., 14–15.

22. Ibid., 16.

23. The most important discussion of English funeral discussions is Geoffrey Gorer, *Death, Grief, and Mourning in Contemporary Britain* (London, 1965). The essay reprinted in this book appeared ten years earlier. Barbara Rotundo told me in a letter of May 1989 that she believes that the British have reacted to Gorer by having more funerals and memorial services.

24. Mitford, *The American Way of Death*, 228.

25. Ibid, 16.

26. Senate Committee on Veterans' Affairs, "National Cemetery System Study: A Study Submitted by the Veterans Administration (Pursuant to Section 3 of Public Law 93–43)." Senate Committee Print no. 24 (Washington, D.C., 21 January 1974), 1. The most prominent veterans' cemetery is Arlington National Cemetery. It has become an extremely popular tourist site, especially since the burials of John F. and Robert Kennedy. See James Edwards Peters, *Arlington National Cemetery: Shrine to America's Heroes* (Kensington, Md., 1986); and Philip Bigler, *In Honored Glory: Arlington National Cemetery: The Final Post* (Arlington, Va., 1987).

27. William L. Ebel, "National Cemetery System," in House Committee on Veterans' Affairs, "The National Cemetery System," in *Hearing before the Subcommittee on Housing and Memorial Affairs*, 26 May 1988, serial no. 100–50 (Washington, D.C., 1988), 27–30. See also Munro MacCloskey, *Hallowed Ground: Our National Cemeteries* (New York, 1968), esp. 88–183.

28. Monument Builders of North America, "Position Paper on Expansion of Veterans Cemeteries," in House Committee on Veterans' Affairs, "The National Cemetery System," 1–3. See also Thomas Rankin, "Government Cemeteries," in *NYSAC Seventeenth Proceedings, 1944*, 66–69, in which he argues for a burial allowance of fifty dollars allotted to the family of the deceased in order to purchase a burial space in a private cemetery, rather than face the cost overruns and expensive maintenance that he associated with publicly owned cemeteries.

29. The course of government regulation is discussed in Bureau of Consumer Protection, "Funeral Industry Practices: Final Staff Report to the Federal Trade Commission and Proposed Trade Regulation Rule (16 CFR Part 453)" (Washington, D.C., 1978), 101–42.

30. Jo Ellen Davis, "Bob Waltrip Is Making Big Noises in a Quiet Industry," *Business Week*, no. 2961 (25 August 1986):66. According to the 1987 annual report of SCI, it owned 461 funeral homes in thirty-three states, the District of Columbia, and five Canadian provinces, and 121 cemeteries in twenty-five states and one Canadian province. In May 1988 SCI purchased Gorham Bronze, one of the two largest producers of bronze memorials in America.

31. For example, see the articles about the formation of White Chapel Memory Gardens in Syracuse in Oakwood Cemeteries Archives, Syracuse, N.Y..

32. This information is based on my interviews with Lawrence Sloane, L. F. Sloane Consulting Group, Albany; Jack Sloane, retired executive director, Oakwood Cemeteries; and R. Gregory Sloane, executive director, Oakwood Cemeteries.

33. The advertisement was published 14 September 1978.

34. This statement was contained in letter to an executive at Trinity from a cemeterian, who provided a copy of the it to me. In 1974 Forest Lawn Memorial-Park experimented with humorous radio commercials as a way to establish a larger market share of Los Angeles funerals; the results were unsuccessful. See "Mortuary Humor Gets a Cold Reception," *Business Week,* no. 2327 (20 April 1974):42–43.

35. "Lot Profit" and "Cemetery Equipment and Maintenance, " in *NYSAC Eighteenth Proceedings, 1946*.

36. See "Auto Hearses," *Cincinnati Enquirer,* 23 April 1911. Memorial Day restrictions are discussed in "Cemetery Rule Changed," *Cincinnati Enquirer,* 11 May 1920. Earlier, some metropolitan cemeteries provided customers with motorized bus service to and through them; see "Motor Transportation for the Cemetery," *Park and Cemetery* 25, no. 10 (December 1915), 294–95.

37. The gardens are described in various Pinelawn Memorial Park brochures.

38. Teresa Hiner Ohlemeier, "Lending to the Funeral Industry," *Journal of Commercial Bank Lending,* January 1982, 18–19.

39. The incident occurred in Syracuse on 18 October 1988 and is discussed in the Syracuse *Post-Standard* and the *Daily Orange,* the student newspaper of Syracuse University.

BIBLIOGRAPHIC ESSAY

The Notes provide a fuller indication of the type and scope of materials consulted for this book than any formal bibliography could. I list manuscript collections and interviews and briefly discuss some of the central secondary sources.

MANUSCRIPT COLLECTIONS

Cedar Hill Cemetery, Newburgh, N.Y., Corporation Files
Cemetery of Spring Grove, Cincinnati, Archives
Levi Chapman Family Papers, Syracuse University
Division of Cemeteries, Department of State, Albany and New York City, Cemetery Files
Elmlawn Cemetery, Buffalo, Corporation Files
Nathaniel Goldstein Papers, 1943–67, Syracuse University
Henry Laurens Papers, microfilm edition
Maple Grove Cemetery, Brooklyn, Corporation Files
Morningside Cemetery, Syracuse, Corporation Files
Mount Auburn Cemetery, Cambridge, Mass, Corporation Files
Frederick Law Olmsted, Olmsted Associates Papers, Library of Congress, Washington, D.C., microfilm edition, reels 12–15
Pinelawn Memorial Park, Pinelawn, N.Y., Corporation Files
Henry Stiles Papers, Long Island Historical Society, Brooklyn
Vestal Hills Memorial Park, Binghamton, N.Y., Corporation Files
White Chapel Memory Gardens, Syracuse, Corporation Files
Caleb Woodhull Family Papers, New-York Historical Society
Woodlawn Cemetery, the Bronx, Corporation Files
Woodlawn Cemetery, Syracuse, Corporation Files

INTERVIEWS

Clint Adams, White Haven Memorial Park, Rochester, December 1981
Donald Attrage, Maple Grove Cemetery, Brooklyn, August 1982
Vincent Boyd, Ferncliff Cemetery, New York City, June 1982
Robert Bruce, Vestal Hills Memorial Park, Binghamton, N.Y., 1981–82
G. Richard Bruns, Woodlawn Cemetery, Syracuse, November 1981
Edwin Casey, Trinity Church Cemetery, New York City, August 1982
Reverend Albert Clody, Diocesan Cemeteries of Buffalo, August 1982
Seth Colby, Forest Lawn Cemetery, Buffalo, August 1982
Andrew Conroy, Cemetery of Spring Grove, Cincinnati, April 1985
Roger Cooper, Riverhurst Cemetery, Binghamton, N.Y., August 1981
Brian Dollery, St. Agnes Cemetery, Albany, May 1982
Benjamin Garland, Garland Funeral Home, Syracuse, June 1981
Clyde Gordon, Cemetery of Spring Grove, Cincinnati, August 1986
Adolph Hansen, Acacia-Resthaven Memory Gardens, Buffalo, August 1982
W. James Huggins, Elmlawn Cemetery, Buffalo, August 1982

Donald Hulbert, Schenectady Memorial Park, Schenectady, May 1982
Bernard Jaffe, Montefiore Cemetery, New York City, June 1982
Ray Krolewicz, Diocesan Cemeteries of Buffalo, August 1982
Edward Laux, Woodlawn Cemetery, the Bronx, June 1982
Alfred Locke, Pinelawn Memorial Park, Pinelawn, N.Y., June 1982
Steven Locke, Pinelawn Memorial Park, Pinelawn, N.Y., June 1982
George Mocko, Cedar Hill Cemetery, Newburgh, N.Y. January 1982
Louis Natalie, Pinelawn Memorial Park, Pinelawn, N.Y., June 1982
Janice Senser, Oakwood Cemetery, Troy, N.Y., May 1982
Jack Sloane, Oakwood Cemeteries, Syracuse, 1981–90
Lawrence Sloane, L. F. Sloane Consulting Group, Syracuse, 1981–90
R. Gregory Sloane, Oakwood Cemeteries, Syracuse, 1981–90
Samuel Steuve, Cemetery of Spring Grove, Cincinnati, August 1986
Frederick Haley, Forest Lawn Cemetery, Buffalo, August 1982
Robert K. Wheeler, Forest Lawn Memorial-Park, Glendale, Calif., April 1982
Robert Wurtz, Mount Calvary Cemetery, Buffalo, August 1982

The Bibliographic Note only includes a portion of the books, articles, pamphlets, and ephemeras in the Notes. Genealogists, local historians, and others have published hundreds of articles on graveyards and cemeteries throughout America. I have focused here, as elsewhere in the book, on the cultural trends within that mosaic of death. A more substantial bibliography is in my Ph.D. dissertation, "The Living among the Dead: New York State Cemetery Landscapes as Reflections of a Changing American Culture to 1949" (Syracuse University, 1984).

SECONDARY SOURCES

General

The most influential survey of Western death customs is Philippe Ariès, *The Hour of Our Death,* trans. Helen Weaver (New York, 1985), which focuses on French Catholic practices from medieval to modern times. This controversial book is conservative in tone and primarily focuses on France, but it is by far the best survey yet written.

There is no American companion to Ariès's work. John R. Stilgoe, *Common Landscape of America, 1580–1845* (New Haven, 1982), James J. Farrell, *Inventing the American Way of Death* (Philadelphia, 1980), and William Lloyd Warner, *The Living and the Dead: A Study in the Symbolic Life of Americans* (New Haven, 1959) each explore aspects or time periods of American customs.

Although there is no history of American death customs, several authors have attempted portraits of them. Quincy Dowd wrote *Funeral Management and Costs: A World-Survey of Burial and Cremation* (Chicago, 1921). Robert W. Habenstein and William M. Lamars, *The History of American Funeral Directing* (Milwaukee, 1981), provide an in-depth view of the development of funeral directing, but only briefly discusses cemeteries. The most widely noted survey of American burial customs is Jessica Mitford, *The American Way of Death,* a less than balanced exploration of American customs by a English commentator.

Early American Graveyards

There have been several excellent studies of early American graveyards, but the best discussion is in Stilgoe, *Common Landscape of America.* A good discussion of American attitudes toward death during this period is Charles Allen Shively, "A History of the Conception of Death in America, 1650–1850" (Ph.D. diss., Harvard University, 1968). Beatrix Rumford, "The Role of Death as Reflected in the Art and Folkways of the Northeast in the Eighteenth and Nineteenth Centuries" (Ph.D. diss., State University of New York at Oneonta, Cooperstown Graduate Program, 1965), is a broader examination of death customs. A more popular, though still useful, survey is Margaret Coffin, *Death in Early America: The History and Folklore of Customs and Superstitions of Early Medicine, Burial and Mourning* (New York, 1976).

Students of early American customs have found gravestones particularly interesting. The most helpful of the many studies include Harriette Forbes, *Gravestones of Early New England and the Men Who Made Them, 1653–1800* (Boston, 1927); Edwin Dethlefsen and James Deetz, "Death's Heads, Cherubs, and Willow Trees: Experimental Archaeology in Colonial Cemeteries," *American Antiquity* 31 (April 1966):502–10; Richard Welch, "Colonial and Federal New York and New Jersey Gravestones," *Journal of Long Island History* 17, no. 1 (Winter 1981):23–34; and Peter Benes, *Masks of Orthodoxy: Old Gravestone Carvings in Plymouth County, 1689–1805* (Amherst, Mass., 1977).

Colonial graveyards obviously were heavily influenced by European practices, especially English ones. English burial grounds are discussed in James Stevens Curl, "The Design of the Early British Cemeteries," *Journal of Garden History* 4, no. 3 (July-September 1984):223–53; Mrs. Basil Holmes, *The London Burial Grounds: Notes on Their History from the Earliest Times to the Present Day* (New York, 1896); and Clare Gittings, *Death, Burial and the Individual in Early Modern England* (London, 1984). French churchyards are described in Richard Etlin, *The Architecture of Death: The Transformation of the Cemetery in Eighteenth-Century Paris* (Cambridge, Mass., 1984).

I have used Trinity churchyard in New York City as the archetype of colonial and early national graveyards. There is not a good history of Trinity churchyard, although the church has produced several booklets. Material is from Morgan Dix, *A History of the Parish of Trinity Church in the City of New York*, 4 vols. (New York, 1905); and Trinity Church, *Churchyards of Trinity Church in the City of New York* (New York, 1969).

Early-Nineteenth-Century Alternatives

The change from graveyard to cemetery was gradual, occurring from the 1790s to the 1830s and requiring Americans to reconsider what the appropriate characteristics of a burial place were. This reconsideration was part of a larger rethinking of the appearance of the city. The best study of the change in burial places is Blanche Linden-Ward, *Silent City on a Hill: Landscape of Memory and Boston's Mount Auburn Cemetery* (Columbus, Ohio, 1989), but, because it was published after I had written this book, I relied on Rudy J. Favretti, "The Ornamentation of New England Towns, 1750–1850," *Journal of Garden History* 2, no. 4 (October-December 1982):325–42.

The most important early-twentieth-century alternative to the graveyard was the New Haven Burying Ground, which was founded in 1796. The person most responsible for the new burial place was James Hillhouse. See *Dictionary of American Biography*, s.v. "Hillhouse, James."

For a fascinating early-nineteenth-century view of New Haven, see Timothy Dwight, *A Statistical Account of the Towns and Parishes in the State of Connecticut* (New Haven, 1811), and *Travels in New England and New York*, 4 vols. (1821–22; reprint, Cambridge, Mass., 1969). Several works have explored the origins and development of the New Haven Burying Ground, including Henry H. Townsend, "The Grove Street Cemetery" (Paper delivered to New Haven Colony Historical Society, 27 October 1947), and Henry T. Blake, *Chronicles of the New Haven Green from 1638–1862* (New Haven, 1898).

The only article on the origins on the Marble cemeteries is St. Clair McKelway's popular piece "The Marble Cemeteries," *The New Yorker* 10, no. 25 (4 August 1934):29–32. The battle over the legislation prohibiting burials has received more attention since it raised issues about public health (see John Duffy, *A History of Public Health in New York City, 1625–1865* [New York, 1968]) and changing concepts of municipal power (see Hendrick Hartog, *Public Property and Private Power: The Corporation of the City of New York in American Law, 1730–1870* [Chapel Hill, 1983]).

The Rural-Cemetery Movement

The rural-cemetery movement has received far more attention than any other cemetery style. The interest of historians in Victorian culture, city building, antebellum middle-class culture, and the melancholy of death has led to numerous works on rural cemeteries. One important work, Blanche Linden-Ward, *Silent City on a Hill,* also discusses the movement's origins in French and English aesthetic theories.

A leading scholar of rural cemeteries is Barbara Rotundo, whose "Mount Auburn Cemetery: A Proper Boston Institution" *(Harvard Library Bulletin* 22, no. 3 [July 1974]:268–79) preceded much of the fashionable activity in this area and set a precedent for high scholarship in it. See also her "Mount Auburn: Fortunate Coincidences and an Ideal Solution," *Journal of Garden History* 4, no. 3 (July-September 1984):255–67.

Père Lachaise has also received a growing amount of attention, partially because of the work left undone by Ariés. The best of the new books is Richard Etlin, *The Architecture of Death: The Transformation of the Cemetery in Eighteenth-Century Paris* (Cambridge, Mass., 1984).

The spread of the rural cemeteries has received considerable attention. The following discuss aspects of the movement: Blanche Linden-Ward and David Sloane, "Spring Grove: The Founding of Cincinnati's Rural Cemetery, 1845–1855," *Queen City Heritage* 43, no. 1 (Spring 1985):17–32; Edward F. Bergman, *Woodlawn Remembers: Cemetery of American History* (Utica, N.Y., 1989); Donald Simon, "Green-Wood Cemetery and the American Park System," in *Essays in the History of New York City: A Memorial to Sidney Pomerantz,* ed. Irwin Yellowitz (Port Washington, N.Y., 1978), 61–77; and David Stannard, "Calm Dwellings: The Brief 'Sentimental Age' of the Rural Cemetery," *American Heritage* 30, no. 5 (August-September 1979):43–55.

Of interest to many scholars are the stunning family monuments. Blanche M. G. Linden, "The Willow Tree and Urn Motif," *Markers: The Annual Journal of the Association for Gravestone Studies* 1 (1979–80):149–56, discusses the end of the colonial era, whereas Kenneth Ames, "Ideologies in Stone: Meanings in Victorian Gravestones," *Journal of Popular Culture* 14, no. 4 (Spring 1981):641–56, and Diana Williams Comb, *Early Gravestone Art in Georgia and South Carolina* (Athens, Ga., 1986), discuss the meaning of antebellum stones. Edmund Gillon, Jr., *Victorian Cemetery Art* (New York, 1972), is the best of several photographic studies.

My discussion of middle-class culture and the implications of changes in family patterns and economic status has been influenced most by Mary Ryan, *The Cradle of the Middle Class* (Cambridge, 1981), and Daniel Boorstin, *The National Experience* (New York, 1965).

The important relationship of cemeteries to the development of not only urban parks but also the entire urban landscape is discussed in Thomas Bender, *Towards an Urban Vision* (Lexington, Ky., 1975); David Schuyler, *The New Urban Landscape: The Redefinition of City Form in Nineteenth-Century America* (Baltimore, 1986); and J. B. Jackson, "The American Public Space," *Public Interest* 74 (Winter 1984):52–61. The state of scholarship regarding Andrew Jackson Downing exemplifies the need for further work on the origins of landscape architecture and urban design; the best biography remains George B. Tatum, "Andrew Jackson Downing: Arbiter of American Taste, 1815–1852" (Ph.D. diss., Princeton University, 1950).

The Cemetery of Spring Grove and Lawn-Park Cemeteries

Despite the interest in rural cemeteries, Adolph Strauch and the Cemetery of Spring Grove have received little attention. James J. Farrell, *Inventing the American Way of Death, 1830–1920* (Philadelphia, 1980), notes the importance of Strauch, as do Linden-Ward and Sloane, "Spring Grove: The Founding of Cincinnati's Rural Cemetery, 1845–1855."

Previously mentioned works by Bender and Schuyler provide the context for the design changes in the lawn-park cemetery. Schuyler's book has covered some of the material regarding the development of America's urban parks, but there are many other aspects to be explored. Kenneth T. Jackson, *Crabgrass Frontier: The Suburbanization of the United States* (New York, 1985), beautifully portrays the suburbanization of America, but does not discuss the cemetery's role in suburbanization.

The history of landscape architecture has been the subject of many scholarly works, including *The Papers of Frederick Law Olmsted*, ed. Charles Capen McLauglin, 5 vols. to date. Other works of interest include Norman T. Newton, *Design on the Land: The Development of Landscape Architecture* (Cambridge, Mass., 1971), William H. Wilson, *The City Beautiful Movement* (Baltimore, 1989); Jon A. Peterson, "The City Beautiful Movement: Forgotten Origins and Lost Meanings," *Journal of Urban History* 2, no. 4 (August 1976):15–34; Thomas S. Hines, *Burnham of Chicago: Architect and Planner* (New York, 1974); and Peter J. Schmitt, *Back to Nature. The Arcadian Myth in Urban America* (New York, 1969).

The literature on national cemeteries has slowly grown with the continuing interest in the Civil War. The most important work remains Monro MacCloskey, *Hallowed Ground: Our National Cemeteries* (New York, 1968). In this area in particular, there is a large amount of unexamined material on design trends, the relationship between the federal government and providers of markers and monuments, and the origins of the battle between public cemeteries and private cemeterians.

The rise of the superintendent coincided with a general move toward professionalization in America, as noted by Burton Bledstein, *The Culture of Professionalism: The Middle Classes and the Development of Higher Education in America* (New York, 1976). A specific example of the impact of a very successful medical professionalism is in Charles Rosenberg, *The Care of Strangers: The Rise of America's Hospital System* (New York, 1987), and Paul Starr, *The Transformation of American Medicine* (New York, 1982).

An unexpected obstacle in my research was that the only examination of the amazing technological changes in domestic care *outside* the home is David G. Halford, *Old Lawn Mowers* (Aylesbury, Eng., 1982).

Commercialism in the Lawn-Park Cemetery and the Memorial Park

The commercial development of the cemetery is not easily confined to a single period, so I cite the most important bibliographic sources from the last half of the nineteenth century and twentieth century.

As with many other aspects of research on cemeteries, the best place to find information on the commercial development of the cemetery business is in industry periodicals, particularly *Cemetery Beautiful, Park and Cemetery, Modern Cemetery*, and the latter's successor, *American Cemetery*. A valuable collection of articles on a variety of topics relating to cemeteries between 1890 and 1915 is *The Cemetery Hand Book: A Manual of Useful Information on Cemetery Development and Management* (Chicago, n.d.). The articles were all reprinted from *Modern Cemetery*. The other essential resource is the *Proceedings of the American Association of Cemetery Superintendents,* begun in 1887 and published until 1943.

Roland Marchand, *Advertising the American Dream: Making Way for Modernity, 1920–1940* (Berkeley, 1985), and T. Jackson Lears, "From Salvation to Self-Realization: Advertising and the Therapeutic Roots of the Consumer Culture, 1880–1930," in *Culture of Consumption: Critical Essays in American History, 1880–1980,* ed. Richard Wightman Fox and T. Jackson Lears (New York, 1983), were helpful in their discussions of the changes in consumerism and advertising. One of the leading advertising men of the 1920s was Bruce Barton, most noted for his very popular book *The Man Nobody Knows: A Discovery of the Real Jesus* (Indianapolis, 1925). On Barton, see Leo P. Ribuffo, "Jesus Christ as Business Spokesman: Bruce Barton and the Selling of Corporate Capitalism," *American Quarterly* 33, no. 2 (Summer 1981):206–31.

Changes in the practices of the insurance and real-estate industries were critical models for the preneed sales campaigns of lawn-park cemeteries and memorial parks. On the insurance industry, see Edward A. Woods, *The Sociology of Life Insurance* (New York, 1928), and Morton Keller, *The Life Insurance Enterprise, 1885–1910: A Study in the Limits of Corporate Power* (Cambridge, Mass., 1963). On the real-estate industry, see Marc Weiss, *The Rise of the Community Builders: The American Real Estate Industry and Urban Land Planning* (New York, 1987), and Robert Fogelson, *The Fragmented Metropolis: Los Angeles, 1850–1930* (Cambridge, Mass., 1967).

Cremation

There is no adequate history of cremation in America. Details are in Paul Irion, *Cremation* (Philadelphia, 1968); James J. Farrell, *Inventing the American Way of Death,* 164–69, and George B. Catlin, "Cremation in Michigan," *Michigan History Magazine* 14, no. 1 (Winter 1930):38–59. For a view of a late-nineteenth-century cremationist activist, see John Storer Cobb, *A Quartercentury of Cremation in North America: Being a Report of Progress in the United States and Canada* (Boston, 1901). For an extensive, though now outdated, bibliography of the worldwide cremation movement, see H. E. Mose, ed., *A List of Books, Pamphlets and Articles on Cremation; including the Collection of the Cremation Association of America at the John Crerar Library* (Chicago, 1940).

Cremation raised important religious and social concerns during the late-nineteenth century. On the atmosphere in which these concerns arose, see John S. Stephenson, *Death, Grief, and Mourning: Individual and Social Realities* (New York, 1985); on the contemporary Catholic view, see James P. Murphy, "The Cremation Movement Is Anti-Catholic," *Catholic World* 73, no. 436 (July 1901):453–62. See also Paul Carter, "If a Man Die, Shall He Live Again?" in the excellent *Passing: The Vision of Death in America,* ed. Charles O. Jackson (Westport, Conn., 1977).

The medical visions embodied in the cremation crusade are similar to those that drove many sanitary reforms in the late nineteenth century. See Robert P. Hudson, *Disease and Its Control: The Shaping of Modern Thought* (New York, 1983); Lloyd G. Stevenson, "Science down the Drain: The Hostility of Certain Sanitarians to Animal Experimentation, Bacteriology and Immunology," *Bulletin of the History of Medicine* 29, no. 1 (January-February 1955):1–10; Martin Melosi, *Garbage in the Cities: Refuse, Reform and the Environment, 1880–1980* (College Station, Tex., 1981); and James Cassedy, "The Flamboyant Colonel Waring: An Anticontagonist Holds the American Stage in the Age of Pasteur and Koch," *Bulletin of the History of Medicine* 36, no. 2 (March-April 1962):163–76.

Anyone interested in reading about cremation as a reform would do best to begin with the marvelous, although somewhat repetitive, pamphlets of the cremationists. See especially Hugo Erichsen, *The Cremation of the Dead Considered from an Aesthetic, Sanitary, Religious, Historical, Medico-legal, and Economic Standpoint* (Detroit, 1887); and Augustus G. Cobb, *Earth-Burial and Cremation: The History of Earth-Burial with Its Attendant Evils, and the Advantages Offered by Cremation* (New York, 1892).

The Memorial Park and Death in the Twentieth Century

Information on Forest Lawn is quite extensive. Besides the apparently never-ending onslaught of Forest Lawn's own publications, there have been three books about the cemetery: Barbara Rubin, Robert Carlton, and Arnold Rubin, *L.A. in Installments: Forest Lawn;* Adela Rodgers St. Johns, *First Step Up toward Heaven: Hubert Eaton and Forest Lawn* (Englewood Cliffs, N.J., 1959); and Ralph Hancock, *The Forest Lawn Story* (Los Angeles, 1964). *L.A. in Installments* is the most valuable and scholarly; see also Bruce Barton, "A Cemetery without Gloom," *Reader's Digest* 31, no. 184 (August 1937):73–76.

My ideas on modernism have been influenced by the *American Quarterly* special issue *Modernist Culture in America,* ed. Daniel Joseph Singal, 39, no. 1 (Spring 1987). As that issue suggests, the relationship of popular and modernist culture is not always obvious in America, at least before World War II. An interesting discussion of this issue is in William Hubbard, "A Meaning for Monuments," *Public Interest* 74 (Winter 1984):17–30.

I found Edwin S. Shniedman's edited collection of essays helpful in exploring the changing attitudes in the twentieth century toward death; see *Death: Current Perspectives* (Palo Alto, Calif., 1976).

Critics of the American Way of Death

Jessica Mitford was only one of a long list of commentators who found the amount of money spent by Americans on funerals and death obsessive, if not obscene. There needs to be more research about the ambivalence Americans feel about private and public expressions of death, and in comparing their feelings with those of Europeans, Asians, and people of other cultures.

The most important studies were by Quincy Dowd, *Funeral Management and Costs;* John Gebhart, *Funeral Costs* (New York, 1928); LeRoy Bowman, *The American Funeral: A Study in Guilt, Extravagance, and Sublimity* (Washington, D.C., 1959); and Mitford's contemporary Ruth Mulvey Harmer, *The High Cost of Dying* (New York, 1963). Why Americans were readier in the early 1960s to discuss and be shocked by facts that were not terribly different from those of previous decades is discussed in chapters eight and nine above.

It is rather surprising that in the Reagan and Bush years the issue of private burial was not as provocative as in previous decades. Yet future research on, and discussions of, American death beliefs, burial habits, funeral process, and cemeteries will surely continue to focus on the American combination of public attitudes and private means.

INDEX

References to figures or legends are in italics.

Acacia-Resthaven, Tonawanda, N.Y., 186, 189

Adams, Abagail, 15

Adams, J. F. A., 148

Adams, John, 15

Adler, Felix, 156

Advertising: on cremation, *242;* current practices in, 237–38; in early cemeteries, 134; by entrepreneurial cemeteries, 134–38; euphemisms in, 211; by funeral directors, 202; for memorial parks, *185;* for Memory Hill Gardens, *226;* for Mount Tamalpais Cemetery, *136;* for New-York Bay Cemetery, *130;* for preneed programs, *177;* by rural cemeteries, 138–39. *See also* Sales manager and selling

African-Americans, burial places of, 15, 83, 91, 188, 256n.46, 268n.66; exclusion of, from Forest Lawn, 187; in national cemetery, 114; in New York City, 25

African Zion Methodist Episcopal Church, N.Y.C., 37

After Many a Summer Dies the Swan (Huxley), 179

Agriculture, nineteenth-century interest in, 46, 73. *See also* Horticulture

AIDS epidemic, 229

Albany, N.Y., 57; Albany Rural Cemetery, 62, 67, 77, 83, 93, 168; Memory Gardens, 186; New Rural Cemetery, 131–32; St. Agnes Cemetery, 67, 70, 93

Alcott, William, 73

Allegheny Cemetery, Pittsburgh, 56

Allen, Francis, 37, 38

Allen, Lewis, 69, 73

Allen, Stephen, 38, 38–39, 40

Alvord, Thomas, 69

American Cemetery Association, 210, 234

American Cemetery Owners Association (ACOA), 160

American Revolution, 11

American Way of Death, The (Mitford), 215, 230–31

Ariès, Philippe, 6, 19, 173, 175

Arminianism, 72, 94

Art: in Forest Lawn, 165, *165,* 167, 169–70, 171–73; on children's gravestones, 72–73; on early American gravestones, 21–22, *23,* 78–79; as landscape focus, 240–41; in memorial parks, 181, 183, 184, *219,* 240; sepulchral, 78, 79; and Spring Grove, 240, 241; and Strauch's new landscape, 99, 103, 104, 109

Association of American Cemetery Superintendents (AACS), 108, 110–12, 222

Atlanta: Oakland Cemetery, 5, 56, 121; West View Cemetery, 121; and rural cemeteries, 55, 93

Automobiles in cemeteries, 239

Bacon, Leonard, 31

Baker, Charles, xxi

Baldwin, Simeon, 32

Ball, Hugh, 183

Ball, Isaac, 37

Barnard, Daniel D., 62, 83

Barton, Bruce, 165, 174

Bayley, Joseph, 38

Beecher, Henry Ward, 149

Beechwoods Cemetery, New Rochelle, N.Y., 67, 93

Bell, Daniel, 164

Bellefontaine Cemetery, Saint Louis, 56, 75, 93

Bells of Green-Wood Cemetery, *87*

Bentley, William, 22

Beugless, John, 147–48, 151

Bigelow, Jacob, 3, 45, 49, 53, 106, 171

Binney, Emily, 79

Boosterism, 68–70, 94, 112

Boston, 8; Copp's Hill Burial Ground, *21;* cremations in, 150; Forest Hills Cemetery, 109; in-city burial grounds prohibited, 44; King's Chapel, 15; and Mount Auburn Cemetery, 44–45 (*see also* Mount Auburn Cemetery)

Bowditch, Nathanial, statue of, 79, 183

Bowler, Robert, 94, 100

Brackett, E. A., 79

Braintree (now Quincy), Mass., Adams graves in, 15

Brick Presbyterian Church, N.Y.C., 22–23

Bright, Henry Arthur, 55–56

Brimmer, George W., 45

Brooklyn, N.Y.: Calvary Cemetery, 67, 93, 142, 151, 209; Cedar Grove Cemetery, 193, 195; Citizen Union Cemetery, 256n.46; Cypress Hills Cemetery, 67, 76, 80, 83, 93; Evergreens Cemetery, 67; Green-Wood Cemetery, 58–69, 93 (*see also* Green-Wood Cemetery); Maple Grove Cemetery and Memorial Park, 131, 181, 193–94, 195, 217; Most Holy Trinity Cemetery, 67; Salem Fields Cemetery, 67, 93, 221

Brookside Cemetery, Watertown, N.Y., 75, 93

Brown, Lancelot "Capability," 103

Brunetti, Ludovico, 143, 147